"A goldmine of useful ideas and helpful exp[...] own a copy." —James Clear, author of [...]

"Josh has done more for my business education than my MBA. *The Personal MBA* walks you through the mental models you need to excel in business. A lifetime of business knowledge in one volume."

—Shane Parrish, founder of *Farnam Street* (fs.blog) and host of The Knowledge Project podcast

"A masterpiece. This is the '*start here*' book I recommend to everyone interested in business. An amazing overview of everything you need to know. Covers all of the basics, minus buzzwords and fluff. One of the most inspiring things I've read in years."

—Derek Sivers, founder of CD Baby and bestselling author of *Anything You Want*

"*The Personal MBA* is the single best business book I've read. Most books focus on a single part of business in isolation, but *The Personal MBA* walks you through every moving part, and gives you the tools to understand how those parts work together to create a complete system."

—Amy Hoy, founder of Noko Time Tracking and Stacking the Bricks

"The only business book I recommend. Josh somehow condenses an entire library of crucial knowledge into a short book that's eminently readable, so you can spend less time reading and more time building your business. It's perfect for both providing an overview and serving as a reference. I revisit *The Personal MBA* more than any other book on my shelf." —Courtland Allen, cofounder of Indie Hackers

"I read *The Personal MBA* cover to cover when it was first released and it had a major impact on how I view business. It's incredible how Josh was able to distill hundreds of books and hundreds of years of business knowledge into this succinct and elegant tome."

—Rob Walling, cofounder of MicroConf and bestselling author of *Start Small, Stay Small*

"Ten years ago, I got an MBA education courtesy of Kaufman's book. His practical business insights and mindset techniques haven't let me down since. *The Personal MBA* is the most distilled, most accelerated MBA on the planet: all of the insights, none of the ego." —Joanna Wiebe, founder of Copyhackers

"My well-worn copy of *The Personal MBA* has been sitting within arm's reach by my desk for the better part of the past decade. Since starting and growing my own business, this book has been my go-to manual for insights, clarity, and wisdom that I never learned in school."

—Shawn Blanc, founder of The Sweet Setup and The Focus Course

"Ten years after reading (and rereading and rereading) *The Personal MBA*, I still refer to it often and use it to make better decisions. Whether it's building a business plan to launch my writing studio, planning my day, or taking a systematic approach to identify and solve problems, I can't think of any other book that's had such a positive impact on my overall productivity and enjoyment of life."

—Daniel Joshua Rubin, playwright and author of *27 Essential Principles of Story*

"*The Personal MBA* should be required reading for anyone in business. This book exposed me to ideas, systems, and best practices that I had never been taught anywhere else. Even after ten years, I still reference it on a regular basis. Buy it, read it, then keep it close. It'll be your constant business companion for years to come."

—Tim Grahl, author of *Running Down a Dream* and founder of Book Launch

"I graduated with an MBA in 2005 before I encountered *The Personal MBA*, but I still felt like I didn't know anything about business. In retrospect, I wish I had read this book before enrolling in an MBA program—it would've helped me be more mindful while completing my degree. Who knows . . . I might have skipped the MBA completely. This is easily the best foundational business book available."

—Roger Hui, senior software manager at RedHat, Inc.

"I used the mental models in *The Personal MBA* to create a profitable business in less than four weeks. Josh quickly dispels many mistaken beliefs about entrepreneurship, and his guidance has made me vastly more productive and successful, and my life more fulfilling." —Evan Deaubl, president and CEO of Tic Tac Code, LLC

"File this book under 'No Excuses.' After you've read it, you won't be open to people telling you that you're not smart enough, not insightful enough, or not learned enough to do work that matters. Josh takes you on a worthwhile tour of the key ideas in business." —Seth Godin, bestselling author of *This Is Marketing*

"No matter what they tell you, an MBA is not essential. If you combine reading this book with actually trying stuff, you'll be far ahead in the business game."

—Kevin Kelly, founding executive editor of *Wired* and bestselling author of *The Inevitable*

THE PERSONAL
MBA

10TH ANNIVERSARY EDITION

Master the Art of Business

JOSH KAUFMAN

PORTFOLIO / PENGUIN

Portfolio / Penguin
An imprint of Penguin Random House LLC
penguinrandomhouse.com

The Personal MBA: Master the Art of Business first published by Portfolio / Penguin, an imprint of Penguin Random House LLC, in 2010.

This revised and expanded edition published by Portfolio / Penguin, an imprint of Penguin Random House LLC, in 2020.

Most Portfolio books are available at a discount when purchased in quantity for sales promotions or corporate use. Special editions, which include personalized covers, excerpts, and corporate imprints, can be created when purchased in large quantities. For more information, please call (212) 572-2232 or e-mail specialmarkets@penguinrandomhouse.com. Your local bookstore can also assist with discounted bulk purchases using the Penguin Random House corporate Business-to-Business program. For assistance in locating a participating retailer, e-mail B2B@penguinrandomhouse.com.

THE LIBRARY OF CONGRESS HAS CATALOGED THE HARDCOVER EDITION AS FOLLOWS:

Kaufman, Josh.
The personal MBA: master the art of business / Josh Kaufman.
p. cm.
Includes index.
ISBN 978-1-59184-352-8 (hc.)
ISBN 978-1-59184-557-7 (pbk.)
1. Management. 2. Management—Study and teaching. 3. Business.
4. Commerce. I. Title.
HD31.K343 2010
650—dc22   2010027919

ISBN 9780525543022 (trade edition)

Printed in the United States of America

11th Printing

Book design by Jaime Putorti

To the millions of business professionals worldwide who work to make people's lives better, in ways large and small.

CONTENTS

Introduction: Why Read This Book? *1*

1   Value Creation *37*

2   Marketing *87*

3   Sales *115*

4 Value Delivery 146

5 Finance 168

6   The Human Mind 216

7   Working with Yourself 260

8 Working with Others *318*

9 Understanding Systems *358*

10 Analyzing Systems *381*

11 Improving Systems *403*

KEY TERMS

A NOTE TO THE READER

Clear language engenders clear thought,
and clear thought is the most
important benefit of education.
—RICHARD MITCHELL,
THE GRAVES OF ACADEME

Many people assume that they need to attend business school to learn how to build a successful business or advance in their career. That's not true. The vast majority of modern business practice requires little more than common sense, simple arithmetic, and knowledge of a few very important ideas and principles.

The Personal MBA is a foundational business book that focuses on the fundamentals. Its purpose is to give you a clear, comprehensive overview of the most important business concepts in as little time as possible.

Each idea in this book is presented in plain language. Connections between these ideas are highlighted for easy reference. Once you know the essentials, you're free to focus on building your career, secure in the knowledge that you're considering the most important matters first.

Most "MBA alternative" books try to replicate the curricula of top-tier business-school programs. That's not the focus of *The Personal MBA*. My aim is to help you build a solid understanding of general business practice from scratch, regardless of your current level of education or business experience.

Your time is valuable. I've made every effort to condense a large and diverse topic into an approachable volume you can read in a few hours. If additional research into specific topics is prudent in your situation, you'll know what to look for and where to begin.

Knowing where to start in common business situations is valuable, whether you're an early-career professional, an entrepreneur, a skilled tradesperson, or an executive with decades of experience. Having a common language to think about what you observe opens the door to major improvements, no matter what you do for a living.

This revised and updated edition of *The Personal MBA* features many new concepts that make the book's coverage of fundamental ideas even more comprehensive. In addition, small edits have been made to improve the clarity of the concepts included in the first two editions, and additional index features have been added to enhance the book's value as a long-term reference.

If you combine reading this book with real-world experience, you'll reap the rewards for the rest of your life. I hope this book helps you make more money, get more done, and have more fun in the process.

PREFACE TO THE 2020 EDITION

It's wonderful when something that works in theory works in practice.

Fifteen years ago, I started *The Personal MBA* as a side project. I wanted to improve my business knowledge and skills in a direct, efficient, and cost-effective way. When I started the project, I was focused on pursuing a career at a large, multinational company. I had no intention of writing a book and no way of knowing that my research would go on to help hundreds of thousands of people worldwide—and change the course of my life in the process.

The Personal MBA has given readers from all walks of life—from early-career professionals just entering the workforce to skilled tradespeople, executives, and entrepreneurs—a more accurate and practical understanding of what businesses are, how they work, how to create a new business from scratch, and how to improve any existing business venture.

For better or worse, when adults decide to get serious about business education, they start looking into MBA programs. Business *degrees* are often a poor investment, but business *skills* are always useful, no matter how you acquire them.

One of the great pleasures of writing a book is hearing from readers who have benefitted from it in some way. In the ten years since *The Personal*

MBA was first published, I've heard from thousands of readers who have used the concepts in this book to start profitable businesses, land major promotions, and improve their personal and professional lives.

Dirk, who lives in Berlin, Germany, decided to learn business on his own instead of attending business school:

> *The Personal MBA* saved me from a $150,000 mistake and gave me a new perspective on my personal education. In 2014, I was no longer happy with my corporate career, and I was seriously considering an MBA from a top European university. Two days before I was scheduled to mail my enrollment paperwork and send my first payment, I read *The Personal MBA* . . . and I completely changed my mind. Instead of going into severe debt, I went on a personal education journey to pursue my desired career: working with start-ups. I traveled, attended conferences, and participated in programs while reading every book I could get my hands on. At a fraction of the cost and time of an MBA, I made the right contacts and learned what I needed to start my career. I've been successfully running my own company for the past five years, and I've worked with over three hundred start-ups.

Michael, who lives in the United Kingdom, used the book to advance his corporate career:

> I came out of university expecting to be prepared for work . . . and I was not. I see *The Personal MBA* as the ultimate primer for continual learning. I read it at least once a month for over two years. I'm currently twenty-six, and I'm leading marketing and product management teams for one of the largest companies in the world. I'm the youngest person ever to have a seat at the leadership table. I recently passed *The Personal MBA* to a new graduate who joined the team. He read it cover to cover several times. Now, I hear a lot of feedback from the team saying that he is "wise beyond his years" and "knows how to ask the right questions." Thank you, Josh.

M. R. uses the book to manage hundreds of employees and deliver essential services to millions of people in Sri Lanka:

I purchased *The Personal MBA* from a bookstall in Malaysia three years ago. I do not have an MBA, but I am practicing management techniques I learned from your book. I have used your ideas about systems to control over $20 million worth of inventory and ensure a smooth flow of materials. In addition, I guided a team to develop a customer support system that is now benefitting 6.2 million customers, and we have identified over 2,000 business processes to implement in a new Enterprise Resource Planning system. Congratulations, and thank you for the hard work you are doing for the benefit of millions of managers around the world.

Elizabeth in Minneapolis, Minnesota, USA is applying these ideas in her personal life:

I never thought I could become so smart without a college education. You showed me how to increase my knowledge and put that knowledge into practice, and you taught me how to succeed at nearly anything if I'm serious about it. I mentor four children, and I'm passing your legacy on to them. I'm very grateful for your work.

These stories are not unique: hundreds of thousands of readers around the world are using the ideas in *The Personal MBA* to advance in their careers, improve their lives, and make the world a better place.

It's an honor to introduce you to this essential body of knowledge, which will serve you well for the rest of your life. Learning these concepts makes it easier to do great work, make good decisions, and take full advantage of your skills, abilities, and available opportunities—no matter what you do (or would like to do) for a living.

Thank you for reading this expanded and revised tenth anniversary edition of *The Personal MBA*. I hope you find this book useful in your pursuits, and I wish you every success.

Josh Kaufman
Fort Collins, Colorado, USA
September 2020

THE PERSONAL
MBA

TENTH ANNIVERSARY EDITION

Introduction

WHY READ THIS BOOK?

Just what the world needs—another business book!

—US CUSTOMS AGENT AT JOHN F. KENNEDY INTERNATIONAL AIRPORT,
AFTER ASKING ABOUT MY OCCUPATION

Life's tough. It's tougher if you're stupid.

—JOHN WAYNE, WESTERN FILM ICON

Since you're reading this book, chances are you want to make something important happen: you want to start a business, get a promotion, or create something new in the world. It's also likely that one or more things are holding you back from achieving your dream:

▶ *Business angst*—the feeling that you "don't know much about business" and therefore could never start your own company or take more responsibility in your current position. Better to maintain the status quo than face your fear of the unknown.

▶ *Certification intimidation*—the idea that "business is complicated" and is a subject best left to trained "experts." If you don't have an MBA or similar expensive credentials, who are you to say you know what to do?

▶ *Impostor syndrome*—the fear that you're already "in over your head" and it's only a matter of time before you're unmasked as a total fraud. No one likes a phony, right?

Here's the good news: everyone has these unfounded fears, and they're normal. Don't let them hold you back from pursuing what's important to you. Businesses are created, operated, and improved by ordinary people just like you; there's no magic or secret knowledge involved. All you need to do is learn a few simple concepts that will change the way you think about how businesses work and allow you to identify promising opportunities.

If you're an entrepreneur, student, tradesperson, executive, or professional who wants to master the fundamentals of sound business practice, this book is for you. No matter who you are or what you're trying to do, you're about to discover a useful new way of looking at business that will help you spend less time fighting your fears and more time doing things that make a difference.

You Don't Need to Know It All

> As to methods, there may be a million and then some, but principles
> are few. The man who grasps principles can successfully select his
> own methods. The man who tries methods, ignoring principles, is
> sure to have trouble.
>
> —HARRINGTON EMERSON, MANAGEMENT CONSULTANT
> AND EFFICIENCY EXPERT[1]

One of the most important things about learning any subject is the fact that *you don't need to know everything*—you need to understand a small set of important concepts that provide most of the value. Once you have a solid scaffold of core principles to work from, building upon your knowledge and making progress becomes much easier.

The Personal MBA is a set of foundational business concepts you can use to get things done. Understanding these fundamental principles will give you a set of tools you can rely on to make good decisions. If you invest the time and energy necessary to learn these concepts, you'll be in the top 1 percent of the human population when it comes to knowing

- How businesses actually work,
- How to start a new business,

▶ How to improve an existing business, and

▶ How to use business-related skills to accomplish your personal goals.

Think of this book as a filter. Instead of trying to absorb all of the business information that's out there—and there's a *lot* out there—use this book to help you learn what matters most, so you can focus on what's important: making things happen.

No Experience Necessary

> People always overestimate how complex business is. This isn't rocket science—we've chosen one of the world's most simple professions.
>
> —JACK WELCH, FORMER CEO OF GENERAL ELECTRIC

Don't worry if you're a complete beginner. Unlike many other business books, this book does not require any prior business knowledge or experience. I don't assume you're the CEO of a large company who makes multimillion-dollar decisions on a daily basis—but this book will still be useful if you are.

If you *do* have business experience, take it from many of my clients and readers from around the world who have MBAs from top schools—you'll find the information in this book more valuable and practical than anything you learned earning your degree.

Together, we'll explore 271 simple concepts that will help you think about business in a new and useful way. After reading this book, you'll have a more comprehensive and accurate understanding of what businesses actually are and what successful businesses actually do.

Questions, Not Answers

> Education is not the answer to the question. Education is the means to the answer to all questions.
>
> —BILL ALLIN, SOCIOLOGIST AND EDUCATION ACTIVIST

Most business books attempt to teach you to have more answers: a technique for this, a method for that. This book is different. It won't give you answers—it will help you ask better questions. Knowing what's important in *every* business is the first step in making good business decisions. The more you know about the essential questions to ask in your current situation, the faster you'll be able to find the answers you need to move forward.

Mental Models, Not Methods

The limits of my language are the limits of my world.

—LUDWIG WITTGENSTEIN, PHILOSOPHER AND LOGICIAN

To improve your business skills, you don't need to learn everything there is to know—mastering the fundamentals can take you far. I call these foundational business concepts "mental models," and together, they create a solid framework you can rely on to make good decisions.

Mental models are concepts that represent your understanding of how something in the world works. Think of driving a car: What do you expect when you press down on the right-side pedal? If the car slows down, you'll be surprised—that pedal is supposed to be the accelerator. The accuracy of your model of the world determines your expectations, decisions, behavior, and—in the long run—your results.

Your brain forms mental models by noticing patterns in what you experience each day. Very often, however, the mental models you form on your own aren't accurate—you're only one person, so your knowledge and experiences are limited. Education is a way to make your mental models more accurate by internalizing the knowledge and experiences other people have collected throughout their lives. The best education helps you learn to see the world in a new, more productive way.

For example, many people believe things like "Starting a business is risky," "To get started, you must create a detailed business plan and borrow a lot of money," or "Business is about who you know, not what you know." Each of these phrases is a mental model, but they're not quite accurate. Correcting your mental models can help you think about what you're doing in a clear, comprehensive way, which will help you make better decisions.

INACCURATE MENTAL MODEL	ACCURATE MENTAL MODEL
Starting a business is risky.	Uncertainty is an ever-present but manageable part of business, and risks can be minimized.
In order to create a successful business, you must write a flawless business plan first.	A written plan is secondary to understanding the critical functions of your business, and no matter how much you prepare, there will *always* be surprises along the way.
You must raise large amounts of capital before you start building your business.	Raising money is necessary only if it allows you to accomplish something that would otherwise be impossible (like building a factory).
It's not what you know, it's who you know.	Personal connections are important, but knowledge is key if you want to use those connections to your best advantage.

After learning the mental models in this book, many of my readers have realized that their picture of what businesses are and how businesses work was inaccurate—getting their venture off the ground would be far easier than they originally imagined. Instead of wasting valuable time and energy feeling intimidated and freaking out, learning these concepts gave them the freedom to stop worrying and start making progress.

This book will help you learn the fundamental principles of business so you can focus your time and energy on doing useful things: creating something valuable, attracting attention, closing more sales, serving more customers, getting promoted, making more money, changing the world. Not only will you be able to create more value for others and improve your own financial situation, you'll have more fun along the way.

My Personal MBA

Self-education is, I firmly believe, the only kind of education there is.

—ISAAC ASIMOV, FORMER PROFESSOR OF BIOCHEMISTRY AT BOSTON
UNIVERSITY AND AUTHOR OF MORE THAN FIVE HUNDRED BOOKS

> This section describes the history of the Personal MBA as a project. You may find this context useful, but the primary value of this book is independent of my personal background. If you'd like to get to the business concepts, feel free to skip ahead to page 32.

People often ask me if I have an MBA. "No," I reply, "but I did go to business school."

As a student at the University of Cincinnati, I was fortunate enough to participate in the Carl H. Lindner Honors-PLUS program, which resembles an MBA at the undergraduate level. The program was funded via scholarships, and as a result I had the remarkable opportunity to experience most of what business schools teach without the crippling burden of debt.

I've also been on the fast track to corporate success. Through the University of Cincinnati's cooperative education program, I landed a management position at a *Fortune* 500 company—Procter & Gamble—during my second year of college. By the time I graduated in 2005, I had an offer to become an assistant brand manager in P&G's Home Care division, a role reserved for graduates of top MBA programs.

As I began my last semester of college, I started focusing less on my coursework and more on the future. My new job would require a solid understanding of business, and almost all of my peers and managers would have MBAs from top-tier schools. I briefly considered enrolling in an MBA program, but it made no sense to pursue an expensive credential to get the kind of job I already had, and my responsibilities would be demanding enough without adding a load of coursework by enrolling in a part-time program.

While considering my options, I remembered a bit of career advice that Andy Walter, the first associate director I reported to at P&G, had given me: "If you put the same amount of time and energy you'd spend completing an MBA into doing good work and improving your skills, you'll do just as well." (Andy doesn't have an MBA—he studied electrical engineering in college. He retired as one of the company's top global IT executives, responsible for leading many of P&G's largest projects.)

In the end, I decided to skip business school, but not business *education*. Instead of enrolling in an MBA program, I hit the books, creating my own personal MBA.

A Self-Directed Crash Course in Business

Many who are self-taught far excel the doctors, masters, and bachelors of the most renowned universities.

—LUDWIG VON MISES, AUSTRIAN ECONOMIST
AND AUTHOR OF *HUMAN ACTION*

I've always been an avid reader, but before I decided to learn everything I could about business, most of what I read was fiction. I grew up in New London, a small farm town in northern Ohio where the major industries are agriculture and light manufacturing. My mother worked as a librarian, and my father was a sixth-grade science teacher, then an elementary school principal. Books were a major part of my life, but business was not.

Before getting my first real job, I knew next to nothing about what businesses were or how they functioned, other than that they were places people went every day in order to draw a paycheck. I had no idea that companies like Procter & Gamble existed until I applied for the job that swept me into the corporate world.

Working for P&G was an education in itself. The size and scope of the business—and the complexity of managing a business of that size—boggled my mind. During my first three years with the company, I participated in making decisions across every part of the business process: creating new products, ramping up production, allocating millions of marketing dollars, and securing distribution with major retailers like Walmart, Target, Kroger, and Costco.

As an assistant brand manager, I was leading teams of thirty to forty P&G employees, contractors, and agency staff—all of whom had competing projects, plans, and priorities. The stakes were huge, and the pressure was intense. To this day, I can't help but marvel at the thousands of man-hours, the millions of dollars, and the complex processes necessary to make a simple bottle of dish soap appear on the shelf of the local supermarket. Everything from the shape of the bottle to the scent of the product is optimized—including the text on the cardboard boxes used to ship inventory to the store.

My work at P&G, however, wasn't the only thing on my mind. My decision to skip business school in favor of educating myself developed from a side project into a minor obsession. Every day I would spend hour after hour reading and researching, searching for one more tidbit of knowledge that would help me to better understand how the business world worked.

Instead of using the summer after graduation to relax and go on vacation, I spent my days haunting the business stacks at the local bookstore, absorbing as much as I could. By the time I officially started working full-time for P&G in September 2005, I had read books spanning every discipline that business schools teach, as well as disciplines that most business schools don't cover in detail, such as psychology, physical science, and systems theory. When my first day at P&G finally arrived, I felt prepared.

As it turned out, my self-education served me well—I was doing valuable work, making things happen, and getting good annual reviews. As time went on, however, I realized three very important things:

1. *Large companies move slowly.* Good ideas often died on the vine because they had to be approved by too many people.

2. *Climbing the corporate ladder is an obstacle to doing great work.* I wanted to focus on getting things done and making things better, not drafting memos, sitting in meetings, and positioning myself for promotion. Politics and turf wars are an inescapable part of the daily experience of working for a large company.

3. *Frustration leads to burnout.* I wanted to enjoy the daily experience of work, but instead I felt like I was running a gauntlet each day. It began to affect my health, happiness, and relationships. The longer I stayed in the corporate world, the more I realized I wanted out. I wanted to decide what to work on, who to work with, and what to prioritize—making entrepreneurship the best path for me long-term.

The Wheat and the Chaff

It is important that students bring a certain ragamuffin, barefoot irreverence to their studies; they are not here to worship what is known, but to question it.

—JACOB BRONOWSKI, WRITER AND PRESENTER OF *THE ASCENT OF MAN*

If there's one thing I'm good at, it's taking in an enormous amount of information and distilling it to the essentials. Even so, sifting through the massive amount of business information available was a huge challenge: thousands of new business books are published every year, and business periodicals, journals, and websites publish new research daily. Some of this information is useful, but most of it is not.

My early business research was haphazard—I went to a bookstore and picked up any book that looked interesting. For every great book I found, I had to wade through ten times as many low-quality texts written by authors who were more interested in creating a three-hundred-page business card than providing useful information.

I started to wonder how much of what's out there—and there's a *lot* out there—I *really* needed to know. How could I separate the valuable information from the rubbish? I only had so much time and energy, so I started searching for a filter: something that would direct me to the useful knowledge and keep me away from the chaff. The more I searched, the more I realized it didn't exist—so I decided to create it myself.

I began tracking which resources were valuable and which ones weren't, then publishing my findings on my website, both as an archive and for the benefit of anyone interested. It was a personal project, nothing more: I was just a recent college graduate doing my best to learn something useful, and publishing my research for others seemed like a good use of time and energy.

One fateful morning, however, the Personal MBA went public—and became much more than a personal project.

The Personal MBA Goes Global

Whoever best describes the problem is the one most likely to solve it.

—DAN ROAM, AUTHOR OF *THE BACK OF THE NAPKIN*

In addition to reading books, I was following several hundred business blogs. Some of the best business thinking was being published on the internet months (or years) before it ever appeared in print, and I wanted to read it all as soon as it was available.

One of the bloggers I followed was Seth Godin. A bestselling author (of books like *Permission Marketing*, *Purple Cow*, and *Linchpin*) and one of the earliest successful online marketers, Seth specializes in bold statements of big ideas designed to challenge you to do more, do better, question the status quo, and make a difference.

One particular morning, Seth was commenting on a recent news story: Harvard was rescinding the admission of 119 previously soon-to-be Harvard MBA students.[2] These prospective students had discovered a way to hack into the Harvard admissions website to view their application status before the official acceptance letters went out. The story became a media frenzy, devolving into a debate about whether MBA students were predisposed to lie, cheat, and steal, or if business schools made them that way.

Instead of being outraged at the bad behavior of the applicants, Seth had a different perspective: Harvard was giving these students a *gift*. By rescinding their admission, the university was returning $150,000 and two years of their lives that would otherwise have been spent chasing a piece of paper. "It's hard for me to understand," he wrote, "why [getting an MBA] is a better use of time and money than actual experience combined with a dedicated reading of 30 or 40 books."

I experienced a moment of unexpected validation, then got to work.

Over the next two days, I created a list of the books and resources I had found most valuable in my studies,[3] then published it on my website with a link to Seth's post, so anyone interested in figuring out how to do what Seth suggested would be able to find it. When it was done, I sent Seth an email with a note of thanks and a link to my post.

Two minutes later, a post went up on Seth's blog directing people to my reading list, and a flood of readers from around the world began visiting my website.

Popular personal-development and productivity blogs and sites like Lifehacker picked up the story, which then spread to social media websites and a wide variety of personal blogs. In the first week of the Personal MBA's existence, thirty thousand people visited my little corner of the internet to see what I was doing. Better yet, they started talking.

Some readers asked questions—where should they start? Others suggested great books they'd read, helping me with my research. A few told me the entire project was naive and that I was wasting my time. Through it all, I kept reading, researching, and developing the Personal MBA in my spare time, and the business self-education movement began to snowball.

In a very short time, the Personal MBA grew from a one-man side project into a global phenomenon. The site, personalmba.com, has been visited by millions of readers since it went live in early 2005, and the project has been featured by the *New York Times*, the *Wall Street Journal*, *Bloomberg Businessweek*, the *Financial Times*, *Time*, *Fortune*, *Fast Company*, and hundreds of other major news organizations and independent websites. In late 2008, I left P&G to focus on research, writing, and improving the Personal MBA full-time.

As much as I enjoyed the interest in my reading list, I soon realized that providing a reading list wasn't enough. People read business books to solve specific challenges or to improve themselves in some tangible way. They're looking for solutions, and a list of books—while valuable—could only do so much.

The books themselves aren't as important as the ideas and knowledge they contain, but many of my readers were missing out because it took hours of turning pages to get to the good stuff. Many readers started with enthusiasm, only to quit after reading a few books—it took too long to reap the rewards, and the demands of work and family life prevented many readers from completing the project.

To help them, I had more work to do.

Munger's Mental Models

I think it's undeniably true that the human brain works in models. The trick is to have your brain work better than the other person's brain because it understands the most fundamental models—the ones that do the most work.

—CHARLES T. MUNGER, BILLIONAIRE BUSINESS PARTNER OF
WARREN BUFFETT, FORMER CEO OF WESCO FINANCIAL, AND
VICE-CHAIRMAN OF BERKSHIRE HATHAWAY

My first glimpse into the future of the Personal MBA came when I discovered the work of Charlie Munger.

Charlie was born in Omaha, Nebraska, just before the Great Depression. As a young man, Charlie skipped high school athletics in favor of reading to satisfy his intense curiosity about how the world worked. His early business experience consisted of working in a family-owned grocery store for $2 a day.

In 1941, Charlie graduated from high school. After two years of studying undergraduate mathematics and physics at the University of Michigan, he enlisted in the US Army Air Corps, where he was trained as a meteorologist. In 1946, after leaving the army, he was accepted to Harvard Law School, even though he had never earned a bachelor's degree, which wasn't required at the time.

Charlie graduated from Harvard Law in 1948 and spent the next seventeen years practicing as an attorney. In 1965, he left the law firm he had created to start an investment partnership, which went on to outperform the market by 19.8 percent compounded annually over fourteen years—an astounding record given his complete lack of formal business education.[4]

Charlie Munger isn't a household name, but most people have heard of Warren Buffett, Charlie's business partner. Munger joined Buffett at Berkshire Hathaway, a floundering textile manufacturer turned investment holding company, in 1978. Together, Buffett and Munger became billionaires.

According to Buffett, Charlie's mental model–centric approach to business is a major contributing factor in the success of Berkshire Hathaway and Buffett's status as one of the world's wealthiest business owners. In Buffett's words: "Charlie can analyze and evaluate any kind of deal faster and more accurately than any man alive. He sees any valid weakness in sixty seconds. He's the perfect partner."[5]

The secret to Charlie's success is a systematic way of understanding how businesses work. Even though he never studied business in college, his relentless self-education in a wide variety of subjects allowed him to construct what he called a "latticework of mental models," which he then applied to making business decisions:

> I've long believed that a certain system—which almost any intelligent person can learn—works way better than the systems most people use [to understand the world]. What you need is a latticework of mental models in your head. And, with that system, things gradually fit together in a way that enhances cognition.
>
> Just as multiple factors shape every system, multiple mental models from a variety of disciplines are necessary to understand that system . . . You have to realize the truth of biologist Julian Huxley's idea that "Life is just one damn relatedness after another." So you must have all the models, and you must see the relatedness and the effects from the relatedness . . .[6]
>
> It's kind of fun to sit here and outthink people who are way smarter than you are because you've trained yourself to be more objective and more multidisciplinary. Furthermore, there is a lot of money in it, as I can testify from my own personal experience.[7]

By basing their investment decisions on their extensive knowledge of how businesses work, how people work, and how systems work, Buffett and Munger created a company worth more than $500 billion—an astounding track record for a meteorologist-turned-lawyer from Omaha with no formal business education.

Discovering Munger's approach to business education was a revelation. Here was a man who, decades before, had decided to do what I was doing—and it had worked beyond all expectation. Munger's method of identifying and applying fundamental principles made much more sense to me than most of the business books I'd read. I decided to learn everything I could about the mental models Charlie Munger used to make decisions.

Charlie has never published a comprehensive collection of his mental models. He's given hints in his speeches and essays—even going so far as to publish a list of the psychological principles he finds most useful in *Poor Charlie's Almanack*, a 2005 biography—but there is no single text that contains Charlie's conception of "everything you need to know in order to succeed in business."

If I wanted to understand the fundamental principles of how every successful businessperson works, I'd have to discover them myself. To do that, I had to rebuild my understanding of business from the ground up.

Connecting the Dots

> In all affairs, it's a healthy thing now and then to hang a question mark on the things you have long taken for granted.
>
> —BERTRAND RUSSELL, RENOWNED PHILOSOPHER AND
> AUTHOR OF *THE PROBLEMS OF PHILOSOPHY*
> AND *THE PRINCIPLES OF MATHEMATICS*

Most business books—and business schools—assume that the student already knows what businesses are, what they do, and how they work—as if it were the most obvious thing in the world. It's not. Business is one of the most complex and multidisciplinary areas of human experience, and trying to understand how businesses work can be difficult, even though they surround us every day.

Businesses are so much a part of daily life that it's easy to take the business world for granted. Day after day, businesses deliver what we want and need with little fanfare or fuss. Look around: almost every material good you're surrounded by right now was created and delivered to you by some sort of business.

Businesses create and deliver so many different things in so many different ways that it makes generalizations difficult: What do apple cider and airlines have in common? As it turns out, quite a bit—if you know where to look.

Here's how I define a business:

Every successful business (1) creates or provides something of value that (2) other people want or need (3) at a price they're willing to pay, in a way that (4) satisfies the purchaser's needs and expectations,

and (5) provides the business sufficient revenue to make it worthwhile for the owners to continue operation.

Take away any of these things—value creation, customer demand,
transactions, value delivery, or profit sufficiency—and you have something
other than a business. Each factor is both essential and universal.

As I researched each of those factors in detail, I found additional universal requirements. Value can't be created without understanding what
people want (market research). Attracting customers first requires getting
their attention, then making them interested (marketing). In order to close
a sale, people must trust your ability to deliver on what's promised (value
delivery and operations). Customer satisfaction depends on exceeding the
customer's expectations (customer service). Profit sufficiency requires
bringing in more money than is spent (finance).

These tasks aren't rocket science, but they're always necessary, no matter who you are or what business you're in. Do them well and your business
thrives. Ignore them and you won't be in business very long.

Every business relies on two additional factors: people and systems.
Every business is created by people and survives by benefiting other people
in some way. To understand how businesses work, you must have a firm
understanding of how people tend to think and behave—how humans
make decisions, act on those decisions, and communicate with others. Recent advances in psychology and neuroscience are revealing why people do
the things they do, as well as how to improve our own behavior and work
in a more efficient and effective way with others.

Systems, on the other hand, are the invisible structures that hold every
business together. At the core, every business is a collection of processes that
can be *repeated* to produce a particular result. By understanding how complex
systems work, it's possible to find ways to improve existing systems, whether
you're dealing with a marketing campaign or an automotive assembly line.

Before writing this book, I spent several years testing its principles with my
clients and readers. Understanding and applying these mental models of business has helped them launch new careers, land job offers from prestigious
organizations in corporate and academic fields, land promotions and pay
raises, start new businesses, and, in several cases, go through the entire product development process (from idea to first sale) in weeks instead of years.

These concepts are important because they *work*. Not only will you be able to create more value for others and improve your career, you'll find it easier to achieve what you set out to do—and you'll have more fun along the way.

For the Skeptics

You wasted $150,000 on an education you could have got for a buck fifty in late charges at the public library.

—MATT DAMON AS WILL HUNTING, *GOOD WILL HUNTING*

This section examines the benefits and detriments of traditional business school programs versus learning business concepts outside of academia. If you have already enrolled in business school, have completed an MBA program, or don't care about the current state of business academia, this section won't be as valuable for you. Feel free to skip ahead to page 32.

This is a book about business concepts, not business schools. However, many people don't believe it's possible to reap the benefits of a comprehensive business education without forking over enormous sums of money for a name-brand diploma from an Ivy League school. This section, which will discuss the merits and downfalls of traditional MBA programs, is for the skeptics.

Should You Go to Business School?

There is a difference between (A) what an MBA does to help you prove your abilities to others and (B) what getting an MBA actually does to improve your abilities.

—SCOTT BERKUN, AUTHOR OF *MAKING THINGS HAPPEN* AND *THE MYTHS OF INNOVATION*

Every year, millions of individuals determined to make a name for themselves have the following thought: "I want to become a successful businessperson. Where should I get my MBA?" Since you're flipping through this book, you've probably wondered the same thing at some point in your life.

Here's the answer: five simple words that will save you years of effort and hundreds of thousands of dollars:

Skip business school. Educate yourself.

This book will show you how to succeed in business—without mortgaging your life.

Three Big Problems with Business Schools

College: two hundred people reading the same book. An obvious mistake. Two hundred people can read two hundred books.

—JOHN CAGE, SELF-TAUGHT WRITER AND COMPOSER

I have nothing against people who work in business schools: by and large, business-school professors and administrators are lovely people who try their best and want to see their students succeed. MBA programs, however, have three major systemic issues:

1. *MBA programs have become so expensive you must mortgage your life to pay the price of admission.* Return on investment is always related to how much you spend, and after decades of tuition increases, MBA programs have become a burden to their students instead of a benefit. The primary question is not whether attending a university is a positive experience: it's whether or not the experience is worth the cost.[8]

2. *MBA programs teach many worthless, outdated, even outright damaging concepts and practices*—assuming your goal is to build a successful business and increase your net worth. Many of my MBA-holding readers and clients come to me after spending tens (sometimes hundreds) of thousands of dollars learning the ins and outs of complex financial formulas and statistical models, only to realize that their MBA program didn't teach them how to start or improve a real, operating business. That's a problem—graduating from business school does not guarantee having a useful working knowledge of business when you're done, which is what you need to be successful.

3. *MBA programs won't guarantee you a high-paying job, let alone make you a skilled manager or leader with a shot at the executive suite.* Developing skills such as decision making, management, and leadership takes real practice and experience, which business schools can't provide in the classroom, regardless of how prestigious the program is.

Instead of spending huge sums of money to learn information of questionable value, you can spend your time and resources learning business concepts that matter. If you're ready and able to invest in improving your skills and abilities, you can learn everything you need to know about business on your own, without mortgaging your life for the privilege.

Delusions of Grandeur

The very substance of the ambitious is merely the shadow of a dream.
—WILLIAM SHAKESPEARE, *HAMLET*

It's easy to figure out why business school is attractive: it's sold as a one-way ticket to a prosperous and comfortable life. It's a pleasant daydream to think that after two years of case studies and happy-hour "networking," corporate recruiters will be shamelessly throwing themselves at you, each of them offering a prestigious and high-paying position at a top firm.

Your rise up the corporate ladder will be swift and sure. You'll be a CAPTAIN OF INDUSTRY, collecting huge bonuses and tabulating the value of your stock options while sitting behind an impressive-looking mahogany desk in the corner office on the top floor of a gigantic glass skyscraper. You'll be the big boss, telling other people what to do until it's time to go play golf or relax on your yacht. You'll be wined and dined all over the world, and the lowly masses will venerate you and your astounding achievements. Everyone will think you're rich, intelligent, and powerful—and they'll be damned right.

What price for the promise of riches, power, and glory? A few thousand dollars in application fees, an effortless scribble on a loan document, and you'll be on your way to the top! Not only that, you'll get a two-year vacation from your day job. What a fantastic deal!

Daydreams and reality are often quite different.

Your Money AND Your Life

There ain't no such thing as a free lunch.

—ROBERT A. HEINLEIN, AUTHOR OF *STRANGER IN A STRANGE LAND* AND *THE MOON IS A HARSH MISTRESS*

For the moment, let's assume you think business school is your ticket to everlasting success. You're in luck—getting into at least one business school is close to guaranteed. If you pay thousands of dollars in application fees, write enough personal statements that strike just the right balance of confidence and humility, and compliment the quality of the school's program in interviews, sooner or later some college or university will bestow upon you the chance to become the next Bill Gates.[9]

Here, though, is where the problems begin: business school is expensive and is getting more expensive each year. Unless you're already wealthy or you land a massive scholarship, your only option is to secure a loan against your future earnings to pay the tuition.

Most prospective MBA students have already graduated from college with an undergraduate degree, so they're often already carrying some level of student loan debt. According to the Institute for College Access and Success—a higher education availability and affordability nonprofit—the average cumulative debt of a student who completed an undergraduate degree in the United States in 2017 is $28,650.[10] For students who choose to pursue an MBA program after undergrad, the total average student loan balance is $66,300.[11] Tuition isn't the only reason graduate students borrow money: day-to-day material needs like rent, groceries, and transportation costs are often funded via student loans.

Sixty-six thousand dollars is a significant chunk of change, assuming you go to an *average* school—but who wants to be average? If you're shooting for offers from top-tier financial-services companies like Goldman Sachs or major consulting companies like McKinsey and Bain (which are historically the highest-paying options for newly minted MBAs), you're going to have to attend a top-ten program, and that'll require a *lot* more than a measly sixty-six grand.

Breaking Out the Benjamins

Who goeth a borrowing, goeth a sorrowing . . . A fool and his money
are soon parted.

—THOMAS TUSSER, SIXTEENTH-CENTURY ENGLISH FARMER AND POET

At the time of publication, top MBA programs charge $50,000 to $80,000 *per year* for tuition.[12] That amount doesn't include fees, student loan interest, or living expenses and is increasing by 5 to 10 percent each year.

It gets worse. According to data compiled by Poets&Quants, a business-school news website, nine business schools exceed $200,000 in direct costs for their two-year, full-time program: Harvard, Stanford, Wharton, NYU, Columbia, Dartmouth, Chicago, MIT, and Northwestern.[13] Tack on 1 to 3 percent in loan origination fees and a 6 to 10 percent compound annual interest rate on the loan balance, plus living expenses in a major metropolitan area and the money you're not earning while in school, and you've calculated the true cost of enrollment. Once you account for everything, the total cost of a top graduate-level business degree can exceed $400,000. Even if you assume a six-figure salary after graduation, the total cost of the degree is a substantial percentage of your future career earnings.

That's assuming you get in, of course—business-school admissions are famous for their competitive selection processes for a reason. The reputation of a business school is built on the success of its graduates, so schools have a direct incentive to admit students who already have what it takes to succeed, MBA or no MBA.

In addition, top schools rely on high-profile donors, well-heeled graduates, and corporate connections to raise funds, recruit future students, and expand their campuses. As a result, wealthy and well-connected applicants are more likely to receive acceptance letters.[14] According to a *Bloomberg Businessweek* survey that polled business graduates from 126 business schools, 44 percent of students reported that they did not borrow money to pay for their degree.[15] That figure doesn't make sense until you consider other forms of financial support: preexisting family wealth, donor admissions, and corporate sponsorship.

Business schools don't *create* wealthy and well-connected people. They *accept* them, then take credit for their success.

If you get in, the school will do what it can to help you get a well-paying job within a few months of graduation, but making things happen will always be *your* responsibility. If you're successful in the years after graduation, the school will hold you up as a shining example of the quality of their program and will use the "halo effect" of your name to recruit more students. If you lose your job and go broke, you'll get neither publicity nor help, but the loan bills will keep rolling in. Sorry about your luck.

Here's what Christian Schraga, a 2002 graduate of the University of Pennsylvania's Wharton School, had to say about his MBA experience in an essay on his website:[16]

> My been-there-done-that experience has taught me that a top MBA program provides some benefits, but at a steep price. If you are currently considering attending a full-time program, please stop to ask yourself whether or not you are willing to take the risk.
>
> Business school is a big risk. Should you choose to enroll, the only certainty is that you will shell out about $125,000. Such a figure correlates to a $1,500/month non-deductible loan repayment and a ten-year period of time in which you will not be able to save a red cent.
>
> If you think that this payment is worth it to earn the pedigree, the fraternity, the two years off, and a shot at the big bucks, then the MBA is right for you. If not, please do something else.

Wise words. If you don't need the sheepskin, don't enroll.

What an MBA Will Actually Get You

Hypocrisy can afford to be magnificent in its promises; for never intending to go beyond promises, it costs nothing.

—EDMUND BURKE, POLITICIAN AND POLITICAL THEORIST

In "The End of Business Schools? Less Success Than Meets the Eye," a study published in *Academy of Management Learning & Education*,[17] Jeffrey Pfeffer of Stanford University and Christina Fong of the University of Washington analyzed forty years of data in an effort to find evidence that business schools make their graduates more successful. Their hypothesis was straightforward:

> If an MBA education is useful training for business, then the following should be true as a matter of logic: (1) having an MBA degree should, other things being equal, be related to various measures of career success and attainment, such as salary; and (2) if what someone learns in business school helps that person be better prepared for the business world and more competent in that domain—in other words, if business schools convey professionally useful knowledge—then a measure of how much one has learned or mastered the material, such as grades in course work, should be at least somewhat predictive of various outcomes that index success in business.

What Pfeffer and Fong found was astonishing and disturbing: business schools do almost nothing, aside from making money disappear from students' pockets.

> Business schools are not very effective: Neither possessing an MBA degree nor grades earned in courses correlate with career success, results that question the effectiveness of schools in preparing their students. And, there is little evidence that business school research is influential on management practice, calling into question the professional relevance of management scholarship.

According to Pfeffer and Fong's study, it doesn't matter if you graduate at the top of your class with a perfect 4.0 GPA or at the bottom with a barely passing grade—getting an MBA has zero correlation with long-term career success. None.

> There is scant evidence that the MBA credential, particularly from non-elite schools, or the grades earned in business courses—a measure of the mastery of the material—are related to either salary or the attainment of higher level positions in organizations. These data, at a minimum, suggest that the training or education component of business education is only loosely coupled to the world of managing organizations.

That's tough to hear if you've forked over a few hundred thousand dollars to buy a degree whose sole purpose is to make you a more successful businessperson.

It gets worse: getting an MBA doesn't even have an impact on your total lifetime earnings. It takes decades of work to dig yourself out of the debt you took on to get the degree. Christian Schraga, the Wharton MBA, estimated that the ten-year net present value (a financial analysis technique used to estimate whether or not an investment is worthwhile) of a top MBA program is approximately negative $53,000 (that's bad). This assumes a pre-MBA base salary of $85,000, a post-MBA salary of $115,000 (a 35 percent increase), marginal tax rate increases (which you'll pay if your job requires moving to a major city), and a discount rate of 7 percent to account for opportunity cost (the opportunities you give up by spending money on business school instead of investing it in something else). In plain English: Schraga used a technique business schools teach to prove that getting an MBA from a top-tier business school is a bad financial decision.

Assuming Schraga's assumptions are accurate, it takes twelve years of solid post-graduation effort *just to break even*—and that's assuming everything goes according to plan. If you graduate into a bad job market, you're screwed.

Where Business Schools Came From

> It is, in fact, nothing short of a miracle that modern methods of instruction have not entirely strangled the curiosity of inquiry.
>
> —ALBERT EINSTEIN, NOBEL PRIZE–WINNING PHYSICIST

MBA programs don't make students more successful because they teach very few things that are useful in the working world. As Pfeffer and Fong state in their paper:

> A large body of evidence suggests that the curriculum taught in business schools has only a small relationship to what is important for succeeding in business . . . If there is, in fact, only a slight connection between the skills needed in business and what is taught in graduate

business programs, then the absence of an effect of the MBA or mastery of the subject matter on the careers of graduates is understandable.

If you look at the curriculum of any business school, you'll notice a few assumptions about what you'll do after you graduate: you'll either be a C-level executive at a large industrial manufacturing or retail operation, become a consultant, become a corporate accountant, or work in finance at an investment bank or hedge fund. The coursework tends to be structured around keeping a massive operation running and/or doing sophisticated quantitative analysis—not doing any of the other essential tasks that 99 percent of working businesspeople do in any given day.

The case for business school relies on the claim that it makes graduates more capable executives, managers, and business owners, but there's no evidence that graduate-level business education makes you a skilled or effective businessperson: situational factors are far more important. In a comprehensive study titled "The MBA Myth and the Cult of the CEO," Dan Rasmussen and Haonan Li shared their research into the effect of MBA credentials on the individual and company performance of more than 8,500 CEOs.[18] Here's how they described one of their primary research interests:

> Do CEO characteristics predict stock price performance? Do CEOs with MBAs perform better than CEOs without MBAs? Do CEOs with MBAs from the best MBA programs outperform other CEOs? Do CEOs who worked at top consulting firms and investment banks outperform other CEOs? More broadly, are the "best and brightest" better at running companies?

Here's the conclusion of Rasmussen and Li's study:

> We found no statistically significant [advantage]—despite testing every possible school with a reasonable sample size. MBA programs simply do not produce CEOs who are better at running companies, if performance is measured by stock price return . . . The actual CEO performance results line up very closely with what we would expect to see by chance. [. . .] How much longer will investors and boards be fooled by randomness and hollow credentialism?

The disconnect between the classroom and the working world makes sense when you realize that the concepts, principles, and techniques most business schools teach were designed for a very different world. Graduate schools of business started popping up at the end of the nineteenth century, during the second Industrial Revolution. The intent of early MBA programs was to train managers to be more scientific in an effort to make large operations more efficient.

Frederick Winslow Taylor, the pioneer of "scientific management" techniques that now form the foundation of modern management training, used a stopwatch to shave a few seconds off the average time a workman took to load iron ingots into a train car. That should give you a good idea of the underlying mind-set of most business-school management programs.

Management was thought of as an exercise in getting people to work faster and do what they're told. The philosopher-kings behind what passed for management psychology were Ivan Pavlov and, later on, B. F. Skinner, who believed that if you discovered and applied just the right stimulus, people would behave however you wanted. This mentality led to the widespread use of financial incentives to influence behavior: salary, bonuses, stock options, and so on, in an effort to encourage business professionals and managers to act in the best interest of corporate shareholders.

There's an enormous (and growing) body of evidence that direct incentives often undermine performance, motivation, and job satisfaction in the real world.[19] Despite more useful competing theories of human action,[20] the search for the magic stimulus continues in business-school classrooms to this day.

In Search of Distribution

> Any technique, however worthy and desirable, becomes a disease when the mind is obsessed with it.
>
> —BRUCE LEE, WORLD-RENOWNED MARTIAL ARTIST

Marketing, on the other hand, was originally a way to get additional store distribution for physical products and keep expensive factory production lines busy. With the widespread adoption of radio and television in the early twentieth century, it became possible to advertise to a large, national audience, paving the way for national brands and national retailers. More advertising resulted in more distribution, which, in turn, resulted in more sales and even more money to spend on advertising, continuing the cycle. As decades passed, this self-reinforcing feedback loop resulted in a few dominant behemoths in each industry. Business schools became obsessed with how to capture market share and create gigantic companies via ever-larger mergers, raising the financial stakes with each acquisition.

For entrepreneurs, venture capital became a must-have aspect of the business-creation process—how else could you afford to build a factory or a national brand in a few short years? Economies of scale in production meant large companies could outcompete smaller rivals by offering similar products at lower prices. Investors wanted to see huge returns on their money—prudence be damned—rewarding speculators who wrote business plans promising a huge exit in a short amount of time. Viable businesses were acquired and gutted in the name of conglomeration and "synergy," all with the blessing of business academia. The sheer enormity of integrating these gigantic, complex business systems was ignored or overlooked, leading most of the companies that attempted such huge mergers to ruin.

Playing with Fire

Beware of geeks bearing formulas.

—WARREN BUFFETT, CHAIRMAN AND CEO OF BERKSHIRE HATHAWAY
AND ONE OF THE WEALTHIEST INDIVIDUALS IN THE WORLD

Finance, in the meantime, increased in complexity. Before the twentieth century, accounting and finance were a matter of common sense and relatively simple arithmetic. The widespread adoption of double-entry bookkeeping (a thirteenth-century innovation) brought many benefits, including increased accuracy and ease of detecting anomalies like theft, at the cost of simplicity.

The introduction of statistics to financial practice enhanced analytical capability at the cost of abstraction, increasing opportunities to fudge the numbers without anyone noticing. Over time, managers and executives began using statistics and analysis to forecast the future, relying on data-bases and spreadsheets in much the same way ancient seers relied on tea leaves and goat entrails. The world itself is no less unpredictable or uncertain: as in the olden days, the signs only "prove" the biases and desires of the soothsayer.

The complexity of financial transactions and the statistical models those transactions relied upon continued to grow until few practitioners fully understood how they worked or respected their limits. As *Wired* revealed in a February 2009 article, "Recipe for Disaster: The Formula That Killed Wall Street," the inherent limitations of financial formulas such as the Black-Scholes option pricing model, the Gaussian copula function, and the capital asset pricing model (CAPM) played a major role in the tech bubble of 2000 and the housing-market and derivatives shenanigans behind the 2008 recession.

Learning how to use complicated financial formulas isn't the same as learning how to run a business. Understanding *what businesses do to create and deliver value* is essential knowledge, but many business programs have de-emphasized value creation and operations in favor of finance and quantitative analysis. In a *New Republic* article, "Upper Mismanagement," journalist Noam Scheiber explores the reasons behind the downfall of American industry:

> Since 1965, the percentage of graduates of highly ranked business schools who go into consulting and financial services has doubled, from about one-third to about two-thirds. And while some of these consultants and financiers end up in the manufacturing sector, in some respects that's the problem . . . Most of GM's top executives in recent decades hailed from a finance rather than an operations background. [. . .] But these executives were frequently numb to the sorts of innovations that enable high-quality production at low cost.[21]

Process improvements are easy to skip if you want the business's short-term profit numbers to look good, even though they're essential to long-term viability. By ignoring the things that make a business operate in an effective and sustainable way, MBA-trained executives have gutted viable companies in the name of quarterly earnings per share.

Meanwhile, the widespread practice of using large amounts of debt as leverage[22] created enormous companies with even more enormous obligations, amplifying returns in good years but making the firms catastrophically unstable during the slightest downturn. The "leveraged buyout" strategy taught in many business-school classrooms—buying a company, financing massive expansion via debt, then selling the business to another company at a premium[23]—turned formerly self-sustaining companies into debt-bloated monstrosities, and the constant flipping of businesses from one temporary owner to the next turned financial markets into a game of musical chairs.

When financial wizardry and short-term returns overshadow prudence and long-term value creation, customers and employees suffer. The only people who benefit are the MBA-trained, executive-level financiers and fund managers running the show, who extract hundreds of millions of dollars in transaction fees and salaries while destroying viable companies, hundreds of thousands of jobs, and billions of dollars of value.

Business is about creating and delivering value to paying customers, not orchestrating legal fraud. Unfortunately for us all, business schools have de-emphasized the former in favor of teaching the latter.

No Reason to Change

Schools teach the need to be taught.

—IVAN ILLICH, PRIEST, THEOLOGIAN, AND EDUCATION CRITIC

The world is changing, but business schools aren't changing with it. With the advent of the internet and the widespread availability of new technologies, successful modern businesses tend to be smaller, require less capital to build, have less overhead, and require fewer employees. According to the US Small Business Administration, small businesses represent 99.9 percent of all firms in the United States,[24] employ close to half of all private-sector workers,[25] have generated 64.9 percent of net new jobs from 2000 to 2018,[26] and represent approximately 44 percent of US gross domestic product (GDP).[27] You wouldn't know that from looking at business school curricula: based on current standards, it seems that most MBA programs believe huge businesses are the only ventures worth managing.

Mass-market advertising is no longer able to convert pennies to dollars in a predictable and reliable way. Inventories (if they exist at all) tend to be smaller, businesses depend on others for critical functions, and industries change and adapt to new developments. Speed, flexibility, and ingenuity are the qualities that successful businesses rely on today—qualities that the corporate giants struggle to acquire and retain and business-school classrooms struggle to teach.

The demands of the stock market push executives to chase short-term earnings at the expense of long-term stability, creating waves of layoffs and severe budget cuts when times get tight or unexpected events occur. At the same time, employees are looking for a greater sense of autonomy, flexibility, and security from their work—and they're finding these things outside of the confines of the traditional corporate job. How do you manage someone who doesn't want to work for you in the first place?

MBA programs are trying to cope, but they're still teaching theories that are outdated, misguided, and even outright wrong, and they have little incentive to change. Why bother, when MBA programs are profitable status symbols for universities and in such high demand? As long as students are still signing up, don't expect business schools to change their approach to business instruction.

The Single Benefit of Business Schools

Institutions will try to preserve the problem to which they are the solution.

—CLAY SHIRKY, PROFESSOR AT NYU AND AUTHOR OF
HERE COMES EVERYBODY AND *COGNITIVE SURPLUS*

The one significant benefit that business schools *do* provide is better access to *Fortune* 500 recruiters, consulting firms, large accounting firms, and investment banks via on-campus recruiting and alumni networks. Upon graduating from a top-tier business school, you'll find it much easier to get an interview with a corporate recruiter who works for a *Fortune* 500 company, investment bank, or consulting firm. The effect is strongest just after graduation, then wears out within three to five years. After that, you're on your own: hiring managers no longer care so much about where you went to school; they care more about what you've accomplished since then.

Hiring managers use MBA programs as a filter when deciding whom to bring in for an interview. HR managers are busy, and since each student in such a program has been prescreened, there's less of a chance the manager will be wasting precious time. Hiring from MBA programs also provides plausible deniability for the recruiter if the hire doesn't work out: "I'm not sure what the issue was—she graduated from Harvard Business School!"

The filtering aspect of MBA programs is very real and difficult to overcome on your own. If you have your heart set on becoming a management consultant, international financier, or *Fortune* 500 fast-track management candidate, you may have to buy yourself a $200,000 interview. If you go this route, be aware of what you're getting yourself into *before* you apply—once you sign your life away, the debt will make it very difficult to change your mind.

If you're more interested in working for yourself or holding down an enjoyable job while having a life, getting an MBA is a waste of time and money. As Dr. Pfeffer, coauthor of the AMLE business-school study, said in a 2006 *Businessweek* article on MBA programs, "If you are good enough to get in, you obviously have enough talent to do well, regardless."[28]

I Owe, I Owe—It's Off to Work I Go

Are you where you want to be if it doesn't work?

—LOUIS L'AMOUR, AUTHOR AND HISTORIAN

Let's say you go ahead and get your MBA. If you're "lucky," you may be hired by a big financial-services or consulting firm, where you'll have the privilege of working ten-plus hours a day for around $100,000 a year. The salary increase is nice, but you'll have a hard time maintaining any sort of life outside of work, and the pressure will be intense and relentless. Even if you don't like your job, you'd better keep pushing if you want to pay off your tuition loans and make your investment "worth it."

Congratulations: you've used your intelligence and drive to condemn yourself to the life of an indentured servant.

If you do good work, you'll become an executive, get a raise, have more responsibility—and work even harder. You'd better not mind enjoying the fruits of your labor alone: top executives have high rates of divorce and family relationship issues. As the saying goes: you can have anything you want, as long as you're willing to pay the price.

If you're not so "fortunate," you'll find a job that pays little more than what you'd be able to command without your MBA. Worse yet, graduating into an iffy job market means that you may leave business school with a $1000-a-month loan payment but without a job to foot the bill. An unforgiving job market won't make student loan payments go away. Regardless of how your life works out, your student loans will always be there, and your phone will ring with the calls of debt collectors until they're repaid.

I can't emphasize this enough: *the quickest and easiest way to screw up your life is to take on too much debt.* The primary reason people spend decades working at jobs they despise is to pay off their creditors. Financial stress can destroy relationships, threaten your health, and jeopardize your sanity. Is a shot at a desk in a corner office really worth it?

With heavy debt loads and questionable returns, MBA programs aren't a good investment—they're a trap for the unwary.

A Better Way

> To educate educators! But the first ones must educate themselves! And for these I write.
>
> —FRIEDRICH NIETZSCHE, PHILOSOPHER AND AUTHOR OF
> *THE WILL TO POWER* AND *THUS SPOKE ZARATHUSTRA*

Fortunately, you have a choice in how you go about educating yourself—a choice that can make you *more* successful than top MBA graduates while saving you hundreds of thousands of dollars. Studying the fundamentals of sound business practice and developing a network on your own can provide most of the benefits of business education at a fraction of the cost. Instead of wasting your time and hard-earned money learning outdated theories you'll probably never use, it's far better to spend your time and energy teaching yourself what you need to know to succeed.

If you're the type of person who's capable of getting into a top MBA program and doing what it takes to succeed after graduation, skipping business school and learning the fundamentals of business by reading this book may be the best decision you ever make.

What You'll Learn in This Book

> When you first start to study a field, it seems like you have to memorize a zillion things. You don't. What you need is to identify the core principles—generally three to twelve of them—that govern the field. The million things you thought you had to memorize are simply various combinations of the core principles.
>
> —JOHN T. REED, REAL ESTATE INVESTOR AND AUTHOR OF *SUCCEEDING*

This book is designed to teach you the fundamentals of sound business practice. Here's a quick preview of what you'll learn:

How businesses work. A successful business, roughly defined, provides (1) something of value that (2) other people want or need at (3) a price they're willing to pay, in a way that (4) satisfies the customer's needs and expectations so that (5) the business brings in sufficient profit to make it worthwhile for the owners to continue operation. Together, the concepts in chapters 1 to 5 describe how every business operates and what you can do to improve your results.

How people work. Every business is created by people and survives by benefiting other people. To understand how businesses work, you need a firm understanding of how people make decisions, act on those decisions, and communicate with others. Chapters 6 to 8 introduce you to a few major concepts in psychology that describe how the human mind processes the world, how you can work in a more effective and efficient way, and how you can create and strengthen professional relationships.

How systems work. Businesses are complex systems with many moving parts that exist within even more complex systems like industries, societies, cultures, and governments. Chapters 9 to 11 will help you understand how complex systems work, as well as help you analyze existing systems and find ways to improve them without provoking unanticipated consequences.

Here are a few things you *shouldn't* expect:

Management and leadership overload. Many business resources (and all business schools) conflate management and leadership skills with business skills; *they're not the same thing.* While management and leadership are important in the practice of business, they aren't the be-all and end-all of business education: without solid business knowledge, it's possible to organize and lead a group of people toward the accomplishment of the wrong objectives. Business is about the profitable creation and delivery of valuable offers to paying customers; management and leadership are a means to this end. We'll discuss the essentials of effective management and leadership in chapter 8, but in their proper context.

CFA/CPA-level finance and accounting. Finance and accounting are very important topics, and we'll discuss the essential concepts and practices in chapter 5, including common mistakes and pitfalls. That said, we have many topics to explore, and finance is not the sole focus of this book. Deep examinations of financial analysis and accounting standards have filled thousands of books much longer than this one, and unless you plan on becoming a chartered financial analyst (CFA) or a certified public accountant (CPA), you should learn the basics of these topics, but leave the details to the specialists.

Fortunately, there's no need to reinvent the wheel: great books on finance and accounting already exist. If you're interested in exploring these topics in more detail after completing chapter 5, I recommend the following books:

Financial Intelligence for Entrepreneurs by Karen Berman and Joe Knight

Simple Numbers, Straight Talk, Big Profits! by Greg Crabtree

Accounting Made Simple by Mike Piper

How to Read a Financial Report by John A. Tracy

In addition, online courses like MBA Math (http://mbamath.com) and Bionic Turtle (http://bionicturtle.com) are available if you want to explore these topics in even greater depth. (Many business schools and corporate-finance training programs recommend or require these courses prior to enrollment.)

Quantitative analysis and modeling. We'll discuss the fundamentals of measurement and analysis in chapter 10, but this book won't turn you into a Wall Street "quant" or a high-flying spreadsheet jockey. Statistics and quantitative analysis are very useful skills when used appropriately, but the actual techniques are very situational and beyond the scope of this book. If you're interested in learning more about statistical analysis after reading chapter 10, I recommend:

Thinking Statistically by Uri Bram

How to Lie with Statistics by Darrell Huff

Turning Numbers into Knowledge by Jonathan Koomey, PhD

For an examination of more advanced methods of analysis, *Principles of Statistics* by M. G. Bulmer is a useful reference.

How to Use This Book

> All truly wise thoughts have been thought already thousands of times; but to make them truly ours, we must think them over again honestly, until they take root in our personal experience.
>
> —JOHANN WOLFGANG VON GOETHE, POET, DRAMATIST, AND POLYMATH

Here are a few tips that will help you get the most from this book:

Browse, skim, and scan. You don't need to read a book cover to cover to benefit: browsing can give you better results with less effort. Feel free to browse and preview concepts until you find a section that grabs your attention, then commit to applying that concept to your work for a few days.

You'll begin to notice significant differences in the quality of your work as well as in your ability to "think like a businessperson."

Keep a notebook and pen handy. The purpose of this book is to give you ideas about how to make things better, so be prepared to capture your thoughts as you have them; it'll make it easier to review the major concepts later. Your notebook will also make it easy to shift from taking notes to creating detailed action plans as they occur to you.[29]

Review this book often. Keep it close to where you work so you can refer to it as you work, particularly before starting a new project. Repetition leads to mastery: the better you internalize these concepts, the more you'll improve your results. I also recommend setting a reminder in your calendar to review this book or your notes every few months to reinforce your understanding and spark new ideas.

Discuss these ideas with your colleagues. Great things happen when everyone you work with knows these concepts and uses the same language to discuss how they apply to your business. After every concept, I've included a link to an online reference page, which you can include in an email, proposal, blog post, or other communication. This helps ensure everyone is on the same page, particularly if the recipient isn't familiar with the concept you're referencing.

There's always more to explore. Each idea has many applications, and it's impossible to explore every ramification of these concepts in a single book. There are many great resources in the world of business literature that can deepen your understanding if you'd like to learn more about a particular mental model. Join me at personalmba.com to explore these ideas in more detail and learn how to apply them to your daily life and work.

Let's begin.

1

VALUE CREATION

Make something people want . . . There's nothing more valuable than an unmet need that is just becoming fixable. If you find something broken that you can fix for a lot of people, you've found a gold mine.

—PAUL GRAHAM, COFOUNDER OF Y COMBINATOR, VENTURE
CAPITALIST, AND ESSAYIST AT PAULGRAHAM.COM

Every successful business creates something of value. The world is full of opportunities to make other people's lives better in some way, and your job as a businessperson is to identify things that people don't have enough of, then find a way to provide them.

The value you create can take on one of several different forms, but the purpose is always the same: to make someone else's life a little bit better. Without value creation, a business can't exist—you can't transact with others unless you have something valuable to trade.

The best businesses in the world are the ones that create the most value for other people. Some businesses thrive by providing a little value to many, and others focus on providing a lot of value to only a few people. Regardless, the more real value you create for other people, the better your business will be and the more prosperous you'll become.

REFERENCE LINK: **personalmba.com/value-creation/**

The Five Parts of Every Business

A business is a repeatable process that makes money. Everything else is a hobby.

—PAUL FREET, SERIAL ENTREPRENEUR AND COMMERCIALIZATION EXPERT

Roughly defined, a business is a repeatable process that:

1. Creates and delivers something of value . . .

2. That other people want or need . . .

3. At a price they're willing to pay . . .

4. In a way that satisfies the customer's needs and expectations . . .

5. So that the business brings in enough **Profit** to make it worthwhile for the owners to continue operation.

It doesn't matter if you're running a solo venture or a billion-dollar brand. Take any one of these five factors away and you don't have a business—you have something else. A venture that doesn't create value for others is a hobby. A venture that doesn't attract **Attention** is a flop. A venture that doesn't sell the value it creates is a nonprofit. A venture that doesn't deliver what it promises is a scam. A venture that doesn't bring in enough money to keep operating is not going to exist very long.

At the core, every business is a collection of five **Interdependent** processes, each of which flows into the next:

1. *Value Creation*—discovering what people need or want, then creating it.

2. *Marketing*—attracting attention and building demand for what you've created.

3. *Sales*—turning prospective customers into paying customers.

4. *Value Delivery*—giving your customers what you've promised and ensuring that they're satisfied.

5. *Finance*—bringing in enough money to keep going and make your effort worthwhile.

If these five things sound simple, it's because they are. Business is not (and has never been) rocket science—it's a process of identifying a problem and finding a way to solve it that benefits both parties. Anyone who tries to make business sound more complicated than this is either trying to impress you or trying to sell you something you don't need.

The **Five Parts of Every Business** are the basis of every good business idea and business plan. If you can define each of these five processes for any business, you'll have a complete understanding of how it works. If you're thinking about starting a new business, defining what these processes might look like is the best place to start. If you can't describe or diagram your business idea in terms of these core processes, you don't understand it well enough to make it work.[1]

REFERENCE LINK: personalmba.com/5-parts-of-every-business/

Economically Valuable Skills

Don't go around saying the world owes you a living. The world owes you nothing—it was here first.

—MARK TWAIN, GREAT AMERICAN NOVELIST

If you want to improve your value as a businessperson, focus on improving skills related to the **Five Parts of Every Business**.

Not every skill or area of knowledge is **Economically Valuable**, and that's okay—there are many things worth pursuing for the sake of relaxation or enjoyment alone. You may enjoy white-water rafting, but it's very unlikely anyone will pay you to shoot the rapids unless you apply your skills for the benefit of others. Make the leap from personal enjoyment to **Products** and **Services**, however, and you'll find yourself getting paid—plenty of adventurous souls are willing to pay for rafting equipment and guides.

As Michael Masterson suggests in *Ready, Fire, Aim*, don't expect skills that aren't related to the Five Parts of Every Business to be economically rewarded. Find a way to use them to create Economic Value and you'll find a way to get paid.

Any skill or knowledge that helps you create value, market, sell, deliver value, or manage finances is Economically Valuable—these are the skills we'll discuss in this book.

REFERENCE LINK: **personalmba.com/economically-valuable-skills/**

The Iron Law of the Market

> Market matters most. And neither a stellar team nor a fantastic product will redeem a bad market. . . . *Markets that don't exist don't care how smart you are.*
>
> —MARC ANDREESSEN, VENTURE CAPITALIST AND COFOUNDER OF NETSCAPE

What if you throw a party and nobody shows up? In business, it happens all the time.

Dean Kamen, a renowned and prolific inventor whose creations include the Stirling engine, the world's first wearable insulin pump, and water-purification devices, poured more than $100 million into the development of the Segway PT, a $5,000, two-wheeled, self-balancing scooter that he claimed would revolutionize personal transportation "in the same way that the car replaced the horse and buggy." When the Segway was made available to the public in 2002, the company announced that it expected to sell fifty thousand units every year.

Five years into the business, the company had sold a total of twenty-three thousand units—less than 10 percent of the initial goal. (The company's financial records are private, but it's safe to say they didn't look good. In 2015, the company was sold to Ninebot, a competitor that sells inexpensive electric scooters, for an undisclosed sum.)

The problem wasn't that the product was poorly designed. The technology that makes the Segway work is sophisticated, and the benefits are significant: the Segway is a convenient, green urban car replacement. The problem was that very few people cared enough to spend $5,000 on a goofy-looking alternative to walking or riding a bike—the massive market that Kamen expected didn't exist.

The same thing happens to new businesses every day. Without enough revenue to sustain it, any business will fail. Your revenue is dependent on people *wanting* what you have to offer.

Every business is fundamentally limited by the size and quality of the market it attempts to serve. The *Iron Law of the Market* is cold, hard, and unforgiving: if you don't have a large group of people who want what you have to offer, your chances of building a viable business are very slim.

The best approach is to focus on making things people want to buy. Creating something no one wants is a waste. Market research is the business equivalent of "Look before you leap." Books like *The New Business Road Test* by John Mullins can help you identify promising markets from the outset, increasing the probability that your new venture will be a success.

In the next few sections, we'll explore how to figure out what people want and need *before* investing your time and hard-earned money into creating something new.

REFERENCE LINK: **personalmba.com/iron-law-of-the-market/**

Core Human Drives

Understanding human needs is half the job of meeting them.

—ADLAI STEVENSON II, POLITICIAN AND FORMER GOVERNOR OF ILLINOIS

If you're going to build a successful business, it's useful to have a basic understanding of what people want. The most well-known general theory of what people want is Maslow's hierarchy of needs, proposed by the psychologist Abraham Maslow in 1943. Maslow's theory was that people progress through five general stages in the pursuit of what they need: physiology, safety, belonging/love, esteem, and self-actualization. Physiology represents the "lowest" level of human need, while self-actualization (the exploration of a person's innate potential) is the "highest."

In Maslow's hierarchy, each lower-level need must be met before a person can focus on higher-order needs. If you don't have enough food or you're in physical danger, you're probably not paying too much attention to how much other people like you or how much personal growth you're experiencing.

In practice, I prefer Clayton Alderfer's version of Maslow's hierarchy, which he called "ERG theory": people seek existence, relatedness, and growth, in that order. When people have what they need to survive, they move on to making friends and finding mates. When they're satisfied with their relationships, they focus on doing things they enjoy and improving their skills in things that interest them. First existence, then relatedness, then growth.

ERG theory explains the general *priority* of human desires, but not the *methods* people use to satisfy them. For that, we must turn to other theories of human action. According to Harvard Business School professors Paul Lawrence and Nitin Nohria, the authors of *Driven: How Human Nature Shapes Our Choices*, all human beings have four **Core Human Drives** that have a profound influence on our decisions and actions:

1. *The Drive to Acquire*—the desire to obtain or collect physical objects, as well as immaterial qualities like status, power, and influence. Businesses built on the drive to acquire include retailers, investment brokerages, and political consulting companies. Companies that promise to make us wealthy, famous, influential, or powerful connect to this drive.

2. *The Drive to Bond*—the desire to feel valued and loved by forming relationships with others, either platonic or romantic. Businesses built on the drive to bond include restaurants, conferences, and dating services. Companies that promise to make us attractive, well-liked, or highly regarded connect to this drive.

3. *The Drive to Learn*—the desire to satisfy our curiosity. Businesses built on the drive to learn include academic programs, book publishers, and training workshops. Companies that promise to make us more knowledgeable or competent connect to this drive.

4. *The Drive to Defend*—the desire to protect ourselves, our loved ones, and our property. Businesses built on the drive to defend include home alarm system manufacturers, insurers, martial arts training programs, and legal services. Companies that promise to keep us safe, eliminate a problem, or prevent bad things from happening connect to this drive.

There's a fifth core drive that Lawrence and Nohria missed:

5. *The Drive to Feel*—the desire for new sensory stimuli, intense emotional experiences, pleasure, excitement, entertainment, and

anticipation. Businesses built on the drive to feel include movie theaters, arcades, concert promoters, and sports teams. Companies that promise to give us pleasure, thrill us, or give us something to look forward to connect with this drive.

Whenever a group of people have an unmet need in one or more of these areas, a market will form to satisfy that need. As a result, the more drives your offer connects with, the more attractive it will be to your potential market.

At the core, all successful businesses sell the promise of some combination of money, status, power, love, knowledge, protection, pleasure, and excitement. The better you articulate how your offer satisfies one or more of these drives, the more attractive your offer will become.

REFERENCE LINK: personalmba.com/core-human-drives/

Social Status

The society which scorns excellence in plumbing as a humble activity and tolerates shoddiness in philosophy because it is an exalted activity will have neither good plumbing nor good philosophy: neither its pipes nor its theories will hold water.

—JOHN W. GARDNER, FORMER PRESIDENT OF THE CARNEGIE CORPORATION

In addition to understanding *Core Human Drives*, it's important to understand that humans are social creatures. Like many other mammals, humans evolved to have a pecking order, a relative ranking of *Power* or status in a group. Competing with other people for status and power brought many benefits, including access to food, mates, resources, and the protection of other group members.

Status considerations are no longer as critical to survival, but our brains developed to place a very high priority on *Social Status*. As a result, status considerations influence the vast majority of a person's decisions and actions.

Social Status is a universal phenomenon: neurotypical human beings care about what other people think of them and spend a significant amount of energy tracking their relative status compared to other members of their group. When opportunities to increase status appear, most people will seize them. When given a choice between different alternatives, people will choose the option with the highest perceived status.

In general, we like to be associated with people and organizations that we think are powerful, important, or exclusive or that exhibit other high-status qualities or behaviors. We also like to ensure other people are aware of our status: for proof, examine what people post on their social-media profiles.

Social Status is a fact of human life; it's not necessarily bad or something to be avoided. On the contrary: status seeking can motivate people to accomplish amazing things. In the words of Alain de Botton, a philosopher and social critic, "If one *felt* successful, there'd be so little incentive to *be* successful."

Unchecked, this urge toward status can lead people to make poor decisions: think of someone who purchases a large house, a luxury car, and designer clothing, only to end up bankrupt or in severe debt. As an individual, paying attention to how much you value status is useful when making buying decisions, particularly when there are other options that can meet the same needs or desires at a lower cost.

As a business professional, it's important to understand that status considerations are present in every level of the Core Human Drives. When you make an offer to a new prospect, they will estimate how your offer will influence their social status. Building **Status Signals** into your offer is almost always an effective way to increase its appeal to your target market.

REFERENCE LINK: **personalmba.com/social-status/**

Ten Ways to Evaluate a Market

So often people are working hard at the wrong thing. Working on the right thing is probably more important than working hard.

—CATERINA FAKE, COFOUNDER OF FLICKR AND HUNCH

If you're thinking of starting a new business or expanding an existing business into a new market, it pays to do some research before you leap.

The **Ten Ways to Evaluate a Market** provide a back-of-the-napkin method you can use to identify the attractiveness of any potential market. Rate each of the ten factors below on a scale of 0 to 10, where 0 is terrible and 10 fantastic. When in doubt, be conservative in your estimate:

1. *Urgency.* How badly do people want or need this right now? (Renting an old movie is low urgency; seeing the first showing of a new movie on opening night is high urgency, since it only happens once.)

2. *Market Size.* How many people are purchasing things like this? (The market for underwater basket-weaving courses is very small; the market for cancer cures is massive.)

3. *Pricing Potential.* What is the highest price a typical purchaser would be willing to spend for a solution? (Lollipops sell for $0.05; aircraft carriers sell for billions.)

4. *Cost of Customer Acquisition.* How easy is it to acquire a new customer? On average, how much will it cost to generate a sale, in both money and effort? (Restaurants built on high-traffic interstate highways spend little to bring in new customers. Government contractors can spend millions landing major procurement deals.)

5. *Cost of Value Delivery.* How much will it cost to create and deliver the value offered, in both money and effort? (Delivering files via the internet is almost free; inventing a product and building a factory costs millions.)

6. *Uniqueness of Offer.* How unique is your offer versus competing offerings in the market, and how easy is it for potential competitors to copy you? (There are many hair salons but very few companies that offer private space travel.)

7. *Speed to Market.* How soon can you create something to sell? (You can offer to mow a neighbor's lawn in minutes; opening a bank can take years.)

8. *Up-front Investment.* How much will you have to invest before you're ready to sell? (To be a housekeeper, all you need is a set of inexpensive cleaning products. To mine for gold, you need millions to purchase land and excavating equipment.)

9. *Upsell Potential.* Are there related secondary offers that you could also present to purchasing customers? (Customers who purchase razors need shaving cream and extra blades as well; buy a Frisbee and you won't need another unless you lose it.)

10. *Evergreen Potential.* Once the initial offer has been created, how much additional work will you have to put in in order to continue selling? (Business consulting requires ongoing work to get paid; a book can be produced once and then sold over and over as is.)

When you're done with your assessment, add up the score. If the score is 50 or below, move on to another idea—there are better places to invest your energy and resources. If the score is 75 or above, you have a very promising idea—full speed ahead. Anything between 50 and 75 has the potential to pay the bills but won't be a home run without a huge investment of energy and resources.

REFERENCE LINK: **personalmba.com/ten-ways-to-evaluate-a-market/**

The Hidden Benefits of Competition

> The competitor to be feared is one who never bothers about you at all, but goes on making his own business better all the time.
>
> —HENRY FORD, FOUNDER OF THE FORD MOTOR COMPANY
> AND ASSEMBLY-LINE PIONEER

One of the most common experiences of a first-time entrepreneur is discovering that your brilliant business idea isn't as original as you'd thought: other businesses are already offering similar products or services. This would shake anyone's confidence—after all, why bother when someone else is doing what you want to do?

Cheer up: there are *Hidden Benefits of Competition*. When any two markets are equally attractive in other respects, you're better off choosing to enter the one *with* competition. Here's why: it means you know from the start there's a market of paying customers for this idea, eliminating your biggest risk.

The existence of a market means you're already on the right side of the *Iron Law of the Market*, so you can spend more time developing your offer instead of proving a market exists. If there are several successful businesses serving a market, you don't have to worry so much about investing in a dead end, since you already know that people are buying.

The best way to observe what your potential competitors are doing is to become a customer. Buy as much as you can of what they offer. Observing your competition from the customer's perspective can teach you an enormous amount about the market: what value the competitor provides, how they attract attention, what they charge, how they close sales, how they make customers happy, how they deal with issues, and what needs they aren't yet serving.

As a paying customer, you get to observe what works in your market and what doesn't before you commit to a particular strategy. Learn everything you can from your competition and then create something even more valuable.

REFERENCE LINK: personalmba.com/hidden-benefit-of-competition/

The Mercenary Rule

Make money your god and it will plague you like the devil.

—HENRY FIELDING, EIGHTEENTH-CENTURY NOVELIST AND SATIRIST

Becoming a **Mercenary** doesn't pay—don't start a business for the money alone. Here's why: starting and running a business *always* takes more effort than you first expect.

Even if you identify a business that will run itself, setting up the systems necessary to run the business requires persistence and dedication. If the only thing that interests you about an opportunity is the money, you'll probably quit well before you find the pot of gold at the bottom of the landfill.

Pay very close attention to the things you find yourself coming back to over and over again. Building or finishing anything is a matter of *starting* over and over again; don't ignore what pulls you. The trick is to find an attractive market that interests you enough to keep you improving your offering every single day. Finding that market is a matter of patience and active exploration.

That said, don't ignore "boring" businesses until you investigate them; if you can find some aspect of the work that interests you and keeps you engaged, mundane markets can be quite attractive. "Dirty" businesses like plumbing and garbage collection aren't sexy, but they can be quite lucrative because there's a significant ongoing need combined with relatively few people willing to step up and meet the demand.

If you find a way to make a necessary but dull market interesting enough to pursue, you may have discovered a hidden vein of gold waiting to be mined.

REFERENCE LINK: **personalmba.com/mercenary-rule/**

The Crusader Rule

The zealous display the strength of their belief, while the judicious show the grounds of it.

—WILLIAM SHENSTONE, EIGHTEENTH-CENTURY POET
AND LANDSCAPE DESIGNER

Being a *Crusader* doesn't pay either. Every once in a while, you'll find an idea so fascinating it becomes hard to think about it objectively. The stars align, heavenly trumpets blare, and suddenly you have the unmistakable impression that you've found your calling.

In all the excitement, it's easy to forget that there's often a huge difference between an interesting idea and a solid business. In your optimism, forget ye not prudence: changing the world is difficult if you can't pay the bills.

Some ideas don't have enough of a market behind them to support a business, and that's okay. That doesn't mean you should ignore them: side projects can help you expand your knowledge, improve your skills, and experiment with new methods and techniques. I'm a huge advocate of pursuing side projects as long as you don't rely on them to produce income. Once you have your financial bases covered, crusade all you want.

Before attempting to launch a business, take the time to do a thorough evaluation using the *Ten Ways to Evaluate a Market*. If you're finding it difficult to be objective, find a trusted colleague or adviser to help you, then test the market before you fully commit. A few hours spent in evaluation can prevent months (or years) of frustration and misplaced effort.

REFERENCE LINK: **personalmba.com/crusader-rule/**

Twelve Standard Forms of Value

Value is not intrinsic; it is not in things. It is within us; it is the way in
which man reacts to the conditions of his environment.

—LUDWIG VON MISES, AUSTRIAN ECONOMIST

In order for your business to successfully provide value to another person,
that value must take on a form they're willing to pay for. Fortunately,
there's no need to reinvent the wheel—*Economic Value* usually takes on one
of twelve standard forms:

1. *Product.* Create a single tangible item or entity, then sell and deliver it for more than what it cost to make.

2. *Service.* Provide help or assistance, then charge a fee for the benefits rendered.

3. *Shared Resource.* Create a durable asset that can be used by many people, then charge for access.

4. *Subscription.* Offer a benefit on an ongoing basis and charge a recurring fee.

5. *Resale.* Acquire an asset from a wholesaler, then sell that asset to a retail buyer at a higher price.

6. *Lease.* Acquire an asset, then allow another person to use that asset for a predefined amount of time in exchange for a fee.

7. *Agency.* Market and sell an asset or service you don't own on behalf of a third party, then collect a percentage of the transaction price as a fee.

8. *Audience Aggregation.* Get the attention of a group of people with certain characteristics, then sell access to that group, in the form of advertising, to another business looking to reach that audience.

9. *Loan.* Lend a certain amount of money, then collect payments over a predefined period of time equal to the amount of the original loan plus interest at a predefined rate.

10. *Option.* Offer the ability to take a predefined action for a fixed period of time in exchange for a fee.

11. *Insurance.* Take on the risk of some specific bad thing happening to the policyholder in exchange for a predefined series of payments, then pay out claims only if the bad thing happens.

12. *Capital.* Purchase an ownership stake in a business, then collect a corresponding portion of the profit as a one-time payout or ongoing dividend.

Let's investigate these **Twelve Standard Forms of Value** in more detail.

REFERENCE LINK: **personalmba.com/12-standard-forms-of-value/**

Form of Value #1: Product

> Business is not financial science . . . it's about creating a product or service so good that people will pay for it.
>
> —ANITA RODDICK, ENTREPRENEUR AND FOUNDER OF THE BODY SHOP

A **Product** is a tangible form of value. To run a Product-oriented business, you must:

1. Create some sort of tangible item that people want.

2. Produce that item as inexpensively as possible while maintaining an acceptable level of quality.

3. Sell as many units as possible for as high a price as the market will bear.

4. Keep enough inventory of finished product available to fulfill orders as they come in.

The book you're holding right now is a good example of a Product. It had to be written, edited, typeset, printed, bound, and shipped to bookstores in sufficient quantities before reaching your hands. Leave out any of these steps and you wouldn't be reading this right now. To make money, a book must be sold for more than it cost to create, print, and distribute.

Products can be durable, like cars, computers, and vacuum cleaners. They can also be consumable: goods like apples, donuts, and prescription medications are products as well. Products don't have to be physical—even though things like software, ebooks, and MP3s don't have a distinct physical form, they are entities that can be sold.

Providing value in Product form is valuable because Products can be **Duplicated**. This book was written only once, but individual copies can be created and delivered millions of times to readers around the world. As a result, products tend to **Scale** better than other forms of value, since they can be Duplicated and/or **Multiplied** (all of these concepts are discussed later).

REFERENCE LINK: **personalmba.com/product/**

Form of Value #2: Service

Everyone can be great because everyone can serve.

—MARTIN LUTHER KING, JR., HUMAN RIGHTS ACTIVIST

Service involves helping or assisting someone in exchange for a fee. To create value via Services, you must be able to provide some type of benefit to the user.

In order to create a successful Service, your business must:

1. Have employees capable of a skill or ability other people require but can't, won't, or don't want to use themselves.

2. Ensure that the Service is provided at high quality.

3. Attract and retain paying customers.

A good example of a Service business is a barbershop. A haircut is not a **Product**: you can't purchase one from a shelf. The Service is the series of actions the stylist uses to transform your current hairstyle into the one you want. In this sense, doctors, freelance designers, massage therapists, lawn-care providers, and consultants are all Service providers.

Services can be lucrative, particularly if the skills required to provide them are rare and difficult to develop, but the trade-off is that they're difficult to duplicate. Services depend on the Service provider's investment of time and energy, both of which are finite; a heart surgeon can only complete so many four-hour operations on any given day.

If you're developing a Service, be sure to charge enough to compensate for the time you'll be investing on a daily basis in providing the Service to your customers. Otherwise, you'll discover that you're working too hard for too little reward.

REFERENCE LINK: **personalmba.com/service/**

Form of Value #3: Shared Resource

The joy that isn't shared, I've heard, dies young.

—ANNE SEXTON, PULITZER PRIZE–WINNING POET, "WELCOME MORNING"

A **Shared Resource** is a durable asset that can be used by many people. Shared Resources allow you to create the asset once, then charge your customers for its use.

In order to create a successful Shared Resource, you must:

1. Create an asset people want to have access to.

2. Serve as many users as you can without affecting the quality of each user's experience.

3. Charge enough to maintain and improve the Shared Resource over time.

Gyms and fitness clubs are a classic example of a Shared Resource. A fitness club may purchase forty treadmills, thirty exercise bikes, six sets of free weights, a set of kettlebells, and other useful but expensive equipment that lasts a long time. The club's members benefit by being able to access this equipment without having to purchase it themselves—instead, they pay an access fee, which is much easier for an individual to afford. (Most gyms combine access to their Shared Resource with **Services** and **Subscriptions**, a common example of **Bundling**, which we'll discuss later.)

Businesses like movie theaters and amusement parks work in much the same way. Whether it means watching the latest big-budget film or riding a roller coaster, Shared Resources allow many people to take advantage of experiences that would otherwise be too expensive.

The tricky part about offering a Shared Resource is carefully monitoring usage levels. If you don't have enough users, you won't be able to spread out the cost of the asset enough to cover up-front costs and ongoing maintenance. If you have too many users, overcrowding will diminish the experience so much that they'll become frustrated, stop using the resource, and advise others not to patronize your business, diminishing your **Reputation**. Finding the sweet spot between too few members and too many is the key to making a Shared Resource work.

REFERENCE LINK: **personalmba.com/shared-resource/**

Form of Value #4: Subscription

Please accept my resignation. I don't want to belong to any club that will accept me as a member.

—GROUCHO MARX, COMEDIAN

A **Subscription** program provides predefined benefits on an ongoing basis in exchange for a recurring fee. The actual benefits provided can be tangible or intangible—the key differences from other forms of value are (a) the expectation of additional value to be provided in the future and (b) the understanding that fees will be collected until the Subscription is canceled.

In order to create a successful Subscription, you must:

1. Provide significant value to each subscriber on a regular basis.

2. Build a subscriber base and continually attract new subscribers to compensate for attrition.

3. Bill customers on a recurring basis.

4. Retain each subscriber as long as possible.

Cable or satellite television service is a great example of a Subscription. After you sign up, the company will continue to provide television service as long as you make the payments. You don't have to call up the company every month to buy another thirty days' worth—the service continues as long as the invoice is paid.

Subscription is an attractive form of value because it provides more predictable revenue. Instead of having to resell to your existing customers every day, Subscriptions allow you to build a steady base of loyal customers over time. This model ensures a certain level of revenue coming in each billing period.

The key to Subscription offers is doing everything you can to keep customer attrition as low as possible. As long as you continue to make your customers happy, only a small percentage of your customer base will cancel each period, giving you the ability to plan your finances with more certainty. Any subscriber attrition you experience can be overcome by enrolling more customers.

REFERENCE LINK: **personalmba.com/subscription/**

Form of Value #5: Resale

Buy low, sell high.

—STOCK TRADER'S MAXIM

Resale is the acquisition of an asset from a wholesale seller followed by the sale of that asset to a retail buyer at a higher price. Resale is how most of the retailers you're familiar with work: they purchase what they sell from other businesses, then resell each purchase for more than it cost.

In order to provide value as a reseller, you must:

1. Purchase a product as inexpensively as possible, usually in bulk.

2. Keep the product in good condition until sale—damaged goods can't be sold.

3. Find potential purchasers of the product as soon as possible to keep inventory costs low.

4. Sell the product for as high a markup as possible, preferably a multiple of the purchase price.

Resellers are valuable because they help wholesalers sell products without having to find individual purchasers. For a farmer, selling apples to millions of individuals would be time-intensive and inefficient: it's far better to sell them all to a grocery chain and focus on growing more apples.

The grocery chain then takes the apples into inventory and sells them to individual consumers at a higher price.

Mass-market retailers like Walmart and Tesco, specialty retailers like CVS and Walgreens, and catalog operations like Lands' End work the same way: purchase products at low prices from manufacturers, then sell them for a higher price as soon as possible.

Sourcing good products at low prices and managing inventory levels are the keys to reselling. Without a steady supply of sellable product obtained at a low enough price to turn a profit, a reseller will have a hard time bringing in enough revenue to keep going. Most successful resellers establish close relationships with the businesses that supply their inventory to ensure they continue to get a reliable supply of good assets at low prices.

REFERENCE LINK: **personalmba.com/resale/**

Form of Value #6: Lease

The human species, according to the best theory I can form of it, is composed of two distinct races: the men who borrow and the men who lend.

—CHARLES LAMB, ESSAYIST

A **Lease** involves acquiring an asset, then allowing another person to use that asset for a predefined amount of time in exchange for a fee. The asset can be pretty much anything: a car, boat, house, bike, or power tool. As long as an asset is durable enough to survive rental to another person and be returned ready for reuse, you can Lease it.

In order to provide value via a Lease, you must:

1. Acquire an asset people want to use.

2. Lease the asset to a paying customer on favorable terms.

3. Protect yourself from unexpected or adverse events, including the loss or damage of the leased asset.

Leasing benefits the customer by allowing the use of an asset for less than the outright purchase price. You may not be able to afford to spend tens of thousands of dollars to purchase a luxury car or a speedboat, but for a few hundred dollars a month, you can Lease one. The same principle applies to housing: leasing makes it possible to live in an expensive building for much less than it would cost to purchase or build it yourself. After your lease is up, the housing unit can be leased by the owner to someone else.

To successfully provide value via a Lease, you must ensure that the revenue from the Lease covers the purchase price of the asset before it wears out or is lost. Most assets have a limited useful life, so you must charge enough to bring in more revenue than the purchase price before the asset loses its value. In addition, be sure to plan for repair and replacement costs to ensure you're charging enough money to cover you in the event your asset is lost or damaged in use.

REFERENCE LINK: **personalmba.com/lease/**

Form of Value #7: Agency

I wish to be cremated. One tenth of my ashes shall be given to my agent, as written in our contract.

—GROUCHO MARX

gency involves the marketing and sale of an asset you don't own. Instead of producing value by yourself, you team up with someone else who has value to offer, then work to find a purchaser. In exchange for establishing a new relationship between your source and a buyer, you earn a commission or fee.

In order to provide value via Agency, you must:

1. Find a seller who has a valuable asset.

2. Establish contact and trust with potential buyers of that asset.

3. Negotiate until an agreement is reached on the terms of sale.

4. Collect the agreed-upon fee or commission from the seller.

Sellers benefit from an Agency relationship because it generates sales that might not otherwise happen. Literary agents are a classic example: a potential author may have an idea for a book but may not know anyone in publishing. By working with an agent who has preexisting connections in the publishing industry, the author is far more likely to land a publishing contract. In exchange for finding a publisher and negotiating the deal, the agent gets a percentage of the book's advance and royalties.

Buyers also benefit from an Agency relationship—good agents can help them find great assets to purchase. Agents often act as a filter for buyers, who trust that the agent will bring to their attention assets worth purchasing and keep them away from bad deals. Residential real estate is a great example: working with an experienced buyer's agent who knows the area often makes purchasing a home in a new town much easier.

The key to Agency is to ensure that your fee or commission is high enough to make the effort worth it. Since most Agency relationships are dependent upon closing a sale, you must spend your time on activities that will result in a completed transaction, and you must ensure that the commission or fee from that transaction compensates you for the time and effort you put into closing the deal.

REFERENCE LINK: **personalmba.com/agency/**

Form of Value #8: Audience Aggregation

So long as there's a jingle in your head, television isn't free.
—JASON LOVE, MARKETING EXECUTIVE

Audience Aggregation revolves around collecting the attention of a group of people with similar characteristics, then selling access to that audience to a third party. Since attention is limited and valuable, gathering a group of people in a certain demographic is quite valuable to businesses or groups that are interested in getting the attention of those people.

In order to provide value via Audience Aggregation, you must:

1. Identify a group of people with common characteristics or interests.

2. Create and maintain some way of attracting that group's attention.

3. Find third parties who are interested in buying the attention of that audience.

4. Sell access to that audience without alienating the audience itself.

Audience Aggregation benefits the audience because it provides something worthy of their attention. Magazines and advertising-supported websites are great examples: readers benefit from the information and entertainment these sources provide in exchange for being exposed to some level of advertising. If the advertising becomes obnoxious, they'll leave, but most people are willing to be exposed to a certain amount of advertising if the content is good.

Audience Aggregation benefits the advertiser because it gets attention, which leads to sales. Think of a conference or trade show: buying a booth in the center of a building full of people interested in what you have to offer can be a smart decision. Done well, advertising attracts attention, attention brings prospects, and prospects lead to sales. As long as the sales bring in more money than the cost of the advertising plus the business's **Overhead**, the advertising can be a valuable tool to bring in new customers, which means the advertiser can continue to support the aggregator by purchasing more advertising.

REFERENCE LINK: personalmba.com/audience-aggregation/

Form of Value #9: Loan

Money talks—but credit has an echo.

—BOB THAVES, CARTOONIST AND CREATOR OF *FRANK AND ERNEST*

A **Loan** involves an agreement to let the borrower use a certain amount of resources for a certain period of time. In exchange, the borrower must pay the lender a series of payments over a predefined period of time, which is equal to the amount of the original loan plus interest at a predefined rate.

In order to provide value via Loans, you must:

1. Have some amount of money to lend.

2. Find people who want to borrow that money.

3. Set an interest rate that compensates you adequately for the Loan.

4. Estimate the probability that the Loan won't be repaid, and avoid preventable losses.

Used responsibly, Loans allow people to benefit from immediate access to products or services that would otherwise be too expensive to purchase outright. Mortgages allow people to live in houses without having hundreds of thousands of dollars in the bank. Auto loans allow people to drive new vehicles in exchange for a monthly payment instead of a 100 percent down payment. Credit cards allow people to purchase products and services immediately, then pay for them over the course of several months.

Loans are beneficial to the lender because they provide a way to benefit from excess capital. The addition of compound interest on top of the original loan (the "principal") means that the lender will collect much more than the value of the original loan—in the case of long-term Loans like mortgages, often two to three times more.

After the Loan is made, little additional work is required on the part of the lender aside from collecting payments—unless the borrower stops making payments. The process of identifying how risky a particular Loan is—a process called underwriting—is an essential skill for lenders, who often require some sort of asset as collateral to protect against the risks of a Loan gone sour. If the Loan is not repaid, ownership of the collateral is transferred to the lender, then sold to recoup any funds lost in the transaction.

REFERENCE LINK: **personalmba.com/loan/**

Form of Value #10: Option

You pays your money and you makes your choice.
—*PUNCH*, NINETEENTH-CENTURY BRITISH COMIC MAGAZINE, 1846

An **Option** is the ability to take a predefined action for a fixed period of time in exchange for a fee. Most people think of Options as financial securities, but they're all around us: movie or concert tickets, coupons, retainers, and licensing rights are all examples of Options. In exchange for a fee, the purchaser has the right to take some specific action—attend the show, purchase an asset, produce a licensed **Product**, or buy a financial security at a particular price—before the deadline.

In order to provide value via Options, you must:

1. Identify some action people might want to take in the future.

2. Offer potential buyers the right to take that action before a specified deadline.

3. Convince potential buyers that the Option is worth the asking price.

4. Enforce the specified deadline on taking action.

Options are valuable because they allow the purchaser the *ability* to take a specific action without *requiring* them to take that action. For example, if you purchase a movie ticket, you have the ability to occupy a seat in the theater, but you don't *have to* if a better opportunity presents itself. When you purchase the ticket, all you're purchasing is the right to exercise the Option to see the movie at the time specified—nothing more.

Options are often used to keep specific courses of action open for a certain period of time before another transaction takes place. For example, in moving to Colorado from New York, my wife, Kelsey, and I put a deposit down on an apartment we hadn't seen in person. The deposit ensured that the landlord wouldn't rent the apartment to someone else before we moved. Once we signed the official rental agreement, the deposit became a standard rental security deposit. If we had decided not to move forward, the landlord would have kept the deposit in compensation for holding the apartment for us and would have been free to find another tenant. Thus, the Option was beneficial for both parties.

Options are often an overlooked form of value—flexibility is one of the **Three Universal Currencies**. Find a way to give people more flexibility and you may discover a viable business model.

REFERENCE LINK: **personalmba.com/option/**

Form of Value #11: Insurance

Take calculated risks. That is quite different from being rash.

—GENERAL GEORGE S. PATTON, COMMANDER OF THE US THIRD ARMY IN
WORLD WAR II

Insurance involves the transfer of risk from the purchaser to the seller. In exchange for taking on the risk of some specific bad thing happening to the policyholder, the policyholder agrees to give the insurer a predefined series of payments. If the bad thing happens, the insurer is responsible for footing the bill. If it doesn't, the insurer gets to keep the money.

In order to provide value via Insurance, you must:

1. Create a binding legal agreement that transfers the risk of a specific bad thing (a "loss") happening from the policyholder to you.

2. Estimate the risk of that bad thing happening, using available data.

3. Collect the agreed-upon series of payments (called premiums) over time.

4. Pay out legitimate claims on the policy.

Insurance provides value to the purchaser by protecting them from downside risk. For example, a house can catch fire in any number of ways, and most homeowners don't have enough cash to purchase another if their home burns to the ground. Homeowners' insurance transfers this risk to the insurer. If the home is destroyed by fire, the Insurance will compensate the homeowner and allow them to purchase a new home. If it isn't, the insurer gets to keep the premium payments.

Insurance works because it spreads risk over a large number of individuals. If an insurer writes policies for thousands or millions of homes, it's highly unlikely that every single one will burn to the ground at once; only a certain number of claims will ever have to be paid. As long as the insurer brings in more in premium payments than it pays in claims, the insurer makes money. Car insurance, health insurance, and warranty coverage for consumer goods work the same way.

The more premiums an insurer collects and the fewer claims the insurer pays, the more money it makes. Insurers have a vested interest in avoiding "bad risks," maximizing premiums, and minimizing payments on claims. Insurers must be vigilant to avoid fraudulent activity, both preventing fraudulent claims and refraining from defrauding purchasers by collecting premium payments without paying legitimate claims. If an insurer fails to pay legitimate claims, they're likely to find themselves in court as policyholders use the legal system to uphold their Insurance contract.

REFERENCE LINK: **personalmba.com/insurance/**

Form of Value #12: Capital

Capital is that part of wealth which is devoted to obtaining further wealth.

—ALFRED MARSHALL, ECONOMIST AND AUTHOR OF
PRINCIPLES OF ECONOMICS

apital is the purchase of an ownership stake in a business. For parties that have resources to allocate, providing Capital is a way to help owners of new or existing businesses expand or enter new markets. Angel investing, venture capital, and purchasing stock in publicly traded companies are all examples of providing value via Capital, which we'll discuss in detail later, in the **Hierarchy of Funding**.

In order to provide value via Capital, you must:

1. Have a pool of resources available to invest.

2. Find a promising business in which you'd be willing to invest.

3. Estimate how much that business is currently worth, how much it may be worth in the future, and the probability that the business will go under, which would result in the loss of your Capital.

4. Negotiate the amount of ownership you'd receive in exchange for the amount of Capital you're investing.

Businesses benefit from Capital investment because it enables them to gather the resources necessary to expand or enter new industries. Some industries, like manufacturing and financial services, require huge amounts of funding to start or expand. By taking on investors, business owners can secure enough funding to move forward.

Investors benefit by acquiring a certain percentage of that company's ownership, which allows them to benefit from the business's activities without active involvement. Instead of leaving their money in a bank account, investors can allocate it to companies that are involved in promising ventures, which may provide a higher rate of return. If the business brings in a lot of cash, investors may benefit from a regular dividend. If it's acquired by another company or is listed on a public stock exchange, investors may receive a percentage of the purchase price as a lump-sum payment or sell their shares of the company on the open market for a profit.

REFERENCE LINK: **personalmba.com/capital/**

Hassle Premium

All human situations have their inconveniences.

—BENJAMIN FRANKLIN, EIGHTEENTH-CENTURY AMERICAN POLITICAL LEADER, SCIENTIST, AND POLYMATH

People are almost always willing to pay for things to be dealt with that they believe are too much of a pain to take care of themselves. Where there's a hassle, there's a business opportunity.

Hassles come in many forms. The project or task in question may:

▶ Take too much time to complete.

▶ Require too much effort to ensure a good result.

▶ Distract from other, more important priorities.

▶ Involve too much confusion, uncertainty, or complexity.

▶ Require costly or intimidating prior experience.

▶ Require specialized resources or equipment that's difficult to obtain.

The more hassle a project or task involves, the more people are willing to pay for an easy solution or for someone to complete the job on their behalf. Here's an example: a homeowner may be willing to pay a one-time fee of $50 for a pool cleaning kit, but they may be willing to pay a cleaning service $100 per *month* to have someone clean their pool for them.

The end result is a clean pool either way, but the cleaning service removes the hassle: the pool owner doesn't have to spend any time or effort to get the same desired result. As a result, the pool cleaning service benefits from the **Hassle Premium**: it's able to collect $1,200 per year—$1,150 more than the DIY option—by eliminating the hassle for the pool owner.

There is a limit, however. Charging $10,000 a month for a pool cleaning service won't work—the vast majority of homeowners don't care about having a clean pool that much. To benefit from the Hassle Premium, you need to understand how much of a hassle the task is to the prospect. The greater the hassle, the higher the potential Hassle Premium.

If you're looking for a new business idea, start looking for hassles. Where there's hassle, there's opportunity. The more hassle you eliminate for your customers, the more you'll collect in revenue.

REFERENCE LINK: **personalmba.com/hassle-premium/**

Perceived Value

> People don't trade money for things when they value their money
> more highly than they value the things.
>
> —ROY H. WILLIAMS, *THE WIZARD OF ADS*

All forms of value are not created equal. Value is in the eye of the beholder.

Perceived Value determines how much your customers will be willing to pay for what you're offering. The more valuable a prospect believes your offer is, the more likely they'll be to buy it and the more they'll be willing to pay.

The most valuable offers do one or more of the following:

▸ Satisfy one or more of the prospect's **Core Human Drives**.

▸ Offer an attractive and easy-to-visualize **End Result**.

▸ Command the highest **Hassle Premium** by reducing end-user involvement as much as possible.

▶ Satisfy the prospect's desire for **Social Status** by providing **Status Signals** that help them look good in the eyes of other people.

It's important to note that Perceived Value is a subjective matter and depends on your prospect's current situation, values, beliefs, and world view. If your prospects don't believe your offer is valuable, they won't be **Receptive** to your offer.

Focus on providing the most significant benefits and the highest status in a way that requires the least amount of end-user effort and frustration and you'll increase the Perceived Value of your offer.

REFERENCE LINK: **personalmba.com/perceived-value/**

Modularity

> Great things are not done by impulse, but by a series of small things brought together.
>
> —VINCENT VAN GOGH, ARTIST

Keep in mind that the **Twelve Standard Forms of Value** aren't mutually exclusive: you can offer any number or combination of these forms to your potential customers to see which ones they like best. This strategy is called **Modularity**.

Most successful businesses offer value in multiple forms. Take the magazine industry, for example. Magazines charge a monthly or annual **Subscription** fee in exchange for a printed magazine delivered by mail on a periodic basis. Simultaneously, they use **Audience Aggregation** to sell access to their subscribers via advertising, which is included in the magazine alongside the content.

Travel websites like Orbitz sell **Options** (airplane tickets) alongside trip-cancellation **Insurance** and display advertising (Audience Aggregation) to website visitors. Movie theaters combine movie showings (a **Shared Resource**) with tickets (an Option) and concession sales (**Products**). Companies like Netflix and Spotify provide digital access to a large library of movies and music (a Shared Resource) in exchange for a monthly fee (Subscription).

In most companies, each of these offers is handled separately, and the customer can pick and choose which offers they want to take advantage of. By making offers Modular, the business can create and improve each offer in isolation, then mix and match offers as necessary to better serve their customers. It's like playing with LEGOs: once you have a set of pieces to work with, you can put them together in all sorts of interesting ways.

REFERENCE LINK: **personalmba.com/modularity/**

Bundling and Unbundling

A bit of this and a bit of that is how newness enters the world.

—SALMAN RUSHDIE, NOVELIST

One of the primary benefits of *Modularity* is that it allows you to take advantage of a strategy called *Bundling*. Bundling allows you to repurpose value that you have already created to create even more value.

Bundling occurs when you combine multiple smaller offers into a single large offer. An example of Bundling occurs in the mobile phone industry, where a mobile phone (a physical *Product*) is bundled with a monthly service plan (a *Subscription*) for a single price. Similarly, buy-one-get-one-free offers at the grocery store are a form of Bundling.

The more offers contained in the bundle, the higher the *Perceived Value* of the offer and the more the business can charge. That's why mobile phone providers offer additional minutes, unlimited text messaging, and internet service on top of the basic service plan. The more benefits provided, the more a customer is often willing to pay on a monthly basis for the entire package.

Unbundling is the opposite of Bundling: it's taking one offer and splitting it up into multiple offers. A good example of Unbundling is selling downloads of a single song instead of the entire album. Customers may not be willing to pay $10 for the album, but they might be willing to pay a dollar or two for the songs they like. Unbundling the album into individual units opens the way to sales that wouldn't otherwise happen.

Bundling and Unbundling can help you create value for different types of customers without requiring the creation of something new. By combining offers and forms in various configurations, you can offer your customers what they want.

REFERENCE LINK: **personalmba.com/bundling-unbundling/**

Intermediation and Disintermediation

The shortest and best way to make your fortune is to let people see clearly that it is in their interests to promote yours.

—JEAN DE LA BRUYÈRE, SEVENTEENTH-CENTURY
PHILOSOPHER AND SATIRIST

Another way of thinking about value creation involves a simple question: how much help would your *Probable Purchaser* find useful?

Think of a complex buying decision, like purchasing a house. You can't just walk into a store, examine all of the potential options, pick the house that suits you best, then walk up to a cash register to purchase it with cash or a credit card. Looking at available homes, clarifying needs and preferences, securing financing, negotiating the purchase price, and completing the legal paperwork takes a nontrivial amount of time, knowledge, and expertise.

That's why residential real estate agents have a market: potential home buyers often don't know the options (particularly if they're not familiar with the area), don't have a lot of experience completing these sorts of *Transactions*, and feel overwhelmed. Real estate agents assist in the search, purchase decision, and closing process, and home buyers are often happy to work with someone who knows what they're doing.

The term for this sort of help is *Intermediation*: adding a party between the buyer and seller responsible for helping one of the parties complete the Transaction or derive value from the purchase.

Intermediation is useful in complex situations where the purchaser benefits from guidance and help from experts. You'll often find Intermediaries in areas where there are a lot of options to choose from—like retailers who decide which items to stock. They're also common in complex negotiations and purchases, like business brokerages who help entrepreneurs put a price on their current business operations, then help them find potential acquiring companies willing to pay what their business is worth. In most cases, the Intermediary also acts as a *Buffer* between the parties, which can shield them from unnecessary pressure or uncomfortable situations.

The opposite of Intermediation is *Disintermediation*: removing unnecessary parties to a Transaction in favor of direct contact between the buyer and seller. Before the internet, most manufacturers had to deal with retailers if they wanted to sell their goods, since mass advertising and distribution opportunities were expensive and limited. The internet allowed manufacturers to attract the attention of potential customers, complete purchases, and deliver their goods direct to their consumers: no retailer required. As a result, more product and service companies can exist in a profitable and sustainable way: the *Margins* that would otherwise be captured by an Intermediary can be redirected toward lower prices, targeted advertising, product development, or *Profit*.

Opportunities exist at both ends of the spectrum: would your potential customers benefit from more help, or less?

REFERENCE LINK: **personalmba.com/intermediation-disintermediation/**

Prototype

It's this simple: if I never try anything, I never learn anything.
—HUGH PRATHER, AUTHOR OF *NOTES TO MYSELF*

The stereotypical product development model is shrouded in secrecy: develop the offer in private, make everyone involved sign nondisclosure agreements,[2] raise millions of dollars in venture capital, spend years making it perfect, then unveil your creation to the astonishment of the world and the thunderous sound of ringing cash registers.

This mentality ruins careers and empties bank accounts. On their own, ideas are worthless—discovering whether or not you can make them work in reality is the most important job of any entrepreneur.

Don't be shy about showing potential customers your work in progress. Unless you work in an industry with unusually aggressive, competent, and well-funded competitors, you don't have to worry about other people "stealing" your idea. Ideas are cheap—what counts is the ability to translate an idea into reality, which is much more difficult than recognizing a good idea.

"Stealth mode" diminishes your early learning opportunities, putting you at a huge early disadvantage. It's almost always better to focus on getting feedback from real customers as soon as you can.

A **Prototype** is an early representation of what your offering will look like. It may be a physical model, a computer rendering, a diagram, a flowchart, or a one-page paper that describes the major benefits and features. It doesn't have to be fancy: all your Prototype has to do is represent what you're offering in a tangible way, so that your potential customers can understand what you're doing well enough to give you good feedback.

For best results, create your prototype in the same form as the finished product. If you're creating a physical product, make a tangible model. If you're making a website, create a working webpage with the basic components. If you're creating a service, create a diagram or flowchart of everything that happens in the process, then act it out. The more realistic your Prototype is, the easier it'll be for people to understand what you're trying to do.

The Prototype is your first attempt at creating something useful, but it won't be your last. Your first will be poor and incomplete, and that's okay. Prototypes are valuable because they allow you to get good feedback from real people before you invest a huge amount of time, money, and effort into the project. The purpose of a Prototype is not to make it perfect: it's to create a tangible focus for your efforts—something you and other people can see, evaluate, and improve.

As you show your Prototype to potential customers, you'll get a steady stream of ideas and feedback that will help you make your offer even better.

REFERENCE LINK: **personalmba.com/prototype/**

The Iteration Cycle

I have not failed. I've just found ten thousand ways that won't work.

—THOMAS EDISON, PROLIFIC INVENTOR

Nobody—no matter how smart or talented they are—gets it right the first time.

For proof, consider any artistic masterpiece. Beneath the finished surface of the *Mona Lisa*, you'll find layer upon layer of draft sketches, false starts, and major alterations. The ceiling of the Sistine Chapel is covered with hundreds of millions of very small brushstrokes, each of which brought the resulting masterpiece one step closer to completion. It took Michelangelo millions of hammer strokes to turn a crude block of marble into *David*.

The **Iteration Cycle** is a process you can use to make anything better over time. There's nothing wasteful about the inevitable changes and revisions that these artists made to their creations: every iteration brought the project one step closer to completion.

Iteration relies on the scientific method, which has five general steps:

1. Observe what's happening and identify something that you'd like to improve.

2. Design an experiment and identify indicators that will tell you whether or not the prospective change is an improvement.

3. Conduct the experiment and collect data.

4. Evaluate the results of the experiment.

5. Accept or reject the change as an improvement.

Iteration is a cycle—once you measure the results of the change and decide whether or not to keep it, you go back to the beginning to observe what's happening, and the cycle repeats.

For best results, define what you're trying to accomplish with each iteration. Are you trying to make the offering more attractive or appealing? Are you trying to add a new feature people will value? Are you trying to make the offering cost less without detracting from its value? The better you can define what you're after, the easier it'll be to understand the **Feedback** you're receiving and the more value you'll extract from each Iteration Cycle.

REFERENCE LINK: personalmba.com/iteration-cycle/

Iteration Velocity

Our goal is to have more at bats per unit of time and money than anyone else.

—ERIC SCHMIDT, FORMER CHAIRMAN AND CEO OF GOOGLE

When creating a new offering, your primary goal should be to work your way through each *Iteration Cycle* as fast as possible. Iteration is a structured form of learning that helps you make your offering better; the faster you learn, the faster you'll improve.

The faster you move through the Iteration Cycle, the better your offering will become—that's *Iteration Velocity*. If you're good, you can move through the process several times each day. The key is to keep each iteration small, clear, and quick, basing each iteration on what you learned via previous iterations.

The Iteration Cycle often feels like additional work because it *is* additional work. That's why so few people do it: it's very tempting to skip all of these "extra" steps and attempt to create the final offering outright.

The major problem with the direct approach is risk: you're sinking a great deal of time, energy, and resources on creating something that may not sell. If the idea's a dud, it's far better to figure that out via a few quick Iteration Cycles than to bet the farm on an idea or market that just won't work.

Iteration may take some additional effort up front, but after you've gone through a few cycles, you'll have a deeper understanding of the market, direct knowledge of what people want enough to pay for, and a clear understanding of whether or not you have a viable offer to make to them.

If you discover that you have what people want, great—full steam ahead. If there's no demand for what you're developing, move on to the next promising idea.

REFERENCE LINK: **personalmba.com/iteration-velocity/**

Feedback

No business plan survives first contact with customers.

—STEVEN GARY BLANK, SERIAL ENTREPRENEUR AND AUTHOR OF
THE FOUR STEPS TO THE EPIPHANY

Getting useful *Feedback* from your potential customers is the core of the **Iteration Cycle**. Useful Feedback from real prospects helps you understand how well your offer meets their needs before development is complete, which allows you to make changes before you start selling.

Here are a few tips to maximize the value of the Feedback you receive:

1. *Get Feedback from real potential customers instead of friends and family.* Your inner circle wants you to succeed and wants to maintain a good relationship with you, so it's likely that they'll unintentionally sugarcoat their Feedback. For best results, be sure to get plenty of Feedback from people who aren't personally invested in you or your project.

2. *Ask open-ended questions.* When collecting Feedback, you should be listening more than you talk. Have a few open-ended questions prepared to give the conversation a bit of structure, but otherwise encourage the other person to do most of the talking. Short who/what/when/where/why/how questions work best. Watch what the user does, and compare their actions with what they say.

3. *Steady yourself and keep calm.* Asking for genuine Feedback (the only useful kind) requires thick skin—no one likes hearing their baby is ugly. Try not to get offended or defensive if someone doesn't like what you've created; they're doing you a great service by telling you so.

4. *Take what you hear with a grain of salt.* Even the most discouraging Feedback contains crucial pieces of information that can help you make your offering better. The worst response you can get when asking for Feedback isn't emphatic dislike: it's total apathy. If no one seems to care about what you've created, you don't have a viable business idea.

5. *Give potential customers the opportunity to preorder.* One of the most important pieces of Feedback you can receive during the iteration process is the other person's willingness to purchase what you're creating. It's one thing for a person to say that they'd purchase something and quite another for them to be willing to pull out their wallet or credit card and place a real order. You can do this even if the offer isn't ready yet—a tactic called **Shadow Testing**. Whenever possible, give the people who are giving you Feedback the opportunity to preorder the offering. If a significant number of people take you up on the offer, you're in good shape: you know that you have a solid offering *and* you boost your cash flow. If no one is willing to preorder, you know you have more work to do before you have a viable offer. By asking why they're not willing to purchase right now, you'll discover their major **Barriers to Purchase**—what's holding them back.

REFERENCE LINK: **personalmba.com/feedback/**

Alternatives

> Until one is committed, there is hesitancy, the chance to draw back, always ineffectiveness. Concerning all acts of initiative and creation, there is one elementary truth the ignorance of which kills countless ideas and splendid plans: that the moment one definitely commits oneself, the providence moves too.
>
> —W. H. MURRAY, MOUNTAINEER AND WRITER

It's Friday night. You're hungry and you're thinking about going out to eat. You've already decided that you value having food prepared for you enough to justify the extra expense. Where should you go for dinner?

If you go to the neighborhood diner, you'll have access to a large variety of decent food at a reasonable price. The place may not be very fancy, but you know you'll be served a pretty good meal without a lot of fuss or expense.

If you go to a swanky hot spot, you'll be treated to attractive decor, impeccable service, and sophisticated cuisine. You'll have an impressive story to tell your friends, as well as the anticipation and excitement of a big night on the town. You'll also have a heftier tab at the end of the evening.

Unless you're *really* hungry, you won't patronize both restaurants on the same evening—it's an either/or decision. At the same time, there's no "right" decision—in fact, you may choose to go to the diner one evening and the trendy restaurant the next. It all depends on what you value most at the moment you decide where to eat.

Now let's flip the situation. You're the owner of the diner, and you're looking for ways to serve your customers better and bring new people into the restaurant. What should you focus on improving? Would expanding your entrée selection, reducing the time it takes to serve customers, or remodeling the restaurant make the biggest difference to the bottom line?

In a perfect world, it would be best to do *all* of these things, but business has been lackluster recently, and you don't have an unlimited budget to work with. You know you need to do something, but it's not clear which improvements—if any—would make the cash register ring more often. What do you do?

As you develop your offering, you can't avoid making choices between competing **Alternatives**. Should you add a particular feature, or not? Should you optimize for market A, optimize for market B, or attempt to please both? If you invest more in the offering, will your customers be willing to pay more to defray the expense?

Examining the possible Alternatives and considering the customer's perspective results in better choices. As you make decisions about what to include and what to leave out, it's essential to appreciate the Alternatives that your potential customers face when they decide whether or not to purchase your offering. Once you're aware of the options, you can examine the combinations and permutations of those Alternatives to present an attractive offer.

REFERENCE LINK: personalmba.com/alternatives/

Trade-offs

I can't give you a surefire formula for success, but I can give you a
formula for failure: try to please everybody all the time.

—HERBERT BAYARD SWOPE, PULITZER PRIZE–WINNING JOURNALIST

A **Trade-off** is a decision that places a higher value on one of several competing options. We live in a world where time, energy, and resources are finite. There are only twenty-four hours in a day, you only have so much available energy, and at any given time there's an upper limit on the amount of money you're able to spend. What do you do when you can't do everything you want?

You can't have everything you want all of the time. Even if your bank account is large enough to purchase a private island, you're still faced with the decision of *which* private island to buy. You may want it all, but you can't have it all, so you do the best you can by choosing the option with the characteristics that matter most to you at the moment you make the decision.

Every minute of every day, you and the people around you are making Trade-offs. Some of these Trade-offs are economic: Which pair of pants should you purchase? Some of them are temporal: Should you visit with friends or go to a movie? Some of them are about effort: Should you go to the team meeting or complete the overdue TPS report?

Predicting how people will make certain Trade-offs is tricky—values change, given the environment and context. Values are preferences—how much we want, desire, or place importance on one particular object, quality, or state of being versus another. What you value this morning may be different from what you value this afternoon or this evening. What you want today may be different from what you want tomorrow.

When making decisions about what to include in your offering, it pays to look for patterns—information about how specific groups of people tend to value some characteristic in a certain context. The decisions you make about what to include and what to leave out will never make everyone happy, so perfection shouldn't be your goal. By paying attention to the patterns behind what your *best* customers value, you'll be able to focus on improving your offering for *most* of your best potential customers *most* of the time.

REFERENCE LINK: personalmba.com/tradeoffs/

Economic Values

A successful business is either loved or needed.

—TED LEONSIS, FORMER EXECUTIVE AT AOL AND OWNER OF THE
WASHINGTON WIZARDS AND WASHINGTON CAPITALS

Every time your customers purchase from you, they're deciding that they value what you have to offer more than they value anything else their money could buy at that moment. As you develop your offering, one of your first priorities should be to find out what your potential customers value more than the buying power of the dollars in their wallets.

Everyone has slightly different values at any given time, but there are a few common patterns that appear when people evaluate a potential purchase. Assuming the promised benefits of the offering are appealing, there are nine common **Economic Values** that people consider when evaluating a potential purchase. They are:

1. *Efficacy*—how well does it work?

2. *Speed*—how soon does it work?

3. *Reliability*—can I depend on it to do what I want?

4. *Ease of use*—how much effort does it require?

5. *Flexibility*—how many things does it do?

6. *Status*—how does this affect the way others perceive me?

7. *Aesthetic appeal*—how attractive or otherwise aesthetically pleasing is it?

8. *Emotion*—how does it make me feel?

9. *Cost*—how much do I have to give up to get it?

In the book *Trade-Off: Why Some Things Catch On, and Others Don't*, Kevin Maney discusses these common values in terms of two primary characteristics: convenience and fidelity. Things that are quick, reliable, easy, and flexible are convenient. Things that offer quality, status, aesthetic appeal, or emotional impact are high fidelity.

Almost every improvement you make to an offer can be thought of in terms of improving either convenience or fidelity. It's incredibly difficult to optimize for both fidelity and convenience at the same time, so the most successful offerings try to provide the most convenience or fidelity among all competing offerings. If you're craving pizza, a table at the original Pizzeria Uno in Chicago is high fidelity; Domino's home delivery is convenient. Pizzeria Uno benefits more from making the dining experience remarkable, while Domino's benefits more from delivering decent pizza as fast as possible.

The **Trade-offs** that are made in the development of new offerings are what give each option its unique identity. Here's an example from the apparel business: Old Navy, Banana Republic, and Gap are owned by the same company, Gap Inc. All three lines make the same types of clothing—shirts, pants, and so on—but offer different Trade-offs.

Instead of attempting to make a single clothing line that's designed to appeal to everyone (which is impossible, since everyone wants something different), the company focused each line around a specific Trade-off. Old Navy emphasizes functionality and low cost. Gap emphasizes style and fashion at a moderate cost. Banana Republic emphasizes aesthetics and **Social Status** at a premium cost. Each line has its own identity and appeals to a different type of potential customer, even though the clothes may be manufactured using the same processes and the revenues end up in the coffers of the same company.

REFERENCE LINK: **personalmba.com/economic-values/**

Relative Importance Testing

Things which matter most must never be at the mercy of things which matter least.

—JOHANN WOLFGANG VON GOETHE, EIGHTEENTH-CENTURY POET, DRAMATIST, AND POLYMATH

The tricky thing about trying to figure out what people want is that people want everything. Here's proof: bring together a group of potential customers for a focus group. Ask each participant to rate the importance of each of the nine **Economic Values** for your offering on a scale of 0 to 10. What will the results look like?

Regardless of your product or service, the results will be the same: your customers want products that provide exceptional results every time, with no effort. Simultaneously, they want the offer to make them rich, famous, attractive, and eternally blissful. They also want it to be free. If you ask them what they'd be willing to give up, they'll answer that everything is important and they won't be happy with less.

The reality outside of the focus group is always quite different. After the group adjourns, each of those participants will go out and purchase something that's not free and not perfect, and they'll be happy with their choice. Why?

As a rule, people never accept **Trade-offs** unless they're forced to make a **Decision**. If the perfect option existed, they'd buy it. Since there's no such thing as the perfect offering, people are happy to settle for the **Next Best Alternative**.

The best way to discover what people value is to ask them to make explicit Trade-offs during the research process. The problem with the hypothetical focus group was that it didn't ask the participants to make any real Decisions—the participants could have everything, so they wanted everything.

Relative Importance Testing—a set of analysis techniques pioneered by statistician Jordan Louviere in the 1980s[3]—gives you a way to determine what people want by asking them a series of simple questions designed to simulate real-life Trade-offs. Here's how it works.

Let's assume we're conducting a Relative Importance Test for the diner previously mentioned. Instead of asking the participant to rank each benefit from 0 to 10, we show the participant something like the following:

A. Orders delivered to table in five minutes or less.

B. Most entrée prices under $20.

C. Appealing restaurant decor.

D. Large variety of menu options.

After this set is shown, the participant is asked the following questions:

1. Which of these items is most important?

2. Which of these items is least important?

Once the participant answers the questions, another set is shown:

E. Unique entrées I can't get anywhere else.

F. Knowing I can always order my favorite dishes.

G. People are impressed that I dine here.

H. Large portions.

Random question sets containing four or five criteria are provided until there are no more possible combinations or the participant's attention wanders, which often occurs around the five- to ten-minute mark.

It won't take the participant long to provide a response to each of these simple questions, but the results are quite revealing. By asking the participant to make an actual choice, you're collecting more accurate information about how the participant would respond when faced with a similar choice in the real world. When the results are aggregated and analyzed, the relative importance of each benefit becomes very clear. The more sets each participant completes, the better you'll be able to judge the relative importance of each benefit.[4]

Relative Importance Testing can help you determine which benefits you should focus on to make your offering maximally attractive.

REFERENCE LINK: **personalmba.com/relative-importance-testing/**

Critical Assumptions

It is better to be roughly right than precisely wrong.
—JOHN MAYNARD KEYNES, ECONOMIST

Imagine that you're interested in opening a yoga studio. The market opportunity looks good: you believe that you've identified an underserved neighborhood with significant demand and residents with enough discretionary income to pay a $100-plus monthly membership fee. You've sketched out what the space would look like and you have a rough idea of the different styles you'd like to offer and whom you'd bring in to teach classes.

You've found a suitable location that you can rent for around $10,000 per month (if you sign a twelve-month lease), and you estimate that you'll need an additional $12,000 per month to pay employee salaries and other monthly operating expenses. You'll also need to spend around $5,000 up front for equipment: mats, blocks, and a computer to handle membership records.

The commercial real estate agent you're working with is putting pressure on you to move fast, saying the location you want may be snatched up by another tenant if you don't commit now. Your current life's savings are enough to cover the start-up costs and three months of projected operating expenses. You're excited, but you want to ensure that you're making the right decision before you move forward. Should you sign the lease?

Stories like this are very common: an excited first-time entrepreneur has a dream of owning a restaurant, bar, or bookstore, so they invest their life's savings and take on significant debt to open the new business. Sometimes these stories work out well. More often than not, in a few months the new entrepreneur is bankrupt and out of business, wondering how things went so terribly wrong.

Critical Assumptions are facts or characteristics that must be true in the real world for your business or offering to be successful. Every business or offering has a set of Critical Assumptions that will make or break its continued existence: if any of these Critical Assumptions turns out to be false, the business idea will be less promising than it appears.

The previous yoga studio example has three primary Critical Assumptions:

1. Individuals in this neighborhood will be willing to commit to pay $100 or more per month for a yoga membership close to their home.

2. The business will be able to attract at least 220 members paying full price within three months.

3. Total monthly revenues will exceed $22,000 for the next twelve months, which is the minimum duration of the lease term.

Let's examine what would happen to the yoga studio if these Critical Assumptions turn out to be false:

1. Initial interest is high, but most of the people who tour the new studio balk at paying $100 per month, saying that they'd rather drive a few miles and pay $75. The studio lowers prices to $75, which

means 300 members are now required to keep the studio afloat. After lowering prices, membership reaches the 220-member mark as planned, but it's not enough to keep the studio open.

2. The studio doesn't attract enough members to pay the bills because yoga enthusiasts in the neighborhood are already locked into twelve-month membership contracts with a studio a few miles away. The studio runs out of money and closes.

3. A very nice competing studio opens up in the same neighborhood around the same time. After three months, the studio only has half of the members it needs to sustain itself. With nine more months on the lease, the financial outlook is bleak.

If you can identify these assumptions in advance and test whether or not they're true, you'll take fewer risks and have more confidence in the wisdom of your decisions.

REFERENCE LINK: personalmba.com/critical-assumptions/

Shadow Testing

Praemonitus praemunitus (forewarned is forearmed).

—ROMAN PROVERB

The best way to validate the truth of your *Critical Assumptions* is to test them, but going through the entire process of starting the business is needlessly risky and expensive. It's much smarter to minimize your risk by testing your offering with real paying customers before you fully commit to making it real.

Shadow Testing is the process of selling an offering before it exists. As long as you're up front with your potential customers that the offering is still in development, Shadow Testing is a very useful strategy you can use to test your Critical Assumptions with real customers.

Real paying customers are always different from hypothetical customers. Shadow Testing allows you to get a critical piece of customer feedback you can get in no other way: whether or not people will pay for what you're developing. In order to minimize the risk you're taking on in committing to the project, your objective should be to start gathering data from real paying customers as soon as possible.

Fitbit is a company that knows the value of Shadow Testing. Founded by Eric Friedman and James Park in September 2008, Fitbit makes a small, wearable exercise and sleep data-gathering device. The Fitbit device tracks your activity levels throughout the day and night, then uploads your data to the web, where it analyzes your health, fitness, and sleep patterns.

It's a neat concept, but creating new hardware is time consuming, expensive, and fraught with risk, so here's what Friedman and Park did. The same day they announced the Fitbit idea to the world, they started allowing customers to preorder a Fitbit on their website, based on little more than a description of what the device would do and a few renderings of what the product would look like. The billing system collected names, addresses, and verified credit card numbers, but no charges were processed until the product was ready to ship, which gave the company an out in case their plans fell through.

Orders started rolling in, and one month later, investors had the confidence to pony up $2 million dollars to make the Fitbit a reality. A year later, the first real Fitbit was shipped to customers. That's the power of Shadow Testing.

REFERENCE LINK: **personalmba.com/shadow-testing/**

Minimum Viable Offer

If you're not embarrassed by the first version of your product, you've launched too late.

—REID HOFFMAN, COFOUNDER OF LINKEDIN

In order to conduct *Shadow Testing*, you need something to sell. Fortunately, you don't have to create the entire offer before you start selling.

A *Minimum Viable Offer* is an offer that promises and/or provides the smallest number of benefits necessary to produce an actual sale. A Minimum Viable Offer is a *Prototype* that's been developed to the point that someone will pull out their wallet and commit to making a purchase. It doesn't have to be complicated: Fitbit's Minimum Viable Offer was a Prototype, a description, and a few computer renderings. All you need to do is convey enough information to convince a real potential customer to buy.

Creating a Minimum Viable Offer is useful because it's impossible to predict with 100 percent accuracy what will work in advance. You don't want to invest a ton of time and money in something that has no chance of working, and the faster you can figure out if your idea will work or not, the better off you'll be.

Since **Feedback** from prospective customers and paid-in-full orders are very different things, creating a Minimum Viable Offer allows you to start collecting data from real customers, testing the idea's **Critical Assumptions**, and reducing the risk of making a business-ending investment decision.

Here's how the hypothetical yoga studio we discussed earlier could use a Minimum Viable Offer and Shadow Testing to evaluate its Critical Assumptions:

Step 1: Create a simple website describing the studio in detail, including location, tentative schedule, teaching staff, sketches of the space, and membership fees. The site includes a sign-up form for visitors to preorder memberships by submitting their credit card information. By signing up, members commit to a twelve-month membership when the studio opens, but they have the opportunity to cancel within the first month if they don't like it. If the studio doesn't open, all preorders are canceled without charge. Total cost: a few hundred dollars.

Step 2: Direct prospective customers to the website. This can be done inexpensively in any number of ways: flyers, door-to-door inquiry, direct mail, and local search-engine advertising. Total cost: a few hundred dollars.

Step 3: Track how many individuals preorder memberships at the full rate via the website or request additional information. Total cost: a few hours of analysis.

This method of testing is simple, fast, and inexpensive. Services like Kickstarter (www.kickstarter.com) are making tests like these easy: all it takes to allow potential customers to preorder is a video, a few sketches or renderings, and basic sales copy. Spending a few hours and a few hundred dollars testing your Critical Assumptions is a very good use of money, particularly if your findings indicate your business idea won't work.

The purpose of starting with a Minimum Viable Offer is to minimize your risk. By keeping the investments small, incremental, and learning oriented, you'll be able to discover what works and what doesn't. If the idea is promising, you're in a great position to make it happen. If your assumptions don't hold true, you're able to cut your losses without losing your shirt or your dignity.

REFERENCE LINK: **personalmba.com/minimum-viable-offer/**

Incremental Augmentation

> Pick three key attributes or features, get those things very, very right, and then forget about everything else . . . By focusing on only a few core features in the first version, you are forced to find the true essence and value of the product.
>
> —PAUL BUCHHEIT, CREATOR OF GMAIL AND GOOGLE ADSENSE

Once your **Minimum Viable Offer** is selling and you've proven that your **Critical Assumptions** are valid, you're in good shape, but you're not finished. If you're committed to making your offer as good as it can be, you'll need to keep making small changes that improve the offer if you want to stay competitive and attract more customers.

Incremental Augmentation is the process of using the **Iteration Cycle** to add new benefits to an existing offer. The process is simple: keep making and testing additions to the core offer, continue doing what works, and stop doing what doesn't.

The process of customizing cars is an example of Incremental Augmentation. Starting with a stock car, the tuner replaces and upgrades parts: a better engine, a spoiler, tinted windows, and chrome hubcaps. The intent of every change is to make the car just a little bit better, until it's the best it can be. When the car is finished, it's a different machine.

Incremental Augmentation helps you improve your offering while minimizing the risk that any single iteration will fail catastrophically. If you're not careful, drastic changes after launch can eliminate the qualities that made your offer attractive or break the systems you use to create the value you're providing to your customers. By making and testing changes, you can improve your offer without betting the farm, helping you create even more value for your customers over time.

Keep in mind that Incremental Augmentation can only take you so far. In order to enter a new market or change the game, you may need to create something new. If that's the case, start over with a new **Prototype** and work your way through the value-creation process from the beginning. When the Prototype is ready, get **Feedback** and use **Testing** to compare the new version with the old version and make sure it's better before you launch it.

REFERENCE LINK: **personalmba.com/incremental-augmentation/**

Field Testing

Any engineer that doesn't need to wash his hands at least three times a day is a failure.

—SHOICHIRO TOYODA, FORMER CHAIRMAN OF
THE TOYOTA MOTOR CORPORATION

A hundred and fifty days a year, Patrick Smith lives in the Colorado wilderness, just as he has for the past fifty years. Smith is the founder of the Colorado School of Outdoor Living and two successful hunting/backpacking companies: Mountainsmith, which he sold in 1995, and Kifaru International, which he created in 1997.

Becoming a Kifaru customer is a quick way to overheat your credit card. Kifaru makes arguably the best hiking and hunting packs and shelters in the world—rugged, lightweight, and well designed. Kifaru packs can carry two hundred pounds comfortably, will last for decades, and sell for hundreds of dollars. It's not uncommon for avid sportsmen and soldiers to shell out thousands of dollars for custom-made Kifaru gear, then wait eagerly for six to eight weeks while the company makes it. Try as you might, it's difficult to find a Kifaru customer who's disappointed in the quality of their gear. More often than not, a new Kifaru customer is a customer for life.

The secret behind Kifaru's quality is **Field Testing**. Smith personally creates, uses, and *Iterates* every single product Kifaru makes for *years* before offering it to customers. By the time the finished product is available, even the most demanding customers have a difficult time finding flaws.

Here's what Smith says about his personal approach to Field Testing:

> The backcountry is definitely both my inspiration and my laboratory. I've figured out how to create designs out there [in the field]. I trust this technique. I get instant feedback about designs because I'm in the backcountry doing the things the design is for, and testing it right then, in the real world arena it's intended for . . . I really do think this is a better design process than sitting in front of a computer in an office in town. I think it's a win/win situation.[5]

Field Testing has a long and distinguished history in the creation of successful businesses. In 1923, W. H. Murphy, of the Protective Garment Corporation of New York, had an associate shoot him in the chest with a pistol in front of a public audience to prove his product worked—a marketing stunt based on extensive Field Testing to verify that the vest was capable of stopping live rounds. Miguel Caballero, a Colombian suit manufacturer who has created bulletproof suits for heads of state like Barack Obama and Hugo Chávez, has continued the tradition by posting videos of people wearing his suits being shot point-blank in the stomach.[6]

Most major automotive manufacturers put new car designs through on- and off-road obstacle courses to test performance and handling in real-world conditions. Software companies like Microsoft and Google extensively Field Test their new products internally with employees before releasing them to customers. Testing internally allows the company to eliminate any bugs before customers ever see the product.

Using what you make every day is the best way to improve the quality of what you're offering. Nothing will help you find ways to make your offer better than being its most avid and demanding customer.

REFERENCE LINK: **personalmba.com/field-testing/**

2

MARKETING

Offering value is not enough. If no one knows (or cares) about what you have to offer, it doesn't matter how much value you create. Without marketing, no business can survive—people who don't know you exist can't purchase what you have to offer, and people who aren't interested in what you have to offer won't become paying customers.

Every successful business finds a way to attract the attention of the right people and make them interested in what's being offered. Without prospects, you won't sell anything, and without completing profitable transactions, your business will fail.

Marketing is the art and science of finding "prospects"—people who are interested in what you have to offer. The best businesses in the world find ways to attract the attention of qualified prospects for a reasonable price. The more prospects you entice, the better off your business will be.

Marketing is not the same thing as selling. While direct-marketing strategies often try to minimize the time between attracting attention and asking for the sale, marketing and selling are two different things.

Marketing is about getting noticed; sales, which we'll discuss in chapter 3, is about closing the deal.

REFERENCE LINK: **personalmba.com/marketing/**

Attention

In an attention economy (like this one), marketers struggle for attention. If you don't have it, you lose.

—SETH GODIN, BESTSELLING AUTHOR OF *PERMISSION MARKETING*,
PURPLE COW, AND *TRIBES*

Modern life is overloaded with demands on your **Attention**. Think of all of the things that are competing for your attention right now: there's work to be done, people to call, email to check, TV to watch, music to listen to, and countless websites to visit. Everyone has too many things to do and too little time to do them all.

Rule #1 of marketing is that your potential customer's available attention is limited. Keeping up with everything in your world would require *way* more attention than you have to work with. To compensate, you filter: you ration your attention, allocating more to things you care about and less to things you don't. So does everyone else, including your potential prospects. To get someone's attention, you have to find a way around their filters.

High-quality attention must be earned. When you're seeking someone's attention, it's useful to take a moment to remember that you're competing against everything else in their world. In order to be noticed, you need to find a way to earn that attention by being more interesting or useful than the competing alternatives.

Attention doesn't matter if people don't care about what you're doing. If all you're looking for is attention, don't bother with all of this business stuff: skipping down the street in a pink bunny suit while yelling at the top of your lungs will get you all the attention you'll ever want. When it comes to business, however, some kinds of attention aren't worth having. You want the attention of prospects who will *purchase* from you—otherwise, you're wasting your time.

It's nice to be the center of attention, but business is about making profitable sales, not winning a popularity contest. Being featured on national television or on a huge website is a wonderful thing, but very often this kind of broad publicity fails to deliver actual sales. Spending time and energy acting like a socialite reduces the amount of resources you can devote to creating real value for your customers, which doesn't help anyone.

Earn the attention of the people who are likely to buy from you and you'll build your business. The mental models in this chapter will show you how.

REFERENCE LINK: personalmba.com/attention/

Receptivity

The shoe that fits one person pinches another; there is no recipe for living that suits all cases.

—CARL JUNG, PIONEERING PSYCHIATRIST AND PSYCHOLOGIST

People ignore what they don't care about. One of the primary functions of the human brain is perceptual filtering: determining what to pay attention to and what to ignore. The fastest way to be ignored by anyone is to start talking about something they don't care about.

Receptivity is a measure of how open a person is to your message. Rabid fans of hit novel series like J. K. Rowling's Harry Potter books are paragons of Receptivity: they're interested in almost anything they can find about their obsession as soon as it's available. From a business perspective, that's ideal—it's difficult to offer something that this audience won't want.

Receptivity has two primary components: *what* and *when*. People tend to be receptive only to certain categories of things at certain times. I love hearing about interesting new business books, but I never want to be on the receiving end of a 3:00 a.m. phone call from a publicist.

If you want your message to be heard, the medium matters. The form of your message has a big influence on how receptive people are to the information that message contains. If the form of your message suggests that it was created just for them, you're far more likely to get your prospect's attention.

Here's an example: Almost everyone will ignore postal junk mail—if it looks commercial or mass-produced, there's a 99 percent chance the recipient will throw it away without a second thought. Change the form, however, and Receptivity changes as well: most people will at least open a hand-addressed envelope, since it's clear someone spent time and effort sending it to them. Taken to an extreme, almost everyone (including busy executives) will open and look through the contents of a large, hand-addressed, overnight FedEx envelope—it's big and expensive and requires effort to send. Even then, if the contents don't match what they're interested in, you'll lose their attention.

REFERENCE LINK: **personalmba.com/receptivity/**

Remarkability

Advertising is the tax you pay for being unremarkable.

—ROBERT STEPHENS, FOUNDER OF GEEK SQUAD

Every time I go for a run, people ask me about my shoes. They don't ask me because they're fashionable: they ask me because they're weird.

Vibram FiveFingers are shoes that look like a cross between a sock and a glove. Wearing them makes you look a bit like a frog: each toe has its own little pocket, giving your feet a slightly amphibian look—odd enough to be noticed.

I picked up a pair of FiveFingers to experiment with barefoot running—the thin rubber sole protects your feet from rocks and glass without adding any unnecessary support, which lets your feet do what they're designed to do. Running or walking in FiveFingers is fun, which is why I keep wearing them.

FiveFingers are just strange enough that people can't help but notice your feet when you wear them—they violate expectations of what shoes are supposed to look like. As a result, people ask me about them—even in as "unfriendly" a place as the streets of New York City. By the end of the conversation, I've told my new acquaintance what they are, why I'm wearing them, how much they cost, and where they can purchase them.

FiveFingers are designed to overcome the number one problem every new offering faces: if no one knows you exist, no one will buy what you have to sell. Every customer who wears a pair of FiveFingers provides Vibram all of the advertising they need to keep growing—for free.

From a business perspective, the *Attention*-grabbing design of FiveFingers is working beautifully. On the street, salespeople confirm that Five-

Fingers are flying off the shelves—new stock sells out almost immediately. According to the *New York Times*,[1] sales of the FiveFingers line have tripled every year since they were introduced in 2006, and in 2009 the company's revenue crossed the $10 million mark in North America—without mass-market advertising. Not bad for funny-looking frog shoes.

Remarkability is the best way to attract Attention. In the classic marketing book *Purple Cow*, Seth Godin uses a wonderful metaphor to illustrate this principle: A field full of brown cows is boring. A purple cow violates the viewer's expectations, which attracts Attention and interest.

If you design your offer to be Remarkable—unique enough to pique your prospect's curiosity—it'll be significantly easier to attract attention.

REFERENCE LINK: **personalmba.com/remarkability/**

Probable Purchaser

There are 6 billion people on this planet. 99.999% of them would rather not give you their money.

—HUGH MACLEOD, CARTOONIST AND AUTHOR OF *IGNORE EVERYBODY*

Assuming that everyone in the world cares about what you have to offer is a huge marketing mistake. You may think that what you have to offer is the greatest thing since sliced bread—in fact, I hope you do! That doesn't change the fact that it's not right for everyone. Whatever you're offering, I can guarantee you that most of the people in this world don't—and will never—care about what you're doing. Harsh but true.

Fortunately, you don't have to appeal to everyone in order to succeed. You just have to attract enough **Attention** to close enough sales to produce enough profit to keep going. To do that, it's best to focus on attracting the attention of the people who will care about what you're doing.

Skilled marketers don't try to get everyone's attention—they focus on getting the attention of the *right people* at the *right time*. If you're marketing Harley-Davidson motorcycles, trying to land an appearance on *The Oprah Winfrey Show* to show off this year's new models probably isn't the best strategy. Likewise, Oprah's core audience is not likely to include tough guys in leather jackets with handlebar mustaches and tattoos, so don't expect her to advertise at a motorcycle trade show any time soon.

Your **Probable Purchaser** is the type of person who is suited to what you're offering. Harley's most profitable customers are "weekend warriors"— middle-aged men with disposable income who want to feel powerful and dangerous while cruising around in their spare time. Oprah's Probable Purchasers are middle-aged women who want to improve themselves and enjoy listening to inspiring and emotional stories.

Harley doesn't try to appeal to Oprah's Probable Purchasers, and vice versa—they each focus on appealing to their specific core audience, to great effect.

Attempting to appeal to everyone is a waste of time and money: focus your marketing efforts on your Probable Purchaser. By spending your limited resources reaching out to people who are already interested in the types of things you offer, you'll maximize the effectiveness of your attention-grabbing activities.

REFERENCE LINK: **personalmba.com/probable-purchaser/**

Preoccupation

You wouldn't worry so much about what others think of you if you realized how seldom they do.

—ELEANOR ROOSEVELT, FORMER FIRST LADY OF THE UNITED STATES

In order to earn the **Attention** of a prospect, you must divert their attention from what they're already doing. That's not an easy task.

Preoccupation is a fact of life for modern marketers: at the beginning of the marketing process, your prospects are paying attention to something else, not you. In order to attract Attention to your offer, what you're doing must be more interesting than your prospect's current subject of attention.

The best way to break a potential prospect's Preoccupation is to provoke a feeling of curiosity, surprise, or concern. Our ancient brains pay close attention to opportunities and threats, scanning the environment for new stimuli that could help or harm us.

The stronger and more emotionally compelling the stimuli, the easier it is to attract Attention. There's a reason marketers use evocative imagery, words, and sounds: our brains are wired to stop what we're doing to evaluate them.

That's not to say that your marketing needs to be garish and loud: there are thousands of subtle ways to attract Attention that can work just as well. Depending on the prospect's environment or emotional state, the threshold of interest you need to generate may be low. If the prospect is bored, restless, or looking for entertainment or distraction, it'll be easier to attract their Attention.

It always pays to assume your prospects begin in a state of Preoccupation. Begin your marketing approach in a way that breaks their Preoccupation and earns their Attention.

REFERENCE LINK: **personalmba.com/preoccupation/**

Levels of Awareness

Promise—large promise—is the soul of an advertisement.

—SAMUEL JOHNSON, EIGHTEENTH-CENTURY ESSAYIST AND LEXICOGRAPHER

The best marketing meets the prospect where they are, not where you want them to be. If you want to attract **Attention** in a way that produces results, you need to be sensitive to how much your **Probable Purchasers** know and care about what you have to offer.

In *Breakthrough Advertising*, Eugene Schwartz suggests that prospects experience five distinct **Levels of Awareness** during the marketing and sales process:

1. *Unaware*—the prospect is not aware of any need or desire for what you have to offer.

2. *Problem Awareness*—the prospect knows they have a need or desire, but they aren't aware of any suitable solutions.

3. *Solution Awareness*—the prospect knows that potential solutions exist, but they aren't aware of your specific offer.

4. *Offer Awareness*—the prospect is aware of your offer, but they're not sure it's right for them.

5. *Full Awareness*—the prospect is convinced your offer is a good solution to their need or desire, they just need to know the price and terms so they can decide whether or not to purchase.

Your approach to attracting Attention depends on your prospect's current Level of Awareness, and your objective with each marketing contact is to move the prospect to a higher Level of Awareness over time.

If your prospect is not aware of any need or desire for your offer, the prospect won't be **Receptive** to information about the benefits or price—as far as they're concerned, your marketing is irrelevant noise. In the same way, marketing that focuses too much on the problem or the benefits of your solution is annoying to prospects who are at the full-awareness stage: they're ready to make a decision, so cutting to the chase is the optimal strategy. Targeting potential customers at specific Levels of Awareness makes it easier to create a compelling message.

This approach extends into the sales process. **Education-Based Selling** helps the prospect understand why purchasing is in their best interest and how they can derive benefits from the **Transaction**.

Levels of Awareness create what many marketers refer to as a "funnel." Your initial marketing efforts create awareness of the offer, but most initial prospects won't purchase for various reasons. As prospects move through the various Levels of Awareness, they're more likely to move from your marketing to your sales process, resulting in an eventual purchase.

REFERENCE LINK: **personalmba.com/levels-of-awareness/**

End Result

No one wants a drill. What they want is the hole.

—L. E. "DOC'" HOBBS, ADVERTISEMENT FOR THE MANHATTAN
MUTUAL LIFE INSURANCE COMPANY, 1946

Most business-opportunity seekers aren't interested in the day-to-day details and responsibilities of running a business. They buy business books and courses because they want to experience a more prosperous, abundant, and hopeful future.

Most drivers don't buy expensive, off-road-capable vehicles because they drive off the road. They buy them because off-road capability makes them feel adventurous and bold, capable of meeting any driving challenge.

Most women don't buy a $20 tube of lipstick for its color alone. They buy it because they believe it will make them more beautiful and desirable.

Most college students don't pay hundreds of thousands of dollars to Harvard or Stanford or Yale just to sit in a class. They go (or, rather, their parents send them) because they believe they'll be perceived as sophisticated, intelligent, and powerful after they graduate.

Marketing is most effective when it focuses on the desired **End Result**, which is usually a distinctive experience or emotion related to a **Core Human Drive**. The actual function of the purchase is important, but the End Result is what the prospect is most interested in hearing about.

It's often far more comfortable to focus on the features: you know what your offer *does*. Even so, it's far more effective to focus on the benefits: what your offer will *provide* to customers.

The End Result is what matters most. By focusing on the End Result, you're homing in on what will cause your prospect to conclude, "This is for me."

REFERENCE LINK: **personalmba.com/end-result/**

Demonstration

The truth is generally seen, seldom heard.

—BALTASAR GRACIÁN, SEVENTEENTH-CENTURY SPANISH PHILOSOPHER

Marketers often try to explain the benefits of their offers, but it's more effective to show the product in action. **Demonstration** increases a prospect's belief in the benefits of your offer by showing them how well it works.

Demonstration is one of the oldest and most effective marketing techniques; it's been used to change public opinion for centuries. The Brooklyn Bridge opened in 1883, but pedestrians didn't trust the structure—it was the longest suspension bridge in the world at the time, and the first bridge that crossed the East River. Early users were nervous.

Six days after the Brooklyn Bridge opened to the public, a woman slipped on the stairs that led up to the bridge. The commotion caused a mass panic, the pedestrian equivalent of theatergoers rushing to the exits to escape a fire. Twelve people died, seven sustained life-threatening injuries, and twenty-eight were wounded in the stampede.[2]

Following this public-relations crisis, the city allowed P. T. Barnum, the famed circus showman, to parade twenty-one elephants and seventeen camels across the bridge. The bridge didn't waver, and public confidence was restored: if the Brooklyn Bridge could accommodate a score of five-ton elephants, it could handle pedestrian traffic.[3]

Many of the most profitable businesses of the twentieth century were built using Demonstration as the primary marketing strategy. Consider the golden age of infomercials: Billy Mays sold more than $1 billion dollars of home products like OxiClean, Mighty Putty, Orange Glo, and Kaboom via direct-response television advertisements.[4] Billy's over-the-top enthusiasm was effective in overcoming the viewer's **Preoccupation** and natural impulse to change the channel, but watching Billy restore a grimy floor or a stained shirt to its original glory made the cash registers ring. Viewers didn't have to take Billy's word for how well the product performed: they could see the results for themselves.

Demonstration can go a long way in establishing belief in your offer's ability to help the prospect. Whenever possible, don't tell your prospects what you can do to help: *show* them.

REFERENCE LINK: **personalmba.com/demonstration/**

Qualification

The product that will not sell without advertising will not sell profitably with advertising.

—ALBERT LASKER, FORMER CEO OF LORD & THOMAS
AND PIONEER OF MODERN ADVERTISING

Believe it or not, it's often wise to turn away paying customers. Not every customer is a good customer: customers who require more time, energy, attention, or risk than they're worth to your bottom line aren't worth attracting in the first place.

Qualification is the process of determining whether or not a prospect is a good customer before they purchase from you. By evaluating a prospect before they buy, you can minimize the chance of wasting your time dealing with a customer who's not a good fit for your business.

Progressive Insurance has turned Qualification into a profitable business strategy. To see Qualification in action, go to the Progressive Insurance website[5] and request a quote for car insurance.

When you request a quote, Progressive asks you a set of basic questions:

1. What type of car do you have?
2. Do you own or lease it? If you own it, are you still making payments?
3. What's your ZIP code?
4. Are you married?
5. Did you go to college?
6. Have you had any at-fault accidents in the past five years?

Progressive then uses your answers to gather data from a series of databases to answer two questions:

(A) Are you the type of person Progressive wants to insure?
(B) If so, how much should they charge to insure you?

If you're the type of person Progressive wants as a customer, they'll quote you a price and encourage you to purchase an insurance policy. If you're not, Progressive will tell you that you can get a better price elsewhere and *encourage you to purchase insurance from one of their competitors.*

Why in the world would a business encourage a hot prospect to purchase from the competition? As you recall from our previous discussion of **Insurance**, the profitability of an insurer depends on collecting as much money as possible in premiums while paying out as little money as possible in claims.

Progressive doesn't want to maximize its total client base: it wants to insure only people who are likely to drive safely and have few accidents, which means attracting customers who will pay premiums for a long time without making claims. Qualification allows Progressive to maximize the number of highly profitable customers it insures while funneling the "bad risks" to its competitors. It's good for customers as well—if they're "good risks," they get lower rates on their car insurance.

Screening your customers can help you filter out the bad customers before they do business with you. The better you define your ideal customer, the better you can screen out the prospects who don't fit that description and the more you'll be able to focus on serving your best customers well.

REFERENCE LINK: **personalmba.com/qualification/**

Point of Market Entry

There is nothing harder than the softness of indifference.

—JUAN MONTALVO, ESSAYIST

Assuming you don't have a small child and aren't expecting one any time soon, you probably don't care about diapers, strollers, cribs, infant toys, day care, or local preschools. Any information you're exposed to about these things is likely to be filtered out by your brain, since it's not relevant to your life at the moment.

But once you're expecting a little bundle of joy to enter your life, you suddenly care a great deal about these things and will probably start searching for information about them. Before hearing the news, you had no reason to care; now you do.

Certain markets have obvious entry and exit points. Learning a newborn is on the way is an example of a *Point of Market Entry*. Once you know you're expecting, you're suddenly *much* more receptive to information about products and services that will help you take care of a child. Attempting to attract the *Attention* of people who don't care about what you do is a waste of time, money, and energy, so it's best to find out *when* people are interested in hearing from you before you reach out.

Attracting your *Probable Purchaser's* Attention just after they've reached the Point of Market Entry is valuable. Companies like Procter & Gamble, Kimberly-Clark, Johnson & Johnson, and Fisher-Price pay an enormous amount of attention to Points of Market Entry, since they have a huge impact on the effectiveness of every baby product–related marketing activity. It's not uncommon for new moms and dads to come home from the hospital with a complimentary "care package" from one or more of these companies containing samples of diapers, diaper rash ointment, formula, and other newborn-care basics.

If you can get a prospective customer's attention as soon as they become interested in what you're offering, you become the standard by which competing offers are evaluated. That's a powerful position that increases the likelihood the prospect will purchase from you.

Discovering where Probable Purchasers start looking for information after crossing the interest threshold is valuable. Before the advent of the internet, most expecting parents started devouring books and talking to more experienced family and friends. Today, newly minted moms and dads search the web first, which is why organic and paid search-engine marketing is often so valuable. By optimizing for keywords your prospective customers are likely to search for, you can ensure that they find you first.

REFERENCE LINK: **personalmba.com/point-of-market-entry/**

Addressability

Sometimes the road less traveled is less traveled for a reason.
—JERRY SEINFELD, COMEDIAN

I grew up in rural Ohio, close to several Amish communities. Contrary to popular belief, the Amish don't reject every modern technology: they decide whether or not a technology is permitted based on whether it strengthens or weakens their local community.[6] Pneumatic and steam systems are common, and many Amish manufacturing businesses use sophisticated power tools. Even so, that doesn't make them a prime target for salespeople: making the sale requires visiting each prospect in their local community, making the sale in person, and being willing to deliver to and support customers in rural environments. That's a lot of work for a single sale, so most marketers and salespeople don't bother.

Addressability is a measure of how easy it is to get in touch with people who might want what you're offering. A highly Addressable audience can be reached with little effort and cost. A non-Addressable audience can be reached only with extreme difficulty or isn't **Receptive** and doesn't want to be reached at all.

Yoga is a good example of a highly Addressable market. It's relatively easy to find places where people are already paying attention to yoga-related information: studios, popular magazines like *Yoga Journal*, conferences, websites, etc. Yoga is a $16 billion industry, and you can tap into some or all of these outlets to help yogis and yoginis learn more about what you have to offer.

Sensitive or embarrassing topics tend to have low Addressability, even if there's a huge need. Chronic medical conditions are a good example: it's difficult to find and reach a large group of people who suffer from an uncomfortable and potentially embarrassing condition like psoriasis or ulcerative colitis. People suffering from these conditions don't gather in the same place or read the same things, and many will avoid being publicly identified as sufferers by joining organizations, so it's hard to find and talk to them.

Doctors, on the other hand, are more Addressable: they have publicly listed addresses and phone numbers, and are willing and able to meet with drug company representatives about new offerings. Since each doctor sees many patients and acts as a gatekeeper for prescription medications, pharmaceutical companies spend so much time and money marketing to MDs.

The internet has improved the Addressability of most markets. People who have a sensitive medical condition are highly likely to search for information on the internet, where they are Addressable via advertising. Blogs, discussion boards, and databases like WebMD make it easier for people who don't know one another to share their experiences and knowledge, making these low-Addressability markets more accessible than ever before.

Addressability is a huge concern when you are developing a new offer. If you have a choice, it's far better to focus on building something for an Addressable audience than it is to go around and hand sell or try to address an audience that is not Addressable or doesn't want to be addressed.

If you choose to serve an Addressable market before committing to an offer, it'll be significantly easier to market your offer without breaking the bank.

REFERENCE LINK: **personalmba.com/addressability/**

Desire

But i really want it!!!

—TWO-YEAR-OLD CHILDREN EVERYWHERE

Effective marketing makes your prospect want what you have to offer. In order for a prospect to be willing to pay you good money for what you're offering, they must want what you have. If your marketing activities don't produce some visceral feeling of **Desire** in your prospects, you're wasting your time and money.

Provoking Desire is the part of marketing that makes most people uncomfortable. It's understandable: pop culture is enamored with the image of the marketer as a shadowy master manipulator, hypnotizing the masses into wanting things they don't want or need. Nothing could be further from the truth.

Here's the reality: it's almost impossible to make someone want something they don't *already desire.* Yes, it's possible to be scammy and manipulative if you misrepresent what you're offering or promise something you can't deliver. Don't mistake that for brainwashing: the quickest way to waste a multimillion-dollar advertising budget is to try to force people to want something they don't already want. The human mind doesn't work that way—we only purchase what we already desire on some level.

The essence of effective marketing is discovering what people already want, then presenting your offer in a way that intersects with that preexisting Desire. The best marketing is similar to **Education-Based Selling**: it shows the prospect how the offer will help them achieve what they desire. Your job as a marketer isn't to convince people to want what you're offering; it's to help your prospects *convince themselves* that what you're offering will help them get what they want.

So what do people want? We've already covered that: the **Core Human Drives** are a starting point that will help you discover what your market wants at the most basic level. The more drives you can connect with your offering, the more effective your marketing activities will be.

REFERENCE LINK: **personalmba.com/desire/**

Visualization

When your work speaks for itself, don't interrupt.

—HENRY J. KAISER, PIONEER OF MODERN SHIPBUILDING
AND FOUNDER OF KAISER PERMANENTE

As soon as you step onto the lot of a car dealership, the salesperson you work with has a single, clear objective: convince you to get behind the wheel of a vehicle for a test drive.

The test drive is used to sell cars all over the world for a very good reason: it works. The test drive is the most effective tool a salesperson has to convince you to purchase a car that day.

Until you're driving a car, it's much easier to treat a potential purchase in a detached way. You're capable of rationally comparing makes and models, features, and prices. You can convince yourself that you're "just looking," with no intention of purchasing anything just yet.

Once you're behind the wheel of a car, however, the emotional parts of your mind take control. You start to imagine what your life would be like if you owned this vehicle. Instead of dispassionately comparing horsepower and acceleration metrics, you can feel the power of the engine and the ease of handling, and you can imagine the respect (or envy) of your neighbors as you pull your attractive new vehicle into the driveway.

You've stopped comparing and started *wanting*. Once you start wanting, you'll probably buy—it's only a matter of time.

B&H Photo Video uses the same strategy in a different market. Roaming the aisles of their Manhattan superstore is an intense sensory experience. You can feel the weight of the camera you're considering, see the buttons and dials up close, and hear the snap of the shutter. Better yet, you can compare the feel of each camera to hundreds of others, all within arm's reach. It's little wonder B&H is one of the most successful photography retailers in the world—after test-driving a few cameras, it's difficult to resist the urge to take one home.

The most effective way to get people to want something is to encourage them to use **Visualization**—to picture what their life would be like if they accepted your offer. As we'll discuss later, in **Mental Simulation**, our minds are designed to imagine the consequences of our actions. You can use this natural tendency to your advantage by helping your prospects imagine the positive experiences they'll have.

If you encourage your prospects to Visualize what their life will look like after purchasing, you increase the probability that they'll purchase from you. The best way to help your customers Visualize is to expose them to as much sensory information as possible—the information their mind uses to conclude, "I want this."

REFERENCE LINK: **personalmba.com/visualization/**

Framing

Everything we hear is an opinion, not a fact. Everything we see is a perspective, not the truth.

—MARCUS AURELIUS, PHILOSOPHER AND EMPEROR
OF ROME, SECOND CENTURY BCE

In a famous experiment conducted by psychologists Amos Tversky and Daniel Kahneman, participants were asked to make a decision about administering medical treatment to a sick population of six hundred people. Participants in the study were given two options: Treatment A would save two hundred lives. Treatment B had a 33 percent chance of saving all six hundred people and a 66 percent possibility of saving no one.

Treatment A and Treatment B are mathematically identical—when you do the math, there's no difference in the expected outcome. The study results, however, revealed a clear psychological preference: 72 percent of participants chose Treatment A, while 28 percent of the participants chose Treatment B.

The experiment was then repeated with two different treatment options. Treatment C would result in four hundred deaths. Treatment D offered a 33 percent chance that no one would die but a 66 percent probability that all six hundred would die. Participants overwhelmingly preferred Treatment D, 78 percent to 22 percent.

What's interesting to note is that Treatments A and C are also statistically identical, but A was overwhelmingly preferred while C was not. Contemplating lives saved versus fatalities significantly altered the preferences of the people making decisions, even though the expected outcomes were the same. We'll explore one of the reasons for this preference in **Loss Aversion**, but for now, let's focus on how the *emphasis* of the various messages changed the results.

Framing is the act of emphasizing the details that are important while de-emphasizing things that aren't by either minimizing certain facts or leaving them out entirely. Proper use of Framing can help you present your offer persuasively while honoring your customer's time and attention.

Framing is a natural part of communication; some form of compression in any message is inevitable. It's not practical to include all of the facts and context when communicating with others—we emphasize some details and leave out others to save time. We Frame because we have to: otherwise, it would take a huge amount of time to communicate even the simplest information to other people. It would take two hours to order a pizza, as you told the person at the other end of the line not only the size and toppings you wanted but how you got their phone number and why on this particular evening you were in the mood for pizza, not hamburgers or sushi.

Since Framing is an ever-present part of communication, it pays to be conscious of it. By being mindful of what you're emphasizing and what you're minimizing, you can communicate the benefits of your offer to your prospects in a clear and concise way, which maximizes your persuasive power.

Framing is not the same as lying or being deceitful. Honesty is always the best policy, and not just from a moral perspective. Misrepresenting your offer may net a few more sales in the short term, but it increases the probability that your customer's expectations will be violated, decreasing their satisfaction and permanently harming your **Reputation**, which we'll discuss later in the **Expectation Effect**.

Using Framing to your advantage will allow you to communicate the benefits of your offer to your **Probable Purchasers** persuasively, as long as you don't leave out information that your customers have a right to know.

REFERENCE LINK: **personalmba.com/framing/**

Free

To charge nobody nuthin' is a guarantee of no profit. Getting attention is not the same as getting paid.

—JOSEPH FERRARA, INTELLECTUAL PROPERTY ATTORNEY

If you want to attract **Attention**, give something valuable away for **Free**.

People love the promise of getting something for nothing. You've probably seen Free samples of food being given away at the supermarket, or received an offer to try a product or service for a certain time at no obligation. Chances are, at least a few of those free offers have led you to purchase more. Offers of Free value continue to exist because they work—the Free value is subsidized by the additional sales that are made because of the offer.

I started my teaching and consulting business by giving away my research and writing for Free on my website. As a result, hundreds of thousands of people find (or are referred to) the Personal MBA, benefit from the information, and come to trust me as a useful resource. More often than not, they give me permission to continue providing even more useful Free information via email.

When I started consulting, I offered to meet with prospective consulting customers by phone for Free—there's no obligation whatsoever on their part, and I didn't hold anything back. Every time I make this offer, I receive hundreds of inquiries and meet many new and interesting people. A good percentage of the people who accept the first consultation become paying customers, making Free the foundation of my teaching and consulting business.

More often than not, offering genuine Free value is a quick and effective way to attract attention. By giving your prospects something useful at no cost up front, you earn their attention and give your potential customers a chance to experience the value you provide. Done well, this strategy will net you sales you wouldn't have made otherwise.

Giving Free value attracts attention, but always remember that attention alone doesn't pay the bills. The siren song of "going viral" encourages many business owners to give away too much in an effort to chase attention rather than establish and improve the profit-generating parts of their business. Attention is necessary to attract paying customers, but if that attention never leads to sales, it won't sustain your business.

For best results, focus on giving away real Free value that is likely to attract real paying customers.

REFERENCE LINK: personalmba.com/free/

Permission

Selling to people who actually want to hear from you is more effective than interrupting strangers who don't.

—SETH GODIN, BESTSELLING AUTHOR OF *PERMISSION MARKETING,*
PURPLE COW, AND *TRIBES*

I just did the unthinkable: I opened the spam folder in my email account. The folder contained 1,555 unread messages, most of which were some variant of:

> *"Hot Russian babes want to chat with YOU!"*
>
> *"Buy Viagra online!"*
>
> *"Eliminate hair loss instantly!"*

I didn't ask for any of these emails—the spammers just sent them, without considering whether or not I wanted them. I have no interest in chatting with "hot Russian babes," I have no use for black-market Viagra, and I *like* being bald.

How likely am I to read these messages, let alone respond to them? Not likely at all—on the contrary, I'll go out of my way to *avoid* paying **Attention** to them, and it'll be a cold day in hell before I purchase what they're pushing.

Many businesspeople assume that the spam approach is the best way to get Attention. Unsolicited phone calls, press releases, mass-market advertising, and "resident"-addressed direct mail are the most common legal equivalents of spam: blanketing a huge, undifferentiated group of people with a standard message in the hopes that a tiny fraction will respond.

In the early days of television and radio advertising, commercial interruptions worked. When there were only three channels, people were more likely to pay Attention during the commercials. By purchasing a single thirty-second prime-time advertising slot on each of the three major networks, you could reach 90 percent of the television-watching population in a single day.

Now, people have the ability to filter out anything they don't want to pay Attention to, either by ignoring the offending message or by shifting their Attention to something else. The moment you start talking about something your prospects don't care about, they're gone.

Asking for **Permission** to follow up after providing **Free** value is more effective than interruption. Offering genuine value earns your prospect's Attention, and asking for Permission gives you the opportunity to focus on communicating with people you *know* are interested in what you have to offer.

Permission is a real asset. Reaching new people tends to be difficult and expensive. It's far easier to follow up with someone you already know—all it takes is an email, a letter, or a phone call, all of which are easy and inexpensive. If you ask the new prospects you meet for Permission to follow up, you're making the most of your outreach activities.

The best way to get Permission is to ask for it. Whenever you provide value to people, ask them if it's okay to continue to give them more value in the future. Over time, your list of prospective customers will grow, and the larger it grows, the higher the likelihood you'll start landing more sales.

Use Permission once you have it, but don't abuse the privilege. Getting Permission to follow up never gives you carte blanche to send them anything you like. Before asking your prospects for Permission to follow up, make it clear what they'll be getting and how it'll benefit them.

If you honor your commitments by continually providing value and refraining from spamming your prospects with irrelevant information, you'll have a powerful asset that can help you build a deeper relationship with the people who are interested in what you're offering.

REFERENCE LINK: personalmba.com/permission/

Hook

If you can do it, it ain't braggin'.

—DIZZY DEAN, HALL OF FAME BASEBALL PLAYER

Complicated messages are ignored or forgotten. Your **Probable Purchasers** are busy—they don't have time to pay **Attention** to all of the information assaulting them every day. If you want people to remember who you are and what you're offering, you have to grab their Attention and hold it—all in a matter of seconds.

A **Hook** is a single phrase or sentence that describes an offer's primary benefit. Sometimes the Hook is a title and sometimes it's a short tag line. Regardless, it conveys the reason someone would want what you're selling.

A classic example of a Hook in the publishing world is the title of Timothy Ferriss's book, *The 4-Hour Workweek*. This short title implies several intriguing benefits: (1) four hours is a lot less than most people work, and most people would like to work less; (2) you can potentially earn as much in four hours a week as in forty-plus hours a week; (3) if you're not working so much, you could do other cool things with your time. That's not bad at all for four short words. When paired with the book's cover image of a guy relaxing in a hammock on a tropical beach, the title goes a long way in convincing people to purchase and read the book.

Apple used a Hook for the launch of the iPod: "1,000 songs in your pocket." At the time, portable music players consisted of bulky CD and cassette players, and advertising for early MP3 players focused on geek speak: megabytes of disk space. Apple's Hook highlighted the primary benefit: instead of carrying around hundreds of tapes or CDs, you could carry your entire music collection in one elegant device.

Apple's five-word tag line worked wonders. In a little under a year, 236,000 first-generation iPods were sold—an astounding start, considering this was the company's first foray into the portable music category. The Hook grabbed Attention, and the quality of the product closed the sale.

When creating a Hook, focus on the primary benefit or value your offer provides. Emphasize what's uniquely valuable about your offer and why the prospect should care. Brainstorm a list of words and phrases related to your primary benefit, then experiment with different ways to connect them in a short phrase. Crafting a Hook is a creative exercise—the more potential options you generate, the faster you'll find one that works.

Once you've created your Hook, use it! Place it on your website, your advertising, your business cards—make it one of the first things potential customers see. The Hook grabs Attention, and the remainder of your marketing and sales activities close the deal.

The better your Hook, the more Attention you'll grab, and the easier it'll be for your satisfied customers to tell their friends about you.

REFERENCE LINK: **personalmba.com/hook/**

Call to Action

All the beautiful sentiments in the world weigh less than a single lovely action.

—JAMES RUSSELL LOWELL, NINETEENTH-CENTURY POET

Attracting a prospect's **Attention** doesn't help if they disappear: if you want to make a sale, you need to direct your prospects to take some kind of action.

Your prospects can't read your mind. If you want your prospects to take the next step you're encouraging, you need to tell them what you want them to do. The most effective marketing messages give the recipient or prospect a single, clear, very short action to take next.

Think about a roadside billboard that says something like "Tony's Hamburgers Are the Best." What will people who see that message do? Nothing, probably. In all likelihood, the billboard is a waste of time and money.

Give them a **Call to Action (CTA)** such as "Take Exit 25 and Turn Right for the Best Burgers in Town," and soon Tony will be serving more hamburgers to hungry travelers.

A Call to Action directs your prospects to take a single, simple, obvious action: Visit a website. Enter an email address. Call a phone number. Mail a self-addressed, stamped envelope. Click a button. Purchase a product. Tell a friend.

The key to presenting an effective Call to Action is to be as clear, simple, and obvious as you can. The more compelling your proposal, the higher the probability your prospect will do what you suggest.

If you're encouraging someone to enter their email address to sign up for a newsletter, say that verbatim multiple times, and make it clear *where* the email address field is, *why* they should fill it out, *what* to click once they've entered their email, and *what* they can expect to happen when they do. If you think you're being too obvious, you're doing it right.

The best Calls to Action ask either for the sale or for **Permission** to follow up. Making direct sales is optimal, since it makes it easy to figure out whether or not your marketing activities are cost-effective. Asking for Permission is the next best thing, since it allows you to follow up with your prospects over time, decreasing your marketing costs and increasing the probability of an eventual sale.

Ensure that every message you create has a clear Call to Action, and you'll increase the effectiveness of your marketing activities.

REFERENCE LINK: **personalmba.com/call-to-action/**

Narrative

A tale in everything.
—WILLIAM WORDSWORTH, NINETEENTH-CENTURY POET

Since the dawn of history, people have been telling stories. Telling stories is a universal human experience, and stories have always been used in the conduct of trade. A good story will make even the best offer even better.

Most compelling **Narratives** around the world follow a common format. The world-renowned mythologist Joseph Campbell called this prototypical storyline the "Hero's Journey" or the "monomyth." People all over the world respond very strongly to this story motif, and you can use this basic format to craft and tell your own stories.

The Hero's Journey begins by introducing the Hero: a normal person who is experiencing the trials and tribulations of everyday life. The Hero then receives a "call to adventure": a challenge, quest, or responsibility that requires them to rise above their normal existence and hone their skills and abilities in order to prevail.

When the Hero accepts the call, they depart their normal experience and enter into a world of uncertainty and adventure. A series of remarkable experiences initiates them into this new world, and the Hero undergoes many trials and learns many secrets in the pursuit of ultimate success.

After persevering in the face of adversity and vanquishing the foe, the Hero receives a mighty gift or power, then returns to the normal world to share this knowledge, wisdom, or treasure with the people. In return, the Hero receives the respect and admiration of all.

Your customers want to be Heroes. They want to be respected and admired by all, to be powerful, successful, and determined in the face of adversity. They want to be inspired by the trials and tribulations of other people who have come before and vanquished the foe. Telling a story about people who have already walked the path your prospects are considering is a powerful way to make them interested in proceeding.

Testimonials, case studies, and other stories are effective in encouraging your prospects to accept your "call to adventure." By telling stories about the customers who have come before, you grab your prospect's *Attention* and show them a path to achieve what they want. The more vivid, clear, and emotionally compelling the story, the more prospects you'll attract.

Tell your prospective customers the stories they're interested in hearing and you'll grab their Attention.

REFERENCE LINK: **personalmba.com/narratives/**

Controversy

If you want an audience, start a fight.

—IRISH PROVERB

Controversy means publicly taking a position that not everyone will agree with, approve of, or support. Used constructively, Controversy can be an effective way to attract *Attention*: people start talking, engaging, and paying Attention to your position, which is a very good thing.

The Personal MBA itself is a good example of the power of positive Controversy. The Personal MBA is about fundamental business principles—what you need to understand about business in order to succeed. I believe that anyone can learn whatever they need to know about business on their own terms, without mortgaging their future earnings by enrolling in a traditional MBA program.

Some people vehemently disagree with that position—particularly graduates of Ivy League business-school programs. MBA graduates and candidates are often quite vocal in their disagreement, which usually takes the form of denouncing the Personal MBA approach to business education on their own websites or publicly disagreeing with me by leaving comments on my website.

That's not a bad thing: this consistent level of mild Controversy has allowed the Personal MBA to grow year after year without paid advertising. By making their thoughts known, the Personal MBA's detractors are spreading the word to people who may not have been aware that there are alternatives to traditional business-school programs.

The Controversy leads many new people to investigate and examine the Personal MBA and make up their own minds about its usefulness. More than a few of them stick around, read my *Free* content, then decide to purchase a book, take a course, or hire me as a consultant. As long as my detractors keep things civil, I welcome the disagreement.

It's okay to have an opinion and take a strong stand. Everyone has a natural tendency to want other people to like them, and disagreement is often uncomfortable. In an effort to be unobjectionable, it's easy to water down your opinions to the point where they offend no one. If your position is agreeable to everyone, it becomes so boring that no one will pay Attention to you.

It's okay to support a position that not everyone else supports. It's okay to disagree with someone, or to call someone out, or to position yourself against something, because Controversy provokes a discussion. Discussion is Attention, which is a very good thing if you want to attract people who will benefit from what you're doing.

That's not to say all Controversy is good Controversy: there's a fine line between being constructively controversial and creating a soap opera. Controversy with a purpose is valuable; Controversy for the sake of Controversy, or Controversy that belittles and demeans, is not. Controversy won't help you if you lose sight of the purpose behind your actions.

As long as you're able to maintain a sense of the bigger picture of how you're trying to help, creating a bit of Controversy can be a very effective tool in encouraging people to seek out more information about what you're doing.

REFERENCE LINK: **personalmba.com/controversy/**

Reputation

Like it or not, the market's perception becomes your reality.

—HOWARD MANN, ACTOR AND COMEDIAN

In my opinion, "branding" is one of the most overused and overhyped ideas in the modern business world. There's nothing magical or complex about building a brand: when business professionals say they want to "enhance their brand" or "build brand equity," they almost always mean "improve their reputation."

Reputation is what people think about a particular offer or company. Reputations arise whenever people talk to one another. Some products and services are worth the price; others are not. Some experiences are worth having; others are not. Some people are good to work with; others are not. No one wants to waste their time or money, so people pay very close attention to what others say about things they're interested in.

Building a strong Reputation is valuable: people are often willing to pay a premium for a good Reputation. One of the reasons well-known consumer brands like Tide and Crest can continue to charge premium prices in near-commodity categories is the strength of their Reputation. Potential customers want to feel certain that the purchase they're considering will benefit them, that others will think highly of their decision, and that they won't be wasting their money. As the venerable corporate saying goes, "No one ever got fired for buying IBM."

It's important to note that your Reputation is not under your direct control—it's the sum total of what others think about everything you do: the products you release, the advertising you promote, the customer service you provide. No matter how hard you try, you can't "manage" your Reputation—you can only try to improve it over time by making people glad they chose to do business with you.

Always remember that the marketplace is the final arbiter of your Reputation, and that it's always watching what you do. When you build a great Reputation, your customers will continue to do business with you and will refer you to others because they think highly of you (and because referring friends to good products and services is a way to build their own Reputations). Building your Reputation takes time and effort, but it's the most effective kind of marketing there is.

REFERENCE LINK: personalmba.com/reputation/

3

SALES

People don't like to be sold, but they love to buy.

—JEFFREY GITOMER, AUTHOR OF *THE SALES BIBLE*
AND *THE LITTLE RED BOOK OF SELLING*

Every successful business sells what it has to offer. Having millions of prospects isn't enough if no one pulls out their wallet and says, "I'll take one." The sales process begins with a prospect and ends with a paying customer. No sale, no business.

The best businesses in the world earn the trust of their prospects and help them understand why the offer is worth paying for. No one wants to make a bad decision or be taken advantage of, so sales consists of helping the prospect understand what's important and convincing them you're capable of delivering on what you promise.

The end of the sales process is an excited new customer and more cash in the bank.

REFERENCE LINK: personalmba.com/sales/

Transaction

There is only one boss: the customer. And he can fire everybody in
the company from the chairman on down, simply by spending his
money somewhere else.

—SAM WALTON, FOUNDER OF WALMART

A **Transaction** is an exchange of value between two or more parties. If I have
something you want and you have something I want, we'd both be better
off if we agreed to trade.

The Transaction is the defining moment of every business. Sales are the
only point in the business cycle where resources flow *into* the business,
which makes completing Transactions essential for the continued existence of the venture. Businesses survive by bringing in more money than
they spend, and there's no way to do that without completing Transactions.

You can only transact with things that are *Economically Valuable*. If you
don't have anything your prospective customers want, they won't buy from
you. This may seem obvious, but it's amazing how many prospective businesspeople enter the market without something the market wants. That's why
developing and testing a *Minimum Viable Offer* is so important: it's the best
way to determine whether or not you've created something valuable enough
to sell before you invest your life savings.

When you're starting a new business, the object is to make your first
profitable Transaction: that's the point where you transition from being a
project to being a business. The concepts in this chapter will help you create profitable Transactions that both parties are happy with.

REFERENCE LINK: **personalmba.com/transaction/**

Trust

> The secret of life is honesty and fair dealing. If you can fake that,
> you've got it made.
>
> —GROUCHO MARX, COMEDIAN

Here's a proposal: send me a certified bank check for $100,000 right now, and in ten years I'll give you the keys to a brand-new, ten-thousand-square-foot villa on Italy's Amalfi Coast. You can't see any example villas, you won't hear from me again until the villa is ready, and there are no refunds. Deal?

Unless you're a trusting soul with cash to burn, probably not. After all, how can you be sure I can build you a seaside mansion for such a paltry sum? How can you be sure I won't just take the money and disappear?

You can't, which is why you shouldn't cut me (or anyone else) a check for a villa on the Mediterranean you've never seen.

Let's reverse the situation: let's assume I'm capable of building this villa, and you're interested in purchasing one. Would it be smart for me to purchase land, break ground, and start building before I'm sure you have the money to pay for it? Probably not—if the deal falls through, I'd have to find another customer or eat the cost.

Without a certain amount of **Trust** between parties, a **Transaction** will not take place. No matter what promises are made or how good the deal sounds, no customer is going to be willing to part with their hard-earned money unless they believe you're capable of delivering what you promise. Likewise, it's usually not smart to accept credit or IOUs from customers you don't know.

Building a trustworthy **Reputation** over time by dealing fairly and honestly is the best way to build Trust. You can also take steps to signal you're trustworthy: online reviews, credit and background check services, and financial arrangements like escrow accounts exist to help overcome an initial lack of Trust between parties in a Transaction. These offerings break down an important mutual barrier to completing a sale: without these indicators of trustworthiness, many Transactions would never take place.

The easier it is to demonstrate your trustworthiness and verify that the other party is trustworthy, the greater the chance of a successful Transaction.

REFERENCE LINK: **personalmba.com/trust/**

Common Ground

A compromise is the art of dividing a cake in such a way that everyone believes he has the biggest piece.

—LUDWIG ERHARD, POLITICIAN AND FORMER
CHANCELLOR OF WEST GERMANY

Common Ground is a state of overlapping interests between two or more parties. Think of your available options as a circle that surrounds you. Your prospects have a circle of available options as well. Your job is to find where those circles overlap, which is much easier if you understand what your **Probable Purchasers** want or need.

Consider the job you're currently in, or the last one you held. Chances are, you accepted that job because you were willing to take on certain responsibilities, and your employer was interested in having you do the work. You were interested in being paid a certain amount, and your employer was willing to pay you at least that much. Your interests overlapped, which resulted in a job offer and a paid position at the company. That's Common Ground.

The same thing happens every time you purchase something from a retail business. They have a **Product** you want to own; you have a certain amount of money they are willing to accept for the Product. If you don't want the Product or the retailer wants more than you're willing to pay, no **Transaction** will take place.

Common Ground is a precondition of any type of Transaction. Without any areas of overlapping interest, there's no reason for a prospect to choose to work with you. After all, it wouldn't make sense to pay more for something than it's worth to you. Why expect your prospects to accept your offer if it's not in their best interest?

Aligning interests is critical to finding Common Ground. Sales isn't about convincing somebody to do something that's not in their best interest. Ideally, you should want what your prospects want: the satisfaction of their desire or the resolution of their problem. The more your interests are aligned with your prospect's, the more they'll **Trust** your ability to give them what they want.

There are always many paths to a successful Transaction, which is the essence of negotiation. Negotiation is the process of exploring different options to find Common Ground: the more potential paths you explore, the greater the chance you'll be able to find one on which your interests overlap. The more open you are to potential options, the higher the likelihood you'll find an area of Common Ground that's acceptable for all parties involved.

REFERENCE LINK: **personalmba.com/common-ground/**

The Pricing Uncertainty Principle

Everything you want in life has a price connected to it. There's a price to pay if you want to make things better, a price to pay just for leaving things as they are, a price for everything.

—HARRY BROWNE, AUTHOR OF *FAIL-SAFE INVESTING*

One of the most fascinating parts of sales is what I call the **Pricing Uncertainty Principle**: all prices are arbitrary and malleable. Pricing is always an executive decision. If you want to try to sell a small rock for $350 million, you can. If you want to quadruple that price or reduce it to $0.10 an hour later, there's nothing stopping you. *Any* price can be set to *any* level at *any* time, without limitation.

The Pricing Uncertainty Principle has an important corollary: you must be able to *support* your asking price before a customer will accept it. In general, people prefer to pay as little as possible to acquire the things they want (with some notable exceptions, which we'll discuss later, in **Social Status**). If you expect people to pay you good money to buy what you're offering, you must be able to provide a **Reason Why** the offered price is worth paying.

It's difficult to support a price of $350 million for a rock—unless that rock is the Hope diamond, a 45.5-carat deep-blue diamond with a long and distinguished history.

The Hope diamond is currently owned by the Smithsonian National Museum of Natural History and is not for sale. If the Smithsonian decided to sell the Hope diamond, however, they could set an asking price of $1 billion. What's to stop them?

Auctions are an example of the Pricing Uncertainty Principle at work—prices change, rising in proportion to how many people are interested and how much they're each willing to spend.

Because they set a low starting price and allow potential buyers to bid against one another, auctions are often an efficient way to establish a true market price for something that is difficult to reproduce and for which no comparable items already exist in the market. That's why rare items like the Hope diamond—if they're sold—are sold at auction. The most expensive diamond ever sold was the rough, 507.5-carat Cullinan Heritage diamond, which went for $35.3 million at auction.[1] Not bad for a rock.

REFERENCE LINK: **personalmba.com/pricing-uncertainty-principle/**

Four Pricing Methods

Pricing is the exchange rate you put on all the tangible and intangible aspects of your business. Value for cash.

—PATRICK CAMPBELL, COFOUNDER AND CEO, PROFITWELL

Let's assume for a moment you own a house you're willing to sell. The *Pricing Uncertainty Principle* says the price could be anything—you have to set it yourself, since houses don't come with built-in price tags. Let's also assume you'd prefer to sell the house for as much as possible. How would you go about setting the largest price a customer will accept?

There are four ways to support a price on something of value: (1) replacement cost, (2) market comparison, (3) discounted cash flow/net present value, and (4) value comparison. These *Four Pricing Methods* will help you estimate just how much something is potentially worth to your customers.

The replacement cost method supports a price by answering the question "How much would it cost to replace?" In the case of the house, the question becomes "What would it cost to create or construct a house just like this one?"

Assume a meteorite scored a direct hit on the house, and there's nothing left—you have to rebuild the house from scratch. What would it take to purchase similar land, pay for an architect to draw up plans, acquire identical materials, and hire construction workers to create the same house? Total up these costs, add a bit of margin to compensate for your time and effort, and you'll have a supportable estimate of how much your house is worth.

Applied to most offers, replacement cost is usually a "cost-plus" calculation: figure out how much it costs to create, add your desired markup, and set your price appropriately.

The market comparison method supports a price by answering the question "How much are other things like this selling for?" In the case of the house, this question becomes "How much have houses like this, in this general area, sold for recently?"

If you look at the surrounding area, there are probably a few other houses similar to the one you own that have been sold within the past year. They're probably not exactly the same—maybe they have an extra bedroom or bathroom, a little less square footage, etc.—but they're close enough. After you adjust for the differences, you can use the sale prices of those "comparable" houses to create a supportable estimate of how much your house is worth.

Market comparison is a very common way to price offers: find a similar offer and set your price relatively close to what they're asking.

The discounted cash flow (DCF)/ net present value (NPV) method supports a price by answering the question "How much is it worth if it can bring in money over time?" In the case of your house, the question becomes "How much would this house bring in each month if you rented it for a period of time, and how much is that series of cash flows worth as a lump sum today?"

Rent payments come in every month, which is quite handy: you can use the DCF/NPV formulas[2] to calculate what that series of payments over a certain period of time would be worth if you received it in one lump sum. By calculating the NPV of the house, assuming you could rent it for $2,000 a month for a period of ten years with 95 percent occupancy and you could earn 7 percent interest on your money by choosing the **Next Best Alternative**, you'll have a supportable estimate of what the house is worth.

DCF/NPV is used only for pricing things that can produce an ongoing cash flow, which makes it a very common way to price businesses when they're sold or acquired—the more profit the business generates each month, the more valuable the business is to the purchaser.

The value comparison method supports a price by answering the question "Who is this particularly valuable to?" In the case of the house, this question becomes "What features of this house would make it valuable to certain types of people?"

Let's assume the house is in an attractive, safe neighborhood with a top-tier public school nearby. These characteristics would make the house more valuable to families who have school-age kids, particularly if they want to attend that school. To potential home buyers in the market, this particular house would be more valuable than the same house in an area with inferior schools.

Here's another example: assume Elvis Presley once owned the house. To certain types of people—wealthy people who love Elvis—this house would be priceless. Elvis's previous involvement with the property could triple or quadruple the price you'd be able to support via the replacement, market comparison, or DCF/NPV methods. By looking at the unique characteristics of what you're offering and the corresponding worth of those characteristics to certain individuals, you can often support much higher prices.

Value comparison is usually the optimal way to price your offer, since the value of an offer to a specific group can be quite high, resulting in a much better price. Use the other methods as a baseline, but focus on discovering how much your offer is worth to the party you hope to sell it to, then set your price appropriately.

REFERENCE LINK: **personalmba.com/4-pricing-methods/**

Price Transition Shock

If you want to grow old as a pilot, you've got to know when to push it, and when to back off.

—CHUCK YEAGER, FIRST PILOT TO BREAK THE SOUND BARRIER

When you change the price of an offer, the effects aren't limited to your current target market. A change in prices can change your typical prospect overnight.

Most people who are new to business assume that the best way to increase sales is to reduce prices. That's not necessarily true. Often, raising your prices is an effective way to attract *more* customers.

Discounts attract customers when the offer is a commodity. If there's no difference between the gasoline at one gas station and another, the station that reduces its gas prices may bring in more customers. Since most service stations make more money from their convenience stores than they make selling gasoline, a gas discounting strategy may lead to higher profits.

In introductory economics courses, this idea is called "price elasticity." Offers with high price elasticity experience major changes in demand when prices go up or down. Offers with low price elasticity experience little fluctuation in demand when prices change. Economists love to draw downward-sloping pricing curves that show demand increasing as prices decrease.

The trouble with the traditional pricing curve is that it can be misleading when the offer isn't a commodity. In practice, raising your prices can *increase* demand by appealing to a more attractive type of customer.

Automobiles are a classic example of this type of price sensitivity: some cars are desirable *because they're expensive.* The typical customer who purchases a Bentley Continental GT is very different from the type of customer who purchases a Toyota Camry.

As you test different pricing strategies, you'll notice thresholds where you stop appealing to certain types of customers and start appealing to customers with very different characteristics. This **Price Transition Shock** can change the experience of operating your business, and you shouldn't take it lightly.

There are two major considerations when setting your prices with Price Transition Shock in mind: (1) potential profitability and (2) ideal customer characteristics. The best strategy is to set your prices to appeal to the prospects that will ensure you work with your most desirable customers in a way that results in the highest profits.

The ideal balance depends on your target market. In some markets, it's easy to serve customers who are attracted to low prices; in others, discount customers can be challenging and rude. Likewise, prospects that don't blink at high prices can be pleasant and cordial or demanding and snooty. The experience depends on the industry and the prospects' expectations.

One of the businesses I've been involved with over the years succeeded in doubling its average order value by eliminating low-priced offers. As a result, profits increased. As a **Second-Order Effect**, the company's typical customer changed for the worse: prospects made unreasonable demands more often and acted in disrespectful ways when those demands weren't met. The short-term financial result was positive, but the change placed extraordinary stress on the staff.

On the other hand, a service business I advise decided to quadruple the price of its standard offer and found that its new positioning appealed to its ideal customers: people who valued the firm's work and took the project seriously. Nonideal customers were turned off by the hike in prices, so they went away. As a result, the company filled its client roster with excellent customers and increased profits by more than 500 percent. The staff is thrilled with the change: they're doing more work for better clients and getting paid more for their expertise.

As you change your prices, the prospects attracted to your offer will also change. So long as you maintain **Sufficiency**, you can choose to appeal to any type of customer you please.

REFERENCE LINK: **personalmba.com/price-transition-shock/**

Value-Based Selling

Price is what you pay. Value is what you get.

—WARREN BUFFETT, CHAIRMAN AND CEO OF BERKSHIRE HATHAWAY AND ONE OF THE WEALTHIEST INDIVIDUALS IN THE WORLD

Imagine that you provide an ongoing service to a *Fortune* 500 corporation that increases their annual revenues by $100 million. Is your service worth $10 million a year? Sure—after all, what company would give up $90 million in ongoing revenue?

Does it matter if providing this valuable service doesn't cost you much money? No—even if it only costs you a hundred dollars a year to provide the service, you're providing a huge amount of value, which supports the comparatively high price.

Does it matter if most business-to-business services cost $10,000 or less? No—you're providing much more value than other services in the market, which justifies a higher price.

Value-Based Selling is the process of understanding and reinforcing the reasons your offer is valuable to the purchaser. In the previous section, we discussed how the value comparison method is often the best way to support a high price on your offer. Value-Based Selling is *how* you support that price. By understanding and reinforcing the **Reason Why** a **Transaction** will be valuable to the customer, you simultaneously increase the likelihood of a Transaction as well as the price the buyer will be willing to pay.

Value-Based Selling is not about talking—it's about listening. When most people think of sales, they imagine a pushy, smooth-talking shyster whose sole priority is to "close the deal." Emulating shady used car dealers is the fastest way to destroy **Trust** and give your potential customers the impression that you care more about your bottom line than about what they want. In reality, the best salespeople are the ones who can listen intently for the things the customer wants.

Asking good questions is the best way to identify what your offer is worth to your prospect. In the classic sales book *SPIN Selling*, Neil Rackham describes the four phases of successful selling: (1) understanding the situation, (2) defining the problem, (3) clarifying the short-term and long-term implications of that problem, and (4) quantifying the need-payoff, or the financial and emotional benefits the customer would experience after the resolution of their problem. Instead of barging in with a premature, boilerplate hard sell, successful salespeople focus on asking detailed questions to get to the root of what the prospect wants.

By encouraging your prospects to tell you more about what they need, you reap two major benefits. First, you increase the prospect's confidence in your understanding of the situation, increasing their confidence in your ability to deliver a solution. Second, you'll discover information that will help you emphasize just how valuable your offer is, which helps you in **Framing** the price of your offer versus the value it will provide.

If you discover why, how, and how much your offer will benefit the customer, you'll be able to explain that value in terms they'll understand and appreciate. Understanding the value you can provide your customers is the golden path to a profitable sale.

REFERENCE LINK: **personalmba.com/value-based-selling/**

Education-Based Selling

Upgrade your user, not your product. "Value" is less about the stuff and more about the stuff the stuff enables. Don't build better cameras—build better photographers.

—KATHY SIERRA, AUTHOR AND COCREATOR OF
THE HEAD FIRST SERIES OF BOOKS

Before moving to Colorado, my wife, Kelsey, was the sales manager of the Mark Ingram Bridal Atelier in New York City, the most prestigious bridal salon in the world. Her job was to help brides from around the world find "the One"—the perfect dress for their dream wedding.

Mark Ingram is the Martha Stewart of the bridal industry—his sense of style is legendary. Gowns by Monique Lhuillier, Lela Rose, and Vera Wang populate his collection. Mark's consultants are so skilled that one of the first three gowns they present is almost always the gown the bride chooses for her wedding. In addition, the shopping experience and customer service are superb—Mark doesn't discount, but brides would rather work with him than purchase their gown from a competitor, even though it'd be less expensive.

Compared with most bridal salons, the Mark Ingram Bridal Atelier sells very high-end gowns. The average sale price of a gown at Mark's atelier is $6,000—four times the national average. To make the sale, Mark's consultants must help the bride (and her parents, who often pay the bill) understand why the gown is worth the price.

It's possible to purchase a less expensive gown from another salon, but cheaper gowns cut corners: they use lower-quality fabrics, skimp on construction, and use machined lace or beading. In addition, alterations are necessary to ensure that the gown fits the bride. Mark's team of bridal seamstresses is the best in the world, and you can only work with them if you purchase a gown from Mark's atelier.

If you care about these things—and most fashion-conscious brides do—it's easy to see why it's worth it to purchase a gown from Mark if you can afford to.

Education-Based Selling is the process of making your prospects better, more informed customers. As a sales consultant, Kelsey worked to do two things: (1) make the bride feel comfortable and relaxed, and then (2) help the bride become more knowledgeable about gowns in terms of how they are made and what to look for when buying one.

Instead of pressuring the bride to "close the sale," Kelsey always took the time to explain the ins and outs of fabric, lace, beading, construction, and alterations to the bride and her family. She invested time in making her brides more knowledgeable, and this made them more likely to purchase an expensive dress from her, both because they had learned to fully appreciate the quality of what she was selling and because she had earned their **Trust**.

Education-Based Selling requires an up-front investment in your prospects, but it's worth it. By investing energy in making your prospects smarter, you simultaneously build Trust in your expertise and make them better customers. Be forewarned, however, that effective education requires your offer to be superior in some way to your competitors'—otherwise, you'll be sending customers away. All the more reason to ensure that you have an offer worth selling.

REFERENCE LINK: **personalmba.com/education-based-selling/**

Next Best Alternative

When others sense your willingness to walk away, your hand is strengthened . . . Sometimes you are better off not getting to yes.

—ROBERT RUBIN, FORMER US SECRETARY OF THE TREASURY

When negotiating, it's always useful to know what the other party is likely to do in the event that an agreement can't be reached. Sometimes, it's just not possible to reach an agreement—there's no **Common Ground**, so both parties agree to go their separate ways. What then?

Your **Next Best Alternative** is what you'll do in the event you can't find Common Ground with the party you're negotiating with. Imagine you're looking for a job, and there are three companies interested in hiring you. You may prefer to work at Company A, but if you can't reach a mutually acceptable agreement, it's easier to be a confident negotiator if you know that Companies B and C are also interested in hiring you. If Company A is your only option and they know it, you're not likely to get a good deal.

The other party always has a Next Best Alternative as well—that's what you're negotiating against. If you're selling a product that costs $100, you are selling against the next best thing that they could do with that $100: save it, invest it, or purchase something else. If you're trying to hire an employee, you're competing against the next best offer they have from another company. The more options the other party has, the weaker your negotiating position.

Understanding the other party's Next Best Alternative gives you a major sales advantage: you can structure your agreement so it's more attractive than their next best option. The more you know about the other party's alternatives, the better you can fine-tune your offer by *Bundling* or *Unbundling* various options.

Having a strong Next Best Alternative keeps negotiations moving. Many professional sports players who are approaching free agency use the opportunity to renegotiate or renew their contracts with their current teams, particularly if other teams express interest in them. If the original team doesn't want to lose the player, they have an incentive to reach an acceptable deal.

In every negotiation, the power lies with the party that is *able and willing to walk away* from a bad deal. In almost every case, the more acceptable alternatives you have, the better your position. The more attractive your alternatives, the more willing you'll be to walk away from a deal that doesn't serve you, resulting in better deals.

REFERENCE LINK: personalmba.com/next-best-alternative/

Exclusivity

The best strategy is always to be very strong.

—CARL VON CLAUSEWITZ, MILITARY STRATEGIST

In most sales situations, it's in your best interest to maintain *Exclusivity*: creating a unique offer or benefit that other firms can't match. If you're the only person or company that offers what your prospect wants, you're in a very strong position to negotiate on favorable terms.

If you want to purchase an iPhone, you have to buy it through Apple: it is the sole source. You may purchase the product directly or through a retailer: either way, Apple gets paid. So long as you want an iPhone and aren't willing to settle for an alternative, Apple wins.

Exclusivity is beneficial for many reasons. Exclusive offers make it much easier to maintain high **Perceived Value**, since there's no direct competition. Substitutes or alternatives may exist, but if a prospect is set on your specific offer, they'll have to obtain it through you, making it far easier for you to set high prices and maintain a healthy **Profit Margin**.

Exclusivity is easiest to maintain when you've created something new, which means an exclusivity strategy makes the most sense for **Products** and **Services**. Resellers often find it difficult to establish exclusivity unless they play a role in the product's manufacture, which is why retailers often create "private label" brands. Costco's famous Kirkland Signature brand is a way of creating exclusivity, as is Trader Joe's strategy of negotiating with manufacturers to create unique products.

If you're the exclusive source for what your prospects want, you win.

REFERENCE LINK: **personalmba.com/exclusivity/**

Three Universal Currencies

> Time will take your money, but money won't buy time.
>
> —JAMES TAYLOR, MUSICIAN

In every negotiation, there are **Three Universal Currencies**: resources, time, and flexibility. Any one of these currencies can be traded for more or less of the others.

Resources are tangible items like money, gold, oil, etc. Resources are physical: you can hold them in your hand. If you want to buy some furniture, you can offer money in exchange. If you're selling your car, the purchaser could (with your agreement) give you a bar of gold or a mint first-edition issue of *Action Comics #1*, which features the first appearance of Superman in print. You're trading one resource for another.

Time is the second universal currency. If you go to work as an hourly employee, you are trading a certain amount of time and effort for a certain amount of resources. You can also trade resources for time: you can offer to pay other people in exchange for their work, which is the essence of employment, contracting, and freelancing.

Flexibility is the third universal currency—one that is usually quite underrated. Becoming a salaried employee isn't a straightforward exchange of resources for time and effort—you're also giving up a certain amount of flexibility. There's an implicit agreement that you won't work on other things when you're supposed to be working for the company, which is a very real **Opportunity Cost**. While you're working, you're giving up the flexibility to do something else.

It's entirely possible to negotiate for a greater or lesser degree of flexibility by trading off effort or resources. For example, you can decrease your effort and increase your flexibility by working part time, in exchange for fewer resources—reduced salary and benefits. Purchasing a house requires less time if you agree to a thirty-year mortgage versus saving up to buy it outright, at the cost of additional resources (interest payments) and decreased flexibility.

It's possible to gain more of any of these desired currencies by finding appropriate **Trade-offs** between one or more of the others. If you'd like additional compensation in the form of a raise or a larger contract, you can give up time or flexibility (such as the ability to use what you make for other purposes) as a Trade-off. If you'd like a bit more flexibility or time off in your working arrangements, you can negotiate a decrease in salary to compensate. If your employer or client wants you to work more or wants to benefit more from your work, you can ask them for more compensation in return.

Keep the Three Universal Currencies in mind when negotiating and you'll be amazed at the range of potential options you'll be able to present to the other party, making it easier to find an option that works for all parties involved.

REFERENCE LINK: **personalmba.com/3-universal-currencies/**

Three Dimensions of Negotiation

> The first thing to decide before you walk into any negotiation is what to do if the other fellow says no.
>
> —ERNEST BEVIN, FORMER BRITISH SECRETARY
> OF STATE FOR FOREIGN AFFAIRS

Most people think of negotiation as sitting down across from the other party and presenting offers and counteroffers. But that's the last phase of the process; the other two happen well before you ever sit down at the negotiating table.

The **Three Dimensions of Negotiation** are setup, structure, and discussion. As David A. Lax and James K. Sebenius discuss in *3-D Negotiation*, each of these phases is essential: by creating an **Environment** that's conducive to a deal and preparing your strategy in advance, you can increase the probability of finding a mutually acceptable solution.

The first phase of every negotiation is the *setup*: setting the stage for a satisfying outcome to the negotiation. The more you can stack the odds in your favor before you start negotiating, the better the deal you'll be able to strike.

▶ Who is involved in the negotiation, and are they open to dealing with you?

▶ Who are you negotiating with, and do they know who you are and how you can help them?

▶ What are you proposing, and how does it benefit the other party?

▶ What's the setting—will you present your offer in person, by phone, or by some other means?

▶ What are all of the environmental factors around the deal—do recent events make this deal more or less important to the other party?

Setup is the negotiation equivalent of **Guiding Structure**—the Environment surrounding the deal plays a huge role in the eventual outcome, so it pays to ensure that the Environment is conducive to getting a good deal before you ever reach the table. By thinking about the setup, you can make sure you're negotiating with the right person—the person who has the **Power** to give you what you want. Research is what gives this dimension of negotiation its power—the more knowledge you gain about your negotiating partner during this phase, the more power you have in the entire negotiation, so do your homework before presenting an offer.

The second dimension of negotiation is *structure*: the terms of the proposal. In this phase, you put together your draft proposal in a way the other party is likely to appreciate and accept:

▶ What will you propose, and how are you *Framing* your proposal to the other party?

▶ What are the primary benefits of your proposal to the other party?

▶ What is the other party's *Next Best Alternative*, and how is your proposal better?

▶ How will you overcome the other party's objections and *Barriers to Purchase*?

▶ Are there *Trade-offs* or concessions you're willing to make to reach an agreement?

Remember, your goal in creating the proposal is to find *Common Ground*: an agreement that both parties will be happy to accept. By thinking through the structure of your proposal in advance, you can prepare a few different options that you believe the other party will want, on terms you're willing to accept.

If you're expecting the other party to balk at the price, for instance, you can prepare arguments to overcome the objection, lower-cost options that provide less value, or alternative offers that would better fit their needs. When the time comes for you to discuss the deal with your negotiating partner, you'll be ready for anything.

The third dimension of negotiation is the *discussion*: presenting the offer to the other party. The discussion is when you talk through your proposal with the other party. Sometimes the discussion happens the way you see it in the movies: in a mahogany-walled boardroom, across the table, toe to toe with the CEO. Sometimes it happens over the phone. Sometimes it happens over email. Whatever the setting, this is the point where you present your offer, discuss or clarify any issues the other party doesn't understand, answer objections and remove Barriers to Purchase, and ask for the sale.

Regardless of what happens during the discussion phase, the end result of every round of discussion is either (1) "Yes, we have a deal on these terms," (2) "We don't have a deal quite yet—here's a counteroffer or another option to consider," or (3) "No, we don't have a deal—there's no Common Ground, so we'll suspend negotiations and reserve the right to talk to somebody else." Discussion continues until a final agreement is reached or the parties decide to quit negotiating, whichever happens first.

If you prepare the Three Dimensions of Negotiation (setup, structure, and discussion) in advance, you'll be far more likely to settle on terms that benefit both parties.

REFERENCE LINK: **personalmba.com/3-dimensions-of-negotiation/**

Buffer

Zeal without knowledge is the sister of folly.

—SIR JOHN DAVIES, ELIZABETHAN POET AND FORMER
ATTORNEY GENERAL OF IRELAND

In all but the most extenuating circumstances, *Common Ground* ensures that every deal is in the best interest of all parties involved. However, there may be parts of the agreement or discussion where one party's gain is the other's loss. If you're interviewing for a job and you attempt to negotiate a higher salary, any increase in your salary is necessarily the employer's loss.

Depending on the situation, these aspects of the negotiation can be tense. You want to push for as much as you can, but if you push too hard, you risk torpedoing the deal and permanently harming your relationship with the other party. In these cases, it's helpful to work with someone who can help you negotiate a good deal without risking the relationship.

A *Buffer* is a third party empowered to negotiate on your behalf. *Agents*, attorneys, mediators, brokers, accountants, and other similar subject-matter experts are all examples of Buffers. Buffers who have expertise in specific types of negotiations can be valuable in helping you get the best deal possible. You don't have to know everything about arcane topics like tort law and tax policy if you enlist the help of an honest and capable Buffer.

When a professional athlete is negotiating a contract to join a professional sports team, he or she enlists the help of both an agent and an attorney. The agent's job is to obtain the best possible compensation for the athlete, and the team's manager and owner know this. They can remain positive about hiring the athlete even while the agent plays hardball. In the end, the athlete's overall compensation is improved despite the agent's fees.

The same thing happens with the athlete's attorney, who can argue for the inclusion or exclusion of certain provisions in the proposed contract. An attorney can make these proposals with much greater force and effect based on their knowledge, experience, and expertise. Together with the agent, the attorney can work with the team owner and manager to ensure that the athlete gets the best deal the team is willing to accept, without adversely affecting the athlete's **Reputation** or goodwill.

Buffers can also be useful in order to add some time or space to a high-intensity negotiation. It's often quite useful not to be the party who has the final say. Being able to say, "I need to discuss this with my agent/accountant/attorney" before giving final approval on a deal is a valuable check step that prevents hasty or unwise decisions.

Be very mindful of **Incentive-Caused Bias** when working with a Buffer. Depending on the arrangement, your Buffer's priorities may be very different from your own. For example, real estate agents act as Buffers between the sellers of property and potential purchasers. If you're looking to buy property, it's often useful to work with a buy-side agent, provided you're aware of how they're compensated.

Agents are usually compensated on a commission basis, so it pays to be wary if you're using them on the buy side of a deal. The Agent is compensated if (and only if) a **Transaction** occurs. Their first priority is to complete a deal—any deal—regardless of whether or not it's the best possible deal for the buyer.

If at all possible, work with a Buffer who is willing to accept a flat fee in exchange for services rendered, whether or not the deal happens. If your Buffer will be paid regardless of what happens, their interests will be more closely aligned with getting you the best deal possible, which enhances their Reputation.

Don't let your Buffer replace your own informed judgment. One of the worst things you can do is relinquish control over your decisions to your Buffer, particularly if your interests aren't aligned. Many unwary investors have found their savings depleted by giving carte blanche to "investment professionals" who are compensated every time a security is bought or sold. By "churning" the account, the broker is able to legally rack up thousands of dollars in unnecessary fees. As a rule of thumb, don't give *anyone* unfettered control over decisions that affect your money.

Buffers can be a valuable resource as long as you're clear about how they'll be rewarded, what they're responsible for, and how you intend to work together.

REFERENCE LINK: **personalmba.com/buffer/**

Persuasion Resistance

Sales are contingent upon the attitude of the salesman, not the attitude of the prospect.

—W. CLEMENT STONE, INSURANCE SALESMAN,
PHILANTHROPIST, AND AUTHOR

One of the things that makes prospects uncomfortable around salespeople is the feeling that they're going to get the "hard sell" or be tricked into agreeing to something that's not in their best interest. This experience is called *Persuasion Resistance*, and it's a major barrier to making sales.

When a prospect senses that someone is trying to convince or compel them to do something they're not sure about, they resist and attempt to move away from the conversation. This is particularly true in situations where the salesperson is trying to force a choice or limit the prospect's available options in some way.

Psychologists call this "reactance," and it appears in early childhood. Every parent has experienced the fallout of telling a child they "can't" or "have to" do something. Prospects react in much the same way when a salesperson attempts to pressure a sale, resisting out of an instinct to preserve their autonomy. The harder the salesperson pushes, the more the prospect resists. That's why hard-sell approaches usually fail to generate sustainable results.

The more effective strategy, in the words of the renowned sales expert Zig Ziglar, is to present yourself to the prospect as an "assistant buyer." Your job is not to sell the prospect a bill of goods: it's to help them make an informed decision about what's best for them. You're not pressuring them to give you their money; you're helping to ensure they invest their resources wisely. This basic *Reinterpretation* of your role in the sales process works: it eliminates the prospect's feeling of pressure by convincing them you're looking out for their best interests.

Salespeople need to be aware of two additional signals that can trigger Persuasion Resistance: *desperation* and *chasing*. Sending either signal during any part of the sales process will reduce the number and size of the **Transactions** you close.

If a prospect feels that you're desperate to make a sale, it diminishes their interest in a matter of seconds. Desperation is a subtle signal that other people don't find your offer desirable, and **Social Proof** starts working against you. In the same way that people don't want to date a person who desperately wants to be in a relationship, prospects don't want to do business with a person who desperately wants or needs their money.

It's much better to present yourself with confidence, in a way that signals your offer is valuable, is a good fit for the prospect, and will be a wise investment of the prospect's money. If you don't genuinely believe that, you need to find something else to sell.

If a prospect senses you're chasing them, their first impulse will be to move away from you. Chasing and being chased are evolutionary patterns: for thousands of years, human beings have chased things that are desirable and they have been chased by threats. Even if we wouldn't label a situation as "chasing" or "being chased," our minds notice and respond without conscious effort.

Chasing a prospect to make a sale is counterproductive, a waste of time and energy. Instead, find ways to use **Framing** to present the situation in a way that encourages the prospect to feel like *they're chasing you*. If your prospect feels like they need to justify why they're good enough to work with you, you're in a very strong position to make a sale on favorable terms.

We'll discuss additional ways our primal minds process our modern **Environment** in **Caveman Syndrome**. For now, it's important to remember that these social signals may seem silly at best or manipulative at worst, but that doesn't make them any less real or important. By understanding how your prospects evaluate offers, you can plan your pitch in a way that minimizes Persuasion Resistance and encourages the prospect to **Desire** what you have to offer.

REFERENCE LINK: **personalmba.com/persuasion-resistance/**

Reciprocation

Gifts are never free: they bind the giver and receiver in a loop of reciprocity.

—MARCEL MAUSS, SOCIOLOGIST AND ANTHROPOLOGIST

Reciprocation is the strong desire most people feel to "pay back" favors, gifts, benefits, and resources provided. If you've ever had the experience of receiving a holiday gift from someone you didn't send anything to, you know how uncomfortable this feels. If someone benefits us, we like to benefit them in return.

As a social force, Reciprocation is one of the primary psychological tendencies that underlie human cooperation. The "You scratch my back, I'll scratch yours" instinct is powerful and forms the foundation of friendships and alliances. Historically, gift giving was how the powerful remained in *Power*: in throwing lavish parties or generously awarding titles and land, leaders increased their influence by amassing a store of favors that could be called in during times of need.

Here's the tricky part: the desire to reciprocate is not necessarily in proportion to the original benefit provided. In *Influence: The Psychology of Persuasion*, Dr. Robert Cialdini provides an example of reciprocation in car sales. Car salesmen often offer prospects a small gift up front. "Can I get you a coffee? Would you like a soda? Some water? Cookies? Is there anything that I can do to make you more comfortable?"

It seems like a common gesture of hospitality. It's not. Accepting this small offer creates a psychological need to Reciprocate, subtly stacking the deck in the salesman's favor. Prospective car buyers who accepted this *Free* offer were far more likely to purchase a vehicle, add optional accessories, and agree to less attractive financing terms. As a result, these customers spent thousands of dollars more than the people who did not accept anything from the salesman while negotiating. That doesn't make rational sense, because the coffee or cookies cost the dealer very little, but Reciprocation makes it more likely that the buyer will "pay back" the favor with a much larger concession.

The more legitimate value you can provide to others up front, the more receptive they'll be when it's time for your pitch. Providing Free value builds your social capital, making it more likely the people you benefit will Reciprocate when you make an offer down the road.

Being generous is one of the best things you can do to improve your results as a salesperson. If you give away value and help others as much as you can, they'll respect you; it will build your *Reputation*, but it will also increase the probability that they will be interested enough when you *do* present your *Call to Action*.

REFERENCE LINK: **personalmba.com/reciprocation/**

Damaging Admission

We confess our little faults to persuade people that we have no large ones.

—FRANÇOIS DE LA ROCHEFOUCAULD, SEVENTEENTH-CENTURY
FRENCH COURTIER AND APHORIST

When Kelsey and I moved from New York City to the mountains of northern Colorado, our new landlords, Ben and Betty, made sure to notify us of two important facts about our new home:

(1) Rock slides were a very real possibility.

(2) Black bears and mountain lions roamed nearby.

These facts didn't prevent us from leasing the apartment, but we were glad to know them in advance, and it increased our estimation of their integrity. We weighed the risks, increased our renter's insurance, purchased a can of bear pepper spray, and signed the lease.

Counterintuitively, making a *Damaging Admission* like this to your prospects can *increase* their *Trust* in your ability to deliver what you promise.

Since Kelsey and I didn't own a car when we lived in Manhattan, we had to purchase one when we moved to Colorado. We found a car we were interested in purchasing online, but making such a large purchase without seeing the vehicle was uncomfortable.

To help alleviate our concerns, the dealership that listed the car went out of their way to photograph every detail—including a small chip in the paint on the left side, which wasn't a big deal. Because they were willing to include even the small flaws in their description before we purchased, we felt more confident that they had thoroughly described the vehicle. We purchased it, and everything was as described. Without making a Damaging Admission, the dealer wouldn't have made the sale.

Your prospects know you're not perfect, so don't pretend to be. People become suspicious when something appears to be too good to be true. If an offer has no obvious downsides, your prospects will start asking themselves, "What's the catch?"

Instead of making them wonder, tell them yourself. By being up front with your prospects regarding drawbacks and *Trade-offs*, you'll enhance your trustworthiness and close more sales.

REFERENCE LINK: **personalmba.com/damaging-admission/**

Option Fatigue

Don't make me think.

—STEVE KRUG, COMPUTER USABILITY EXPERT

Let's say you're in the market for a new computer. Should you choose the fastest available processor, the least powerful option that's half the price, or the middle-of-the-road option? How much storage do you need? How much internal memory is enough to run your software without slowing you down? Which display size should you select? Should you purchase a portable computer, a desktop system, or a tablet?

This matrix of decisions is overwhelming to most computer purchasers. Choosing the best option seems like it should be easy, but it's not: if there are five separate variables, and three options for each variable, there arc 243 possible combinations to consider. That's enough to short-circuit anyone's brain.

Option Fatigue is often a major barrier to buying decisions: if a prospect is overwhelmed by *Decisions*, they often choose to resolve their discomfort by abandoning the purchase instead of completing it. Every choice the prospect must make decreases the probability of closing the deal.

In general, the best approach is to guide the purchaser to select from two or three predefined options that represent good starting points for certain types of customers, then customize that option further if necessary. That's why computer manufacturers like Apple and Dell present a few preconfigured computers designed to appeal to certain types of customers, then allow you to upgrade or downgrade individual components later in the purchasing process. The same number of options exist, but the cognitive load on the prospect is much lower.

You don't have to present every available option from the outset: making a few strategic recommendations can keep your prospects engaged in a way that results in more sales.

REFERENCE LINK: **personalmba.com/option-fatigue/**

Barriers to Purchase

Selling begins when the prospect says no.

—SALES MAXIM

Assume for a moment you present an offer to a prospect, and their reply is something along the lines of "No—that doesn't work for me." Time to give up and move on?

There's always a reason a prospect says no. The fact that they're even talking with you implies that they have at least *some* interest in your offer—otherwise, the conversation would end. There's still hope of closing the sale, if you start asking the right questions.

Selling anything is the process of identifying and eliminating **Barriers to Purchase**: risks, unknowns, and concerns that prevent your prospects from buying what you offer. Your primary job as a salesperson is to identify and eliminate barriers standing in the way of completing the **Transaction**. Eliminate your prospect's objections and barriers and you'll close the deal.

There are five standard objections that appear in sales of all kinds:

1. *It costs too much.* **Loss Aversion** makes spending money feel like a loss—by purchasing, the prospect is giving something up, and that makes people hesitate. (Some people even experience this sense of loss *after* they make a purchase decision, a condition called "buyer's remorse.")

2. *It won't work.* If the prospect thinks that there's a chance the offer won't (or can't) provide the promised benefits, they won't purchase.

3. *It won't work for me.* The prospect may believe that the offer is capable of providing benefits to other people but that they're different—a special case.

4. *I can wait.* The prospect may believe they don't have a problem worth addressing right now, even if it's very clear to you that they do.

5. *It's too difficult.* If the offer takes any effort whatsoever on their part, the prospect may believe that their contribution will be too hard to manage.

To overcome these objections, it makes sense to build them into the structure of your initial offer. Since these objections are very common, anything that you can do to alleviate them before the prospect considers the offer will make the sales process much easier.

Objection 1 ("It costs too much") is best addressed via *Framing* and *Value-Based Selling*. If you're selling a piece of software to a business that can save them $10 million a year, and you're asking $1 million a year for a license, your software isn't expensive—it's almost *Free*. If it's clear that the value of your offer far exceeds the asking price, this objection is moot.

Objections 2 and 3 ("It won't work" / "It won't work for me") are best addressed via *Social Proof*—showing the prospect how customers *just like them* are already benefiting from your offer. The more like your prospect's situation your stories and testimonials are, the better. That's why *Referrals* are such a powerful sales tool—customers tend to refer people who have similar situations and needs, and the Referral itself helps break down these objections.

Objections 4 and 5 ("I can wait" / "It's too difficult") are best addressed via *Education-Based Selling*. Often, your prospects haven't fully realized they have a problem, particularly in the case of *Absence Blindness*. If the business doesn't realize it's losing $10 million in the first place, it's difficult to convince them that you can help. The best way to get around this is to focus your early sales efforts on making your customers smarter by teaching them what you know about their business, then use *Visualization* to help them imagine what their involvement would look like if they decide to proceed.

Once you have the prospect's *Attention* and *Permission*, there are two possible tactics if they still have these objections: (1) convince the prospect that the objection isn't true, or (2) convince the prospect that the objection is irrelevant. The approach you'll use depends on the objection raised, but some combination of Framing, Value-Based Selling, Education-Based Selling, Social Proof, and Visualization will usually do the trick.

If the prospect still doesn't buy, that often means there's a **Power** issue—your negotiating partner may not have the budget or the authority to agree to your proposal. Always try to negotiate with the decision-maker—that way, if they refuse your offer, you know that it's because it wasn't a good fit for them, and you can move on to more promising prospects.

REFERENCE LINK: **personalmba.com/objections-barriers-to-purchase/**

Risk Reversal

If you want a guarantee, buy a toaster.

—CLINT EASTWOOD, ACADEMY AWARD–WINNING DIRECTOR AND ACTOR

People, as a rule, hate losing. They hate feeling stupid. They hate making bad decisions or wasting money. They hate taking risks.

When it comes to closing sales, *you* are that risk. In every **Transaction**, the purchaser is taking on some risk. What if this offer doesn't work as promised? What if it doesn't meet their needs? What if purchasing from you is a waste of money?

These questions are always in the back of your prospect's mind as they're considering purchasing from you. If you don't eliminate these questions, it's very likely they'll ruin the sale.

Risk Reversal is a strategy that transfers some (or all) of the risk of a Transaction from the buyer to the seller. Instead of making the purchaser shoulder the risk of a bad Transaction, the seller agrees in advance to make things right if—for whatever reason—things don't turn out as the purchaser expected.

Take the bedding industry, for example. Look around, and you'll see a lot of over-the-top offers: twelve-month, 100 percent money-back guarantees, no questions asked! A customer could sleep on a bed for a year, decide they didn't like it, and call up the store to return it for a full refund. Crazy, right?

It's not crazy at all: this strategy eliminates the purchaser's perception of risk, which is a major *Barrier to Purchase*. If a customer makes a purchase and it doesn't work out, they don't have to feel stupid about wasting their money—and they don't have to feel angry at the company or at themselves for making a bad decision. All they need to do is take advantage of the guarantee and return it—no big deal. As a result, they'll go through with the Transaction—there's no downside, so why not?

This approach is sometimes called the "take the puppy home" strategy. If you visit a pet store and meet an adorable puppy, but you're not sure whether or not you're ready to commit, the pet store will often tell you to take the puppy home on a trial basis. "If it doesn't work out," the salesperson says, "you can always bring it back."

The puppy almost never comes back, of course. The promise of an easy return is the key to making the sale: the salesperson is happy to accept the small risk of a return to secure the sale, the new owners feel less anxious about their decision, and the puppy gets a new home. Everyone wins.

Adopting a Risk Reversal strategy is uncomfortable because sellers *also* hate to lose. No seller wants to feel used or taken advantage of, and it's often easy to feel that way if a customer obviously gets value from the offer and asks for a refund anyway.

The difference is that the purchaser is purchasing from one seller—the seller is selling to many purchasers. Your customers experience this risk with every purchase they make, and it's a big deal. Since you're serving many customers, you can spread the cost of a return across the total number of customers you serve.

Yes, you'll lose money on customers who are obviously taking advantage of your generosity, and that never feels good. In compensation, by eliminating the risk that every purchaser feels, you'll close many more sales and come out way ahead in terms of total revenue and profit.

If you want to maximize your sales, it almost always makes sense to offer a very strong, risk-reversing guarantee and to extend the risk-free period as much as possible. If you don't already have a Risk Reversal policy, implement one and you'll see your sales increase.

REFERENCE LINK: **personalmba.com/risk-reversal/**

Reactivation

Every company's greatest assets are its customers, because without customers there is no company.

—MICHAEL LEBOEUF, BUSINESS PROFESSOR AND AUTHOR OF
HOW TO WIN CUSTOMERS AND KEEP THEM FOR LIFE

Sales is the process of convincing prospects to become customers. Winning new customers, however, is often costly and time intensive. What if there was another way to bring in more revenue at very little additional cost?

Reactivation is the process of convincing past customers to buy from you again. If you've been in business for a while, you'll have some "lapsed" customers—people who have already purchased from you but haven't purchased for quite some time. You know they're interested in what you have to offer, and you probably already have their contact information. Why not present them with a new offer to make them active customers once again?

Netflix is a company that uses Reactivation in a brilliant way. If you cancel a Netflix subscription, three to six months later you'll receive a postcard and/or email with an offer to resubscribe at a reduced rate. If you don't reply, they'll send another message every few months until you resubscribe or request to be removed from their marketing system. Since Netflix is a **Subscription** business, every reactivated customer means an additional monthly stream of income, which greatly enhances the **Lifetime Value** of each customer.

Reactivation is often a quicker, simpler, and more effective approach to increasing revenue than attracting new customers. Your old customers already know and **Trust** you, and they're aware of the value you provide. You have their information—you don't have to find them. Your cost of customer acquisition (a component of **Allowable Acquisition Cost**) is low—all you have to do is contact them and present an attractive offer.

Reactivation is much simpler if you have **Permission** from your customers to follow up. Your list of prospective customers is a valuable asset, but your list of past customers is just as valuable. By obtaining Permission from your customers to follow up with them, you increase the probability of Reactivation if they—for whatever reason—stop buying from you.

Most point-of-sale (POS) systems keep track of customer data: who purchased and when the sale was made. It's relatively simple to extract a list of customers who haven't purchased from you in a while, then present them with a Reactivation offer via email, phone call, or postal mail. Reactivation campaigns are the easiest and most profitable marketing activities you'll ever try.

Make it a priority, every three to six months, to contact your lapsed customers with another offer to see if you can encourage them to start buying again. You'll be amazed by the results.

REFERENCE LINK: **personalmba.com/reactivation/**

4

VALUE DELIVERY

A satisfied customer is the best business strategy of all.

—MICHAEL LEBOEUF, BUSINESS PROFESSOR AND AUTHOR OF
HOW TO WIN CUSTOMERS AND KEEP THEM FOR LIFE

Every successful business delivers what it promises to its customers. There's a term for a person who takes other people's money without delivering equivalent value: "scam artist."

Value delivery involves everything necessary to ensure that every paying customer is a happy customer: order processing, inventory management, delivery/fulfillment, troubleshooting, customer support, etc. Without value delivery, you don't have a business.

The best businesses in the world deliver the value they've promised to their customers in a way that surpasses the customers' expectations. The more happy customers a business creates, the more likely it is that those customers will purchase from the company again. Happy customers are also more likely to tell others about what you do, improving your **Reputation** and bringing in even more potential customers.

Successful businesses satisfy their customers most of the time in the midst of a changing environment. Unsuccessful businesses fail to make their customers happy, lose them, and eventually fail.

REFERENCE LINK: **personalmba.com/value-delivery/**

Value Stream

Great design is eliminating all unnecessary details.

—MINH D. TRAN, TECHNOLOGIST AND DESIGNER

When I worked at Procter & Gamble, one of the most fascinating things about my job was understanding how products were created and delivered. Here's a quick look at how a bottle of Dawn dishwashing liquid is made:

1. Raw materials are delivered to the factory.

2. The materials are combined to create dishwashing liquid, which is stored in large vats.

3. Plastic bottles are blown into shape using molds, then filled with the liquid and capped.

4. Adhesive labels are applied to each bottle.

5. Each bottle is inspected, boxed, then loaded onto a pallet.

It's a textbook example of a value-creation process, which begins with raw materials and ends with a finished **Product**, ready to be shipped. Here's what happens next:

6. Pallets are wrapped, stacked, and stored for shipment in a warehouse.

7. When orders from customers are placed, pallets are moved into position for loading onto a truck.

8. A truck picks up the pallets and delivers them to the customer's closest distribution center.

9. The customer puts the pallets on a delivery truck.

10. The truck delivers the pallet to a store that needs additional inventory.

11. The store unwraps the pallet, unboxes the product, and transfers it to the shelf, where it will remain until purchased by the consumer.

That's a lot of steps for a little bottle of dish soap. Those steps are worth studying.

A **Value Stream** is the set of all steps and all processes from the start of your value-creation process all the way through the delivery of the end result to your customer.

You can think of the Value Stream as a combination of your value-creation and value-delivery processes. Even though the purposes of these core processes are very different, treating them as one big process can help you improve your ability to deliver the value you create.

The Toyota Production System (TPS) was the first large-scale manufacturing operation to systematically examine its entire Value Stream on a regular basis. Analyzing the production system in great detail paved the way for an ongoing series of small, incremental improvements: Toyota engineers make more than 1 million improvements to the TPS each year. As a result, the company reaps huge rewards in speed, consistency, and reliability, which has greatly improved Toyota's **Reputation** as a company with very high-quality products—that is, until the **Paradox of Automation** damaged that Reputation, which we'll discuss in detail later.

The best way to understand your Value Stream is to diagram it. Tracing the steps or transformations your offer goes through from the beginning to the end is an enlightening process that can show you just how efficient your value-delivery process is. It's very common for processes to contain unnecessary steps or awkward transitions. Creating a complete diagram of your entire Value Stream takes effort, but it can help you streamline your process, making the entire system perform better.[1]

In general, try to make your Value Stream as small and efficient as possible. As we'll examine later in the book when we discuss systems, the longer your process, the greater the risk of things going wrong. The shorter and more streamlined your Value Stream, the easier it is to manage and the more value you'll be able to deliver.

REFERENCE LINK: **personalmba.com/value-stream/**

Distribution Channel

Unless a person is a clam digger, a trapper, or an old-style pick-and-shovel prospector, it's virtually impossible these days to be a success all by oneself.

—BENJAMIN F. FAIRLESS, FORMER PRESIDENT OF US STEEL

Once a sale is made, you must deliver what you promised to your customer. A **Distribution Channel** describes how your form of value is delivered to the end user.

There are two basic types of Distribution Channels: direct-to-user and intermediary.

Direct-to-user distribution works across a single channel: from the business to the end user. **Services** are a classic example: when you get a haircut, the value is provided by the business itself to you, with no intermediary.

Direct-to-user distribution is simple and effective, but it has limitations—you have full control of the entire process, but you can only serve as many customers as your time and energy allow. Once demand for your offer outpaces your ability to deliver it, you're risking disappointing your customers and diminishing your **Reputation**.

Intermediary distribution works across multiple channels. When you purchase a **Product** from a store, that store is engaging in **Resale**. The store (in most cases) doesn't manufacture the Products—it purchases them from another business.

The business that created the Product can sell it to as many stores as it wants, a process called "securing distribution." The more distribution a Product has, the more sales the business is likely to make—the more stores selling the Product, the more opportunities for sales.

Intermediary distribution can increase sales, but it requires giving up a certain amount of control over your value-delivery process. Trusting another business to deliver your offer to your customers frees up your limited time and energy, but it also increases **Counterparty Risk**—the risk that your partner will screw up and diminish your Reputation.

Imagine you're in the business of selling cookies and you secure distribution at a local supermarket. The supermarket purchases cookies from you, places them on their shelves, and sells them to their shoppers at a premium. Instead of buying cookies from you, shoppers purchase them via the supermarket: classic intermediary distribution.

It's easy to see the benefits of this approach, but there are drawbacks. Let's say your cookies are damaged in the supermarket's truck on the way to the store: they break, they crumble, and the box they're delivered in is crushed. The supermarket's shoppers won't know what happened, but if it happens often, they'll assume that *you* create a low-quality Product, damaging your Reputation.

Securing distribution can be valuable, but keep an eye on your intermediaries. Distribution isn't a set-it-and-forget-it strategy—if you're working with multiple Distribution Channels, plan to devote time and energy to making sure they're representing your business well.

REFERENCE LINK: **personalmba.com/distribution-channel/**

The Expectation Effect

Never promise more than you can perform.

—PUBLILIUS SYRUS, FIRST-CENTURY BCE SYRIAN APHORIST

Zappos has perfected the art of selling shoes online.

Selling shoes over the internet is a tough business—customers can't try them on, and no one wants to be stuck with shoes they don't like and will never wear. To compensate, Zappos applies classic **Risk Reversal** to every order—they offer free shipping and no-questions-asked returns if you don't like the **Products** you order. Those two policies eliminate the risk of making a bad purchase, so customers are more willing to try Zappos out.

That's not, however, the reason Zappos has developed such a solid **Reputation** in this market. The secret lies in an unexpected benefit the company doesn't advertise.

When you order from Zappos, it's likely that you'll receive a pleasant surprise: your shoes will often arrive a few days ahead of schedule.

Zappos could advertise "free expedited shipping," but they don't—the surprise is far more valuable.

A customer's perception of quality relies on two subjective criteria: expectations and performance. You can characterize this relationship in the form of a quasi-equation, which I call the *Expectation Effect*: Quality = Performance–Expectations.

Customer expectations have to be high enough for a customer to purchase from you in the first place. After the purchase is made, however, the performance of the offering must *surpass* the customer's expectations in order for them to be satisfied. If performance is better than expectations, the customer's perception of quality will be high. If performance is lower than expectations, the perception of quality will be low—no matter how good the offer is in absolute terms.

Apple's first-generation iPhone was a massive success—customers expected something good, and they received a device that delivered benefits beyond their expectations. Apple's second-generation iPhone, the 3G, wasn't as well received—prelaunch expectations were so high that there was almost no way the company could surpass them, and a few glitches in the roll-out process took center stage.

The iPhone 3G was a better phone in the absolute—it was faster and had several new features, more memory, and a lower price. To many customers, however, it didn't *feel* better—Apple failed to deliver on their expectations, and the company's *Reputation* suffered. The same thing happened again with the launch of the fourth-generation iPhone—a small antenna glitch soured many customers on the device, even though the new version was better than the old in every other respect.

The best way to surpass expectations is to give your customers an unexpected bonus in addition to the value they expect. The purpose of the value-delivery process is to ensure that your customers are happy and satisfied, and the best way to ensure customer satisfaction is to at least meet the customers' expectations, surpassing them whenever you can.

Do whatever you can do to provide something that unexpectedly delights your customers. Zappos's free upgraded shipping is more valuable as a surprise—if it were part of the deal, it would lose its emotional punch.

When you perform well above your customers' expectations, they'll be satisfied with the experience.

REFERENCE LINK: **personalmba.com/expectation-effect/**

Predictability

I have always believed that for a product or service to thrive, it must
deliver quality. A fine product or service is its own best selling point.

—VICTOR KIAM, FORMER OWNER OF REMINGTON PRODUCTS
AND THE NEW ENGLAND PATRIOTS

Aaron Shira, one of my best friends growing up, cofounded a painting
company with his brother, Patrick, in Columbus, Ohio, USA. Shira Sons
Painting specializes in large-scale painting projects—they've painted universities, military bases, megachurches, and multimillion-dollar homes.
Having started from scratch, they're now the preferred painting company
for several major general contractors in the Columbus area.

How did two young guys break into a competitive market filled with
contractors who have been in business longer than they've been alive?
Simple: when you hire Aaron and Pat, you can be *certain* the job will be
done right and on time.

Contractors are notoriously unpredictable: they often show up late, take
too long, do sloppy work, and/or have bad attitudes. The secret of Aaron
and Pat's success is **Predictability**—they do great work every single time,
they deliver on schedule, and they're always pleasant to work with. As a
result, they're booked solid—an impressive achievement, particularly in a
soft construction market.

When purchasing something of value, customers want to know what
they can expect—they want their experience to be predictable. Pleasant
surprises can provide a customer with a great experience, but if you're not
able to deliver what the customer expects in a predictable manner, it doesn't
matter how many bonuses you offer. People love pleasant surprises, but
they hate to be caught off guard.

There are three primary factors that influence the Predictability of an
offer: uniformity, consistency, and reliability.

Uniformity means delivering the same characteristics every time. Coca-
Cola was one of the first large companies to combine solid marketing with
large-scale product uniformity. Product uniformity in the beverage industry is an astounding feat: creating, bottling, and distributing soda is a

complex process. A little too much sugar or flavoring, slightly more air, or an introduction of bacteria can drastically alter the final product.

No one wants their favorite soda to taste different every time they drink it. When you open a can of Coke, you expect the same product as you had the last time, no matter where you are in the world. If even 0.1 percent of the cans of Coca-Cola sold were flat or sour, people would stop buying.

Consistency means delivering the same value over time. One of the reasons "New Coke" failed in the mid-1980s was that customers expected Coke to taste a certain way, and the company delivered something new under the same name. Violating consistency led to a swift decline in sales, followed by a swift increase when the Coca-Cola Company restored the original formula.

Violating the expectations of loyal customers is not the way to success—if you're offering something different, present it as something new.

Reliability means being able to count on delivery of the value without error or delay. Ask Microsoft Windows users what they hate most about their computers, and they'll always tell you, "System crashes." Unreliability is a huge frustration for a user, particularly when Predictability is at a premium. How would you feel if you were building a house and a contractor didn't show up on time?

Improving Predictability has major **Reputation** and value perception benefits. The more Predictable your standard offering is, the more you'll be able to increase the perceived quality of the **Products** and the **Services** that you offer.

REFERENCE LINK: **personalmba.com/predictability/**

Quality

Strive for perfection in everything. Take the best that exists and make it better. If it doesn't exist, create it. Accept nothing nearly right or good enough.

—HENRY ROYCE, ENGINEER AND COFOUNDER OF ROLLS-ROYCE

What makes something "good"?

Quality, in the broadest sense, is "fitness for purpose": Does the offer deliver the intended benefits, and is it suitable for use in the intended **Environment**?

Quality is often subjective—some aspects, like manufacturing **Tolerances**, can be measured, but fuzzy factors, like "Does the end user like using it," are more difficult to quantify.

In 1987, David A. Garvin, a professor at Harvard Business School, proposed a practical framework managers and executives can use to define, measure, and improve quality.[2] I like to think through Garvin's eight factors in terms of questions:

1. *Performance*—how well does it serve the intended purpose?

2. *Features*—how many useful or valuable benefits does it offer?

3. *Reliability*—what is the probability it will break, malfunction, or fail when used?

4. *Conformance*—how well does it meet established standards? Are defects common? Are acceptable replacements available if I need them?

5. *Durability*—how long will it work?

6. *Serviceability*—if something goes wrong, is it easy to fix?

7. *Aesthetics*—is the subjective experience of using it pleasurable, attractive, or reassuring?

8. *Perception*—does it have a good **Reputation** and deliver better results than anticipated, to avoid the **Expectation Effect**?

The nice thing about this deconstruction is that it can serve as a **Checklist** of how to improve your offer over time. Nothing is perfect: there is always something you can do to improve the Quality of your offer.

REFERENCE LINK: **personalmba.com/quality/**

Quality Signals

Tis the same to him who wears a shoe, as if the whole earth were covered with leather.

—RALPH WALDO EMERSON, PARAPHRASING SHANTIDEVA,
EIGHTH-CENTURY BUDDHIST SCHOLAR

Car aficionados love the roar of a powerful motor pushed to the limit. There's just one problem: advances in manufacturing have resulted in better isolation between the engine compartment and the passenger cabin, which reduces engine noise. The sound is still there, but the driver can't hear it.

If you can't hear the motor when you hit the accelerator, does it really make a sound?

Many major car manufacturers (like BMW, Ford, Porsche, and Volkswagen) have adopted a workaround: they play engine noise—in some cases, *artificial* engine noise—through the vehicle's audio system when the driver presses the accelerator and the engine reaches certain RPM thresholds.[3]

Some drivers don't like the artifice, but there's a good argument to be made for the auditory sleight of hand: engine noise is an important aesthetic signal of **Quality** that increases customer satisfaction. People enjoy the sound, even if it's engineered.

Quality Signals are elements of an offer designed to increase the user's perception of Quality in a direct, tangible way. When performance is difficult to see, hear, feel, or otherwise notice, Quality Signals provide important reassurance that the offer is performing as intended.

Quality Signals don't just increase customer satisfaction: having a "reason to believe" the offer is able to produce the promised results makes marketing and sales efforts easier and more effective.

Dish detergent doesn't need to produce fluffy white bubbles in dishwater in order to work, but the presence of bubbles is a tangible indicator the detergent is present. Soap manufacturers like Procter & Gamble don't add a "sudsing agent" to soap without good reason: the additional raw materials increase the cost and complexity of production, but increased customer satisfaction makes it a worthwhile investment.

Quality Signals are a form of **Demonstration** that's built into the offer: they provide a noticeable indicator of performance, so users are less likely to undervalue the benefits of the offer due to **Absence Blindness** or unmet expectations.

REFERENCE LINK: **personalmba.com/quality-signals/**

Throughput

However beautiful the strategy, you should occasionally look at the results.

—WINSTON CHURCHILL, PRIME MINISTER OF
GREAT BRITAIN DURING WORLD WAR II

Throughput is the rate at which a system achieves its desired goal. By understanding and improving the process you use to create and deliver the value you've promised to your customers, you can improve quality and customer satisfaction.

Throughput is a measure of the effectiveness of your **Value Stream**. Throughput is measured in the formula [units/time]. The more units you create per increment of time, the higher the Throughput.

In order to measure Throughput, you need a clear objective:

Dollar throughput is a measure of how fast your overall business system creates a dollar of profit. Assume a standard time unit, like an hour/day/week/month—how many dollars does your business system produce on average during that time? The faster your business produces dollars of profit, the better.

Production throughput is a measure of how much time it takes to create an additional unit for sale. How long does it take to go from raw materials to a finished item rolling off the production line? The faster the production throughput, the more items you'll have available to sell and the faster you'll be able to respond to new demand for those items.

Satisfaction throughput is a measure of how much time it takes to create a happy, satisfied customer. It takes "fast casual" restaurants like Chipotle Mexican Grill approximately three minutes from the time the customer enters the restaurant to the time they receive their order. The less time that it takes to create a happy customer, the more customers you can serve in an hour and the more happy customers you can create every day. The longer customers have to wait, the fewer customers you can serve in an hour, and the less satisfied they will be with the experience.[4]

The best way to begin increasing Throughput is to start measuring it. How long does it take for your business system to produce a dollar of profit? How long does it take to produce another unit to sell or a new happy customer?

If you don't know your Throughput, make it a priority to find out—measuring Throughput is the first step toward improving it.

REFERENCE LINK: **personalmba.com/throughput/**

Duplication

> The problems of this world are only truly solved in two ways: by extinction or duplication.
>
> —SUSAN SONTAG, AUTHOR AND POLITICAL ACTIVIST

Duplication is the ability to reproduce something of value. Factory production is the quintessential example of Duplication: one design, many copies. Instead of reinventing the wheel over and over again, Duplication allows you to design the wheel once, then make as many of them as you wish.

The better your ability to Duplicate your offer, the more value you can provide. The more time and effort it costs to make something, the less available it tends to be. Duplication allows you to make copies of your offer, making it more widely available in a cost-effective way.

Consider this book. In the olden days, books used to be copied and bound by hand. It would take a scribe months (sometimes years[5]) of full-time work to copy a single book. As a result, books were expensive and difficult to obtain.

How times have changed. This book was written only once, but via the wonder of large-scale printing equipment, it can be reproduced in a fast, reliable, and inexpensive way. As a result, tens of millions of copies can be made and distributed all over the world and can be purchased for a few dollars. That's the magic of Duplication.

The internet has made Duplication of some forms of value even easier. As Kevin Kelly remarked in his essay "Better Than Free,"[6] the internet is an enormous, inexpensive copy machine. When I write a post for my website, it can be Duplicated by my web server for next to nothing and delivered to a reader on the other side of the world in a few milliseconds.

Duplication of information—text, images, music, video—is close to free. The value of this information, however, can be quite significant.

If you want to create something that you can sell without your direct involvement, the ability to Duplicate your offer is essential. If you have to be personally involved with every customer, there's an upper limit on the number of customers you can serve in a given amount of time. Combining Duplication with **Automation** allows you to deliver value to more people— and close more sales as a result.

REFERENCE LINK: personalmba.com/duplication/

Multiplication

> All growth depends upon activity. There is no development physi-
> cally or intellectually without effort, and effort means work.
>
> —CALVIN COOLIDGE, THIRTIETH PRESIDENT OF THE UNITED STATES

McDonald's knows how to **Duplicate** Big Macs. Starbucks knows how to Duplicate triple soy vanilla lattes. Here's what McDonald's and Starbucks have in common: both businesses can Duplicate entire stores, which is why there are thousands of each all over the world.

Multiplication is Duplication for an entire process or system. McDonald's began as a single restaurant in California; Starbucks began as a single coffee shop in Seattle. By learning to Duplicate the entire business system that is a McDonald's or Starbucks store, each company opened new possibilities for growth.

Walmart did the same thing. Starting with a single store in Fayetteville, Arkansas, USA, Walmart Multiplied at an astounding rate, spreading rapidly across the Midwest United States, then across the nation, then around the world.

Walmart's success lies in Multiplying two interconnected systems: stores and distribution centers. Distribution centers Multiply the ability to receive inventory from suppliers and deliver it to stores. Stores replicate a proven system of receiving, displaying, and selling that inventory to paying customers.

Multiplication is what separates small businesses from huge businesses.

There's an upper limit on what any single business system can produce. By creating more identical business systems based on a proven model, Multiplication can expand a business's ability to deliver value to more customers. That's the major benefit of franchising: instead of reinventing a business model, opening a franchise helps Multiply a model that already works.

The easier it is to Multiply your business system, the more value you can deliver.

REFERENCE LINK: **personalmba.com/multiplication/**

Scale

Ut sementem feceris, ita metes. (You reap what you sow.)
—MARCUS TULLIUS CICERO, FIRST-CENTURY-BCE
ROMAN STATESMAN AND ORATOR

Think of a skilled quilter who specializes in creating quilts by hand. Assuming each quilt takes a week to produce, having one active customer a week is great: creating and delivering a single quilt to a single customer is no problem at all.

Having two customers at once is challenging: Customer 2 has to wait until Customer 1 is served. If the quilt maker receives a thousand orders in a single day, that's a huge issue—there's no way to keep up with the demand without keeping customers waiting, which creates an undesirable level of **Scarcity**.

Scale is the ability to **Duplicate** or **Multiply** a process as volume increases. Scalability determines your maximum potential volume. The easier it is to Duplicate or Multiply the value provided, the more scalable the business.

Contrast the handmade-quilt business with a scalable business like Starbucks. Assume the average Starbucks has the capacity to serve a hundred beverages an hour—any demand above that and the store starts getting overcrowded. The solution? Build another Starbucks, even if it's right across the street—not an uncommon sight in cities like New York.

Scalability is often limited by the amount of required human involvement in a process. Starbucks is able to enhance its ability to Duplicate lattes via **Automation**. Starbucks employees are involved in making drinks, but the process is semiautomated: a machine makes the espresso, many of the ingredients are prepared ahead of time, and so on. The overall level of human attention or intervention that's required to make a good drink is quite small, which is why Starbucks can crank out so many drinks every hour.

If your goal is to create a business that doesn't require your direct daily involvement, scalability should be a major consideration. **Products** are often the easiest to Duplicate, while **Shared Resources** (like gyms, etc.) are easiest to Multiply.

Humans don't Scale. Individual people only have so much time and energy each day, which is a **Constraint** that doesn't change with the volume of work to be done. On the contrary—as we'll discuss later, in **Performance Load**, a person's effectiveness usually goes down as the demands on them increase.

As a result, **Services** are often difficult to Scale, since they tend to rely heavily on the direct involvement of people to deliver value. As a general rule, the less human involvement required to create and deliver value, the more scalable the business.

REFERENCE LINK: **personalmba.com/scale/**

Accumulation

> Sometimes when I consider what tremendous consequences come from little things, I am tempted to think: there are no little things.
>
> —BRUCE BARTON, ADVERTISING EXECUTIVE BEST KNOWN
> FOR CREATING THE BETTY CROCKER BRAND

At this very moment, a Toyota engineer somewhere in the world is making a very small change to the Toyota Production System, one of the most efficient manufacturing systems in the world.

Alone, the change may not look like much—a small tweak, a slight restructuring, a bit of material or effort saved. Taken together, however, the effects are huge—Toyota employees implement more than one million improvements to the TPS every year. It's little wonder that Toyota is now the world's largest and most valuable automotive manufacturer.[7]

Over time, the **Accumulation** of small helpful or harmful behaviors and inputs produces huge results. According to *Lean Thinking*, by James P.

Womack and Daniel T. Jones, Toyota's approach is based on the Japanese concept of *kaizen*, which emphasizes the continual improvement of a system by eliminating *muda* (waste) via a lot of very small changes. Many small improvements produce huge results.

Accumulation isn't always positive. Think of what would happen to your body if you consumed nothing but fast food, candy bars, and soda for a decade. Eating a single candy bar isn't a big deal, but eating hundreds of candy bars is. Fortunately, the opposite is true as well: small improvements in your diet, a little more exercise, and a little more sleep can have major effects on your health over time.

Incremental Augmentation is an example of the power of **Accumulation**. If your offer improves with every **Iteration Cycle**, it won't be long before your offer is many times more valuable to your customers than it was before. Small changes to your value-delivery process can save you a ton of time and effort in the long run.

The more small improvements you make over time, the better your results.

REFERENCE LINK: **personalmba.com/accumulation/**

Amplification

> In nature, there are neither rewards nor punishment—there are consequences.
>
> —ROBERT G. INGERSOLL, POLITICAL LEADER AND ORATOR

Think of a typical can of soda. When cans were first used to sell beverages, they were cylindrical, flat-topped, and made of steel. Over time, steel was phased out in favor of aluminum, pull tabs were introduced to make opening easier, and the can was "necked"—tapered slightly at the top.

"Necking" a can has two major effects. First, it makes it easier to drink from, which users like. Second, it reduces the amount of metal necessary to produce a structurally sound can: the walls of a typical beverage can are now around ninety micrometers thick (instead of about two millimeters), saving an enormous amount of raw materials.

According to the Can Manufacturers Institute, approximately 94 billion beverage cans are manufactured every year in the United States.[8]

When you multiply the cost savings of modern can designs across billions of cans and several decades, a few very small changes have saved the beverage industry hundreds of billions of dollars.

That's **Amplification**: making a small change to a scalable system produces a huge result. The effect of any improvement or system optimization is amplified by the size of the system. The larger the system, the larger the result.

When McDonald's comes up with a new sandwich, they're not limited to just selling it in one of their stores—they can start selling it in all of their stores around the world. When Starbucks comes up with a new drink, it can be made available to customers in every Starbucks location with little additional effort.

The best way to identify Amplification opportunities is to look for things that are **Duplicated** or **Multiplied**. If Starbucks found a way to produce a shot of espresso using fewer coffee beans, it would make a huge difference in the amount of coffee they'd need to buy. If they discovered a way to make that espresso shot in ten seconds instead of twenty, it would reduce the time it takes to serve a customer and increase the number of customers a single store could serve in an hour.

Scalable systems amplify the results of small changes. Small changes to scalable systems produce massive results.

REFERENCE LINK: personalmba.com/amplification/

Barrier to Competition

Don't compete with rivals—make them irrelevant.

—W. CHAN KIM, AUTHOR OF *BLUE OCEAN STRATEGY*

How much attention are you paying to what your competitors are doing? The more time and energy you spend following your competition, the less time and energy you have to build your business.

Think of a company like Apple—there's no other company in the technology world that focuses less on keeping up with what other companies are providing. Instead, they focus on building something new and **Remarkable**, then perfecting it as much as possible.

Apple's competitors, on the other hand, seem to be locked in a never-ending scramble to keep up. After Apple launched the iPhone in 2007, BlackBerry scrambled to create the Storm, which replicated many of the same features. By the time the Storm launched, the iPhone had already gone through several *Iteration Cycles*, making it very difficult for BlackBerry to compete. To date, Apple has sold hundreds of millions of iPhones worldwide, becoming one of the most valuable companies in the world in the process. In contrast, BlackBerry's share of the global mobile device market is now approximately 0 percent, down from a high of 20 percent in 2009.[9]

In the same vein, instead of trying to compete with commodity laptop manufacturers like Asus, HP, and Dell in the category of netbooks (small, low-powered computers designed for portability), Apple avoided the market for years. That changed when the iPad was launched in 2010—an offer that redefined the market instead of competing with preexisting netbooks on features. In the first two months of its existence, the company sold more than two million units. By choosing to innovate instead of compete, Apple successfully captured a leadership share of a very competitive market.

Every improvement you make to your *Value Stream* makes it harder for potential competitors to keep up, creating a *Barrier to Competition*. By increasing your ability to create and deliver value in an efficient and effective way, you make it more difficult for competitors to compete with you by doing what you're doing.

Every benefit you deliver and every customer you serve make it harder for competitors to replicate you. Don't focus on competing—focus on delivering even more value. Your competition will take care of itself.

REFERENCE LINK: **personalmba.com/barrier-to-competition/**

Force Multiplier

Man is a tool-using animal. Without tools he is nothing, with tools he is all.

—THOMAS CARLYLE, NINETEENTH-CENTURY ESSAYIST AND HISTORIAN

One of the things that make humans unique is our ability to create and use tools. Tools are important because they multiply the effect of physical force, thought, or attention. The more a tool *Amplifies* or concentrates your effort, the more effective the tool.

If you try pounding on a nail with your bare hands, you'll be able to exert *some* force, but it won't be enough to drive the nail into something solid. (Besides, you'll probably hurt your hand.)

Using a hammer multiplies the magnitude of the force you're exerting and concentrates that force into a small area, making it easy to drive a nail in a single stroke. Saws, screwdrivers, and other tools work the same way— they amplify and concentrate the force you generate to produce more output.

The most effective tools amplify force in the greatest magnitude. A power saw is far more effective at multiplying force than a handsaw is. A dump truck can carry more than a wheelbarrow. A rocket can launch a payload farther than a slingshot.

Investing in **Force Multipliers** makes sense because you can get more done with the same amount of effort. If you need to dig the foundation to build a new house, a $10 shovel from your local hardware store will work, but a backhoe will get the job done faster and easier. If building homes is your business, buying or leasing a backhoe is worth the cost.

Force Multipliers can be expensive—the more effective they are, the more expensive they tend to be. Factory production and distribution systems are examples of large-scale Force Multipliers—they make it possible to deliver value to thousands (or millions) of paying customers in a very short time. They may cost thousands (or millions) of dollars, but they can give you capabilities that would otherwise be out of reach.

As a general rule, the only good use of debt or outside capital in setting up a system is to give you access to Force Multipliers you would not be able to access any other way. If your business requires tooling up a factory, you probably don't have $10 million sitting in your bank account. Taking a **Loan** from a bank or accepting **Capital** from an outside investor may be your best option, provided you use those funds to purchase and maintain Force Multipliers, not to pay yourself or maintain rent on a fancy office.

Always choose the best tools that you can obtain and afford. Quality tools give you maximum output with a minimum of input. By investing in Force Multipliers, you free up your time, energy, and attention to focus on *building* your business instead of operating it.

REFERENCE LINK: **personalmba.com/force-multiplier/**

Systemization

If you can't describe what you are doing as a process, you don't know what you're doing.

—W. EDWARDS DEMING, PRODUCTION MANAGEMENT EXPERT
AND PIONEER OF STATISTICAL PROCESS CONTROL

Even if you make everything up as you go along, there is still a process involved, assuming that multiple steps are needed to get from point A to point B. Instead of "winging it," clarifying your process through **Systemization** can provide a few major benefits.

A system is a process made explicit and repeatable—a series of steps that has been formalized in some way. Systems can be written or diagrammed, but they are *always* **Externalized** in some way.

The primary benefit of creating a system is that you can examine the process and make improvements. By making each step in the process explicit, you can understand how the core processes work, how they're structured, how they affect other processes and systems, and how you can improve the system over time.

Google is a great example of the power of systems. Every time you use the Google search engine, thousands of computers spring into action to deliver your results. Google's search algorithm (a fancy programming word for system) defines how these computers work together, and Google employees refine the details of how the system works. Each year, Google engineers make thousands of improvements to the primary search engine algorithm,[10] making it better able to point you to what you're looking for.

As a result, the Google algorithm has become so efficient that your search results are returned in approximately 0.2 seconds with zero human intervention—an astounding achievement. If Google hadn't spent most of their early time and energy defining and systemizing the search process, the company wouldn't exist.

Systems also help teams of people stay on the same page. As we'll discuss in chapter 8, communication is necessary for people to work well together, and the more people you're working with, the more communication you need. Developing systems and clear processes for certain events and tasks can help everyone do what must be done with a minimum of misunderstanding and fuss.

If you can't systematize your process, you can't automate it. Imagine what it would be like if Google relied on a team of human librarians to generate search results. It'd be a nightmare—you'd wait days (or weeks, or months) to get your results.

The key to Google's quality and speed is **Automation**: by defining the rules of how the system operates, the search-engine programmers are able to automate the day-to-day operation of the system. As a result, Google developers are free to focus their efforts on continually *improving* the system instead of on *operating* the system.

Most people resist creating business systems because it feels like extra work. We're all busy, and it's easy to feel like you don't have time to create and improve systems because there's already too much work to do. Useful systems make your work easier—if you're feeling overloaded, the best thing you can do to solve the issue is spend time creating good systems.

Systemization and Automation have a few major drawbacks, which we'll explore in detail in chapters 10 and 11. For now, recognize that effective systems are the lifeblood of a business—they allow you to create, market, sell, and deliver what you have to offer.

The better your systems, the better your business.

REFERENCE LINK: **personalmba.com/systemization/**

Triage

> The art of being wise is the art of knowing what to overlook.
>
> —WILLIAM JAMES, NINETEENTH-CENTURY DOCTOR
> AND PIONEERING PSYCHOLOGIST

A few years ago, I found myself in the emergency room of Mount Sinai Hospital in New York City at 2:00 in the morning, suffering from extreme abdominal pain. As soon as I arrived, a nurse saw me, took detailed notes on my symptoms, then directed me to the waiting area.

I waited three hours to see the doctor on call. That was a *good* thing.

Triage is the process of identifying and handling the most important matters first, allowing less urgent matters to wait. Hospital emergency rooms are equipped to deal with a wide variety of ailments, ranging from trivial to life-threatening. There are a limited number of doctors and nurses available to provide care, and in the most severe cases, seconds matter. The first task of the triage nurse is to identify who needs care right away and who can afford to wait.

In my case, the mystery stomach pain was extreme at the beginning, but it was already improving by the time I arrived at the hospital, and I wasn't exhibiting any of the signs of someone who needed critical care. By the time the doctor on call had capacity to see me, my symptoms had resolved, and a few quick tests confirmed there was nothing urgent or critical. While I waited, the doctors and nurses had tended to dozens of patients with severe issues that required immediate attention.

Triage, as a strategy, applies to much more than medical care. Not every task on your to-do list has the same impact: some tasks are more important and valuable than others; some are time sensitive, while others are not. Triage can help you focus on your *Most Important Tasks* and not feel bad about letting less important tasks slip.

The same idea applies to most business systems. Most businesses have some sort of customer-support queue, and some requests are more urgent or important than others. If you have a large, long-term client who is experiencing issues, it is both rational and wise to prioritize resolving their problem before responding to someone with a small free trial account.

Your ability to Triage relies on your ability to collect information relevant to the situation. It's often helpful to create a defined hierarchy of priority for each context, then customize the questions you ask to ensure you have the relevant information needed to categorize each case.

In a business context, this technique is often referred to as "lead scoring." Defining metrics like the strength of each prospect, the projected *Lifetime Value* of a customer, or the urgency and importance of each incoming request helps you *Systematize* the support process so you can handle the most important cases first.

REFERENCE LINK: **personalmba.com/triage/**

5

FINANCE

He had heard people speak contemptuously of money: he wondered if they had ever tried to do without it.

—W. SOMERSET MAUGHAM, *OF HUMAN BONDAGE*

In my experience, people enjoy learning about value creation, marketing, sales, and value delivery—they're easy to understand and visualize.

When it comes to finance, however, eyes glaze over. Finance conjures up images of "bean counting," mathematical formulas, and spreadsheets overflowing with numbers. It doesn't have to be that way—finance is quite easy to understand if you focus on what's most important.

Finance is the art and science of watching the money flowing into and out of a business, then deciding how to allocate it and determining whether or not what you're doing is producing the results you want. Accounting is the process of ensuring the data you use to make financial decisions is as complete and accurate as possible. It's not any more complicated than that. Yes, there can be fancy models and jargon, but in the end, you're using numbers to decide whether or not your business is operating the way you intended and whether or not the results are enough.

Every successful business must bring in a certain amount of money to keep going. If you're creating, marketing, selling, and delivering value, there's money flowing into and out of the business every day. In order to continue to exist, every business must bring in sufficient revenue to justify all of the time and effort that goes into running the operation.

Everyone has bills to pay and groceries to buy, so the people involved in the business need to make enough money to justify the time and energy they're investing, or they'll quit and do something else. Every business must capture some amount of the value it creates as revenue, which is used to pay expenses and compensate the people who make the business run.

The very best businesses create a virtuous cycle: they create huge amounts of value while keeping their expenses low, so they make more than enough money to keep going without capturing too much value. As a result, they're able to simultaneously pad their pocketbooks and improve the lives of their customers, since the continued existence of the business makes everyone involved better off.

Finance helps you watch your dollars in a way that makes sense.

REFERENCE LINK: **personalmba.com/finance/**

Profit

> Remind people that profit is the difference between revenue and expense. This makes you look smart.
>
> —SCOTT ADAMS, CARTOONIST AND CREATOR OF *DILBERT*

It doesn't matter if your business brings in $100,000,000 a year in revenue if you spend $100,000,001. Business is not about what you make—it's about what you keep.

Profit is a very simple concept: it's bringing in more money than you spend. In order for a business to continue to exist, the total revenue it collects must exceed the total expenses it accumulates at some point in the foreseeable future. If it doesn't, it'll cease to be a business—the operation will run out of resources and close, or it'll become a project subsidized by the Profits of another business. Nothing can operate at a loss forever.

Profit is important because it allows businesses to stay in operation. Without generating Profits, a business can't compensate its owners, who may be investing considerable time, money, and energy into the operation. If the owners don't find their investment worthwhile, they'll close the business.

Profit also provides a cushion that allows the business to weather unexpected events. If a business is barely generating enough revenue to cover its expenses, and those expenses suddenly rise, the business is in a great deal of trouble. The more profitable the business, the better it will be able to handle **Uncertainty** and **Change**, and the more options it has to respond to the unforeseeable.

Profit is a very important consideration, but it's not the be-all and end-all of business. Some people believe that the purpose of a business is to maximize the amount of Profit generated, but that's not the only reason businesses are created. For some people (like me), business is more of a creative endeavor—a way to explore what's possible, help others, and support yourself at the same time. From this perspective, as long as you're making *enough* Profit, your business will continue to be successful.

The concepts you'll learn in this chapter will help you ensure that your business creates enough Profit to keep going.

REFERENCE LINK: **personalmba.com/profit/**

Profit Margin

I never lost money by turning a profit.

—BERNARD BARUCH, FINANCIER AND PHILANTHROPIST

rofit Margin (often abbreviated to "margin") is the difference between how much revenue you capture and how much you spend to capture it, expressed in percentage terms. Here's the formula for Profit Margin:

((Revenue – Cost) / Revenue) × 100 = % Profit Margin

If you spend \$1 to get \$2, that's a 50 percent Profit Margin. If you're able to create a **Product** for \$100 and sell it for \$150, that's a **Profit** of \$50 and a Profit Margin of 33 percent. If you're able to sell the same Product for \$300, that's a margin of 66 percent. The higher the price and the lower the cost, the higher the Profit Margin. In any case, your Profit Margin can never exceed 100 percent, which only happens if you're able to sell something that cost you nothing.

Profit Margin is not the same as "markup," which represents how the price of an offer compares to its total cost. Here's the formula for markup:

((Price – Cost) / Cost) × 100 = % Markup

If the cost of an offer is $1 and you sell it for $2, your markup is 100 percent, but your Profit Margin is only 50 percent. Margins can never be more than 100 percent, but markups can be 200 percent, 500 percent, or 10,000 percent, depending on the price and the total cost of the offer. The higher your price and the lower your cost, the higher your markup.

Most businesses try to keep each offer's Profit Margin as high as possible, which makes sense: the higher the margin, the more money the business gets to keep from each sale. Regardless, there are many market pressures that can lead to a decline in margins over time: aggressive pricing by competitors, new offers that decrease demand for older offers, and rising input costs.

Businesses often use Profit Margin as a way of comparing offers. If a company has more than one offer in the market, it tends to favor the offers with the highest margins. If a business needs to cut costs, it often starts by eliminating offers with the lowest margins.

When examining a business, pay close attention to Profit Margin. The higher the margin, the stronger the business.

REFERENCE LINK: **personalmba.com/profit-margin/**

Value Capture

You can get anything you want in this life if you help enough other people get what they want.

—ZIG ZIGLAR, RENOWNED SALES TRAINER AND SPEAKER

Every business must capture some percentage of the value it creates in the form of revenue as *Profit*. If it doesn't, the business will have a difficult time generating enough resources over time to continue operation.

Value Capture is the process of retaining some percentage of the value provided in every *Transaction*. If you're able to offer another business something that will allow it to bring in $1 million of additional revenue, and you charge $100,000, you're capturing 10 percent of the value created by the Transaction.

Value Capture is tricky. In order to be successful, you need to capture enough value to make your investment of time and energy worthwhile, but not so much that there's no reason for your customers to do business with you. People buy because they believe they're getting more value in the Transaction than they're spending.

The more value you capture, the less attractive your offer becomes. Capture too much and your prospects won't bother purchasing from you. Movies are great, but would you pay $5,000 for two hours of entertainment?

There are two dominant philosophies behind Value Capture: maximization and minimization.

Maximization (the approach taught in most business schools) means that a business should attempt to capture as much value as possible—capturing less than the maximum amount of value possible is unacceptable, and choosing to leave value "on the table" is considered a dereliction of duty.

In the short run, it's easy to see the appeal of maximization—more Profit is a good thing for the owners of a company. But the maximization approach tends to erode the reason customers purchase from a business in the first place.

Would you spend $999,999 in order to make $1 million? It may be rational (after all, you'd be $1 ahead), but most people won't bother. Customers purchase from you because they're receiving more value than they're giving up in the purchase. The less they receive, the less they'll want to buy from you.

The *minimization* approach means that businesses should capture as little value as possible, as long as the business maintains **Sufficiency**. While this approach may not bring in as much short-term revenue as maximization, it preserves the value customers see in doing business with the company, which is necessary for the business's long-term success.

When something is a good deal, customers tend to continue to patronize the business and spread the word to other potential customers. When a business tries to maximize revenue by nickel-and-diming its customers or trying to capture too much value, customers flee.

As long as you're bringing in enough to keep doing what you're doing, there's no need to fight for every last penny. Create as much value as you can, then capture enough of that value to make it worthwhile to keep operating.

REFERENCE LINK: **personalmba.com/value-capture/**

Sufficiency

Know contentment and you will suffer no disgrace; know when to
stop and you will meet with no danger. You can then endure.

—LAO TZU, SIXTH-CENTURY-BCE CHINESE PHILOSOPHER

Once, a powerful executive went on vacation—his first in fifteen years. As
he was exploring a pier in a small coastal fishing village, a tuna fisherman
docked his boat. As the fisherman lashed his boat to the pier, the executive
complimented him on the size and quality of his fish.

"How long did it take you to catch these fish?" the executive asked.

"Only a little while," the fisherman replied.

"Why don't you stay out longer and catch more?" the executive asked.

"I have enough to support my family's needs," said the fisherman.

"But," asked the executive, "what do you do with the rest of your time?"

The fisherman replied, "I sleep late, fish a little, play with my children,
take a siesta with my wife, and stroll into the village each evening, where
I sip wine and play guitar with my friends. I have a full and busy life."

The executive was flabbergasted. "I'm a Harvard MBA and I can help
you. You should spend more time fishing. With the proceeds, you could
buy a bigger boat. A bigger boat would help you catch more fish, which
you could sell to buy several boats. Eventually, you'd own an entire fleet.

"Instead of selling your catch to a middleman, you could sell direct to
the consumer, which would improve your margins. Eventually, you could
open your own factory, so you'd control the product, the processing, and
the distribution. Of course, you'd have to leave this village and move to
the city so you could run your expanding enterprise."

The fisherman was quiet for a moment, then asked, "How long would
this take?"

"Fifteen, twenty years. Twenty-five, tops."

"Then what?"

The executive laughed. "That's the best part. When the time is right,
you'd take your company public and sell all of your stock. You'd make millions."

"Millions? What would I do then?"

The executive paused for a moment. "You could retire, sleep late, fish a little, play with your children, take a siesta with your wife, and stroll into the village each evening to sip wine and play guitar with your friends."

Shaking his head, the executive bade the fisherman farewell. After returning from vacation, the executive resigned from his position.

I'm not sure where this parable originated, but the message is useful: business is not necessarily about maximizing **Profits**. Profits are important, but they're a means to an end: creating value, paying expenses, compensating the people who run the business, and supporting yourself and your loved ones. Dollars aren't an end in themselves: money is a tool, and the usefulness of that tool depends on what you intend to *do* with it.

Your business does not have to bring in millions or billions of dollars to be successful. If you have enough Profit to do the things you need to do to keep the business running and make it worth your time, you're successful, no matter how much revenue your business brings in.

Sufficiency is the point where a business is bringing in enough Profit that the people who are running the business find it worthwhile to keep going for the foreseeable future. Paul Graham, venture capitalist and cofounder of Y Combinator (an early-stage venture capital firm), calls the point of Sufficiency "ramen profitable"—being profitable enough to pay your rent, keep the utilities running, and buy inexpensive food like ramen noodles. You may not be raking in millions of dollars, but you have enough revenue to keep building your venture without going under.

You can't create value if you can't pay the bills. If you're not bringing in sufficient revenue to cover the operating expenses, that's a major issue. In order to keep going, you must be able to pay the employees and the owners for the time, effort, and attention they're giving to the venture. If these people don't find their investment sufficiently worthwhile, they'll stop doing what they're doing and start doing something else.

You can track financial Sufficiency using a number called "target monthly revenue" (TMR). Since employees, contractors, and vendors are usually paid on a monthly basis, it's relatively simple to calculate how much money you'll need to pay out each month. Your target monthly revenue helps you determine whether or not you've reached the point of Sufficiency: as long as you bring in more than your TMR, you've reached Sufficiency. If not, you have work to do.

Sufficiency is subjective—it's up to you to decide how much is enough to make your time and effort worthwhile. If your financial needs are meager, you don't need that much revenue to keep going. If you're spending millions of dollars on payroll, office space, and expensive systems, you'll need much more revenue to maintain Sufficiency.

The faster you can reach the point of Sufficiency, the better the chance your business will survive and thrive. The more revenue you generate and the less money you spend, the quicker you'll reach the point of Sufficiency.

Once you reach the point of Sufficiency, you're successful—no matter how much (or how little) money you make.

REFERENCE LINK: **personalmba.com/sufficiency/**

Valuation

> The whole value of the dime is knowing what to do with it.
> —RALPH WALDO EMERSON, NINETEENTH-CENTURY ESSAYIST AND POET

We've talked about how to estimate the value of an offer, but how do you calculate the worth of a company?

Valuation is an estimate of the total worth of a company. The higher a business's revenues, the stronger the company's **Profit Margins**, the higher its bank balance, and the more promising its future, the higher its Valuation.

Many companies base their financial decisions on what will increase the business's Valuation. Higher estimates of value are beneficial for many reasons. If a company is private, having a high Valuation makes it easier to borrow money. If the company is public, a high Valuation leads to a high share price and a profit opportunity for the shareholders. If another business seeks to acquire the company, a high Valuation leads to a big payday for the business's owners or shareholders.

Valuation is also important if you intend to take on investors. The amount of **Capital** you raise, as well as the total amount of ownership you give to your investors in exchange, depends on the business's Valuation at the time of investment. The higher the business's Valuation, the more money you'll be able to command for every share you sell to the investor.[1]

It's important to note that **Perceived Value** applies just as much to businesses as it does to individual offers. When people believe a company has bright future prospects, the company's Valuation increases. If people believe the company is in trouble, the Valuation decreases. This dynamic explains why some companies, like Amazon, have share prices of more than one hundred times the company's most recent earnings per share report, while troubled companies sometimes sell for less than the liquidation value of their current assets.

Valuation is important to consider if you intend to sell shares of the company to investors or are positioning your business for future acquisition. If you own your own business and never intend to sell it, Valuation considerations become less important. If you're an executive of a public company, building a business you'd like to sell someday, or investing your capital in a company, Valuation may be on the top of your mind every day.

REFERENCE LINK: personalmba.com/valuation/

Cash Flow Statement

Lack of money is the root of all evil.

—MARK TWAIN, GREAT AMERICAN NOVELIST

In order to understand how well a company is performing, it's useful to look at financial reports that track the business's performance. Where should you begin?

I recommend starting with the **Cash Flow Statement**. We'll examine the other basic types of financial statements in a moment, but examining the Cash Flow Statement is the best place to begin.

The Cash Flow Statement is straightforward: it's an examination of a company's bank account over a certain period of time. Think of it like a checking-account ledger: deposits of cash flow in, and withdrawals of cash flow out. Ideally, more money flows in than flows out and the total never goes below zero.

Every Cash Flow Statement covers a specific period of time: a day, a week, a month, a year. The time period of the report depends on the purpose. Shorter periods, like days and weeks, are most useful for making sure the company doesn't run out of cash. Longer periods, like months and years, are more useful for tracking performance over time.

Cash tends to move in three primary areas: *operations* (selling offers and buying inputs), *investing* (collecting dividends and paying for capital expenses), and *financing* (borrowing money and paying it back). Cash Flow Statements usually track these sources separately to make it easy to see where the cash flows come from.

The nice thing about cash is that it doesn't lie. Barring outright fraud, cash either is in the bank account or it's not. If the company spends a lot of money, but less is coming in, the business's cash position will decrease over time. There's little room for "creative interpretation."

Many investors use a metric called "free cash flow" when evaluating companies. This metric comes from the Cash Flow Statement: it's the amount of cash a business collects from operations minus cash spent for capital equipment and assets, which are necessary to keep the company operating. The higher a company's free cash flow, the better: it means the business doesn't have to keep investing huge amounts of **Capital** in order to continue bringing in money.

In every business, cash represents **Options**: the ability to create new offers, invest in marketing and sales, hire employees, purchase equipment, acquire another company, etc. As a general rule, the more cash your business has at its disposal, the more Options it has and the more **Resilient** the business becomes.

REFERENCE LINK: **personalmba.com/cash-flow-statement/**

Income Statement

> When I was young, I thought money was the most important thing in
> life. Now that I'm old, I know it is.
>
> —OSCAR WILDE, RENOWNED SATIRIST

Cash is important, but it's not the whole picture. Cash is not **Profit**, and Profit is what we're after. It's possible to have a nice, comfortable cash position for a while but lose money with every sale.

Imagine a retailer that buys products from a manufacturer on credit: it receives inventory but doesn't have to pay the manufacturer for ninety days. For three months, the sales roll in, and the retailer's cash position grows and grows. To the untrained eye, things look great.

After ninety days, the manufacturer's invoice comes due. When you total the cost of the products and the retailer's operating expenses, you discover the truth: the company lost money, even though the cash balance looked great for three months. If the retailer doesn't do something, it'll eventually run out of money and close. Businesses can't exist without Profits for long.

The retailer's error was relying on cash accounting without understanding its limitations. For many types of businesses, cash accounting is ideal: it's simple and easy to understand. As long as you bring in more cash than you spend and you don't run out of money, life is good. I've run my businesses using cash accounting for years. I get paid before I provide products and services, and I don't have an inventory to manage. My business isn't complicated, so my accounting and financial tracking don't need to be complicated.

For other businesses, relying on a **Cash Flow Statement** isn't enough. If the business manages an inventory or extends credit to customers, a simple cash flow analysis can be misleading. In order to determine whether or not your sales are profitable, you need to be able to track which sales and expenses are related. By matching each sale with the expenses incurred in the process of making that sale, it's possible to see if you're making a Profit immediately, eliminating unpleasant surprises.

First, the company must change the way it accounts for expenses. Instead of recording revenue when cash flows in and an expense when cash flows out, the company must begin tracking revenue and expenses on what's called an "accrual" basis.

In accrual accounting, revenue is recognized when a sale is made (i.e., a product is purchased, a service is rendered, etc.), and the expenses associated with that sale are incurred in the same time period.

Accountants call this the "matching principle," and one of the primary jobs of an accountant is to match revenue and expense records. This is harder than it sounds: an incredible amount of judgment is required, and ambiguous areas are common. (If you've ever wondered what accountants do all day, this is a big part of the job.)

The result of this effort is an **Income Statement**, which is sometimes called a "profit and loss statement," "operating statement," or "earnings statement." Regardless of the label, the Income Statement contains an estimate of the business's Profit over a certain period of time, once revenue is matched with the related expenses.

The general format for an Income Statement looks like this:

Revenue – Cost of Goods Sold – Expenses – Taxes = Net Profit

Income Statements are very useful: there's a reason businesses go to the trouble of creating them. By matching expenses with revenue, Income Statements make it easier to look at the company's profitability and make decisions that will improve the company's bank balance in the weeks and months to come.

That said, it's important to recognize that Income Statements, by nature, include many estimates and assumptions. They have to: large expenses like equipment purchases may involve a huge cash outlay, but the Income Statement attributes only a small piece of the expense to each sales period, a practice called **Amortization**. This practice helps match the expense to the associated revenue: looking at a huge negative Cash Flow Statement for that period would be misleading.

The matching principle, for all of its benefits, introduces many sources of potential bias in the Income Statement. By changing when revenue is recognized and how expenses are matched to that revenue, accountants and finance professionals can make the "profit" line skyrocket or plummet by changing a few assumptions or formulas.

Exploring every source of potential bias in the Income Statement is way beyond the scope of this book. If you're interested in more detail on this topic, I highly recommend *Financial Intelligence for Entrepreneurs* by Karen Berman and Joe Knight with John Case.

If you suspect your business needs accrual accounting to generate an accurate Income Statement, don't do it yourself; talk to a CPA or CFA as soon as possible. The more accurate and reliable your Income Statement is, the better you'll be able to manage your business: money well spent.

REFERENCE LINK: **personalmba.com/income-statement/**

Balance Sheet

If you would know the value of money, go try and borrow some.

—BENJAMIN FRANKLIN, EIGHTEENTH-CENTURY AMERICAN
POLITICAL LEADER, SCIENTIST, AND POLYMATH

A **Balance Sheet** is a snapshot of what a business owns and what it owes at a particular moment in time. You can think of it as an estimate of the company's net worth at the time the Balance Sheet was created.

Balance Sheets always cite a specific day and use this calculation:

Assets – Liabilities = Owner's Equity

Assets are things the company owns that have value: products, equipment, stock, etc. *Liabilities* are obligations the firm hasn't yet discharged: loans, financing, etc. What's left over when you discharge all of the business's liabilities is *owner's equity*, the company's "net worth."

For smaller businesses, the Balance Sheet is pretty straightforward: count your cash on hand, add the estimated market value of any assets you own, and subtract all debt and current obligations. Voilà: you've created a basic Balance Sheet.

For larger businesses, the Balance Sheet is more complicated, and there are more entries to keep track of. Common assets include cash, accounts receivable (credit that you've extended to customers), inventory, equipment, and property. Common liabilities include long- and short-term debt, accounts payable (credit that other firms have extended to you), and other obligations. Owner's equity includes the value of the company's stock, capital from investors, and retained earnings (profit that hasn't been paid to the company's shareholders).

What makes the Balance Sheet "balance" is the secondary form of the calculation, which is a rearrangement of the first equation:

Assets = Liabilities + Owner's Equity

This calculation looks odd at first: why would you ever want to add liabilities and owner's equity?

Here's why: when a business borrows money, it receives the amount of cash borrowed. That goes on the **Cash Flow Statement**, and the influx of money makes it look like the business had a very good month if you don't notice it's a loan. When you think about it, the company's financial picture didn't change: the business now has more assets (more cash), but it also has a new liability (more debt). The company's "net worth" didn't change at all.

The second formula is useful because it reflects this relationship. Let's assume you're starting a business and you borrow $10,000. Before you borrow the money, your Balance Sheet looks like this:

$0 = $0 + $0 (you have no assets, no liabilities, and no equity)

After you borrow the money, your Balance Sheet looks like this:

$10,000 = $10,000 + $0 (you have $10,000 in assets, $10,000 in liabilities, and no equity)

Both sides of the Balance Sheet are the same. The Balance Sheet always balances. If it doesn't balance, you've made an error.

Since Balance Sheets are snapshots of a moment in time, it's common to review several of them at a time. For example, a company might include Balance Sheets calculated on the last day of its fiscal year for the past two or three years. Comparing the Balance Sheets makes it easy to see how assets, liabilities, and owner's equity have changed over time.

Balance Sheets are valuable because they answer many important questions about the financial health of a business. By examining a company's Balance Sheet, you can determine whether or not the company is solvent (i.e., its assets are greater than its liabilities), if it's having trouble paying its bills, or how the company's value has changed over time.

Balance Sheets, just like *Income Statements*, are full of assumptions and estimates that can introduce bias in the numbers. What's the value of a brand name or *Reputation*? What percentage of the company's accounts receivable will be paid? How valuable is the business's current inventory? Don't skip the footnotes: by examining the assumptions behind the entries on the Balance Sheet, you'll develop a more accurate picture of the strength of the business.

REFERENCE LINK: **personalmba.com/balance-sheet/**

Financial Ratios

In the real world, the tests are all open book, and your success
is inexorably determined by the lessons you glean from the free
market.

—JONATHAN ROSENBERG, FORMER SENIOR VICE PRESIDENT
OF PRODUCTS AT GOOGLE

Once you've compiled your business's basic financial reports, you can examine them in many different ways. One of the most effective strategies is to calculate a *Financial Ratio*: a comparison of two important elements of your business.

Financial Ratios are beneficial because they allow you to make comparisons between businesses. Instead of poring over raw financial data, looking at a Financial Ratio helps you decide at a glance whether or not certain parts of the business are healthy. Looking at how these *Ratios* change over time helps you see how the business is changing over time. Comparing the Ratios to industry averages makes it easy to see if the company is performing like a typical company in the industry or if something is odd.

Profitability ratios indicate a business's ability to generate *Profit*. The higher your revenue and the lower your costs, the higher your profitability ratios. We've already discussed *Profit Margin*, which is a very basic profitability ratio. "Return on Assets," which is calculated by dividing net profit by total assets, tells you what percentage of every dollar invested in the business was returned as profit.

Leverage ratios indicate how your company uses debt. "Debt-to-equity ratios," which are calculated by dividing total liabilities by shareholders' equity, tell you how many dollars a company has borrowed for every $1 in owner's equity. If the Ratio is high, it's a signal the company is highly *Leveraged*, which could be a bad sign. Other Ratios, like "interest coverage," calculate how much of the business's profit goes to pay off interest on debt.

Liquidity ratios indicate the ability of a business to pay its bills. Running out of cash is a serious issue, so ratios like the "current ratio" (current assets divided by current liabilities) and the "quick ratio" (current assets, minus inventory, divided by current liabilities) make it easy to determine how close a company is to bankruptcy, or if the business is sitting on cash instead of investing money in growth or improvement.

Efficiency ratios indicate how well a business is managing assets and liabilities. The most common use is inventory management: having too little inventory is a bad thing, but having too much is also bad. Calculating the average number of days an item is in inventory, how long it takes to sell out current inventory, and "day sales outstanding," a measure of how long it takes to collect the cash from sales, are helpful when making changes in production, managing inventory on hand, and planning future capital investments.

There are thousands of Financial Ratios, and covering them all is way beyond the scope of this book. Financial analysts tend to choose a small set of important Ratios based on the industry: it makes no sense to calculate "inventory turns" for a barbershop, unless the shop also happens to sell hair products. Every business has a small number of important Ratios to consider; it's worthwhile to do a bit of research to see what they are for your industry.

We'll discuss other Ratios in chapter 10; the technique is useful in many areas outside of finance. For now, remember that Financial Ratios are useful for sanity-checking profit, debt, cash, and efficiency without spending too much time.

REFERENCE LINK: **personalmba.com/financial-ratios/**

Cost-Benefit Analysis

> I must study the plain physical facts of the case, ascertain what is possible, and learn what appears to be wise and right. The subject is difficult, and good men do not agree.
>
> —ABRAHAM LINCOLN, SIXTEENTH PRESIDENT OF THE UNITED STATES

The purpose of financial analysis isn't to produce impressive-looking spreadsheets: it's to make better decisions. If the data you're examining doesn't lead to changes that improve your business, you're wasting your time. The core of finance is examining a potential action, consulting the data you have at your disposal, and deciding what (if anything) to do.

Cost-Benefit Analysis is the process of examining potential changes to your business to see if the benefits outweigh the costs. Instead of acting on a change the moment you think of it, you take a step back to evaluate the true cost of the action and whether or not you believe it's the best thing you can do with your limited time, energy, and resources.

When conducting a Cost-Benefit Analysis, it's important to include costs and benefits that aren't purely financial. Noneconomic costs, like enjoyment, can play a large role in whether or not a project is worth pursuing. Google's famous cafeteria benefits are a good example: the company provides free, high-quality food to employees around the clock. This policy looks like a huge cost until you consider the benefit: by providing breakfast, lunch, dinner, and snacks, the company is encouraging employees to be at work as much as possible. The cost is offset by the increase in productivity and team cohesion, which is very significant.

Removing chronic frustrations and small inefficiencies can be just as beneficial. I recently spent a few hundred dollars to upgrade my computer's hard disk to a solid-state drive that is six times faster. My applications and programs now launch in less than a second, instead of requiring a five- to ten-second wait. That doesn't sound like much, but small improvements *Accumulate* over time. I spend most of my work time on the computer, and it's a huge difference. I'm happier and I'm getting more work done: money well spent.

Before making a decision, evaluate the total costs and benefits. A little evaluation will ensure you spend your money in the most effective ways.

REFERENCE LINK: **personalmba.com/cost-benefit-analysis/**

Four Methods to Increase Revenue

> Money is plentiful for those who understand the simple laws which govern its acquisition.
>
> —GEORGE S. CLASON, *THE RICHEST MAN IN BABYLON*

Believe it or not, there are only four ways to increase your business's revenue:

1. Increase the number of customers you serve.

2. Increase the average size of each *Transaction* by selling more.

3. Increase the frequency of Transactions per customer.

4. Raise your prices.

Imagine you're operating a restaurant and you want to increase the amount of revenue that your restaurant brings in. Here's how to apply these strategies:

Increasing the number of customers means you're trying to bring more people in the door. This strategy is relatively straightforward: more visitors to your restaurant will equal more tabs, which (assuming the average Transaction size stays the same) will bring in more money.

Increasing average Transaction size means you're trying to get each customer to purchase more. This is often done through a process called "upselling." When a customer purchases an entrée, you offer them appetizers, drinks, and dessert. The more of these items the customer purchases, the more they spend, and the more revenue you collect.

Increasing the frequency of Transactions per customer means encouraging people to purchase from you more often. If your average customer comes in once a month, convincing them to patronize your business once a week will increase your revenue. The more frequently they visit your establishment, the more revenue your restaurant will bring in, assuming the average transaction size stays the same.

Raising your prices means you'll collect more revenue from every purchase a customer makes. Assuming your volume, average Transaction size, and frequency stay the same, raising your prices will bring in more revenue for the same amount of effort.

Remember the lesson of **Qualification**: not every customer is a good customer. Some customers will sap your time, energy, and resources without providing the results that you're looking for. If you're spending a lot of energy serving customers who don't come in often, have a low average Transaction size, don't spread the word, and complain about the price, it doesn't make sense to attract more of those customers.

Always focus the majority of your efforts on serving your ideal customers. Your ideal customers buy early, buy often, spend the most, spread the word, and are willing to pay a premium for the value you provide.

The more ideal customers you can attract, the better your business.

REFERENCE LINK: **personalmba.com/4-methods-to-increase-revenue/**

Pricing Power

You can determine the strength of a business over time by the
amount of agony they go through in raising prices.

—WARREN BUFFETT, CHAIRMAN AND CEO OF BERKSHIRE HATHAWAY, AND
ONE OF THE WEALTHIEST INDIVIDUALS IN THE WORLD

Imagine doubling your current prices. If you'd lose less than half of your
customers, it's probably a good move.

Pricing Power is your ability to raise the prices you're charging over time.
The less value you're capturing, the greater your Pricing Power. Serving
customers takes time, energy, and resources—the more you earn per customer served, the better your business. Changing your prices can help you
maximize your results while minimizing your effort and investment.

Pricing Power is related to a concept economists call "price elasticity."
If customers are very sensitive to the price of your offer, you'll lose many
customers with even a slight increase in price, meaning demand is "elastic."
Established semicommodity markets like toothpaste are good examples:
unless you're able to create something new and unique that customers
badly want, increasing your prices is a good way to ensure that everyone
stops buying your product and starts buying from your competitor.

If your customers aren't price sensitive, you could quadruple the price
with little change in sales. Take luxury goods, for example—customers
purchase them because they're expensive **Status Signals** that are exclusive
because they're costly. Increasing the price of designer handbags, clothing,
and watches is likely to make those items *more* desirable, not less.

Economists like to spend time graphing and calculating price elasticity,
but it's not necessary—unless you already have accurate **Norms**, you can't
know how much Pricing Power you have until you change your prices and
watch what happens. Fortunately, unless you're an established player in a
large and active market (in which case you'll have Norms to work with),
changing your prices very rarely has permanent effects unless your prices
are broadly publicized and scrutinized; you can experiment to find what
works.

Pricing Power is important because raising your prices allows you to
overcome the adverse effects of inflation and increased costs. Historically,

currency issued by any government tends to decrease in value over time—there are many strong incentives for officials to increase the supply of currency, which debases that currency's **Purchasing Power.**

As a result, it takes more currency to purchase the same products and services necessary to stay in business, increasing your business's financial **Sufficiency** needs. Without adequate Pricing Power, your business may not be able to maintain Sufficiency in the face of higher expenses.

The higher the prices you can command, the easier it will be to maintain profit Sufficiency. If you have a choice, choose a market in which you'll have Pricing Power—it'll be much easier to maintain Sufficiency over time.

REFERENCE LINK: **personalmba.com/pricing-power/**

Lifetime Value

The purpose of a customer isn't to get a sale. The purpose of a sale is to get a customer.

—BILL GLAZER, ADVERTISING EXPERT

Imagine operating a lemonade stand on the sidewalk of a popular tourist destination. Each cup of lemonade costs $1. You may be busy serving customers, but each customer you serve is just passing by—you'll probably never see them again.

Contrast that with the insurance business. Assume the average customer pays a premium of $200 per month for term life insurance—that's $2,400 in premiums per customer per year. If the typical customer remains with the same insurance agency for the entire thirty-year term, each client is worth $72,000 in premium payments over the lifetime of their relationship with the company. That's a big difference.

Lifetime Value is the total value of a customer's business over the lifetime of their relationship with your company. The more a customer purchases from you and the longer they stay with you, the more valuable that customer is to your business.

One of the reasons **Subscriptions** are so profitable is that they maximize Lifetime Value. Instead of making a single sale to a customer, Subscription businesses focus on providing value—and collecting revenue—for as long as possible. The longer a customer remains Subscribed and the higher the price they pay, the higher the Lifetime Value of that customer.

The higher your average customer's Lifetime Value, the better your business. By understanding how much your average customer purchases and how long they tend to buy from you, you can place a tangible value on each new customer, which helps you make good decisions. Losing a single lemonade-stand customer isn't a huge deal—losing an insurance client is.

All told, it's much better to operate in markets where customers have a high Lifetime Value. The higher the Lifetime Value of your customer, the more you can do to keep them happy and the more you can focus on serving customers well. Maintain a long-term relationship with profitable customers and you win.

REFERENCE LINK: **personalmba.com/lifetime-value/**

Allowable Acquisition Cost

> Any business can buy incremental unit sales at a negative profit margin, but it's simpler to stand on the corner handing out $20 bills until you go broke.
>
> —MORRIS ROSENTHAL, PUBLISHER

Think back to the lemonade stand: how much could you spend to attract a single paying customer? Not much—you're only earning $1 per cup of lemonade, so you can't afford to spend much on marketing to individuals.

Contrast that with the insurance agency: if the *Lifetime Value* of a customer is $72,000, how much could you spend to attract a new customer? Much more.

Getting people's attention and acquiring new prospects costs time and resources. Once you understand the Lifetime Value of a prospect, you can calculate the maximum amount of time and resources you're willing to spend to acquire a new prospect.

Allowable Acquisition Cost (AAC) is the marketing component of Lifetime Value. The higher the average customer's Lifetime Value, the more you can spend to attract a new customer, making it possible to spread the word about your offer in new ways.

Having a customer with a high Lifetime Value even allows you to lose money on the first sale. Guthy-Renker sells a topical acne treatment called Proactiv using long-form television infomercials, which are expensive—they hire celebrity endorsers and spend millions to produce and air those commercials. At first glance, it doesn't make any sense: the first sale is for the "low, low price" of $20. How on earth are they not losing money hand over fist?

The answer is *Subscription*. When a customer purchases Proactiv, they aren't just buying a single bottle of face goo—they're signing up to receive a bottle every month in exchange for a recurring payment. The Lifetime Value of each new Proactiv customer is so high that it doesn't matter that Guthy-Renker "goes negative" on the initial sale—the company makes a ton of money, even if it loses money on a few customers who don't continue with the program.

The first sale is sometimes called a "loss leader"—an enticing offer intended to establish a relationship with a new customer. Banks and financial services firms will often encourage qualified prospects to open an account by giving them hundreds of dollars in free waivers, gifts, or, in some cases, cash.

These enticements may absorb up to a year's worth of Subscription revenue, but the company comes out ahead when you consider the *Lifetime Value* of each customer. When every new client is worth tens of thousands of dollars of future income, spending a few hundred dollars to establish a new account makes perfect sense.

To calculate your market's Allowable Acquisition Cost, you'll need to know your desired *Profit Margin*. Start with your average customer's Lifetime Value, then subtract your *Value Stream* costs—the *Variable Costs* required to create and deliver the value promised to that customer over your entire relationship with them. Then subtract your *Overhead* divided by your total customer base, which represents the *Fixed Costs* required to stay in business over that period of time: that's your net income before marketing expenses. Multiple the Lifetime Value by your desired Profit Margin, then subtract that result from your net income before marketing expenses. That's your maximum Allowable Acquisition Cost.

Here's an example: if your average Lifetime Value is $2,000 over a five-year period, and the cost of value creation and value delivery is $500, that leaves you with $1,500 in revenue per customer served. Assuming your Overhead expenses are $500,000 over the same five-year period and you have 500 customers, your Fixed Costs are $1,000 per customer, which leaves you with $500 in net income before marketing expenses. If you're shooting for a minimum 15 percent Profit Margin, you can afford to spend up to $200 per customer on marketing expenses ($500 − 0.15 × $2,000 = $200). If your assumptions are correct, any customer you can attract for $200 or less will be worth the investment, giving you a clear budget for future marketing campaigns.

The higher the Lifetime Value of your customers, the higher the Allowable Acquisition Cost. The more each new customer is worth to your business, the more you can spend to attract a new customer and keep them happy.

REFERENCE LINK: **personalmba.com/allowable-acquisition-cost/**

Overhead

Beware of little expenses; a small leak will sink a great ship.

—BENJAMIN FRANKLIN, EIGHTEENTH-CENTURY AMERICAN
POLITICAL LEADER, SCIENTIST, AND POLYMATH

The larger your rent or mortgage payment, the more money you need to make each month to pay your expenses. The same general principle applies to businesses.

Overhead represents the minimum ongoing resources required for a business to continue operation. This includes all of the things you need to run your business every month, regardless of whether you sell anything: salaries, rent, utilities, equipment repairs, and so on.

The lower your Overhead, the less revenue the business requires to continue operation and the faster you'll reach your point of financial **Sufficiency**. If you don't spend much, you don't have to make much to cover your expenses.

Overhead is a critical metric to track if you are building your company on a fixed amount of **Capital**. Venture capitalists and other forms of investment can provide "seed capital"—a fixed amount of money you can use to start the business. The more money you raise in Capital and the more slowly you spend it, the more time you have to make the business work.

The faster you "burn" through your Capital, the more money you need to raise and the faster you need to start bringing in revenue. If you burn through all of your start-up Capital and can't raise more, game over. That's why investors and savvy entrepreneurs watch the business's "burn rate" very closely—the slower the business spends money, the more time you have to find a sustainable business model.

The lower your Overhead, the more flexibility you'll have and the easier it will be to sustain your business operations.

REFERENCE LINK: **personalmba.com/overhead/**

Costs: Fixed and Variable

Watch the costs and the profits will take care of themselves.

—ANDREW CARNEGIE, NINETEENTH-CENTURY INDUSTRIALIST

There's an old business adage: you have to spend money to make money. There's some truth to that statement, but not all expenses are created equal.

Fixed Costs are incurred no matter how much value you create. Your *Overhead* is a Fixed Cost: no matter what you do in any given month, you still have to pay your salaried employees and the lease on your office space.

Variable Costs are related to how much value you create. If you're in the business of creating cotton T-shirts, the more T-shirts you produce, the more cotton fabric you'll need. Raw materials, usage-based utilities, and hourly workers are all Variable Costs.

Reductions in Fixed Costs *Accumulate*; reductions in Variable Costs are *Amplified* by volume. If you can save $50 per month on your phone bill, that savings Accumulates to $600 per year. If you can save $0.50 on each T-shirt you produce, you'll save $500 on every 1,000 T-shirts you make.

The better you understand your costs, the more likely you are to find ways of producing as much value as possible without spending everything you make.

REFERENCE LINK: **personalmba.com/costs-fixed-variable/**

Incremental Degradation

Quality, quality, quality: never waver from it, even when you don't see how you can afford to keep it up. When you compromise, you become a commodity and then you die.

—GARY HIRSHBERG, COFOUNDER OF STONYFIELD FARM

Believe it or not, many of the chocolate products found in the candy aisles of grocery stores are no longer "milk chocolate"—they're "chocolate-flavored candies." What gives?

To make high-quality chocolate, you have to buy high-quality cocoa beans, which are ground up to make cocoa butter. Cocoa butter is then combined with sugar, water, and emulsifiers, which help the oils in the cocoa butter "stick" to the water-saturated sugar. The liquid chocolate is then heated, poured into molds, and cooled to produce solid chocolate.

Over the years, mass-market chocolate manufacturers decided to use cheaper ingredients to keep costs down and increase their **Profit Margins**. Instead of buying high-quality cocoa beans, they bought less expensive beans from mediocre sources—who would notice? Then they replaced cocoa butter with vegetable oils—so much so that food regulatory bodies wouldn't allow them to call it "milk chocolate" anymore. They added more emulsifiers, preservatives, and other chemical additives to keep the zombified chocolate together and make it last forever on the shelf.

Sounds appetizing, right?

Saving money doesn't help you if you degrade the quality of your offer. At the time, these "cost-saving" measures didn't appear to have a huge impact on the chocolate's quality—they seemed to be a **Trade-off** worth making. Over time, however, the accumulated effects undermined the taste and quality of the product. People noticed, and so did the manufacturers: you can now buy "premium" versions that contain the original high-quality ingredients.

Finance and accounting executives get their bean-counting reputations from focusing primarily on cutting costs—reducing expenses in an effort to make an offer or business more profitable. Cutting costs can help you increase your Profit Margin, but it often comes at a steep price: the **Incremental Degradation** of your offer.

If your goal is to increase your profitability, cutting costs can only take you so far. Creating and delivering value will *always* cost at least some amount of money, so there is a lower limit to how much you can cut costs before the cuts begin to diminish the value you provide. Cutting costs that are wasteful or unnecessary is a good idea, but **Diminishing Returns** always kick in—be careful not to throw the baby out with the bath water.

Creating and delivering more value is a much better way to enhance your bottom line. You can never spend less than nothing, but there's no upper limit on the amount of value you can provide or revenue you can collect.

Control your costs, but don't undermine the reason customers buy from you in the first place.

REFERENCE LINK: **personalmba.com/incremental-degradation/**

Breakeven

It is unusual, and indeed abnormal, for a concern to make money during the first several years of its existence. The initial product and initial organization are never right.

—HARVEY S. FIRESTONE, FOUNDER OF THE FIRESTONE
TIRE AND RUBBER COMPANY

Assume your business is bringing in $100,000 per month, and you're spending $50,000 each month in operating expenses. Are you making money?

It depends.

When you create a new business, it often takes a while before you're able to bring in more than you spend. Systems need to be created, employees hired and trained, and marketing efforts launched before revenue starts coming in. During your ramp-up period, those expenses add up.

Let's assume our hypothetical business took a year's worth of $50,000-per-month expenses to launch—that's $600,000. Now that the business is bringing in $50,000 per month more than it needs to cover operating expenses, it can start to recoup that initial investment.

Breakeven is the point where your business's total revenue to date is equal to its total expenses to date—it's the point where your business starts creating wealth instead of consuming it. Assuming the business keeps bringing in $100,000 each month and expenses stay the same, it'll take twelve months to pay down the initial investment. After that, the business will be making money—before that, it just *looks* like the business is profitable.

Your Breakeven point will change month-to-month. Revenue fluctuates, as do expenses. Keeping a running tally of how much you spend and how much revenue you collect from the start of your business's operations is the only way to figure out whether or not you've made money.

The more revenue you bring in and the less you spend on an ongoing basis, the faster you'll reach Breakeven, making your business truly self-sustaining.

REFERENCE LINK: personalmba.com/breakeven/

Amortization

Before every action, ask yourself: Will this bring more monkeys on my back? Will the result of my action be a blessing or a heavy burden?

—ALFRED A. MONTAPERT, AUTHOR OF *THE SUPREME PHILOSOPHY OF MAN: THE LAWS OF LIFE*

You've created the toy of the century: a stuffed animal that looks and acts like a real dog but doesn't need to be fed, watered, or let out in the middle of the night. Kids go crazy for your **Prototype**, and parents are already throwing their credit cards at you to make sure they get one the minute it's available. It's a foregone conclusion that you'll sell millions.

There's only one problem: in order to make these faux dogs affordable, you'll have to tool up a major factory, which will cost at least $100 million. Your bank account has nowhere near $100 million in it—that's a lot of money. How can a business afford something as expensive as a factory and still make money?

Amortization is the process of spreading the cost of a resource investment over the estimated useful life of that investment. In the case of the faux dog factory, let's assume the factory is capable of producing 10 million units during its useful life. On a per-unit basis, that brings the cost per unit of the factory down to $10. If you sell every unit you produce for $100, there's room for a very healthy **Profit Margin**.

Amortization can help you determine whether or not a big expense is a good idea. As long as you have a reliable estimate of how much it will cost and how much you can produce, Amortization helps you figure out whether or not investing large amounts of **Capital** makes sense.

For example, a book designer may choose to purchase a copy of Adobe InDesign, the software often used by professionals to typeset books. Compared to most software packages, InDesign is pricey: a single-user license costs $700. Is it worth it?

The answer depends on how many books the designer uses the software to typeset. If they never complete a project, they've wasted their money. If they use it to typeset ten books for $1,000 each, they've earned $10,000 by making a $700 investment—not bad at all. Amortized across ten projects, the cost of the software is only $70 a project, or 7 percent of the revenue each project brings in. The designer's credit card may hurt when the purchase is made, but the tool offers the ability to earn more money than would be possible otherwise.

Amortization depends on an accurate assessment of useful life, which is a prediction. Amortization doesn't work well if you don't sell what you produce or if your equipment wears out faster than expected. Predictions are a tricky business—if you're wrong in your estimate, your investment may cost a lot more on a per-unit basis than you originally assumed.

Crocs makes funny-looking rubber shoes. After Crocs became an unexpected hit, the company ramped up for huge volumes: they opened a factory in China and started producing millions of shoes on the expectation that they'd continue to sell each unit produced. As it turned out, Crocs were a fad—sales plummeted, and the company was stuck with a lot of expensive manufacturing capacity and huge amounts of inventory it couldn't sell. Amortization couldn't save the company from careening toward bankruptcy.

Using Amortization to figure out whether or not a big investment is worth it is smart—just remember you're making a prediction, and every prediction you make has unavoidable risks.

REFERENCE LINK: **personalmba.com/amortization/**

Purchasing Power

The job of the entrepreneur is to make sure the company doesn't run out of cash.

—WILLIAM A. SAHLMAN, PROFESSOR AT HARVARD BUSINESS SCHOOL

Here's an old business adage you may have heard: "Cash is king."

It's true. You can have millions of dollars in orders on the books, but without cash in the bank, it doesn't matter. IOUs don't pay the bills—if you can't pay your employees or keep the lights on, you're done.

Purchasing Power is the sum total of all liquid assets a business has at its disposal. That includes your cash, credit, and any outside financing that's available. More Purchasing Power is always better, as long as you use that power wisely.

Purchasing Power is what you use to pay your **Overhead** and your suppliers. As long as you continue to pay them, you're in business. As soon as you run out of Purchasing Power, you're finished. Game over.

Always keep track of how much Purchasing Power you have available. How much cash do you have in the bank? How much available credit do you have access to? The more Purchasing Power you have, the better off you are.

Keeping track of your available Purchasing Power makes it *much* easier to run a business. Instead of worrying about paying the bills, Purchasing Power gives you room to breathe, secure in the knowledge that you're not going to suddenly run out of money. That frees up a great deal of mental and emotional energy you can put to better use—figuring out how to improve your business.

Always pay close attention to how much Purchasing Power you have left—it's the difference between a business that stays open and a business that fails.

REFERENCE LINK: **personalmba.com/purchasing-power/**

Cash Flow Cycle

All truth is found in the cash account.

—CHARLIE BAHR, MANAGEMENT CONSULTANT

Money flows through a business in predictable ways. If you understand how revenue, expenses, receivables, and credit work, you can ensure that you continue to have enough *Purchasing Power* on hand to continue operation and maximize your available options.

The *Cash Flow Cycle* describes how cash flows through a business. Think of your business's bank account like a bathtub. If you want the water in the bathtub to rise, you add more water and keep it from leaking out via the drain. The more water that flows in and the less that flows out, the higher the level of water in the tub. Revenues and expenses work the same way: your bank account is a *Stock* of cash that increases or decreases based on your income and payments.

Receivables are promises of payment you've accepted from others. Receivables are attractive, because they feel like a sale—someone has promised to give you money, which is great. There's a catch, however: receivables don't translate into cash until the promise is fulfilled. IOUs are not cash—the faster that promise is translated into payment, the better your cash flow. Many businesses have closed with millions of dollars of "sales" on the books.

Debt is a promise you make to pay someone at a later date. Debt is attractive because you can benefit from a purchase now while holding on to your cash until later. The later you pay, the more cash you have at your disposal. Debt can be useful, but there's also a catch: debts cost additional money in the form of interest. Very often, you'll also have to pay back a portion of your debt over time, which is called "debt service," which you can treat as another type of expense. If you can't cover your debt service, you're in trouble.

Maximizing your cash tackles the issue in a direct way: bring in more revenue and cut costs. Increasing your *Profit Margin*, making more sales, and spending less of what you bring in will improve your cash flow.

Deferring payment or negotiating a longer repayment period with your creditors can also help alleviate a cash crunch. If you have a supplier, vendor, or partner who is willing to let you pay later in exchange for receiving materials or capabilities now, that allows you to keep more cash in your bank account now. You must watch this *Habit* carefully: debts can get out of hand if you don't keep track of how much you owe and when it's due. When done properly, however, paying creditors later can be quite useful, particularly for marketing expenses. Borrowing $1 to make $10 is a good trade; it's even better if you're able to do that for months before the first bill comes due.

To improve your cash situation, it's best to speed up collections and reduce the extension of credit. The faster you get paid, the better your cash flow situation. Ideally, try to get paid immediately, even before buying raw materials and delivering value.

It's common in many industries to extend credit to customers, but that doesn't mean you have to as well. Always remember that you're a business, not a bank (unless your business involves *Loans*)—collect any outstanding payments as soon as possible.

If necessary, you can increase your Purchasing Power by taking on additional debt or opening lines of credit. It's best to avoid using debt or lines of credit if you don't need to, but increasing available credit increases your Purchasing Power. Think of these accounts as backup funding sources— for emergency use only.

The more Purchasing Power you have, the more *Resilient* your business is and the better your ability to handle the unexpected.

REFERENCE LINK: **personalmba.com/cash-flow-cycle/**

Segregation of Duties

The challenge for capitalism is that the things that breed trust also breed the environment for fraud.

—JAMES SUROWIECKI, AMERICAN BUSINESS JOURNALIST

The larger and more complex a business becomes, the easier it is for employees, contractors, and vendors to embezzle funds, steal merchandise, or otherwise defraud the business.

Accountants and finance professionals rely on a system called *Segregation of Duties* to prevent all sorts of shady activities. The system, which is intended to reduce cases of fraud and theft, limits a single person's ability to complete the following business processes:

1. *Authorization*: reviewing, approving, or overseeing a **Transaction**.

2. *Custody*: receiving, accessing, or controlling any assets related to that Transaction.

3. *Record keeping*: creating and storing accounting records related to each Transaction.

4. *Reconciliation*: verifying that two sets of records, like internal company Transaction records and external bank statements, match with respect to timing and amount.

The core principle behind Segregation of Duties is multiparty verification: no individual in the organization is able to complete all four of these processes concerning a single Transaction. In most cases, any specific person might be able to complete one or two of these activities on their own, but the rest must be done and/or verified by another individual.

The classic example of multiparty verification is common corporate banking practice: any check, bank transfer, or other instrument of payment above a certain threshold requires the signature of two authorized officers of the company. Unless two signatures are present, the payment isn't valid and is flagged for investigation.

This simple rule prevents all sorts of financial shenanigans. What prevents a CEO from deciding to double their own salary without approval from the owners or the board of directors? Easy: authorization of the increase by the payroll manager, along with records kept by the payroll system, which can be used to identify and prove the CEO's misconduct.

What prevents the payroll manager—who has direct access to the payroll system—from doubling their own salary? **Cash Flow Statements** and **Internal Controls** by company executives, which can expose a higher-than-expected expense the payroll manager can't hide.

What prevents the CEO and the payroll manager from conspiring to increase *both* of their salaries without approval? Bank statements and transaction records, which can signal to the chief financial officer (CFO) or other executive officers that something fishy is going on. Every part of the system is overseen by more than one individual, so misconduct is more difficult to commit and easier to spot.

Segregation of Duties is also useful when dealing with physical assets and cash. Having more than one person responsible for ordering, receiving, and keeping records of every order and delivery makes it more difficult to divert money or assets in inappropriate ways, since the scheme would require more than one person to cooperate. Ordering and inventory fraud is more difficult to get away with if there's another individual who's expecting to receive an order that doesn't arrive or is charged with auditing the inventory records to ensure everything is accurate.

Most fraudulent activity occurs when someone in a position of power or responsibility recognizes the potential opportunity to cheat and believes there's a low probability of being detected.[2] Segregation of Duties is a simple and direct way to reduce fraud by cutting it off at the source: it reduces potential opportunities for misconduct, raises the probability someone will discover the wrongdoing, and increases the number of people who would have to work together to defraud the business.

REFERENCE LINK: **personalmba.com/segregation-of-duties/**

Limited Authorization

Folly is often more cruel in the consequence than malice can be in the intent.

—GEORGE SAVILE, FIRST MARQUESS OF HALIFAX

There's another simple and effective way to prevent potential misconduct. **Limited Authorization** is a straightforward principle: it's best to limit each individual's ability to act in areas that are outside the scope of their responsibilities.

If access to an asset or authorization isn't required or necessary, it should be withheld by default. If access or authorization is needed in special cases, it should be granted on a temporary basis and in a way that preserves **Segregation of Duties** by requiring more than one person to authorize the action. The fewer the people capable of authorizing a payment from the business's bank account, the lower the likelihood of inappropriate payments, and the easier it is to identify bad actors, fraud, or security breaches.

This principle is useful outside of financial controls. Imagine a software company that grants all of its employees and contractors complete, unlimited, and unsupervised access to its software systems. There might be advantages to doing this: everyone in the company would have the ability to fix or improve any aspect of the system at any time. There is, however, a severe risk inherent in this approach: everyone in the company would also have the ability to break any part of the system at any time.

In the worst case, a disgruntled employee or contractor would be able to shut down the system, access sensitive information, alter critical data, or delete backups and *Fail-safes* in a way that would make recovery impossible. There's also nothing preventing a well-meaning employee or contractor from accomplishing the same thing by accident. If any of those things happened, it would cause severe damage, up to and including the potential bankruptcy and closure of the company.

Granting authorization is an exercise in balancing *Friction* and *Cognitive Switching Penalties* against risk: there's a *Middle Path* between granting too much access and granting too little. Authorization is something that should change over time on the basis of *Trust*, *Earned Regard*, and current responsibilities.

REFERENCE LINK: **personalmba.com/limited-authorization/**

Opportunity Cost

> Business, more than any other occupation, is a continual dealing with the future; it is a continual calculation, an instinctive exercise in foresight.
>
> —HENRY R. LUCE, PUBLISHER AND FOUNDER OF TIME INC.

Let's say you decide to quit your $50,000-a-year job and start a business. Starting the business will have costs of its own, but it will also cost you the $50,000 you would have made had you stayed at your job.

Opportunity Cost is the value you're giving up by making a *Decision*. We can't do everything at once—we can't be in more than one place at a time or spend the same dollar on two different things.

Whenever you invest time, energy, or resources, you're choosing not to invest that time, energy, or resources in any other way. The value that would have been created by your **Next Best Alternative** is the Opportunity Cost of that decision.

Opportunity Cost is important because there are always other options. If you're working for a company that's paying you $30,000 a year and you have the option to move to a company that's paying $200,000 a year for the same work, why would you stay? If you're paying your employees or contractors less than they could make elsewhere for the same work, why would they work for you? If your customers can spend $20 to get something you're charging $200 for, why would they buy from you?

Opportunity Cost is important because it's hidden. As we'll discuss later, in **Absence Blindness**, humans have a hard time paying attention to what's *not* present. Paying attention to what you're giving up by making a Decision helps you consider all of your options before making a decision.

Obsessing over Opportunity Cost too much, however, can drive you crazy. If you're a natural maximizer (like I am), it's tempting to overanalyze every Decision to make sure you've chosen the very best option available, which can go well past the point of **Diminishing Returns**. Don't get bogged down with all of the options available—consider only what appear to be the best alternatives at the time of your decision.

If you pay attention to the Opportunity Costs of your decisions, you'll make much better use of the resources at your disposal.

REFERENCE LINK: **personalmba.com/opportunity-cost/**

Time Value of Money

> They always say time changes things, but you actually have to change them yourself.
>
> —ANDY WARHOL, ARTIST

Would you rather have $1 million today or $1 million five years from now?

The answer is obvious: Why wait? Having the money now means you can spend it now, or invest it now. A million dollars, invested at a **Compounding** interest rate of 5 percent, will be $1,276,281.56 five years from now. Why give up the extra $270,000 if you don't need to?

A dollar today is worth more than a dollar tomorrow. How *much* more depends on what you choose to do with that dollar. The more profitable options you have to invest that dollar, the more valuable it is.

Calculating the **Time Value of Money** is a way of making **Decisions** in the face of **Opportunity Costs**. Assuming you have various options of investing funds with various returns, the Time Value of Money can help you determine which options to choose and how much you should spend, given the alternatives.

Let's go back to the $1 million example: Assume someone offers you an investment that will deliver $1 million risk free in one year's time. What's the maximum amount you should be willing to pay for it today?

Assuming your **Next Best Alternative** is another risk-free investment with a 5 percent interest rate, you shouldn't pay anything more than $952,380. Why? Because if you took that amount and invested it in your Next Best Alternative, you'd have $1 million: $1,000,000 divided by 1.05 (the 5 percent interest/discount rate) equals $952,380. If you can buy the first investment for less than that amount, you'll be ahead.

The Time Value of Money is a very old idea—it was first explained in the early sixteenth century by the Spanish theologian Martín de Azpilcueta. The central insight that a dollar today is worth more than a dollar tomorrow can be extended to apply to many common financial situations.

For example, the Time Value of Money can help you figure out the maximum you should be willing to pay for a business that earns $200,000 in profit each year. Assuming an interest rate of 5 percent, no growth, and a foreseeable future of ten years, the "present value" of that series of future cash flows is $1,544,347. If you pay less than that amount, you'll come out ahead as long as your assumptions are correct. (Note: this is the "discounted cash flow method" we discussed in the section on the **Four Pricing Methods**.)

The Time Value of Money is a versatile concept, and a full exploration of it is beyond the scope of this book. For a more in-depth examination, I recommend picking up *The McGraw-Hill 36-Hour Course in Finance for Nonfinancial Managers* by Robert A. Cooke.

REFERENCE LINK: https://personalmba.com/time-value-of-money/

Compounding

Improve by 1% a day, and in just 70 days, you're twice as good.

—ALAN WEISS, CONSULTANT

Here's a surefire way to become a millionaire: save $10 a day for forty years in a way that earns 8 percent interest. Saving $10 a day isn't difficult—you can save $300 a month by eliminating unnecessary expenses. And you can earn 8 percent by investing that money in the stock market: the S&P 500 produced an average annual return of 8 percent return over the past five decades.

Here's what's even more amazing: you'll only contribute $146,110 over that forty-year span. How, then, do you end up with over $1 million?

Compounding is the **Accumulation** of gains over time. Whenever you're able to reinvest gains, your investment will build upon itself exponentially—a positive **Feedback Loop**.

A simple example of Compounding is a savings account. Let's say your savings account earns 5 percent interest. After a year, $1 in your bank account is going to be worth $1.05. In year two, you don't start with $1—you start with $1.05. In year three, you'll have $1.10. In year four, you'll have $1.15. Fourteen years after you make the initial deposit, you'll have $2.

That doesn't sound like much until you consider that this relationship **Scales**. If you start with $1 million, you'll have $2 million after fourteen years. Not bad at all.

Compounding is important because it creates the possibility of huge gains in short periods of time. If you reinvest the revenue your business generates and your business is growing rapidly, you can multiply your original investment many times over. Compounding is the secret that explains how small companies that reinvest their profits become large companies in a few short years.

Accumulating gains produces huge results over time. The trick is to be patient enough to wait for the reward.

REFERENCE LINK: **personalmba.com/compounding/**

Leverage

Using "other people's money" sounds like a great way to make a fortune.
Borrow some money, make a fortune, pay back your lender, and keep the
rest. What could be better?

Making money by borrowing from others can be savvy, provided you're
aware of the risks.

Leverage is the practice of using borrowed money to magnify potential
gains. Here's an example: let's assume you have $20,000 you'd like to in-
vest in real estate. You could use that money as a 20 percent down payment
on a $100,000 property, borrowing $80,000, but that ties up all of your
money in a single investment.

Instead of using the $20,000 for a single down payment, you could take
the same pool of money and invest in four $100,000 properties, each with
a down payment of $5,000. That strategy requires borrowing $95,000 four
times—a total of $380,000 in loans.

Here's where the magic happens. Let's assume all of the properties double
in value, and you sell them. In the first scenario, you'd make $100,000 on a
$20,000 investment—a 5x return on your $20,000 down payment. In the second scenario, you'd make $400,000 on the very same $20,000 down payment—
a 20x return on investment. Leverage seems like a no-brainer, right?

Not so fast—what will happen if the value of each property drops, and
you sell them all to get back as much money as possible? Assuming the
property value drops by 50 percent, in the first scenario you'd lose $50,000.
In the second scenario, the use of Leverage will magnify your losses to
$200,000—four times as much.

Leverage is a form of financial **Amplification**—it magnifies the potential
for both gains and losses. When your investment pays off, Leverage helps
it pay off more. When your investment tanks, you lose more money than
you would otherwise.

One of the major contributing factors of the recession of 2008–2009 was the use of enormous amounts of Leverage by investment banks. It wasn't uncommon for banks to Leverage their investments by a factor of thirty or forty. Millions (or billions) of dollars were made or lost when the value of a particular stock went up or down by a single percentage point. When the market crashed, a bank's losses were magnified by the amount of Leverage it had taken on, which was more than enough to threaten the entire firm's existence.

Using Leverage is playing with fire—it can be a useful tool if used properly, but it can also burn you. Never use Leverage unless you're fully aware of the consequences and are prepared to accept them. Otherwise, you're putting your business and personal financial situation at risk.

REFERENCE LINK: **personalmba.com/leverage/**

Hierarchy of Funding

Money often costs too much.

—RALPH WALDO EMERSON, NINETEENTH-CENTURY ESSAYIST AND POET

Imagine you've invented an antigravity device that can levitate solid objects without requiring much power. Your invention will revolutionize the transportation and manufacturing industries, making many new products possible. Demand for your invention is a given—all you need to do is create enough devices to fill the demand.

There's a problem, however—estimates indicate that tooling up a production line with the equipment you need to build these devices will cost $1 billion, but you don't have $1 billion to spare. Your device solves a huge problem, but the next step is out of reach. What do you do?

Funding can help you do things that would otherwise be impossible with your current budget. If your business requires expensive equipment or many workers to create and deliver value, you'll probably need outside funding. Few of us have enormous sums of money in our bank accounts waiting to be used, but it's easy to reach out to those who do.

Funding is the business equivalent of rocket fuel. If your business needs to move faster and is already pointed in the right direction, judicious use of financing can help you accelerate the operation's growth. If the business has structural issues, it will explode, and not in a good way.

In order to obtain access to funding, it's often necessary to give up a certain amount of control over the business's operations. Businesspeople won't give you money for nothing—they always ask for something in return.

Remember, providing **Capital** is a form of value for many businesses. In exchange for resources, your lenders or investors are looking for value in return—interest, lease payments, or a share of your company's profits. They're also looking for a way to decrease their risk of losing everything if the business goes under. To alleviate this risk, they ask for control: the ability to influence the operations of the business. The more money you ask for, the more control they'll want.

I think it's useful to imagine a **Hierarchy of Funding**: a ladder of available options. Every businessperson starts on the bottom and climbs as far up the ladder as necessary. The higher you climb, the more funding you get and the more control you give up in exchange.

Let's examine the Hierarchy of Funding, starting at the bottom:

Personal cash is by far the best form of financing. Investing cash you already own is quick and easy and requires no approval or paperwork. Most entrepreneurs begin by financing themselves out of cash as much as possible.

Personal credit is another low-cost method of financing. As long as your needs don't exceed a few thousand dollars, it's easy to finance expenses via personal credit. Approval is quick if you have good credit, and payment over time helps increase your cash flow. You risk ruining your personal credit rating (a form of **Reputation**) if you can't make your payments, but for many entrepreneurs, that's a risk worth taking.

I financed my entire business out of cash and personal credit. If your needs are modest, using personal credit to finance your start-up costs is a good option as long as you watch your budget.

Personal loans are often made by friends and family. If you need more money than you can cover via personal cash and personal credit, **Loans** from friends and family are not uncommon. Just be wary: the risk that you won't be able to pay them back is very real and can have a devastating effect on important personal relationships. For that reason, I'd advise avoiding asking your parents or grandparents to gamble their life savings on your idea—there are better ways.

Unsecured loans are usually made by banks and credit unions. You fill out an application and ask for a certain amount of money, and the bank will evaluate your ability to pay the loan back with interest over a certain time period. The loan can be either a lump sum or a line of credit that can be used at any time. The bank doesn't ask for collateral for smaller amounts (a few thousand dollars), so the interest rate will probably be a bit higher than on a credit card or secured loan.

Secured loans require collateral. Mortgages and automotive loans are good examples of secured loans: if you don't make the payments, the lender can legally seize the property promised as collateral. Because the lender can then sell that property to recoup their funds, secured loans are much larger than unsecured loans—tens or hundreds of thousands of dollars.

Bonds are debt sold to individual lenders. Instead of asking a bank for a loan, the business asks individuals or other companies to loan them money. Bond purchasers give money to the business, which is paid back at an agreed-upon rate for a certain amount of time. When the time expires (i.e., the bond "matures"), the company must give back the original loan amount in addition to the payments already made. The legal and regulatory process that surrounds the bond market can be complicated, so bond issues are usually conducted through an investment bank.

Receivables financing is a special type of secured lending unique to businesses. Receivables financing can make millions of dollars in credit available, but at a cost: the collateral for the loan is control over the business's receivables. Since the bank controls the receivables, they can ensure their loan is paid before anything else, including employee salaries and vendor commitments. Large amounts of funding are available, but you're giving up a great deal of control to the lender.

Angel capital is where we shift from Loans to Capital. An "angel" is an individual private investor—someone who has excess wealth they'd like to invest in a private business, usually $10,000 to $1 million. In exchange, they'll own 1 to 10 percent of the business.

Taking on an angel investor is a bit like taking on a silent partner—they give you Capital, and in exchange you give them partial legal ownership of the business. Some angels offer advice and are available for consulting, but they don't have the power to make business decisions.

Venture capital takes over where angels leave off. Venture capitalists (VCs) are wealthy investors (or groups of investors who pool their funds) with very large sums of Capital available: tens (or hundreds) of millions of dollars in a single investment. Funding via venture capital happens in "rounds" that start small, then grow as more Capital is needed. Later rounds can dilute the ownership percentage of current shareholders, so there's often a great deal of negotiation involved. VCs also require large amounts of control in exchange for large amounts of Capital, which usually means seats on the company's board of directors.

Public stock offerings involve selling partial ownership of the company to investors on the open market. This is usually done via investment banks: companies that will provide a business with enormous amounts of Capital in exchange for the shares of that company to sell on the public stock market. The investment banks make money by selling the shares they've purchased at a premium to individual investors on the open market. An "initial public offering" (IPO) is the first public stock offering a company offers on the open market.

Any investor who purchases shares is a partial owner of the company, which includes the right to participate in management decisions via electing the board of directors. Whoever owns the most shares in the company controls it, so "going public" creates the risk of a hostile takeover: the mass purchasing of shares in an effort to control the company.

Public stock offerings are usually used by angel and venture capital investors to exchange ownership for money. Investors can collect their returns in one of two ways: reaping dividends that distribute the **Profits** of the company or selling their shares to another investor. Public stock offerings enable investors to sell their shares in exchange for money, so it's common for angels and VCs to push successful companies to "go public" or be acquired by another company in order to "cash out" of the investment.

The more control you must give up for each dollar of funding obtained, the less attractive the source of funding. The more people you're required to consult with before making decisions, the slower your company will operate. Investors increase **Communication Overhead**, which can adversely affect your ability to get things done.

It's also not uncommon for investors to remove executives of a company that's not performing well, even if those executives are the founders of the company. Even high-flying executives aren't immune: when Apple was performing poorly in the 1990s, the board of directors fired Steve Jobs from the company he cofounded. A word to the wise: before you take on large amounts of Capital, be aware of how much **Power** the business's board of directors will have over the operation of the company.

Funding can be useful, but be wary of giving up control over your business's operations—unless the funds are essential, err on the side of maintaining your autonomy.

REFERENCE LINK: **personalmba.com/hierarchy-of-funding/**

Bootstrapping

Felix qui nihil debet. (Happy is he who owes nothing.)
—ROMAN PROVERB

How much financing you need depends on what you're trying to do. If you're grasping for the brass ring—accumulating enormous wealth by building a massive public company—you'll probably need financing. If your intent is to be self-sufficient and free to make your own decisions, it's much better to avoid financing in favor of retaining control.

Bootstrapping is the art of building and operating a business without funding. Don't assume that the only way to create a successful business is by raising millions of dollars of venture capital—it's not true. By limiting yourself to the use of personal cash, personal credit, the business's revenue, and a little ingenuity, you can build successful businesses without seeking funding at all. My business operates via a checking account, a savings account, and a business credit card, and I like it that way.

Bootstrapping allows you to grow your business while maintaining 100 percent control over the business's operations. You don't have to get anyone else's approval to make the decisions you think are best. The drawback is that growing the business can take much longer. Prudently used, funding can help make things happen faster than they'd happen otherwise.

If you accept funding, make sure that you use it to do things that you couldn't do any other way. **Force Multipliers** are useful but expensive—taking on funding in order to get access to critical capabilities can be smart. Otherwise, try to operate from cash and operating revenue as much as possible.

For best results, Bootstrap as far as you can go, then move up the **Hierarchy of Funding** only as needed. Having 100 percent ownership and control of a profitable, self-sustaining business is a wonderful thing.

REFERENCE LINK: personalmba.com/bootstrapping/

Return on Investment

Wise are those who learn that the bottom line doesn't always have to be the top priority.

—WILLIAM A. WARD, APHORIST

When you invest in something, you expect it to provide more value than you paid for it. Knowing how to estimate how much you'll receive versus how much you'd invest is a very useful skill.

Return on Investment (ROI) is the value created from an investment of time or resources. Most people think of ROI in terms of currency: if you invest $1,000 and you collect $100 in profit, that's a 10 percent return on your investment: ($1,000 + $100) / $1,000 = 1.10, or 10 percent. If your ROI is 100 percent, you've doubled your initial investment.

Return on Investment can help you decide between competing alternatives. If you deposit money in a savings account, the return on your investment will be equal to the interest rate that the bank gives you to hold your money. Why put your money in an account that pays 1 percent interest if you can deposit that money in an account that pays 2 percent, with no difference in fees?

The usefulness of Return on Investment extends far beyond money: you can use it for the other **Universal Currencies** as well. Return on invested time is an useful way to analyze the benefits of your effort. If you were forced to work twenty-four hours a day nonstop for a year in exchange for $1 million, would you do it? When you look at the return versus the cost to your time and sanity, it's not worth it.

The return on every investment is always related to how much the investment costs. The more you spend (in terms of both money and time), the lower your return. Even "sure bets" like buying a house or getting a college degree aren't wise if you pay too much for them. Every estimate of return is speculative—you never know how it'll turn out. Calculating returns is an exercise in predicting the future, which is fundamentally impossible.

Every future ROI estimate is a semieducated guess. You can only know your ROI for certain *after* the investment is made and the returns collected. Nothing in this world is a sure bet—always take into account the risk of something going wrong before making an investment, no matter how high the potential ROI appears to be.

REFERENCE LINK: **personalmba.com/return-on-investment/**

Sunk Cost

If at first you don't succeed, try, try again. Then quit. There's no point in being a damn fool about it.

—W. C. FIELDS, COMEDIAN

After returning from World War II, my grandfather started the Kaufman Construction Company, building storefronts, homes, union halls, and apartment buildings in Akron, Ohio. In 1965, after twenty-five years in the business, he kicked off his most ambitious project: a five-story, twenty-six-unit apartment building on Portage Path.

The "Baranel" was to be built on the lots of two older homes, which had been purchased and demolished for the job. Steel rebar and bricks had been ordered, and excavation was proceeding as planned. The expected cost of the project was $300,000, roughly $2.4 million in today's dollars.

The project proceeded smoothly until the excavators found huge hidden deposits of blue clay, which could make the foundation unstable. To continue the project, thousands of cubic feet of clay and dirt would have to be excavated to reach bedrock, and additional concrete and rebar would be required to fill the massive hole. Completing the building would cost far more than originally expected, but it was difficult to determine how much.

Instead of walking away, Grandpa decided to finish the project—he'd already spent so much money on the land and excavation that it felt wrong to "waste it" without having something to show for the effort and investment. He found a few investors, put up another apartment building and the family home as collateral, and the project continued.

By the time the building was complete, they'd spent more than three times as much money as originally planned: approximately $1 million, more than $8 million in today's dollars when adjusted for inflation. It was more than the building was worth. Grandpa spent the rest of his career handling angry investors and lawyers. It's a sad story, but one worth learning from.

Sunk Costs are investments of time, energy, and money that can't be recovered once they've been made. No matter what you do, you can't get those resources back. Continuing to invest in a project to recover lost resources doesn't make sense—all that matters is how much more investment is required versus the reward you expect to obtain.

Avoiding the perils of Sunk Costs is easy to understand conceptually but much harder to put into practice. When you sink years of work into a career you realize you don't want, or millions of dollars into a project that unexpectedly requires millions more, it's difficult to walk away. You've invested so much that it feels wrong to "give it up for nothing." In reality, there's nothing you can do about your past investment—it's gone. All you can do is act based upon the information you have now.

Making mistakes is inevitable: no one is perfect. You *will* make a few decisions that, in retrospect, you'll wish you hadn't—count on it. If you could turn back time, you'd try a different approach, but you can't. There will always be other projects, provided you don't double down on a risky project to recover your losses. Throwing good money after bad is not a winning strategy.

Don't continue to pour concrete into a bottomless pit—if it's not worth the additional investment, walk away. You never have to earn back money in the same way you lost it. If the reward isn't worth the investment required to obtain it or the risk, don't invest.

REFERENCE LINK: **personalmba.com/sunk-cost/**

Internal Controls

If something cannot go on forever, it will stop.

—HERBERT STEIN, ECONOMIST

One of the major benefits of tracking your financial and operations data over time is the ability to notice patterns in your revenue, costs, and **Value Stream**. Over time, these patterns become useful for budgeting, supervising operations, complying with laws and regulations, and preventing theft and fraud.

Internal Controls are a set of specific **Standard Operating Procedures** a business uses to collect accurate data, keep the business running smoothly, and spot trouble. The better a company's Internal Controls, the more reliable its financial reports, and the more confidence you can have in the quality of the company's operations. Internal Controls are most useful in three areas:

Budgeting is the act of estimating future costs and taking steps to ensure that these estimates aren't exceeded without good reason. Budgets are very important in controlling **Profit Margins**, the **Cash Flow Cycle**, and **Leverage**. If part of your business breaks the budget in a given time period, you can take action to correct the situation.

Supervision is important in businesses that rely on employees or outside firms for important parts of their business process. By establishing controls related to delivery time, quality, cost, and systems failures, it's possible to conduct evaluations and make changes in operations if necessary if standards appear to slip or performance targets aren't met.

Compliance is necessary when a business operates in an industry affected by government regulations. The company may be obligated to collect and report certain data in the course of operations. Internal Controls ensure that this data is complete and accurate, preventing risks, significant losses, and potential legal issues.

Theft and fraud prevention is important to protect against the risk of financial loss at the hands of an unscrupulous party. Solid Internal Controls make it easier to notice something is amiss, identify the responsible party, and resolve the situation with a minimum of fuss.

In all of these areas, it's useful to have a dispassionate third party audit your data and control processes. Auditing is necessary to find and correct errors, particularly in large businesses with many moving parts. Auditing helps ensure the quality of the company's data and can increase the confidence of lenders, investors, shareholders, and regulatory bodies regarding the business's practices. In all cases, the auditing party should have no interest in the outcome: this *Segregation of Duties* helps ensure the results are accurate, particularly if they're not pretty.

Financial controls also help you to benchmark your company against other companies in your market. Every year, the Risk Management Association (RMA) compiles a huge amount of data from businesses in all industries. The RMA data set makes it easier to discover what solvent businesses of various sizes spend on marketing, sales, and value delivery over a given period of time.

Banks and investors rely on RMA data to determine whether or not a business they're examining is typical. If the company's costs are in line with revenues, outside parties are likely to assume the business has a lower risk profile. If the company is spending three times the typical amount on sales and marketing, it can be a signal of trouble, inefficiency, or shady accounting.

Industry groups can also be a useful source of data. Many markets have trade associations that collect and share information about successful businesses. By comparing your business's data to that of other companies in your market, you can get a better picture of how well you're performing and where your business could use improvement.

REFERENCE LINK: **personalmba.com/internal-controls/**

6

THE HUMAN MIND

Now that we've covered the essentials of how businesses work, we're going to shift gears into understanding how people work.

Businesses are built *by* people *for* people. As we discussed in value creation and value delivery, if people didn't have needs and wants, businesses wouldn't exist. Likewise, if no one was able or willing to fulfill those needs and wants, businesses couldn't operate.

Understanding how we take in information, how we make decisions, and how we decide what to do or what not to do is important if you want to create and sustain a successful business venture. Once you have a clear picture of how the human mind works, it's easy to find better ways to get things done in an efficient and effective way.

REFERENCE LINK: **personalmba.com/human-mind/**

Caveman Syndrome

Imagine for a moment what it would be like to have lived a hundred thousand years ago. Your senses are on full alert as you walk along the banks of a river, scanning for food: fish swimming in the stream, edible plants, or animals to catch. The sun is nearing its apex, and you've already walked six miles today—your callused feet will take you six miles more before the day is done.

In a few hours, you'll stop for some water and find shade: the mid-afternoon sun is hot, and rest will help you conserve energy.

As you walk, your eyes settle on a small bush about twenty feet away. Your heart leaps—you recognize the pattern of the leaves and you know that both the leaves and roots are good to eat. You start to dig at the earth around the base of the plant to expose the roots, intending to place the entire shrub into the simple woven basket you have strapped to your back.

Suddenly, you notice a movement out of the corner of your eye. Four feet away, a massive cobra has drawn itself up to strike, displaying its distinctive patterned hood and sharp fangs. There's no time to think—adrenaline surges, your pulse races, and you jump out of the way, then run away as fast as you're able, leaving the food behind.

You run until it's clear that the threat is gone and then you spend a few minutes recovering, trembling from the exertion and the stress as the adrenaline wears off. You're disappointed about losing the food, but it wasn't worth risking your life.

Once you recover, you resume your search for food and shelter from the midday sun. Tonight, you'll return to your tribe to share what food you've found.

You know everyone well, since there are only forty or so people in the tight-knit group. You've banded together primarily for protection from wild animals and other tribes, who sometimes attempt to seize your tribe's resources via raids. Together, you make spears and nets to catch fish, turn flint into knives and axes for hunting and defense, and create baskets and clay pots to store food.

When you return to your tribe's camp, an antelope is roasting on the fire—a group of hunters in your tribe literally chased it to death, a technique called persistence hunting. In the evening, you'll sit around the fire the group has built to cook food and keep predators away, and you'll discuss the day and tell stories until you drift off to sleep. Tomorrow, you'll do it all over again.

Human biology is optimized for conditions that existed a hundred thousand years ago, not for the world in which we live today. Food is everywhere; predators are not. You no longer have to be in constant motion; instead, you probably spend most of your time occupied by sedentary activities, like computer and office work. As a result, we face many new threats to our brains and bodies, like obesity, heart disease, diabetes, Alzheimer's disease, and cancer.

I call this state of affairs *Caveman Syndrome*: your brain and body aren't optimized for the modern world. Part of the challenge of working in the modern world is that our brains and bodies are tuned for physical and social survival, not sixteen-hour workdays. Business hasn't been around long enough for our biology to adapt to the new demands we're placing upon ourselves.

Don't be too hard on yourself—you weren't built for the type of work you're currently responsible for. No one is—we're all running demanding new software on ancient hardware.

REFERENCE LINK: **personalmba.com/caveman-syndrome/**

Performance Requirements

Now no joy but lacks salt / That is not dashed with pain / And weariness and fault

—ROBERT FROST, "TO EARTHWARD"

Coffee and all-nighters can only take you so far. If you want to do good work, taking care of yourself isn't optional. If you don't give your body what it needs to run, you'll run out of gas long before you reach your goals.

Your mind is first and foremost a physical system. Oftentimes, what we experience as mental fatigue or emotional distress is a signal from our body that we're not getting enough of something we physically need: nutrients, exercise, or rest.

If you want to get things done, you can't run on "empty"—the human body has *Performance Requirements*. Just as a car can't run with an empty gas tank or a broken spark plug, your body can't operate for long without a few necessary inputs. When you have a lot of work to do, it's common to think that taking care of yourself is a secondary concern. It's not—taking care of yourself should be your *primary* concern if you want to get important things done without burning out.

Nutrition, exercise, and rest are the inputs your body converts into productive energy. Poor (or too little) input reduces the quantity and quality of your output. Here are a few basic guidelines to help you get the most out of each day:

Eat high-quality food and drink water. **Garbage In, Garbage Out**—pay attention to what you put into your body. Avoid refined sugar and processed foods as much as possible—to paraphrase food writer Michael Pollan, if your great-grandparents wouldn't recognize it as food, don't eat it. Use caffeine in moderation and only in the morning—herbal tea and flavored water are good substitutes for soda after noon, and carrying a water bottle makes it much easier to stay hydrated.

Exercise. According to *Brain Rules* by John Medina, even low-intensity physical activity increases energy, improves mental performance, and enhances your ability to focus. Going for a walk or run, jumping rope, or doing a bit of yoga can help clear the cobwebs in your mind and give you more energy for the rest of the day. My preferred form of strength training is swinging a kettlebell or steel mace—inexpensive and effective weight-lifting tools that don't take up much space. With proper technique, you can get a full-body workout in twenty minutes or so. (Just don't hit anything.)[1]

Get at least seven to eight hours of sleep each night. Sleep helps consolidate the results of **Pattern Matching** and **Mental Simulation**, so don't skimp on rest. I find it useful to set an alarm to remind me to *go to bed*, giving me enough time to wind down before retiring for the night. Planning for eight to nine hours in bed will ensure you get enough time in deep and REM sleep.

Get some sun, but not too much. Light helps set your circadian rhythm, which affects your sleeping patterns. I regularly use a light-therapy device[2] to ensure that I'm getting enough light, particularly in the winter months. Getting as little as ten minutes of sunlight in the morning is an easy way to improve both your sleep and your mood.

I experiment with new ways to improve my energy, productivity, and mood—I recommend you do the same. **Guiding Structure** can help make these lifestyle changes much easier—changing the structure of my environment has helped me make many changes with little effort. Don't be afraid to try something new to see if you notice an improvement—just be safe.

REFERENCE LINK: **personalmba.com/performance-requirements/**

The Onion Brain

> The views expressed here do not necessarily represent the unanimous view of all parts of my mind.
>
> —MALCOLM MCMAHON, ARCHBISHOP OF LIVERPOOL

Most of us identify with the voice inside our head that's commenting on the world around us. That voice is sometimes electric with excitement, but more often it's uncertain, concerned, or scared.

Fortunately, "you" are not that voice.

"You" are only a small part of your brain. The voice in your head is just a radio announcer, commenting on what your brain is doing. It is not *you*—your consciousness is what your brain uses to solve problems it can't handle on autopilot.

Since human behavior has its roots in the brain, it's very useful to understand how your brain is constructed. Here's a brief (and oversimplified) look at how your brain works.

Humans have an **Onion Brain**—our brain has several layers, which sit on top of one another. At the core is a structure called the *hindbrain*, which is responsible for keeping you alive. The hindbrain is responsible for all of the physiological functions necessary for survival: heart rate, sleeping, waking, reflexes, muscle movements, and biological urges.

Located at the base of the brain, the hindbrain is sometimes called the "lizard brain" because this basic neurological structure appears in all of our biological precursors, including reptiles and amphibians. The hindbrain is primarily responsible for generating signals that are passed down through your spinal cord and nerves to every part of your body, resulting in your physical actions.

Above your hindbrain is the *midbrain*, which is responsible for processing sensory data, emotion, memory, and **Pattern Matching**. Our midbrain predicts what will happen next, then sends that information to the hind-brain, which readies our body for immediate action. The midbrain is the radio announcer, and the hindbrain is the radio.

Sitting just above the midbrain is a thin, folded layer of tissue—the *forebrain*. This small sheet of neural matter is responsible for the cognitive capabilities that make us human: self-awareness, logic, deliberation, *Inhibition*, and *Decision*.

Developmentally speaking, the forebrain is very new and likely evolved to help us handle ambiguity. Most of the time, our midbrain and hind-brain run the show—we're operating on instinct and autopilot. That changes, however, when we face something unexpected or unfamiliar, which confounds the midbrain's ability to predict what will happen next. That's when the forebrain kicks into gear, gathering data and considering options.

After some deliberation and analysis, the forebrain decides what to do based on what appears to be best at the time. Once a Decision is made, the midbrain and hindbrain assume normal operation and carry out the de-cision.

Neuroscientists are probably ready to shoot me at this point, but this very basic model of the brain is accurate enough to be useful.[3] My friend P. J. Eby uses a great analogy to explain the relationship between the dif-ferent parts of your mind: your brain is a horse, and "you" are the rider. Your horse is intelligent—it moves on its own, can identify challenges, and will balk at things that appear dangerous or scary. But you, the rider, are there to set a direction and reassure the horse that it's safe to proceed.

One of the best things you can do to get more done is to dissociate yourself from the voice in your head. The radio announcer has the atten-tion span of a two-year-old after drinking a triple espresso. Its job is to highlight things in your environment you may be interested in paying at-tention to—things that may fulfill one of your *Core Human Drives* or present some danger. That doesn't mean the voice is always right or that you must take everything it says as gospel truth.

Meditation is a simple practice that can help you separate "you" from the voice in your head. There's nothing mystical or magical about meditation—you sit, breathe in and out, and watch what your "monkey mind" does without associating yourself with it. After a while, the voice becomes quieter, improving your ability to keep yourself on the course you choose.

A few moments of quiet meditation every day can be the difference between feeling scared and overwhelmed and feeling in control of your destiny.

REFERENCE LINK: **personalmba.com/onion-brain/**

Perceptual Control

The behavior of an organism is the output of control systems, and is performed with the purpose of controlling perceptions at desired reference values. Behavior is the control of perception.

—WILLIAM T. POWERS, SYSTEMS THEORIST

In the hallowed halls of businesses (and business schools) around the world, B. F. Skinner is the hidden king.

Skinner was one of the major intellectual forces behind the "behaviorist" movement in psychology—the idea that biological systems always respond a certain way to certain stimuli. Control the stimuli and you can control the behavior. "Condition" the organism with rewards and punishments, and the organism will learn how to behave.

Over the decades, behaviorism has fallen out of vogue in psychology—research has made it clear that there's *far* more to behavior than the carrot and the stick. But that understanding hasn't extended to business practice—in corporations and business-school classrooms around the world, the search continues for the magic incentive that will make people do what businesses want.

In reality, human behavior is much more like a thermostat. A thermostat is a very simple system: all it consists of is a sensor, a set point, and a switch. The sensor measures the temperature of the surrounding **Environment**. When the temperature is within a given range, the thermostat does nothing. When the temperature is below the set point, the switch turns the heater on. Once the temperature is above the set point, the switch turns the heater off.

This relationship is called **Perceptual Control**—the thermostat controls the temperature of the room by comparing the perceived temperature against the set point, then taking an action if and only if that perception is "out of control." Once the action brings the perception under control, the system stops acting until the set point is violated once again.

Living organisms—including human beings—are very complex Perceptual Control systems: we act in ways to keep our perceptions of the world within acceptable boundaries. We don't put on a coat because cold weather *forces* us to—we put on a coat *because we feel cold* and we don't *want* to feel cold. If the light entering our eyes is too bright, we find shade, pull down the blinds on the windows, or put on sunglasses—the action controls the perception, and the action we take depends on the Environment we find ourselves in at the time.

In *Making Sense of Behavior: The Meaning of Control*, William T. Powers uses the following example to explain how control systems account for the wide range of behaviors human beings exhibit: Imagine a ship in the middle of an ocean during a wild storm. The ship is rising and falling at random, pitching back and forth as it's buffeted by the waves.

A rock on the deck of the ship is not a control system. The rock doesn't *want* anything, so it has nothing to control—it just tumbles wherever the forces of physics take it. A human being on the deck of the ship, however, *wants* to stay upright, and will therefore take many different actions to continue to stay standing: changing balance, moving, holding on to handrails, etc. If the human stumbles and falls, they'll take whatever actions they can to get back on their feet once more.

The Environment dictates which actions are possible to bring the perception under control. Control is not planning—it's adjusting to changes in the Environment as they happen. The human in the storm doesn't have the capability to predetermine what actions they'll take to stay on their feet—as the Environment changes, their actions will change in response, depending on the resources and options available at the moment.

Perceptual Control explains why the same stimulus often produces different responses. A good example of why the stimulus/response model doesn't paint the whole picture is the classic incentive of many employers: paid overtime. If you want your hourly employees to work more, you should pay more overtime, right?

Not necessarily. Workers who are controlling for income (i.e., they don't have enough and want more) will probably work more overtime, but what about workers who already feel they're making enough money or have priorities that are more important than work? A few of those workers will work the same amount of time, and some will work *less*—they're controlling for a certain amount of income, then spending their time doing other things that are important to them, like being with their family or pursuing a side project. Raising overtime pay will allow them to reach that point faster, so they'll spend *less* time at work.

The overtime incentive produces three different results, two of which are complete opposites—working more and working less. So much for behaviorism.

Perceptual Control represents a fundamental shift in understanding why people do the things they do. Once you understand that people act to control their *perceptions*, you'll be better equipped to influence how they act.

REFERENCE LINK: personalmba.com/perceptual-control/

Reference Level

Action comes about if and only if we find a discrepancy between what we are experiencing and what we want to experience.

—PHILIP J. RUNKEL, PROFESSOR OF PSYCHOLOGY AND EDUCATION, UNIVERSITY OF OREGON

At the heart of every **Perceptual Control** system is a **Reference Level**—a range of perceptions that indicate the system is "under control." When a perception is within the system's Reference Level, nothing happens. When the perception violates the Reference Level by being too high or too low, the system will act to bring the perception back under control.

There are three kinds of Reference Levels: set points, ranges, and errors.

A *set point* is a minimum or maximum value. The thermostat is an example of a system that has a set point—whenever the temperature falls below a certain value, the heater kicks on. Your body's production of melatonin is another set point—once it reaches a particular threshold, you'll start falling asleep.

Business financial controls are managed as set points: as long as your revenue is above a certain set point and your expenses are below a certain set point, you're okay. If you suddenly spend three times what you normally spend or your revenue falls below your point of **Sufficiency**, that triggers action—you want to find out why you overspent and how to bring your expenses back under control.

A *range* is a spread of acceptable values. The difference between a range and a set point is the existence of an upper *and* lower limit to the perception being controlled. With a set point, the perception must be above or below a certain level to be under control; with a range, the perception must be between *two* set points to be under control.

For example, your body has a system for regulating the level of glucose in your blood, which it uses for energy. Too much or too little blood glucose can be life threatening, so your body works to keep the level within an acceptable range by releasing insulin, which causes extra glucose to move into (or out of) the cells in your body. As long as your blood glucose is within the acceptable range, nothing happens. When the reference range is violated, your body starts working to bring the situation back under control.

An *error* is a set point defined as zero—any perception that's not zero is out of control. Think of the pain receptors in your skin. Most of the time, they do nothing, which means everything is under control. If you cut or burn yourself, however, the receptors send a signal that something is wrong, and you'll act to remedy the situation. Customer-service complaints are a business example—if you don't receive any, everything is under control. If your in-box is filling with complaints, you know something needs to be fixed.

If you want to change a behavior, you must either change the system's Reference Level or change the **Environment** in which the system is operating. Think back to the thermostat—if you want to turn the heater off, you can change the set point to a lower temperature. If you're aware that your expenses will be three times what they were last month because you're launching a huge marketing campaign, your finances are no longer out of control. If you're in the process of getting a tattoo, pain receptors firing in your skin is an acceptable situation.

The perceptions themselves haven't changed, but you'll no longer act to bring the perception under control because *it already is under control.* Changing the Reference Level changes the behavior of the system.

Defining and redefining Reference Levels can help you change your behavior. If you're worried that your spending is out of control, you can create a budget that will give you information on what your target monthly revenue needs to be in order to maintain financial Sufficiency. If you're worried that your weight is too high or low, a visit to your doctor can help you calibrate your expectations and self-perception against medical data. If you're working twelve-hour days and you decide that no more than eight is acceptable, your work habits will change.

Change the Reference Level, and your behavior will change as a result.

REFERENCE LINK: **personalmba.com/reference-level/**

Conservation of Energy

> The fundamental principle of human action is that men seek to grat-
> ify their desires with the least exertion.
>
> —HENRY GEORGE, AUTHOR OF *THE SCIENCE OF POLITICAL ECONOMY*

Here's a truth of human nature: people are lazy. The critical insight is that being lazy is a feature, not a bug.

Think what would happen if one of your ancient ancestors ran around all day for no good reason until they collapsed from exhaustion. If a predator or enemy appeared, they'd have no reserves left to respond to the threat—a very bad situation. As a result, we've evolved to avoid expending energy unless absolutely necessary, a *Habit* I call *Conservation of Energy*.

Over the past several decades, researchers have studied marathoners and ultramarathoners (people who run fifty to one hundred miles at a stretch) to learn more about how the body responds to pain. Here's what they've found: when you're so tired that it feels like you're about to kick the bucket any second, physiologically, you're *not even remotely close to dying.* The signals your brain is sending to your body are a ruse that serves as a warning, prompting you to keep some energy in reserve, just in case energy is needed later.

Unless a *Reference Level* is violated, people will conserve energy by not acting. Think of two roommates who have different standards of household cleanliness. To one, the presence of dirty dishes in the sink is a problem—in their mind, any dishes at all is "out of control," which prompts action to fix the situation. To the other roommate, the situation may not be out of control until the sink is overflowing, at which point they'll expend some energy washing dishes. Different Reference Levels, different actions.

If you think your weight, health, and physique are just fine, you probably won't change your diet or start exercising. If you're comfortable with your social circle and confidence, you probably won't do much to improve your social skills or expand your circle of acquaintances. If you think you're making enough money, you probably won't do much to earn more.

Conservation of Energy explains why some people stay in dead-end jobs for decades, even though they know the position isn't great. If the work is okay, the bills get paid, and the job never becomes stressful or frustrating enough to violate expectations, people won't go out of their way to get a promotion, find another job, or start a new business. People only start to expend effort if their Reference Levels are violated in some way, so if their expectations aren't violated, they don't act.

Sources of information that change your Reference Levels are valuable in prompting action. One of the things that prompted me to build courses and offer consulting was the knowledge that some business authors and coaches were able to spend all day learning and helping others and be paid very well for their expertise. That was enough to violate my Reference Levels about work at the time—if they could get paid for doing what I loved to do, why should I have to spend all day in a day job that was just okay? The more I learned about what people did to make this possible, the more I wanted to do to make it a reality for myself.

Before Roger Bannister's record-breaking performance in 1954, running a mile in under four minutes was considered beyond the physical limitations of the human body. After Bannister proved it was possible, the psychological barrier was broken: by the end of 1957, sixteen runners had accomplished the feat. The only thing that changed was the Reference Level: these athletes knew it was possible and wanted to do it, so they did.

Good books, magazines, blogs, documentaries, and even competitors are valuable if they violate your expectations about what's possible. When you discover that other people are doing something you once considered unrealistic or impossible, it changes your Reference Levels in a very useful way. All you need to know is that something you want is possible, and you'll find a way to get it.

REFERENCE LINK: **personalmba.com/conservation-of-energy/**

Guiding Structure

In the long run—and often in the short-run—your willpower will never beat your environment.

—JAMES CLEAR, AUTHOR OF *ATOMIC HABITS*

Let's say you decide to remove refined sugar from your diet. There's overwhelming evidence that it's not good for your health, and you're convinced your quality of life would improve if you can kick the habit. There's just one problem: sugar tastes good, and you experience cravings that are difficult to resist. How can you make it easier to change your eating habits?

One of the most effective strategies is simple: don't purchase products with refined sugar at the grocery store, get rid of any food with added sugar in your house, and purchase a few healthy snacks that meet your new criteria. If sugar isn't available when and where you experience hunger, and if there are easy alternatives to your typical choices, there's no need to resist temptation: the structure of your immediate *Environment* makes your new behavior automatic. A few minutes of willpower applied to altering the world around you can make it much easier to act in the ways you've decided to act.

Guiding Structure means the structure of your Environment is the largest determinant of your behavior. If you want to successfully change a behavior, *don't try to change the behavior by itself.* Change the structure that influences or supports the behavior, and the behavior will change. If you don't want to eat ice cream, don't buy it in the first place.

In Homer's *Odyssey*, Odysseus and his crew prepare to sail past the island of the Sirens—bird women who sing songs so beautiful and alluring that unwitting sailors lose all reason and shipwreck themselves. Instead of relying on strength of will to resist the temptation of the Sirens, Odysseus changes the structure of the Environment, plugging his men's ears with beeswax and tying himself to the ship's mast. Temptation thus avoided, the ship makes safe passage.

Change the structure of your Environment, and your behavior will change as a result. Add a bit of **Friction** or eliminate certain options, and you'll find it much easier to focus on what you're trying to accomplish.

A great example of Guiding Structure is the "sterile cockpit rule" that the Federal Aviation Administration (FAA) instituted in 1981. Most airline accidents happen below ten thousand feet, where distractions can be deadly. Above ten thousand feet, pilots can talk about anything they want, but below ten thousand feet, the only discussion permitted is about information related to the flight in progress. By eliminating distractions, the sterile cockpit rule reduces errors and accidents.

Change the structure of your Environment, and you'll be amazed at how your behavior will change in response.

REFERENCE LINK: **personalmba.com/guiding-structure/**

Reorganization

Not all those who wander are lost.

—J. R. R. TOLKIEN, AUTHOR OF *THE LORD OF THE RINGS*

Whenever a perception violates the system's **Reference Level**, action will occur to bring the perception back under control. Sometimes that response is well defined—as we discussed earlier, your body knows what it needs to do to regulate blood glucose. Often, however, you don't know what is wrong—or how to fix it.

Think of a perception as abstract as "job satisfaction"—there's a set point in your mind that stands for "how happy I should be at work," and your perception of job satisfaction is an average of your actual experiences at work. Pleasant experiences move the average higher, and unpleasant experiences move the average lower.

If your perception of job satisfaction is lower than you think it should be (your Reference Level), your brain will kick into action—"I'm not as happy as I should be . . . *Something* needs to change."

Here's the problem: you may not know what that something is. Would you be happier if you changed assignments, worked for a new boss, left the company, or started working for yourself? Who knows? That's where **Reorganization** comes in.

Reorganization is random action that occurs when a Reference Level is violated but you don't know what to do to bring the perception back under control. The "quarter-life" or midlife crisis many people experience is a perfect example of Reorganization. You don't quite know what to do to eliminate the angst you're feeling, so you start doing things that aren't normal for you, like quitting your job to backpack across Europe or getting a tattoo and buying a motorcycle.

Reorganization feels like you're lost, depressed, or crazy—that's normal. Your brain starts spitting out all kinds of off-the-wall things in an effort to find something to fix the situation. Sometimes, when I'm stressed out, I'll start to think that being a janitor sounds appealing—the work's not difficult, you don't have to think so much, and you still get paid. That doesn't mean it's a good idea, but this type of thought process is normal—my brain is just trying out random ideas to bring certain systems back under control.

Reorganization is the neurological basis of learning. As we'll discuss in **Pattern Matching**, our minds are learning machines that associate specific behaviors with specific effects. If your mind hasn't already learned what to do in a certain situation, the best way to solve the problem is to try new things in an effort to gather data. That's what Reorganization is for—it's the impulse to consider or try new things to see what works.

One of the most important things to understand about Reorganization is that it's best not to fight it. Even though it's sometimes tempting to try to convince yourself that everything is okay, resisting or repressing the impulse to try something different slows down your learning.

There's nothing odd or abnormal about dark nights of the soul—they're a signal that some perception about your life is out of control, and Reorganization is required to gather more data about how to fix it. Once you learn how to bring the perception back under control, Reorganization stops.

When you're feeling lost, take heart—it's just your brain gathering the information it needs to make good decisions. Embracing the impulse to try something new will help you exit Reorganization faster than you would otherwise.

REFERENCE LINK: personalmba.com/reorganization/

Conflict

The significant problems we face cannot be solved at the same level of thinking we were at when we created them.

—ALBERT EINSTEIN, NOBEL PRIZE–WINNING PHYSICIST

Let's take a moment to examine everyone's favorite character flaw: procrastination.

Everyone procrastinates to a certain extent: with too many things to do, putting off tasks until they feel urgent is a natural response. How can you focus on something due in the future when there's something that needs to be done *now*?

What's particularly frustrating are the times we know we have time to get something done in advance, but we just don't feel like doing it *right now*. Part of us wants to work, and part of us wants to *not* work. If you try to force yourself to work, you find that you're so distracted that you don't get much done. If you try to rest, part of you feels bad that you're not working, which means you're not resting.

Entire days can pass where you neither really work nor really rest, but you feel exhausted from the effort of getting nothing done. What gives?

Conflicts occur when two control systems try to change the same perception. When you're procrastinating, one of your brain's subsystems is trying to control "getting things done," while another is trying to control "getting enough rest." Since both systems are trying to control the same perception—physical action—the systems fight to move the perception in the direction they want it to go.

The situation is akin to a heater and an air conditioner fighting to control the temperature in a single room. As long as their respective **Reference Levels** are mutually exclusive, neither system will ever be under control—they'll continue to expend effort to move the system in the direction they're controlling for. Even if one system brings the perception back under control temporarily, it won't be long before the other system ensures it's out of control once more.

Procrastination is an example of an inner Conflict, but Conflicts happen *between* people as well. Conflicts occur when people are controlling for different outputs that require the same input. Think of two children fighting over the same toy. It's the procrastination/temperature battle all over again, only the control systems are people. As long as one child has the toy, the other will be upset. As a result, the toy moves back and forth, and both children are upset.

Think about senior leaders in a large company squabbling over how a limited budget will be allocated, and you'll have a good idea of where Conflicts come from. If $1 million is allocated to one vice president, that means all of the other VPs can't use it, so they protest—corporate politics at its best.

One of the things that make interpersonal Conflict challenging is that we can never truly control the actions of another human being. We can influence, persuade, inspire, or negotiate, but we can never act upon another person's perceptions or change their Reference Levels in a direct way.

Conflicts can only be resolved by changing Reference Levels—how success is defined by the parties involved. Attempting to resolve a Conflict by calling attention to unacceptable behavior is ineffective in the same way that willpower can't change behavior in a direct way—it's not addressing the root cause of the Conflict.

Each party in the Conflict has a different Reference Level, which is primarily influenced by the situation or *Environment*. The only way to resolve the conflict is to change each party's Reference Level, which is best done by changing the structure of the situation.

In the case of procrastination, Conflict can be ended by scheduling firm times for work and rest, ensuring enough of each. In *The Now Habit*, Neil Fiore recommends creating an "unschedule" that prioritizes rest over work. When your brain is sure that you'll be receiving all of the relaxation and enjoyment you need, and that you only have a certain amount of time to get things done, it's easier to focus on doing productive work.

In the case of the competing heater and air conditioner, the situation can only exist as long as you maintain the conflicting temperatures on the thermostats. Change the Reference Levels and you resolve the Conflict.

In the case of squabbling children (or vice presidents), you can change the situation by ensuring that each combatant gets roughly the same toy, gets no toy at all, or changes their measure of success from "getting mine" to "working together."

Change the situation that creates the Reference Levels each party is using to measure success, and you'll eliminate the Conflict.

REFERENCE LINK: **personalmba.com/conflict/**

Pattern Matching

Your memory is a monster; you forget—it doesn't. It simply files things away. It keeps things for you, or hides things from you—and summons them to your recall with a will of its own. You think you have a memory; but it has you!

—JOHN IRVING, NOVELIST AND ACADEMY AWARD–WINNING SCREENWRITER

Long before you knew what gravity was, you knew that a ball would move toward the ground if you released it. The first few times you let go of a ball, it would always fall to the ground. It didn't take many such experiences for you to learn that any object you released would fall. Gravity is a name for something your brain learned by itself.

One of the most interesting things about the brain is its ability to learn and recognize patterns. Think of Pavlov's famous dogs: ring a bell, and they'll start to salivate. Pavlov taught them a pattern: every time the bell rings, food is on the way. It didn't take long for the dogs to learn the pattern, so they began to respond even before the food appeared.

Our brains are natural *Pattern Matching* machines. The brain is busy trying to find patterns in what we perceive, then associating new patterns with other patterns that are stored in memory. This Pattern Matching process happens without conscious effort. By paying attention to the world around you, your brain is collecting new patterns and adding them to memory.

Humans learn patterns primarily via experimentation. If a small child wants to be held by its mother, it doesn't take long to try several different approaches and learn which response produces the desired result: "If I cry,

Mom is going to pick me up and hold me." From then on, the child will rely on the pattern whenever it desires the result.

You can think of your memory as the database of patterns you've learned via past experience. Patterns get stored in our long-term memory, waiting to be used to determine responses to new or uncommon situations. Recall is optimized for speed, not accuracy—the brain stores information contextually, which helps you recall related patterns when you need them. That's why the best way to find a set of lost keys is to mentally walk through all of the places you've been—the context makes it easier to recall the information.

The more accurate patterns you've learned, the more options you have when solving new problems. Pattern Matching is one of the primary reasons experienced people tend to make better decisions than inexperienced people—they've learned more accurate patterns via their experience. Having a larger mental database to draw from is what gives experts their expertise.

Pattern Matching is one of the foundational capabilities of our mind and how it works. The more accurate patterns you have stored in your memory, the better you can respond to whatever life throws at you.

REFERENCE LINK: **personalmba.com/pattern-matching/**

Mental Simulation

I saw the angel in the marble and carved until I set him free.

—MICHELANGELO, SCULPTOR AND ARTIST

Quick: imagine jumping into the middle of an active volcano. Is it a good idea?

Answering this question took you only a few fractions of a second, even though you've never jumped into a volcano or seen anyone who has. What you've done is quite extraordinary: How is it possible to know the answer to a question you've never considered before?

Mental Simulation is our mind's ability to imagine taking a specific action, then simulate the probable result before acting. Our minds try to predict what will happen in the future based on what's happening around us and what actions we're considering. Anticipating the results of our actions is a significant advantage: it enhances our ability to solve novel problems.

Mental Simulation relies on our memory—the database of patterns we've learned via perception and experience. When you imagined jumping into a volcano, your brain couldn't find any personal experiences, but it did find relevant **Associations**: lava is hot, hot things burn, burns are painful and dangerous, painful and dangerous things are bad. This set of Associations is used to simulate the probable result in the blink of an eye, resulting in a snap judgment: VERY BAD IDEA.

Mental Simulation is powerful and versatile—it can be used to test even the most arbitrary actions without risk. Given any goal or scenario, Mental Simulation is what your brain uses to connect point A to point B, where point A is where you are now and point B is what you're imagining. The only limitation on what you can simulate is your imagination.

For example, how would you go about visiting Antarctica? It's a random question, but when you hold the **End Result** in mind for a few seconds, your brain starts connecting the dots, based on the patterns you've learned. "I could call a travel agent . . . Cruises go to Antarctica all the time . . . I'd have to fly to Argentina . . . I'd have to buy a warm coat," etc. All of this thinking just happens, without much effort on your part—it's what your brain is designed to do.

Mental Simulation only works if you supply a "point B," even if the action or goal is arbitrary—you can simulate the path to even the most unrealistic and absurd destination you can imagine. Think of using a vehicle GPS system—the system can give you accurate directions, but it won't work unless you enter a destination. That destination can be your best friend's house or someplace random, like Albuquerque, New Mexico. Either way, unless you supply a **Goal**, the system can't operate. The same rule applies to Mental Simulation—no destination, no simulation.

Mental Simulation is particularly powerful if you learn how to apply it on demand, which we'll explore in detail when we discuss **Thought Experiments**.

REFERENCE LINK: **personalmba.com/mental-simulation/**

Interpretation and Reinterpretation

We don't see things as they are. We see things as we are.

—ANAÏS NIN, AUTHOR AND DIARIST

Have you ever received an email from someone that made you very angry, only to find out later that you misunderstood the tone or intent of the message? Your mind reached a conclusion that wasn't true based on what you thought you perceived, only to discover there was a different way of interpreting the message that also made sense.

Our minds are always simulating different courses of action, but sometimes there's not enough information to ensure that a perceived pattern is accurate. Since you're not omniscient, your mind never has complete data, so it fills in missing pieces by interpreting what you sense via the patterns you have stored in memory. In the absence of information to the contrary, you'll jump to conclusions by relying on the interpretation your mind creates.

This capacity to fill in the blanks even happens on the physiological level. In our field of vision we have two complete blind spots—the points where our optic nerves connect to our eyes. We literally cannot see in those spots, but our brains take in all of the surrounding information and fill in the blanks. As a result, we appear to have a solid field of vision, even though it's an illusion created by our brain's ability to interpret information.

The human brain relies on prior patterns and information to make **Interpretations** in the absence of information. Think of the spam folder in your email account—it uses a collection of previous spam messages to estimate the probability that any new incoming message is also spam. The messages don't self-identify as spam, but the computer's spam filter can spot them anyway, using information from past emails as a guide.

Your brain does the same thing every time you decide you like someone right after meeting them—your brain is relying on patterns you've learned via past experiences with other people to make a snap judgment.

These snap Interpretations can also be altered—a process called **Reinterpretation**. Think of meeting an attractive person who becomes quiet and aloof whenever you're around. At first glance, their behavior may signal to you that they're shy or don't like you very much. If one of your friends tells you that they're interested in you, however, your Interpretation of that person's past behavior can change in an instant.

Reinterpretation is possible because your memory is impermanent. Our memories aren't like computer disks—every time we recall a memory, it doesn't resave to the same location in the same state. Every time we recall something, the memory is saved in a different location, with a twist: the new memory will *include any alterations we've made to it.*

It's possible to change your beliefs and **Mental Simulations** by recalling and Reinterpreting past events. Mental Simulation and Interpretation rely on patterns stored in memory. If you want to change the results of your brain's simulations, the best approach is to alter the mental database of information those simulations are based on. Reinterpretation is how you change the database.

In *Re-Create Your Life*, Morty Lefkoe teaches a process that can be used to Reinterpret past events in a simple and useful way:

1. Identify the undesirable pattern.

2. Name the underlying belief.

3. Identify the source of the belief in memory, including as much sensory detail as possible.

4. Describe possible alternate Interpretations of the memory.

5. Realize that your original belief is an Interpretation, not reality.

6. Choose to reject the original belief as "false."

7. Choose to accept your Reinterpretation as "true."

Here's an example of how I used Lefkoe's process: One possible way of Interpreting my brand-management career at P&G is that I was a miserable failure—I was on the **Management** fast track, and I couldn't "cut it," so I "washed out." For a while, I believed that was true, but that belief didn't serve me very well. When I tried to explore alternate paths, my mind predicted that my "failure" would extend to my new projects as well. As long as my mind relied on this Interpretation to simulate the future, I was stuck in a self-defeating cycle.

There's another way of Interpreting my previous career at P&G: My experience taught me a lot about how large corporations work, and I learned more about what I'm good at, what I don't enjoy doing, and how I want to invest my time. Working at P&G helped me discover a path that didn't work for me, so I stopped following that path and started experimenting with other approaches that better fit my strengths and desires until I found a new career option that worked for me—a major victory and a huge life improvement.

Which Interpretation is "true"? Both are valid Interpretations. My mind wasn't malfunctioning when it created the first Interpretation, but that Interpretation didn't serve me very well. Reinterpreting the situation and accepting the second version as "true" was much more useful—without it, you probably wouldn't be reading this book.

Reinterpret your past and you'll enhance your ability to make great things happen in the present.

REFERENCE LINK: **personalmba.com/interpretation/**

Motivation

BUT I DON'T WANNA!!!
—TWO-YEAR-OLD CHILDREN EVERYWHERE

Motivation is something that you probably think about all the time, using phrases like "I'm feeling motivated to get this done" or "I'm not feeling very motivated to do this right now." Since so many of us rely on the term to explain our daily experience, it's worthwhile to understand what we're talking about.

Motivation is an emotional state that links the parts of our brain that feel with the parts that are responsible for action. Going back to the **Onion Brain** as a basic model, Motivation is the link between the midbrain (which perceives the world) and the hindbrain (which sends signals to our body to take action). In most cases, Motivation is automatic—our mind perceives a difference between the way things are and the way we want them to be, and the body acts to eliminate the difference.

You can break down the experience of Motivation into two basic desires: moving *toward* things that are desirable and moving *away* from things that aren't. Things that fulfill our **Core Human Drives** appear desirable, so we experience an impulse to move toward them. Things that appear dangerous, scary, or threatening are undesirable, so we experience an impulse to move away from them.

In general, "moving away" takes priority over "moving toward." The reason comes back to **Caveman Syndrome**—running away from a lion takes priority over cooking lunch.

Let's say you have an exciting opportunity to start a new business. A feeling of excitement may cause you to move toward that opportunity. At the same time, if the opportunity requires you to leave a high-paying job, which feels risky, you may be compelled to move away from the very same opportunity, resulting in **Conflict**. As long as the risk outweighs the excitement, you'll hesitate, even if there's very little chance you'll ever be in danger if you take the leap. This safety mechanism in our minds developed for very good reasons, but today, most of the decisions we make don't have life-and-death consequences.

Motivation is an emotion—*not* a logical, rational activity. Just because your forebrain *thinks* you should be motivated to do something does not mean you'll become motivated to do that thing. (If only it were that easy, right?) Very often, **Mental Simulations**, patterns, Conflicts, and **Interpretations** hidden in the midbrain can get in the way of making progress toward what we want to accomplish. As long as there are "move away from" signals being sent, you'll have a hard time feeling motivated to move toward what you want.

In the same vein, you can't "motivate" other people by yelling at them to work faster—all the drill-sergeant approach accomplishes is making them want to move away from you. They may comply with you temporarily if they perceive some threat to themselves in noncompliance, but you can bet that they'll move away from working with you at the first available opportunity.

Eliminate the inner conflicts that compel you to move away from potential threats and you'll find yourself experiencing a feeling of Motivation to move toward what you want.

REFERENCE LINK: **personalmba.com/motivation/**

Inhibition

Inhibition is the ability to stop: to delay our response until we are
adequately prepared to make it.

—MICHAEL J. GELB, AUTHOR OF *HOW TO THINK LIKE LEONARDO DA VINCI*

Believe it or not, most of your daily actions require very little conscious
thought.

Most of the time, our bodies and minds are on autopilot—our minds sense
the world around us, compare our *Environment* and actions against internal *Reference Levels*, and act in accordance with our perceptions, desires, and values.
Think about driving a car: with practice, your body does everything necessary
to keep the car on the road, without requiring much conscious thought.

Every once in a while, however, it pays to ignore the autopilot and do
something different. If you stumble across a bear in the woods, the last
thing you want to do is run, even though that's what your instincts may be
telling you to do. If you run, the bear is likely to decide you look like lunch
and chase you down.

Instead of running, it's more effective to stand your ground and make
yourself appear as big and loud and threatening as you can. Appearing to
be a threat requires you to inhibit your natural response, but it'll cause the
bear to see *you* as a threat and decide to leave you alone.

Inhibition is the ability to temporarily override our natural inclinations.
If you've ever put up with one of your siblings (or colleagues) acting immature, obnoxious, or annoying, Inhibition prevented you from doing
something you would have regretted later.

Willpower is the fuel of Inhibition. As we discussed in the section on
the *Onion Brain*, the forebrain's job is ambiguity resolution, decision making,
and Inhibition. Whenever we inhibit our natural responses to our Environment, willpower is at work. Our midbrain and hindbrain are the autopilot, and the forebrain is the override. In that sense, "free will" is a bit
misleading—"free won't" is a more accurate description.

REFERENCE LINK: **personalmba.com/inhibition/**

Status Signals

The People's Theatre, what nonsense! Call it the Aristocrat's Theatre
and the people will come.

—JULES RENARD, NINETEENTH-CENTURY FRENCH AUTHOR

Every minute of every day, a nontrivial part of your brain has been devoted
to keeping track of how you measure up against the rest of the world.
Without very much effort, you could make a list of things like:

▶ Who is more attractive than you.

▶ Who is stronger than you.

▶ Who is wealthier than you.

▶ Who is more influential than you.

▶ Who is more powerful than you.

▶ Who is more famous than you.

▶ Who is better than you are in some specific area of skill (regardless of whether or not you're skilled in that area at all)

Humans are social creatures—we're built to survive and thrive in
groups. Group behavior confers many advantages when it comes to ensuring survival in an often hostile **Environment**, but it also introduces intragroup
competition for scarce resources.

The individuals who prosper within the group tend to be the ones who
most successfully compete on obvious reproductive survival dimensions
(like beauty, wealth, strength, coalition-building, or group influence) *and*
those who innovate by inventing a new dimension to compete on. That's
why humans have direct incentives to explore, create, and build skill in
millions upon millions of different areas: being "the best" in something is
a straightforward way to increase **Social Status**.

Relative status is often tricky to calculate precisely, so we rely on **Status
Signals**: tangible indicators of some intangible quality that increases a person's Social Status or group affiliation. Rare or expensive items, awards,
honors, victory in recognized competition, and verifiable public acclaim
are all examples of Status Signals.

Status concerns permeate human desires and actions. Have you ever dreamt of being a movie star? Performer or musician? Professional athlete? Astronaut? CEO? Politician or world leader? Celebrity? Those are all occupations that carry significant Social Status, and the status is a huge part of the compensation for the otherwise extreme demands and sacrifices required to break into, compete in, and maintain position in those fields.

Ever wanted to buy a Bentley, Lamborghini, Ferrari, or Tesla Model S? A private jet or your own yacht? A private island? That's status-motivated cognition: all of these things, aside from their utility, signal wealth.

Ever wanted to win a Nobel Prize, be *Time* magazine's Person of the Year, win an Oscar, or be awarded some prestigious medal of honor? These sorts of awards signal importance, skill, or influence.

Ever felt envy when someone accomplishes something impressive, purchases something cool, or receives some sort of difficult-to-attract attention? The benefit in question doesn't harm or diminish you in any way, but their good fortune does change your perceived relative status, even if the tangible benefit is minimal.

This sort of pattern of thought and behavior operates at all levels. A substantial amount of our cognitive resources are devoted to tracking our current status and changes in our status relative to others. Likewise, many things that factor into our emotions and behavior boil down to a single question: "Will this improve my Social Status in some meaningful way?"

A Rolex doesn't tell time any better than a Timex, but that's not the point: it's an obvious signal of wealth. In the same way, an Olympic gold medal is poor compensation on a currency-per-hour basis for the years of intense training it takes to win. Not only that, does it really matter, in the grand scheme of things, who was able to run a little faster or play a game a little better than the second-best competitor? Again, that's not the point: An Olympic gold medal is a recognized symbol of victory in worldwide competition. It's not about the value of the materials or the value of the skill. It's about the status conferred to the winner.

Status seeking is a part of human nature and can be harnessed for good or ill. Learning to recognize status-motivated behavior—in yourself and in other people—will help you understand why people tend to act in certain predictable ways, help you avoid common pitfalls, and improve your ability make wise decisions.

REFERENCE LINK: **personalmba.com/status-signals/**

Status Malfunction

Human beings, who are almost unique in having the ability to learn from the experience of others, are also remarkable for their apparent disinclination to do so.

—DOUGLAS ADAMS, HUMORIST AND AUTHOR
OF THE HITCHHIKER'S GUIDE SERIES

Competition for status is often extreme. The greater the potential perceived status increase, the higher the risk of serious error or *Malinvestment*.

I call this tendency *Status Malfunction*: the more attractive an option looks in terms of status, the more likely it is to have significant drawbacks or pitfalls (given extreme competition for that status), and the more likely you are to ignore or undervalue those drawbacks and pursue that option anyway.

Let's go back to the Olympic medal example. Everyone pays attention to the gold medalists and ignores the fact that most Olympic hopefuls struggle to pay their day-to-day living expenses. Maintaining an intense training schedule is often not compatible with running a business or holding down a full-time job, and sponsorship opportunities are limited.[4]

To the victors go the spoils, both in terms of status and financial opportunities like sponsorships: for the rest of the field, the price of being ready for competition is monetary hardship and an uncertain future.

I happen to know several performers who grace Broadway stages. The benefits of that path are easy to see: if you're cast in a leading role, you literally have your name in lights, perform in front of tens of thousands, and have the opportunity to build a legion of adoring fans. The drawbacks are often underappreciated by novices: the vast majority of auditions will lead to rejections, every project is speculative, pursuing one opportunity might remove you from consideration for others, and the demands of the work make it challenging to support a family.

If you land a role, you'll find producers have most of the power because there are other actors willing to take your place: their **Next Best Alternative** is always better than yours, which reduces your negotiating power. Even in the best cases and at the highest levels, shows have limited runs: no matter how well you perform, you'll be unemployed and looking for a new gig in a few months. It's a glamorous life, but it's also a difficult one.

The same dynamic exists for performers of all kinds: there are more people willing to do the work than there are positions to fill. It's a winner-take-all market, and there are only a few temporary winners at any given time.

That's not to say that you should never compete for high-status roles: for the winners, the benefits can be quite substantial. Understanding Status Malfunction helps you take a mental and emotional step back from the **Mystique** of status, examine your options and potential opportunities with a clear mind, and understand the day-to-day realities of what you're getting yourself into before you commit.

Status Malfunction is also a way to identify opportunities that other people overlook. As I mentioned in the section on the **Mercenary Rule**, businesses like trash disposal, plumbing, and oil extraction aren't high status, but they can be quite lucrative. Many fortunes have been built by entrepreneurs and business owners willing to do high-quality work in low-status markets.

There are millions of ways to get better results in important areas of life if you're willing to ignore alluring distractions and focus on doing what works.

REFERENCE LINK: **personalmba.com/status-malfunction/**

Loss Aversion

Our doubts are traitors, and make us lose the good we oft might win,
by fearing to attempt.

—WILLIAM SHAKESPEARE, *MEASURE FOR MEASURE*

A few years ago, my wife, Kelsey, decided to withdraw some funds from an investment account. When the brokerage deposited the money into her bank account, they deposited an additional $10,000 by mistake.

It shouldn't have been a big deal—it was a simple mistake. On an emotional level, however, Kelsey felt like she was "losing" the extra money, even though it wasn't hers at all.

Loss Aversion is the idea that people hate to lose things more than they like to gain them. There are very few relationships that psychology is able to quantify, but this is one of them: people respond twice as strongly to potential loss as they do to the opportunity of an equivalent gain. If you look at your investment portfolio and notice that it's increased by 100 percent, you'll feel pretty good. If you notice that your portfolio went down 100 percent, you'll feel *horrible*.

Loss Aversion explains why threats usually take precedence over opportunities when it comes to **Motivation**. The threat of loss used to require immediate attention, because losses were costly—even life threatening. Dying or losing a loved one to a predator, sickness, exposure, or starvation is universally a horrible experience, so we're built to do everything in our power to prevent that from happening. The potential losses we face now are rarely as serious, but our minds still give them automatic priority.

Loss Aversion also explains why uncertainty appears risky. Depending on the study you look at, anywhere between 80 and 90 percent of adults think it would be great to own their own business and work for themselves. If that's true, why don't more people start businesses? Loss Aversion keeps them from acting: the threat of losing a steady (and somewhat predictable) job commands more **Attention** than the opportunity to create a new, self-sustaining business. Starting a business involves the specter of potential loss, which prevents people from getting started in the first place.

Loss Aversion is particularly pronounced in recessions and depressions. Losing a job, a home, or a significant percentage of your retirement fund isn't life threatening, but it feels horrible all the same. As a result, people tend to become more conservative, avoiding risks that could make things worse. Yet some of those risks—like starting a new business—may present a major opportunity to make things better.

The best way to overcome Loss Aversion is to use **Reinterpretation** to consider the risk of loss as "no big deal." Casinos are in the business of overcoming Loss Aversion every single day—in a sense, the ostentatious buildings on the Las Vegas Strip are enormous monuments to human stupidity. How do casinos encourage people to play games in which they're *mathematically certain* to lose money?

Casinos win by abstracting the loss. Instead of having players gamble with currency, which is perceived as valuable, the casino converts currency into chips or value on debit cards, which don't *feel* as valuable. As the player loses this "fake" money over time, the casino will provide "rewards" like free drinks, T-shirts, room upgrades, or other benefits to alleviate any remaining sense of loss. As a result, losing becomes "no big deal," so players continue to play—and continue to lose money night after night.

Loss Aversion is why **Risk Reversal** is so important if you're presenting an offer to a potential customer. People hate to lose, which makes them feel stupid and taken advantage of. As a result, they'll go to great lengths to ensure that they don't lose, and the best way to ensure that they don't make a stupid decision is to not buy your offer in the first place. If you're in the business of making sales, that's a big problem. Eliminate this perception of risk by offering a money-back guarantee or similar offer of Risk Reversal and people will feel the decision is less risky, resulting in more sales.

REFERENCE LINK: **personalmba.com/loss-aversion/**

Threat Lockdown

How little can be done under the spirit of fear.

—FLORENCE NIGHTINGALE, PIONEER OF PROFESSIONAL NURSING

You're fast asleep when something goes bump in the night. Almost immediately, you're alert—your heart rate increases, your pupils dilate to take in more light and detail, and stress hormones like adrenaline and cortisol flood your bloodstream. Your mind identifies the likely source of the noise, escape routes, and potential defensive weapons. In the blink of an eye, you're ready to defend yourself against the threat, whatever it might be.

When your mind perceives a potential threat—real or imaginary—your body prepares to respond. This automatic physiological response is designed to help you do one of three things to eliminate the threat: fight, flee, or freeze. As long as you're in "protection mode," it's difficult to do anything other than fixate on the threat. Until you search the house, there's no way you'll be able to go back to sleep—your body will only come out of protective mode after you're sure there's no threat to face.

The subconscious choice to fight, flee, or freeze is dependent on your brain's automatic **Mental Simulation** of the situation. If your brain predicts you can win if you fight, you'll fight. If your brain predicts you can "win" by getting away, you'll flee. If your brain predicts you can't get away, you'll freeze in the hope that the threat will pass you by. Freezing makes your brain go into **Threat Lockdown**—protection mode—which makes it difficult to do anything other than fixate on the threat.

Threat Lockdown is a constructive response designed to help you defend yourself, but like many ancient instincts, it often malfunctions in our modern environment. The threats you face are far less acute today, but they are often chronic.

In the olden days, when the threat was a predator or an angry tribal chief, the lockdown response was constructive, since it focused our energy on staying alive and/or part of the tribe. Even though the thoughts that run through our heads on a daily basis have little in common with those of our ancient ancestors, the hardware those thoughts are running on— our brains—is still the same and is on the lookout for very old threats in a very new environment. As a result, we eat too much and exercise too little, and the instinctive behaviors of fighting, freezing, or running away aren't very constructive when dealing with an angry boss or an overdue mortgage payment.

Periodic turmoil in the stock market is an excellent example of Threat Lockdown in action. The stock market crash in late 2008 sparked a flurry of panic and hand-wringing, even among people who were in no danger of losing their homes or jobs. The mere *possibility* of bad things happening grinds businesses to a halt at the very time increased productivity is needed to keep the firm in good shape. Instead of focusing on doing good work, employees spend most of their time and energy worrying about what the future holds and gossiping about who's next on the chopping block, decreasing the overall amount of value created and increasing the likelihood that the firm's future will get worse.

Threat Lockdown can become a vicious cycle. If you're ever in the unfortunate situation of having to lay off workers, it's best to make cuts fast and all at once, then reassure remaining employees that no more cuts will be made. Rumors of layoffs or workers wondering "if I'll be next" is a recipe for Threat Lockdown.

If you're experiencing Threat Lockdown, *don't try to repress the threat signal.* Many studies have shown that active repression doesn't make a perception go away—instead, it makes the signals stronger. Think of what a small child does when they want to get your attention, but you ignore them—they'll increase the commotion they make until they're sure you've noticed them. Your brain does the same thing—repression only makes the threat signals stronger. Sending a mental "message received, safe to proceed" signal to your brain is a simple and effective way to make yourself stop fixating on the issue so you can consider appropriate responses.

The key to dealing with Threat Lockdown is to convince your mind that the threat no longer exists. You can do that in one of two ways: (1) you can convince your mind there was never any threat, or (2) you can convince your mind the threat has passed. Convincing your mind there was never a threat is the equivalent of searching your house in the dark at midnight—the search proves that no threat exists, so it's safe to leave protective mode. Convincing your mind that the threat has passed does the same thing—the threat is gone and can no longer harm you, so it's safe to carry on.

Sometimes it's difficult to defuse Threat Lockdown, particularly if you've been in it for a long time. Because protective mode is physiological, it's often best to use physiological means to calm yourself down. Exercise, sleep, and meditation can help calm your mind by metabolizing or counteracting the stress hormones that have been flooding your body. When you're feeling overwhelmed, going for a quick run or lifting weights can do wonders for your state of mind.

Notice the threat signal, then do what you can to prove to your mind the threat no longer exists, and you'll break yourself out of Threat Lockdown.

REFERENCE LINK: **personalmba.com/threat-lockdown/**

Cognitive Scope Limitation

One death is a tragedy. A million deaths is a statistic.

—KURT TUCHOLSKY, SATIRIST

If you ever have a chance to walk through the middle of Times Square in New York City during tourist season, you'll soon realize that, to most of the people moving toward you, *you are not a person*. You are an object—an obstacle standing between where they are and where they want to go. As a result, they'll run you over with impunity.

No matter how intelligent a person is, there's an upper bound on the amount of information a single mind can process, store, and respond to. Above that limit, information may be considered in abstract terms, but it's not treated as urgent and important as information related to that individual's personal experience or concerns.

"Dunbar's number" is a theoretical cognitive limit on the number of stable social relationships humans can maintain at one time. According to Robin Dunbar, a British anthropologist, humans have the cognitive capacity to keep track of somewhere around 150 close personal connections. Beyond this limited circle, we start treating people less like individuals and more like objects, and groups of people beyond this limit are likely to splinter off into subgroups over time.

If you've ever wondered why you don't write letters to your elementary school classmates, Dunbar's number is a decent hypothesis—you're too busy maintaining your ties to people who are in your immediate social circle.

There's some controversy regarding the actual quantity of connections where **Cognitive Scope Limitation** kicks in (the Bernard-Killworth median, a competing estimate, is 231), but there's little doubt that such a limit exists. When a disaster strikes somewhere around the world that affects millions of people, we may feel bad, but we don't feel a *million times* what we would feel if that disaster affected a close friend or family member. The more remote the connection, the less such an impact affects us individually.

The tourists in Times Square aren't evil—they're just overwhelmed. More than 380,000 people pass through Times Square every day,[5] and our minds aren't capable of handling that much information at once.

On an abstract level, these people still realize that you're a human being, but there's so much going on in the area that it's difficult for them to treat you like one. The mind gets overwhelmed, so it starts simplifying reality to compensate.

The same thing happens to executives of large companies. Rationally, they may be aware that they're responsible for hundreds of thousands of employees and millions of shareholders, but no matter how intelligent they are, their brains aren't capable of processing the magnitude of that reality. As a result, executives can hurt a lot of people without even realizing it. The CEO of a large company may not care if thousands of frontline workers are laid off—at the highest levels, it's easy to think of "human resources" as numbers on a spreadsheet, not individual human beings.

Whenever you see an executive making a boneheaded decision like dumping toxic waste into a river millions of people drink from, or downsizing thousands of jobs while handing out millions of dollars in bonuses, it's probably *not* because they're rotten to the core. As scary as it sounds, it's probably because they *haven't thought too much about it*—the scope and scale of what they're managing is too complex to handle, so their mind processes the decision abstractly instead of viscerally.

Personalizing an issue is a way to hack this universal limitation. In the absence of brain upgrades, it's not possible to expand the scope of information our minds are capable of processing. In order to get around this limitation, it's useful to personalize decisions and issues by imagining they affect someone close to us.

In the case of the boneheaded executive, they'd feel very different about their decision if their *mother's* water was polluted, or their *child's* job was eliminated. Instead of considering the issue abstractly, personalizing it makes it easier to feel the effects of the decision viscerally, which makes it easier to make better decisions.

In *Green to Gold*, Daniel C. Esty and Andrew S. Winston describe several ways of making it easier to internalize the results of large decisions. The "newspaper rule" and the "grandchild rule" are effective ways of personalizing the results of your decisions. The "newspaper rule" is a simulation of the following: assume your decision was publicized on the front page of tomorrow's *New York Times*, and your parents and/or significant other read it. What would they think? Imagining the personal consequences of your decisions in this way is a much more accurate way to evaluate the impact of short-term decisions.

The "grandchild rule" is a way of evaluating decisions with long-term consequences. Imagine that, thirty or forty years from now, your grandchild gives you feedback on the results of your decision. Will they laud you for your wisdom or reprimand you for your stupidity?

Personalize the results of your decisions and actions, and you'll be far less likely to run afoul of Cognitive Scope Limitation.

REFERENCE LINK: personalmba.com/cognitive-scope-limitation/

Association

In general, we are least aware of what our minds do best.

—MARVIN MINSKY, COGNITIVE SCIENTIST AND
ARTIFICIAL INTELLIGENCE RESEARCHER

Who cares which golf clubs Tiger Woods uses? Who cares which shoes Michael Jordan wears? Who cares which purse Taylor Swift is carrying?

Your mind cares. Remember, your brain is taking in information all the time and is using it to create patterns that describe how the world works. Rationally, these things may not matter—you probably know that using the same golf clubs Tiger Woods uses won't magically correct your atrocious slice. When it comes time to buy golf clubs, however, your mind will be drawn to the clubs that make you feel good, and more likely than not, you'll find the clubs Tiger uses quite appealing.

The human mind stores information contextually, including cues like *Environment* and *Correlation*. Because the brain is a *Pattern Matching* machine, it's trying to figure out what's associated with what. As a result, your mind forms *Associations*—even between things that aren't logically connected.

For decades, the Coca-Cola Company has been associating Coke with a single emotion: happiness. Do a quick search for Coke commercials on the internet: you won't find any images of layoffs or funerals. What you will find is a litany of happy moments: Adrien Brody cruising in his car, parades of whimsical creatures celebrating as a bottle of Coke exits a vending machine, and Charlie Brown winning the race for a runaway Coke-bottle balloon in the Macy's Thanksgiving parade. Even holidays aren't immune: the company invented the modern image of Santa Claus, who just so happened to be holding a bottle of Coca-Cola.

It's possible to influence behavior by using associative cues, even Associations that make no logical sense. Coca-Cola's advertisements don't convince soda consumers that Coke is better in some functional respect (*"Now with 37 percent more sugar!"*), but they do make people feel good whenever they think about Coke. When a customer is standing in the supermarket deciding which soft drink to buy, those feelings make a big difference in each customer's final choice.

Consider beer commercials, which usually feature attractive women and confident men. Your rational mind knows that drinking a certain type of beer won't make you more attractive or confident, but Correlation is powerful—your brain will make the Association anyway. As a result, beer ads influence behavior, even though no one takes the images they contain seriously.

Presenting your prospects with positive Associations can influence how they think about what you offer. Celebrity endorsements work because they tie into strong Associations people already have with the endorsers, associations that rub off on the product or service being endorsed. Everyone knows James Bond is a fictional character, but when Daniel Craig is featured wearing a tuxedo in a watch advertisement, the "sophisticated international spy" Association is transferred to the timepiece.

Cultivate the right Associations, and potential customers will want what you have even more.

REFERENCE LINK: personalmba.com/association/

Absence Blindness

Facts do not cease to exist because they are ignored.

—ALDOUS HUXLEY, ESSAYIST AND AUTHOR OF *BRAVE NEW WORLD*

Here's a curious fact about human beings: we have a hard time realizing that something isn't there.

When I worked in P&G's Home Care division, one of my first projects was testing the viability of a **Product** that *prevented things from getting dirty*.

You still had to clean, but it took more time for things to get dirty again, so the Product saved the user significant time and effort.

Once the Product went into testing, however, it was apparent that the idea wasn't feasible. The Product worked, but users didn't realize it—they had a hard time believing the Product did something, since they couldn't see anything happening. After the test phase was complete, the project was canceled.

Absence Blindness is a cognitive bias that prevents us from identifying what we can't observe. Our perceptual faculties evolved to detect objects that are present in the **Environment**. It's far more difficult for people to notice or identify what's missing.

Examples of Absence Blindness are everywhere. Here's a common example: great **Management** is boring—and often unrewarding. The hallmark of an effective manager is anticipating likely issues and resolving them in advance, *before* they become a problem. Some of the best managers in the world exhibit a quiet sort of competence: there's little drama, and everything gets done on time and under budget.

The problem is, no one sees all of the bad things that the great manager *prevents*. Less skilled managers are more likely to be rewarded, since everyone can see them "making things happen" and "moving heaven and earth" to resolve issues—issues they may have created themselves via poor Management.

Make a note to remind yourself to reward the low-drama manager who gets things done with little fuss. It may not seem like their job is particularly difficult, but you'll miss them when they're gone.

Absence Blindness makes prevention grossly underappreciated. In the case of the Product I was working on, people had a hard time believing that something they couldn't see working was effective. If you're trying to sell the absence or prevention of something, you're fighting an uphill battle, even if your Product is great. Always state benefits in positive, immediate, concrete, and specific terms by focusing on things the user can experience.

Absence Blindness also makes it uncomfortable for people to "do nothing" when something bad happens, *even if doing nothing is the best course of action*. Often, the best course of action is to choose not to act, but that can be difficult for humans to accept.

The economic "boom and bust" cycle most markets experience is partially a consequence of Absence Blindness. According to Ludwig von Mises in *Human Action*, economic "bubbles" are created when a government tries to encourage an economy to grow by reducing interest rates, making it easier to borrow money. By making access to **Capital** easier, this policy leads investors to speculate, paying abnormally high prices for assets they'd otherwise avoid, like tulips,[6] internet companies with no revenue,[7] and risky mortgage-backed securities.[8] Eventually, the bubble "pops" when investors realize that the assets they've been speculating on aren't worth what they paid, leading to a sudden crash in the price of the overvalued asset.

Because of **Loss Aversion**, people start freaking out and start clamoring for an immediate solution to the collapsing market. More often than not, the "solution" is to reduce interest rates even more to encourage the economy to start growing again—a self-reinforcing **Feedback Loop** that does nothing but exacerbate the issue by creating the conditions necessary for an even larger bubble to form down the road.

To fix the issue, the best course of action is to stop manipulating interest rates, which caused the issue in the first place. Absence Blindness makes doing nothing psychologically uncomfortable—after all, "we can't sit here and do nothing while the world burns!" As a result, people usually prefer the government to act, even if the action the government takes makes things *worse* in the long run.

Experience makes it easier to avoid Absence Blindness. Experience is valuable primarily because the expert has a larger mental database of related patterns and thus a higher chance of noticing an absence. By noticing violations of expected patterns, experienced people are more likely to get an "odd feeling" that things "aren't quite right," which is often enough warning to find an issue before it becomes serious.

In *Sources of Power: How People Make Decisions*, researcher Gary Klein tells the story of a team of firefighters putting out a fire on the first floor of a house. When water was sprayed at the base of the fire, the fire didn't respond as expected—it didn't diminish at all. The chief noticed and ordered everyone out—something just didn't feel right. A few minutes later, the house collapsed—the fire had started in the basement, destroying the foundation. If the team had stayed inside, they would have died. That's the power and benefit of experience.

The only reliable way I've found to overcome Absence Blindness is by using **Checklists**. By thinking in advance what you want something to look like and translating that *Visualization* into visible reminders you can refer to while making decisions, Checklists can help you remember to look for the absence of qualities in the moment. (We'll discuss creating Checklists in great detail in chapter 11.)

REFERENCE LINK: **personalmba.com/absence-blindness/**

Contrast

The world is full of obvious things which nobody by any chance ever observes.

—SIR ARTHUR CONAN DOYLE, AUTHOR OF THE SHERLOCK HOLMES BOOKS

If you walk into a department store to buy a business suit, you're likely to notice a few expensive options. The store will very rarely sell these suits—that's not their purpose. Compared to a $3,000 suit, a $400 suit doesn't seem expensive—even if the same suit could be purchased at another store for $200.

The same principle applies to the order in which products are presented by the salesperson. After choosing a suit, you'll be directed to shirts, shoes, and accessories. Compared to $400 for a suit, what's another $100 on shoes? $80 for a belt? $60 for a few shirts? $50 for a few ties? $40 for a set of cuff links? Compared to the suit, the accessories seem inexpensive, so why not?

Here's what Jordan Smart, one of my clients, reported:

> I went shopping last year on Black Friday, looking to get some slightly more formal clothes . . . I went out with the intent of buying a set of shirts and two blazers. I thought for a while on buying ties to go with it, and decided that the one or two I had in my closet already would suffice.
>
> I went shopping at two stores. In the first, I picked out a set of shirts, and as I was leaving, the salesman asked if I needed ties to go with them. I politely told him no, and privately congratulated myself on sticking to my resolution.

At the second store, I tried on a few blazers and decided to purchase them. Again, the salesman asked if I needed ties to go with my blazers. At that point, I very clearly remember thinking about the price of the blazers and thinking to myself, "Well, I'm spending this much money anyway," and proceeded to buy a set of ties.

I didn't think anything of it until I learned about contrast. Looking back at the receipt, I realized I'd spent more on the ties than I had spent on the blazers.

Our perceptions are influenced by information gathered from the surrounding environment. Is $10,000 a lot of money? It depends on your circumstances. If you have $10 in your bank account, $10,000 is an enormous sum. If you have $100 million, it's a rounding error.

Our perceptual faculties are optimized to notice **Contrast**, not to compare what we perceive with things that aren't there, which is the root of **Absence Blindness**. Everything we notice and every decision we make is based on information gathered from the surrounding **Environment**. That's why camouflage works—it reduces the contrast between an object and its surrounding Environment, which makes it harder to notice.

Contrast is often used to influence buying decisions. In the business world, Contrast is often used as pricing camouflage. In the case of the $60 shirt, it may be possible to buy the exact same shirt at another retailer for $40, but the less expensive shirt *isn't present in the store where the comparison is taking place*. What *is* present is the $400 suit, which makes the $60 shirt look like a bargain.

Compared with a $2,000 computer, a $300 extended warranty appears inexpensive, even though it increases the total purchase price by 15 percent. Compared with a $30,000 vehicle, spending $1,000 for leather seats feels like a bargain. Compared with buying a $400,000 house, spending $20,000 to remodel the kitchen feels like no big deal.

Framing is a way to control the perception of Contrast. For example, I often use the phrase "$149,000 less than a top-tier business program" when marketing my business courses. Compared with buying a book, my course looks expensive; compared with the cost of an MBA program, it's a bargain.

Take advantage of Contrast when presenting your offer, and you'll increase the odds that your potential customers will view your offer favorably.

REFERENCE LINK: **personalmba.com/contrast/**

Scarcity

The way to love anything is to realize it might be lost.
—G. K. CHESTERTON, ESSAYIST

Because of **Conservation of Energy**, people have a natural tendency to decide to "do things later" unless there's a compelling reason to act immediately. As a businessperson, "later" is a big issue, because "later" turns into "never" if the customer forgets about you. How can you encourage your customers to act immediately?

Scarcity encourages people to make decisions quickly. Scarcity is one of the things that overcomes our tendency to conserve—if you want something that's scarce, you can't afford to wait without the risk of losing what you want. **Loss Aversion** ensures that this possibility feels bad enough to prompt us to take action *now*.

As a result, adding a Scarcity element to your offer is a great way to encourage people to take action. Scarcity makes people understand that they'll lose something valuable if they wait, making it more likely they'll choose to act if they desire what is being offered.

The more scarce the value, the more intense the desire. In 1996, the Tickle Me Elmo doll was the hot toy of the Christmas season. Elmo was already a popular television character, but limited quantities of the toy drove parents into a buying frenzy. Otherwise rational people started mobbing retailers when new stock became available and were willing to spend hundreds (sometimes thousands) of dollars for a toy that cost $28.99 retail.

Here are a few ways you can add an element of Scarcity to your offer:

1. *Limited quantities*—inform prospects that you're offering a limited number of units for sale.

2. *Price increases*—inform prospects that the price will go up in the near future.

3. *Price decreases*—inform prospects that a current discount will end in the near future.

4. *Deadlines*—inform prospects that the offer is only good for a limited period of time.

Scarcity that appears artificial can backfire. For example, putting an artificial limit on sales of ebooks, downloadable software, or electronic music files makes no sense—everyone knows electronic files can be **Duplicated** at close to zero cost, so the Scarcity feels manipulative, which makes people want to buy from you less. Price increases with deadlines, on the other hand, tend to work well—raising the price after a certain number of orders or a certain amount of time is a reasonable policy and is less likely to come across to the customer as unreasonable or manipulative.

Add an element of Scarcity to your offer and you'll encourage people to buy now instead of "later."

REFERENCE LINK: **personalmba.com/scarcity/**

Novelty

Why is it that when I ask for a pair of hands, a brain comes attached?

—HENRY FORD, FOUNDER OF THE FORD MOTOR COMPANY
AND ASSEMBLY-LINE PIONEER

At the height of World War II, Norman Mackworth took Royal Air Force radar operators away from their jobs for a special mission: staring at a clock for two hours at a time.

Mackworth was a psychologist who specialized in studies of vigilance—the ability to maintain high levels of **Attention** on a single object for long periods of time. Radar operators were natural test subjects—their job consisted of looking at blips on a radar screen in a dark room for hours on end.

Most of the time, very little on the radar screen changed. When something abnormal appeared on the screen, however, it could be an emergency: inbound enemy airplanes on a bombing mission. The radar operator's job was to be alert enough to notice anomalies immediately, but the task was difficult—boredom often led to mistakes that cost lives.

To simulate this challenging environment, Mackworth created the "Mackworth Clock," a device designed to test how well people pay attention over time. The "clock" featured a second hand that worked like the one on a normal clock, with a twist—it would randomly skip a second, ticking two notches instead of one. The test subject's job was to press a button every time they noticed the skip.

Here's what Mackworth found: after ten minutes of staring at the clock, the quality of the subject's attention went down—*way* down. The maximum period of sustained attention even highly motivated operators (who were given substantial bonuses for performance) were able to sustain was thirty minutes—any longer and they'd zone out.

Novelty—the presence of new sensory data—is critical if you want to attract and maintain attention over a long period of time. One of the reasons people can focus on playing games or surfing the internet for hours at a time is novelty—every new viral video, blog post, social-media update, and news report reengages our ability to pay attention.

In *Brain Rules*, John Medina shares how he's able to keep the attention of his students in classes that last more than an hour: he plans his class in modules that last no more than ten minutes. Each module starts with a *Hook*—an interesting story or anecdote, followed by a brief explanation of the key concept. Following this format ensures that his audience retains more information and doesn't zone out. (That's the primary reason this book is organized in short sections that take less than ten minutes to read.)

Even the most remarkable object of attention gets boring over time. Human attention requires novelty to sustain itself. Continue to offer something new, and people will pay attention to what you have to offer.

REFERENCE LINK: **personalmba.com/novelty/**

7

WORKING WITH YOURSELF

To think is easy. To act is difficult. To act as one thinks is the most difficult.

—JOHANN WOLFGANG VON GOETHE, POET, DRAMATIST, AND POLYMATH

Your body and mind are the tools you use to get things done. Learning how to work with yourself in an efficient and effective way makes accomplishing what you set out to achieve easier and more enjoyable.

In today's busy business environment, it's easy to get stressed about everything that needs to be done. Learning how to work in an efficient and effective way can be the difference between a fulfilling career and a draining one.

In this chapter, we'll discuss how to decide what to do, set and achieve goals, track your daily tasks, overcome resistance, and get more productive work done without burning out.

REFERENCE LINK: **personalmba.com/working-with-yourself/**

Akrasia

Some of the greatest battles will be fought within the silent chambers of your own soul.

—EZRA TAFT BENSON, FORMER US SECRETARY OF AGRICULTURE

In one of his most famous stand-up comedy routines, Jerry Seinfeld describes his difficulties going to bed:

I never get enough sleep. I stay up late at night, 'cause I'm Night Guy . . . "What about getting up after five hours' sleep?" Oh, that's Morning Guy's problem . . . that's not my problem, I'm Night Guy . . . Night Guy always screws Morning Guy. There's nothing Morning Guy can do.

The routine is funny because it's so familiar. All of us have had the experience of knowing or feeling that we should do something or that an action would be in our best interest . . . but we don't do it. The term for that experience is **Akrasia** (pronounced "ah-KRAH-see-ah").

Akrasia and procrastination are related, but they're not the same thing. Procrastination occurs when you've decided to complete a task but you keep putting it off until later without deciding to do it later. If you have "answer email" on your to-do list, but you browse the internet for hours without answering any email, that's procrastination.

Akrasia is a deeper issue: it's a general feeling that you "should" do something, without necessarily deciding to do it. The "should" feeling doesn't lead to decision or action, even if the action seems to be in your best interest. Most people experience Akrasia when considering changing **Habits** they no longer want ("I should quit smoking"), taking a new action ("I should donate to that nonprofit"), or contemplating an uncomfortable topic ("I should look into life insurance and talk to a lawyer to write a will"). The "should" feeling sticks around, but never leads to action, generating intense frustration.

Akrasia is a very old problem: discussions about the source of Akrasia go back to Socrates, Plato, and Aristotle. The term comes from the Greek ακρασία, which means "lacking command (over oneself)." Socrates and Plato believed that Akrasia was a moral defect, while Aristotle argued that it stems from a mistaken opinion about what a person "should" do. Even though philosophers have been debating the topic for centuries, they haven't discovered a cure.

Akrasia is one of the most widespread and persistent barriers to getting things done. In order to spend your time making progress, instead of fighting both sides in a battle of wills, it's useful to have a strategy for recognizing and combating Akrasia when you see it.

In my experience, Akrasia has four general parts: a task, a desire, a "should," and an emotional experience of resistance. Within this framework, there can be many potential sources of resistance:

▶ You can't define what you want.

▶ You believe the task will bring you closer to something you don't want.

▶ You can't figure out how you're going to get from where you are right now to where you want to be.

▶ You idealize the desired **End Result** to the point that your mind estimates a low probability of achievement, resulting in **Loss Aversion**.

▶ The "should" was established by someone else, not you, prompting **Persuasion Resistance**.

▶ A competing action in the current **Environment** promises immediate gratification, while the reward of the task in question will come much later. (Psychologists call this "hyperbolic discounting.")

▶ The benefits of the action are abstract and distant, while other possible actions will provide concrete and immediate benefits. (Psychologists call this "construal level theory" or "near/far" thinking.)

Akratic situations can take many forms: eating a cookie versus "becoming healthier" by sticking to a diet. Browsing the web versus exercising. Staying in a bad relationship versus moving on. Dreaming about a new business idea versus testing it. Whenever you "should" do something, but resist doing it, you're experiencing Akrasia.

Akrasia is a slippery problem, and there's no easy, universal solution. That said, there are many strategies and techniques that are useful in preventing and resolving akratic situations. We'll discuss them in this chapter.

REFERENCE LINK: personalmba.com/akrasia/

Monoidealism

Just do it.

—NIKE BRAND SLOGAN

When we're trying to "be productive," what are we trying to do?

Ideally, you want to focus the full powers of your energy and **Attention** on a single subject at a time.

Monoidealism is the state of focusing your energy and attention on only one thing, without conflicts. Monoidealism is often called a "flow" state, a term coined by psychologist Mihaly Csikszentmihalyi. This is the state of human attention at its most productive: clear, focused Attention and effort directed at one (and only one) subject for an extended period of time.

My friend P. J. Eby is a former computer programmer who specializes in helping people use their minds in a more productive way. Here's how he defines Monoidealism:

> When somebody says "just do it," they are trying to communicate that you should not do anything else. It might better be phrased as, "Do it, without thinking about anything, not even about what you're doing. In fact, don't even do it, just watch yourself doing it, but don't actually try to do anything."
>
> Properly, "monoidealism" is simply the state in which you have exactly one thing on your mind, with no conflicts. It's a condition that results in one naturally taking action in relation to the thought, rather than a technique in and of itself . . . The usefulness of a particular [productivity] technique for a particular individual will largely depend on whether it addresses their particular stumbling blocks in achieving a monoideal state.

When you're "just doing it," you're in "flow"—a Monoideal state. There are no distractions, no interruptions, no self-judgments, no doubts. When your mind is in 100 percent "do" mode, you get a lot done.

So how do you get yourself into a Monoideal state?

First, eliminate potential distractions and interruptions. Depending on the level of cognitive activity required to complete your work, it'll take ten to thirty minutes before your mind becomes absorbed in what you're doing.

Phone calls, coworkers "dropping by to pick your brain," and other unanticipated demands on your Attention will break your Monoideal state, so priority number one is ensuring that you don't get distracted. I often use earplugs or play instrumental music to eliminate background noise, and disconnect the phone when I don't want to be interrupted.

Turning off my internet connection while I'm writing also makes it much easier for me to maintain a Monoideal state.[1] Otherwise, I'm way too likely to browse the web when the going gets tough. Using similar *Guiding Structure* techniques is a good way to prevent your Attention from straying.

Second, eliminate inner *Conflicts*. Sometimes it's difficult to get started because you're experiencing a Conflict between two *Perceptual Control* systems in your mind. Eliminating these Conflicts before you start working helps you achieve a Monoideal state faster than you would've otherwise. If you feel resistance to getting started, it's useful to spend some time and energy exploring that Conflict more deeply *before* you keep working.

While writing this book, I experienced several periods of frustrating resistance. Instead of trying to ignore the resistance or push through it, exploring that resistance using *Mental Simulation* and *Reinterpretation* helped me uncover a hidden Conflict: I wasn't happy with how my work was turning out, and doing more of what wasn't working would be a waste. Spending some time revising the structure of the book resolved that Conflict, simultaneously making the book better and eliminating the source of the resistance.

Third, kick-start the attention-focusing process by doing a "dash." Since it can take ten to thirty minutes to get into the zone, setting aside ten to thirty minutes for a quick burst of focused work can make it much easier to get into the zone quickly. If you're not productive by the time the dash is over, you have permission to stop and do something else. That's rarely the case: once you get started, it's easy to keep going.

One technique I often use is called the Pomodoro Technique,[2] named by its creator, Francesco Cirillo, after those funny little kitchen timers shaped like a tomato (*pomodoro* in Italian). Here's how the technique works: Set a kitchen timer for twenty-five minutes. Your job is to focus on a single task for the entire duration—if you get stuck, just keep focusing until the timer goes off. After the twenty-five-minute work period is over, you can take a five-minute break, bringing the total duration to half an hour—a block of time any of us can fit into our schedule here and there.

What I love about the Pomodoro Technique is that it accomplishes two goals at once: it makes it easy to get started, and it gives you permission to ignore distractions. Even if you're not excited about what you need to do, saying to yourself "it's only twenty-five minutes" is a great way to overcome the initial resistance to getting started. The Pomodoro Technique is also a good excuse to ignore distractions: if the phone rings, reminding yourself that "a Pomodoro is indivisible" is an effective way to give yourself permission to ignore it, maintaining your Monoideal state.

If you eliminate distractions and Conflicts before you start your dash, you'll transition into a Monoideal state a few minutes into the work period.

Meditation is a form of Monoidealism "resistance training." Simple meditations like focusing on your breathing, then bringing your focus back to your breath if and when your Attention strays is a way to practice the skills used to maintain your Attention in the face of distractions. As little as ten minutes of simple meditation every day can improve your ability to focus.

REFERENCE LINK: personalmba.com/monoidealism/

Cognitive Switching Penalty

Rule your mind or it will rule you.

—HORACE, FIRST-CENTURY-BC ROMAN POET

Every project and every task that you decide to work on takes a certain amount of **Attention**, energy, and focus to get done. The question is: How can you accomplish everything you need to do in an efficient and effective way?

Many people rely on multitasking: trying to do more than one thing at the same time. While people assume this makes them more efficient, Monoidealism and multitasking are complete opposites. Neurologically, it's impossible for your brain to multitask. When you're trying to do more than one thing at a time, you're not parallel processing—you're rapidly switching your Attention from one thing to another. While you're paying attention to Task A, you're ignoring Task B until you switch back to it.

As a result, productive multitasking is a myth. According to several recent neurological studies,[3] the more tasks you try to pay attention to at any given time, the more your performance at all of them suffers. That's why it's never a good idea to talk on a mobile phone while driving—by trying to focus on two things at once, you decrease your reaction times to the same level as someone who's driving while intoxicated.[4]

Every time you switch the focus of your Attention from one subject to another, you incur the **Cognitive Switching Penalty**. In order to take action, your brain has to "load" the context of what you're doing into working memory. If you switch the focus of your Attention, you're forcing your brain to spend time and effort thrashing, loading and reloading contexts over and over again. That's why it's possible to spend an entire day multitasking, get nothing done, and feel exhausted at the end—you've burned all of your energy context-switching instead of making progress.

The Cognitive Switching Penalty is a **Friction** cost: the less you switch, the lower the cost. That's why Monoidealism is so efficient—by focusing your Attention on only one thing at a time, you're allowing your brain to load the context into working memory *once*, which means you can focus your energy on accomplishing the task at hand.

To avoid unproductive context switching, a batching strategy is best. Eliminating distractions can help prevent unnecessary interruptions, but it's entirely possible to waste energy thrashing even if you have the entire day free. The best approach to avoid unnecessary cognitive switching is to group similar tasks together.

For example, I find it difficult to make progress on creative tasks (like writing or shooting training videos) between client calls. Instead of attempting to juggle both responsibilities at the same time, I batch them together. I usually focus on writing for a few uninterrupted hours in the morning, then batch my calls and meetings in the afternoon. As a result, I can focus on both responsibilities with my full Attention.

I use a similar strategy when doing chores, updating financial reports, or running errands: I'll dedicate a block of uninterrupted hours to finishing those tasks. As a result, I accomplish everything I need to do in very little time.

Paul Graham, a venture capitalist, programmer, and essayist, calls this batching strategy "Maker's Schedule/Manager's Schedule."[5] If you're trying to create something, the worst thing you can do is to try to fit creative tasks in between administrative tasks—context switching will kill your productivity. The "Maker's Schedule" consists of large blocks of uninterrupted time; the "Manager's Schedule" is broken up into many small chunks for meetings. Both schedules serve different purposes—don't try to combine them if your goal is to get useful work done.

A simple rule of thumb I use to plan my day is the 3-10-20 method: in one day, I have the capacity to finish three major tasks and ten minor tasks. A major task is any activity that requires more than twenty minutes of focused concentration; all other tasks are minor. If a major task is interrupted, restarting it counts as a new task.

For example, one day's major tasks might be writing a proposal, consulting with a client, and reviewing a book. Between these major tasks, I might make a short phone call, process and answer incoming emails, read a few articles, do the dishes, and clean my office.

As long as I set aside large chunks of time for my major tasks, I can accomplish everything in a single day. If I'm interrupted in the middle of a major task, that task won't be done that day, or another major task will have to slip. Keeping in mind that there's a limit to what I can accomplish in a single day makes it easier to keep **Stress and Recovery** in balance.

Eliminate unproductive context switching and you'll get more done with less effort.

REFERENCE LINK: **personalmba.com/cognitive-switching-penalty/**

Four Methods of Completion

I am only one, but I am one. I cannot do everything, but I can do something. And because I cannot do everything, I will not refuse to do the something I can do. What I can do, I should do. And what I should do, by the grace of God, I will do.

—EDWARD EVERETT HALE, NINETEENTH-CENTURY
UNITARIAN CLERGYMAN AND WRITER

There are only four ways to "do" something: completion, deletion, delegation, and deferment.

Completion—doing the task—is the option most people think about. If you keep a to-do list, you're probably assuming that those tasks are all your responsibility to get done. That's not quite true—completion is best for important tasks that only you can do particularly well. Everything else can be handled in another manner.

Deletion—eliminating the task—is effective for anything that's unimportant or unnecessary. If something on your task list is unimportant, don't feel bad about eliminating it. If it's not worth doing, it's not worth doing well or quickly—don't hesitate to get rid of it.

Delegation—assigning the task to someone else—is effective for anything another person can do 80 percent as well as you can. In order to delegate, you must have someone to delegate *to*. Employees, contractors, or outsourcers can all help you get more things done by completing tasks on your behalf.

If you don't have anyone to delegate routine tasks to, working with a virtual-assistant company can be quite useful. For less than $100 a month, you can enlist a team of professionals to help you get things done. If you have little experience with delegation, it's an experiment worth trying.

Deferment—putting the task off until later—is effective for tasks that aren't critical or time dependent. Don't feel bad about putting some things off; the best way to bog yourself down is to try to handle too many things at the same time. Saving noncritical tasks for later is a good way to keep your attention and energy focused on what's most important.

In *Getting Things Done*, David Allen recommends keeping a "someday/maybe" list of things you'd like to do someday but that aren't that important right now. Creativity researcher Scott Belsky recommends a similar approach in *Making Ideas Happen*: create a "back burner" list of tasks you want to get to eventually but that aren't a priority right now. Reviewing this list every few weeks is enough to identify tasks you're ready to promote to active projects.

Use all four options when processing your to-do list and you'll get more done than you ever thought possible.

REFERENCE LINK: **personalmba.com/4-methods-of-completion/**

Most Important Tasks

You've got to think about the big things while you're doing small things, so that all the small things go in the right direction.

—ALVIN TOFFLER, TECHNOLOGY RESEARCHER AND FUTURIST

Not all tasks are created equal—some are more important than others.

You only have so much time and energy to get things done each day. Of all of the things that are on your to-do list right now, some of them are important, and some of them aren't important. If you want to make the most of your limited time and energy, it pays to focus on completing the tasks that will make the biggest difference first, before spending your time and energy on anything else.

A **Most Important Task** (MIT) is a critical task that will create the most important results you're looking to achieve. Everything on your plate is not equal in importance or value, so don't treat everything on your task list the same. By taking a few minutes to identify a few tasks as important, you'll make it easier to focus on doing them first.

At the beginning of every day, create a list of two or three MITs, then focus on getting them done as fast as possible. Keep this list separate from your general to-do list or task-tracking system. I use a three-by-five index card or David Seah's "Emergent Task Planner,"[6] a free downloadable PDF that makes it easy to plan your day.

When creating your list of MITs, it's useful to ask a **Self-Elicitation** question: "What are the two or three most important things that I need to do today? What are the things that—if I got them done today—would make a huge difference?" Write only those tasks on your MIT list, then try to get them done first thing in the morning.

Combining this technique with **Parkinson's Law** by setting an artificial deadline is very effective. If you set a goal to have all of your MITs done by 10:00 a.m., you'll be amazed at how fast you can complete the day's Most Important Tasks.

Having a list of two or three MITs helps you maintain a **Monoideal** state by giving you permission to say no to interruptions that aren't as important. If you're working on your MITs and someone calls you, it's easier to ignore the call or tell the caller, "I'm working under deadline—I'll get back to you later." By definition, everything that's not an MIT is not as important, so it's easier to say no to noncritical interruptions.

Achieve your MITs first thing in the morning and then you'll have the rest of the day to handle anything else that comes up.

REFERENCE LINK: **personalmba.com/most-important-tasks/**

Goals

Setting a vague goal is like walking into a restaurant and saying, "I'm hungry. I want some food." You'll stay hungry until you order something.

—STEVE PAVLINA, AUTHOR OF
PERSONAL DEVELOPMENT FOR SMART PEOPLE

Much has been made in business literature about the importance of having **Goals**. Well-formed Goals accomplish two things: they help you visualize what you want and make you excited about achieving it. A Goal is a statement that clarifies *precisely* what you want to achieve, which makes it easy for your brain to use **Mental Simulation** to **Visualize** what achieving that Goal looks like. If the **End Result** you're looking for is vague or fuzzy, you're making it difficult for your mind's automatic planning systems to find ways to get what you want. Well-formed Goals also play a key role in **Motivation**— the better defined your Goal, the easier it is to get excited about doing the things required to get what you want.

Fuzzy Goals like "I want to climb a mountain" aren't very helpful because they don't give your brain any material to work with. Which mountain? Where? When? Why? Without answers to these questions, you probably won't do anything at all.

Well-formed Goals pass the "Everest Test." Useful Goals look like this: "I want to climb to the summit of Mount Everest before my fortieth birthday and take a panoramic picture to frame on my wall as a trophy." This Goal is easy for your brain to simulate—Mount Everest is in Nepal, so you'll have to arrange travel. You'll also have to improve your climbing skills, find a guide, buy equipment, purchase a suitable camera, etc. Once you make a conscious **Decision** to achieve the Goal, your mind starts finding ways to get it done.

Goals are most useful if they're **Framed** in a Positive, Immediate, Concrete, Specific (PICS) format:

▶ *Positive* refers to Motivation—your Goal should be something you move *toward*, not away from. Goals like "I don't want to be fat anymore" are a recipe for **Threat Lockdown**—you're reinforcing the negative instead of using **Reinterpretation** to change your mind's prediction to get excited about improving. For best results, eliminate **Conflicts** first, then move toward what you want to achieve.

▶ *Immediate* refers to time scale: your Goals should be things that you decide to make progress on now, not "someday" or "eventually." If you don't want to commit to working on a particular Goal now, put it on your someday/maybe list and focus on something else.

▶ *Concrete* means you're able to see the results in the real world. Goals are achievements—you should know when you've accomplished what you set out to achieve. Setting Goals like "I want to be happy" won't work because they're not concrete—how would you know when you're done? When you reach the top of Mount Everest, you've achieved something in the real world—that's concrete.

▶ *Specific* means you're able to define what, when, and where you're going to achieve your Goal. Climbing Mount Everest before a certain date in the near future is specific, which makes it easy for your mind to plan how you'll go about accomplishing it.

For best effect, your Goals should be under your control. Goals like "I want to lose twenty pounds" are soul crushing because they're *not* under your control—losing weight is a result, not an effort. If your weight randomly moves up a few pounds on a given day, it's easy to feel defeated, even though you had no choice in the matter. For best results, make your Goals actions that are within your **Locus of Control**, like doing a minimum of thirty minutes of exercise every day and controlling the number of calories you consume.

To track your Goals, any simple notebook or reference system will do. I capture all of my Goals in a simple text file, which I print out and keep in my to-do notebook. Whenever I'm thinking about what I need to do,

I have my list of Goals handy for easy reference, which makes it easy to determine which tasks are most important.

It's okay to change your Goals. Sometimes we think we want something, only to find out later that we don't want it so much anymore. Don't feel bad about that—it's called learning. If you find yourself working toward a Goal you no longer feel good about, work on something else.

REFERENCE LINK: personalmba.com/goals/

States of Being

I may not have gone where I intended to go, but I think I have ended up where I intended to be.

—DOUGLAS ADAMS, HUMORIST AND AUTHOR OF THE
HITCHHIKER'S GUIDE SERIES

One of the common mistakes I see people make when setting **Goals** is assuming everything is an achievement.

Think of statements like "I want to be happy," "I want to feel excited," and "I want to be successful." How do you know if you've achieved what you set out to do? Can you achieve happiness, excitement, or success if your day-to-day experience changes?

A **State of Being** is a quality of your present experience. Emotional experiences aren't achievements because they fluctuate over time—you can be happy right now and upset an hour from now. "Being happy" is not an achievement—it's a quality of your present experience.

States of Being are *decision criteria*, not Goals. It's okay to want to "be happy" or "be successful," but treating these desires as Goals is a recipe for frustration. Instead of treating these states as achievements, it's far better to think of them as decision criteria—ways of understanding whether or not your actions are leading to your desired results.

States of Being help you answer the question "Is what I'm doing right now working?" For example, if you want to feel happy, you may notice that spending time with close friends and family members creates the experience you want, so making time for those things is obviously important. If you want to feel calm, but your job is making you stressed out all the time, it's clear the situation needs to change—what you're doing isn't working.

Breaking down complex States of Being into smaller parts is even more useful. Instead of using complex States of Being like "success" and "happiness" as decision criteria, it's far better to decide what these states mean to you. For example, I define "being successful" as "working on things I enjoy with people I like," "feeling free to choose what I work on," and "having enough money to live without financial stress." Together, these States of Being provide a much more useful definition of success—if that's how I'm experiencing the world, I'm "successful."

The same goes for "happiness." Instead of being a single State of Being, "being happy" is a combination of "having fun," "spending time with people I enjoy," "feeling calm," and "feeling free." When those States of Being describe my experience in the present moment, I'm "happy." Breaking down "happiness" into its component parts helps me ensure I'm doing things that will help me experience it more fully and more often.

Decide what States of Being you want to experience, and you'll have a powerful set of decision criteria you can use to evaluate the results of your actions in an entirely new and useful way.

REFERENCE LINK: personalmba.com/states-of-being/

Habits

We are what we repeatedly do. Excellence, then, is not an act, but a habit.

—WILL DURANT, HISTORIAN, PARAPHRASING ARISTOTLE, ANCIENT GREEK PHILOSOPHER

What about things you want to do on a daily basis, like exercising? Is that a *Goal* or a *State of Being*? Trick question: they don't belong in either category.

Habits are regular actions that support us. Exercising, brushing your teeth, taking vitamins, following a particular diet, or keeping in touch with friends and family are all examples of Habits that keep us happy and healthy. Due to the power of *Accumulation*, small Habits can add up to huge results over time.

Most Habits take on one of four common forms: things you want to *start* doing, things you want to *stop* doing, things you want to do *more*, and things you want to do *less*. For example, you might want to start exercising regularly, stop watching television, drink more water, or spend less money.

Habits usually require a certain amount of willpower to create. Therefore it's best to use the techniques we discussed in the section on **Guiding Structure** to make it easier to instill the Habits you want to adopt. If you want to go to the gym first thing in the morning, packing your gym bag and laying out workout clothing the night before makes it easier to go, since you've structured your environment to require less effort to act.

Habits are easier to install if you look for *triggers* that signal when it's time to act. For example, if you want to take vitamins, it's easier to remember to take them if you use another habitual action as a trigger for the action. Instead of relying on your mind to remember to take your vitamins in the middle of the day, you can use brushing your teeth in the morning or evening as a reminder.

For best results, focus on installing *one* Habit at a time. If you try to install too many Habits at once, you probably won't succeed at adopting any of them for long. Focus on installing one Habit until taking action feels automatic, then move on to the next.

REFERENCE LINK: **personalmba.com/habits/**

Priming

Many an object is not seen, though it falls within the range of our visual ray, because it does not come within the range of our intellectual ray, i.e., we are not looking for it. So, in the largest sense, we find only the world we look for.

—HENRY DAVID THOREAU

Have you ever been interested in a particular type of car, only to start noticing them *everywhere*? I have—it feels like someone suddenly unloaded hundreds of the exact make and model of the car you like all over the highway.

That's not true, of course—the universe isn't playing tricks on you. The cars were always there; you just never noticed them before. Before you decided you were interested in a particular type of car, your brain filtered those cars out of your awareness.

Once you became interested, however, your brain stopped filtering out that information, and you started noticing every time that particular car drove by. In a sense, you programmed your brain to notice certain things about the *Environment* around you. All it took was becoming interested in something specific to remove the filter.

Priming is a method of programming your brain to alert you when particular information is present in your Environment. One of the fascinating ramifications of our brain's *Pattern Matching* function is that we're always scanning the Environment for useful information. If you tell your mind specifically what you want to find, it will alert you whenever your senses notice it.

Priming is a way to influence your brain's Pattern Matching capabilities. By taking a few moments to decide what you're interested in and what you're looking for, you can program your mind to alert you when it notices something relevant. Some people call this "intuition"—Priming is how you put your intuition to productive use.

Here's an example of how I use Priming: in the book *10 Days to Faster Reading*, Abby Marks-Beale recommends a technique I refer to as "purpose setting": taking a few minutes before you start reading to figure out (1) why you want to read this material and (2) what kind of information you're looking for. Jotting down a few notes before picking up the book reinforces what you're looking to find.

After defining your purpose, you then pick up the book and flip through it quickly, paying particular *Attention* to the table of contents, section headings, and index—condensed sources of information about what the book contains and how the material is structured. Jotting down terms and concepts that appear to be important helps prime your brain to notice them when they appear later.

This process only takes a few minutes, but the impact it has on your reading speed is profound. Once you've primed your mind to notice important concepts, you can work your way through the entire book at lightning speed. As you read, your brain filters out unimportant material and homes in on the material you're interested in learning.

As a result, it's possible to extract most of the useful content in almost any nonfiction book in less than twenty minutes. When I go to a library or bookstore, this technique allows me to read several books in less than an hour. Without using this method, there's no way I could have created the Personal MBA reading list as it exists today, let alone written this book.

One of the ways people "get lucky" when they're working toward a particular **Goal** is via Priming. One of the reasons Goal setting is useful is because it's an easy way to prime your brain to look for things that will help you get what you want. If your goal is to climb Mount Everest, you're far more likely to notice when tickets to Nepal are 70 percent off while browsing a travel website. If you read the same thing before setting the Goal, you'd probably filter it out—you'd have no reason to pay Attention.

Take some time to prime your brain to notice what's important to you and you'll find it.

REFERENCE LINK: **personalmba.com/priming/**

Decision

> In every moment of every day I must decide what I am going to do the next moment; and no one can make this decision for me, or take my place in this.
>
> —JOSÉ ORTEGA Y GASSET, PHILOSOPHER AND ESSAYIST

A **Decision** is the act of committing to a specific plan of action. The word "decide" comes from the Latin *decidere*, which means "to cut off." When you make a Decision, you're cutting off the other possible avenues that you could explore, leaving only the path you're committing to. If you're not cutting off viable options, you're not making a Decision.

No matter how good your personal productivity system is, it can't make Decisions for you. No matter how sophisticated your task-tracking system is, it will never be able to tell you the best thing to do at any given moment. Constructing a system to make Decisions for you is a pipe dream—all systems can do is help provide information you can use to make *better* Decisions. Making the Decision will always be your responsibility.

No Decision, large or small, is *ever* made with complete information. Since we can't predict the future, we often attribute the feeling of indecisiveness to a lack of information. What's happening is mental thrashing—your forebrain's job is to resolve ambiguities and make Decisions, so your midbrain will continue to send signals until your forebrain does its job. Once a Decision is made—whatever it is—the thrashing stops.

Don't feel you need to have all of the information before you decide—the world is too complicated to make accurate predictions. Retired general Colin Powell famously advocates collecting half of the information available, then making a Decision, even though your information is incomplete. "Don't wait until you have enough facts to be 100 percent sure, because by then it is almost always too late . . . Once [you've acquired 40 to 70 percent of the available information], go with your gut."[7]

If that's a winning strategy for life-and-death battle decisions, it'll work for life's daily Decisions as well. Collect just enough information to make an informed Decision, then make your Decision and move forward.

Failure to make a Decision is itself a Decision. Life doesn't stop if you refuse to choose—the world will keep moving forward, and you may be forced to take action by default. Abdicating responsibility for your Decisions doesn't mean you're not making them—you're just allowing yourself to be a victim of circumstance.

For best results, make your Decisions in a conscious, deliberate way. In my experience, many people have difficulty figuring out what to do because they hesitate to make a Decision—**Loss Aversion** prompts them to leave all of their options open, "just in case." Without a Decision, however, their brain can't use **Mental Simulation** to figure out how to get from where they are now to where they think they want to be, so their minds thrash around unproductively.

Saying to yourself, "I am deciding to do X right now," makes it much easier to proceed. Once a Decision is finally made, your brain's Mental Simulation planning circuits will kick into gear, and you'll start moving again.

If you're having difficulties making a Decision, Steve Pavlina, the author of *Personal Development for Smart People*, recommends using this question as the tiebreaker: "Out of the available options, which experience do I want to have?" If you're having a difficult time making a particular

Decision, it's probably because your brain is having a hard time figuring out which one is best. It's an uncomfortable situation, but what it means is that *it doesn't really matter which one you choose*. If that's true, you can choose the experience you find more interesting.

When Kelsey received an enticing job offer in New York City, we spent weeks torn between staying in Cincinnati and moving to the big city. There were many uncertainties involved with moving: Where would we live? Could we afford it? What about my job? It was enough to give us both a bad case of **Threat Lockdown**.

In the end, we realized there wasn't a clear winner, so it didn't matter which one we chose. Living in New York was an experience we both wanted to have, so we decided to move. Almost immediately, we felt a sense of clarity and relief. Instead of continuing to thrash, making a Decision allowed us to move forward, even in the face of **Uncertainty**.

REFERENCE LINK: **personalmba.com/decision/**

Five-Fold Why

Ask the next question, and the one that follows that, and the one that follows that.

—THEODORE STURGEON, AUTHOR OF *MORE THAN HUMAN*

Very often, we're not aware of *why* we want what we want. Conducting a "root-cause analysis" is a useful way to discover the motivations behind our desires.

The **Five-Fold Why** is a technique to help you discover what you actually want. Instead of taking your desires at face value, examining the root cause of what you want can help you define your core desires.

Applying the Five-Fold Why is easy: whenever you set a **Goal** or objective, ask yourself *why* you want it. If you want to become a millionaire, ask yourself why you want to have $1 million.

Don't try to force an answer—just ask yourself the question in a spirit of curiosity and wait until your mind generates a response on its own. When your mind provides an answer, ask why again. Continue to ask yourself why until you get a "because I want it" response, which indicates you've reached the root cause of your original Goal.

Here's an example of how to apply the Five-Fold Why to the classic Goal "I want to be a millionaire":

1. *Why do I want $1 million?* Because I don't want to be stressed about money.

2. *Why don't you want to be stressed about money?* So I don't feel anxious.

3. *Why don't you want to feel anxious?* So I feel secure.

4. *Why do you want to feel secure?* So I feel free.

5. *Why do you want to feel free?* Because I want to feel free.

The root desire isn't having $1 million—it's feeling free. Is it possible to feel free without having $1 million? Yes—there are many ways to feel free that have nothing to do with money. Taking an alternate approach that addresses the real desire may be more effective than your original Goal.

Discover the root causes behind your Goals and you'll discover new ways to get what you want.

REFERENCE LINK: **personalmba.com/five-fold-why/**

Five-Fold How

> Go as far as you can see; when you get there you'll be able to see farther.

—THOMAS CARLYLE, NINETEENTH-CENTURY ESSAYIST AND HISTORIAN

After applying the **Five-Fold Why**, you'll probably discover that what you want is quite different from what you thought you wanted. Now that you've identified the root cause of your original **Goals**, it's time to figure out how to get what you really want.

The **Five-Fold How** is a way to connect your core desires to physical actions. Let's use the previous example: the core desire is to feel free. How would you go about doing that?

1. Paying off an outstanding debt

2. Reducing your work hours, finding another position, or becoming an entrepreneur

3. Moving to a new city or country

4. Breaking off a restricting personal relationship

Once you find a "how" that looks like a good idea, ask how again. Let's say that quitting your job and starting a business would give you the greatest sense of freedom. How would you go about doing that? Fill in the details, and what was at first a fuzzy idea becomes more and more defined.

Continue asking "how" until you've defined your plan in terms of **Next Actions** (discussed next). The purpose of the Five-Fold How is to create a complete chain of actions from your big idea all the way down to things that you can do *right now*.

Done properly, each action gives you an experience of what you want as you do it. If paying off a debt would make you feel free, connecting the dots in this way enables you to feel more and more free *every time you make a payment*, which makes it much easier to keep going.

Connect your big Goals to small actions you can take now and you'll achieve what you set out to accomplish.

REFERENCE LINK: **personalmba.com/five-fold-how/**

Next Action

If we attend continually and promptly to the little that we can do, we shall ere long be surprised to find how little remains that we cannot do.

—SAMUEL BUTLER, NINETEENTH-CENTURY NOVELIST

Often, what we want to achieve can't be done in a single sitting. Projects are **Goals** that take more than one action to complete, and the larger the project is, the more difficult it is to anticipate all of the actions that must be done.

Climbing Mount Everest is a project—one fraught with complexity and **Uncertainty**. How do you work on a project so large it threatens to overwhelm you?

Simple: focus only on the action you need to take next to move toward your Goal.

The **Next Action** is the next specific, concrete thing you can do right away to move a project forward. You don't have to know everything that must be done to make progress on a project—all you need to know is the very next thing you can do to move the project forward.

David Allen, the author of *Getting Things Done*, coined the term to describe one of the core steps of his "fundamental process":

1. Write down a project or situation that is most on your mind at this moment.

2. Now describe in a single written sentence your intended desired outcome for this problem or situation. What needs to happen to mark this "done"?

3. Next, write down the very next physical action step required to move the situation forward.

4. Put those answers in a system you trust.

According to Allen, these questions help you clarify what "done" and "doing" look like. If you define what "done" looks like, you can focus your attention and energy on doing the things that will get you to "done."

Writing this book was a massive undertaking—it took me years to compile the research and a little over a year to write the text. "Write the book" is not an action—it's a project. There's no way I could've finished the manuscript in one sitting, but it *was* possible to write a small section of the book in less than an hour. After I broke up the book into well-defined sections, it was much easier to make progress, since each individual task was less overwhelming.

To keep yourself from feeling overwhelmed, track your projects and tasks separately. Here's what I do: I always carry around a notebook that contains a three-by-five index card.[8] The card contains a short list of my active projects. The notebook contains my to-do list: the Next Actions that will move my projects forward, which I process using a system called Autofocus, which was created by Mark Forster.[9] The system helps me use my intuition to identify what I can do *right now* to make progress. As long as my projects are tied to my Goals and are aligned with my preferred **States of Being**, it's only a matter of time before I complete them.

Focus on completing the Next Action and you'll complete the entire project.

REFERENCE LINK: **personalmba.com/next-action/**

Externalization

Words are a lens to focus one's mind.

—AYN RAND, PHILOSOPHER AND AUTHOR OF *ATLAS SHRUGGED*
AND *THE FOUNTAINHEAD*

One of the quirks about how your mind works is that it handles information from *outside* your head better than the thoughts that are rattling around *inside* your head.

If you've ever worked with a personal trainer or coach, you know what I mean. When exercising by yourself, it's very easy to listen to the little voice inside your head that says, "This hurts—you should stop," even if you'll get better results by continuing.

When you're working with someone else, the little voice goes away, since there's a person in your **Environment** who's encouraging you to push yourself just a little bit more. As a result, you get a better workout.

Since we respond more to stimuli in our Environment than our own internal thoughts, there's a simple method we can use to improve our productivity—we can convert our internal thoughts into an external form our minds are better equipped to use.

Externalization takes advantage of our perceptual abilities in a very intelligent way. By converting our internal thought processes into an external form, Externalization gives us the ability to reinput information into our own brains via a different channel, which gives us access to additional cognitive resources we can use to process the same information in a different way.

There are two primary ways to Externalize your thoughts: writing and speaking. Writing (or drawing, if you prefer) is the best way to capture ideas, plans, and tasks. Not only does writing give you the ability to store information in a form you can reference later, it gives your mind the opportunity to examine what you know from a different angle. Challenges and issues that seem insurmountable while they're bouncing around in your frontal lobe can often be solved after putting them onto paper.

Capturing your ideas on paper makes them easier to share with others, in addition to archiving your thoughts for later reference and review. As the saying goes, "The palest ink is clearer than the fondest memory." Notebooks and journals, regularly used, are worth their weight in gold.

Speaking—to yourself or to another person—is another effective method of Externalization. Vocal Externalization explains why most of us have had the experience of solving our own problems while talking with a friend or colleague. By the time you're done talking, you're likely to have more insight into your problem—even if your listener didn't say a word.

The key to vocal Externalization is to find an audience who is willing to listen and avoid interrupting you as you talk through an issue. Even talking to yourself or an inanimate object can help: explaining your problem to a rubber duck, teddy bear, action figure, or other anthropomorphic object sitting on your desk can work if you can get over the initial awkwardness. More often than not, "rubber ducking" the problem makes it easier to solve.

However you choose to Externalize your thoughts, don't keep them locked up in your head. Experiment with different approaches to find which method works best for you. To help keep your mind clear during the day, schedule a small amount of dedicated time to Externalize. Early mornings or late evenings work best for this purpose.

However you do it, the more you Externalize, the clearer your thoughts will become, and the faster you'll make progress toward your goals.

REFERENCE LINK: personalmba.com/externalization/

Self-Elicitation

How do I know what I think until I hear what I say?

—E. M. FORSTER, NOVELIST AND SOCIAL ACTIVIST

Externalization is most useful if you use it as a tool to examine your plans, Goals, and actions. Jotting down the events of the day in a diary format is useful for later review, but using a journal or confidant as a problem-solving tool is even more useful.

Self-Elicitation is the practice of asking yourself questions, then answering them. By asking yourself good questions (or working with someone who asks good questions), you can grasp important insights or generate new ideas very quickly.

The *Five-Fold How* and *Five-Fold Why* are specific examples of Self-Elicitation. By asking yourself questions, you're exploring options you didn't consider and *Priming* your brain to notice related information.

In *Self-Directed Behavior,* David L. Watson and Roland G. Tharp explain a very useful self-questioning technique you can use to discover the reasons behind behaviors that don't serve you. The ABC Method (Antecedent, Behavior, Consequences) is a set of questions to ask yourself whenever you notice a behavior you want to change.

By recording answers to the following questions in a journal, logging when specific behaviors occur, and noting the frequency or duration of those behaviors, it's possible to discover patterns in your behavior or thought processes. Once you know the pattern, it's easier to change the behavior.

ANTECEDENT

—*When did it happen?*

—*Whom were you with?*

—*What were you doing?*

—*Where were you?*

—*What were you saying to yourself?*

—*What thoughts were you having?*

—*What feelings were you having?*

BEHAVIOR

—*What were you saying to yourself?*

—*What thoughts did you have?*

—*What feelings were you having?*

—*What actions were you performing?*

CONSEQUENCES

   —What happened as a result?

   —Was it pleasant or unpleasant?

When you don't know where to begin, it's often difficult to know with certainty which questions are important. The solution is simple: ask yourself, "What are the best questions I could ask myself about this situation?" This metaquestion applies in every situation and will help you generate a working list of relevant issues to explore. Once you have a working list of questions, you can follow up with related questions that will help you find answers, like "Who can I ask?" "What could I read?" and "What could I try?"

Asking yourself good questions helps you discover good answers. Make it a *Habit* to ask yourself good questions and you'll be surprised how easy it is to overcome the challenges you face.

    REFERENCE LINK: **personalmba.com/self-elicitation/**

Thought Experiment

> To be able to ask a question clearly is two-thirds of the way to getting it answered.
>
> —JOHN RUSKIN, NINETEENTH-CENTURY ART CRITIC AND SOCIAL THEORIST

As we discussed in the section on *Mental Simulation*, our minds are trying to predict the future. Now it's time to learn how to simulate potential courses of action in an intentional way.

Counterfactual—"what if"—questions allow you to access your brain's simulation capabilities. You can think of *Thought Experiments* as applied imagination—you pose a "what if" or "what would happen if" question to your mind, then sit back and let your brain do what it does best.

Based on the patterns, *Associations*, and *Interpretations* you have stored in memory, your brain will produce what it believes to be the most likely result. All you have to do is suspend judgment, pose the question, let your mind wander, and wait for the answer.

Thought Experiments are one of our most powerful (and underused) capabilities. Instead of waiting for your brain to simulate a potential course of action, a well-constructed Thought Experiment allows you to "force" your brain to run the simulations you want it to run.

Thought Experiments are useful because of their flexibility: you can imagine *anything you want*, even if an actual experiment would be too expensive or risky. The subject of your simulation can be arbitrary; the only limit to the things you can simulate is your imagination. If you want to simulate what would happen if you suddenly quit your job and moved to Tahiti, there's nothing stopping you. You could even simulate what would happen if you lived ten thousand years in the future or set up shop on Jupiter.

Thought Experiments can help you discover hidden opportunities you may have assumed weren't available. While I was working at P&G, I often dreamed of working for myself and developing the Personal MBA full-time, but I always assumed this possibility was "a year or two away." A year later, it was still "a year or two away." Working for myself was a pleasant daydream, but I assumed it wasn't realistic without examining the possibilities.

That changed after I started using Thought Experiments in a more systematic way. While traveling on business in September of 2008, I wrote a question in my notebook: "What would have to be true if I left my job by early November?" I didn't think the question was realistic, but it was ambitious enough to be interesting, so I **Inhibited** my judgment and simulated the question anyway.

When you run a Thought Experiment, you assume the event or end state you're simulating *is already true*. When you supply your mind with an artificial destination, it will start to fill in the blanks between point A and point B. When I ran the simulation on leaving my job, I assumed that it was *definitely going to happen*, then figured out how it would be possible.

As I ran the simulation, other questions presented themselves. How much revenue was coming in from the Personal MBA? How many clients would I need to have? What other projects would I work on, and how much money would I need to bring in to be financially **Sufficient**? As these questions presented themselves, I answered them as best I could.

By the time I finished the Thought Experiment, I had discovered it was possible for me to leave my job at P&G *that day*, instead of "in a year or two." When I returned to work the following Monday, I resigned. My last day of corporate work was four days before my twenty-eighth birthday.

In my experience, time spent examining counterfactuals and potential actions is never wasted. Instead of assuming what you want isn't realistic or possible, Thought Experiments allow you to figure out what it would take to make what you want real. After doing a simulation, you'll always come away with a greater understanding of what it takes to do something or what would need to be true in order to make something work.

REFERENCE LINK: **personalmba.com/thought-experiment/**

Parkinson's Law

> It's called a "Work Breakdown Structure" because the Work remaining will grow until you have a Breakdown, unless you enforce some Structure on it.
>
> —DAVID AKIN, PROFESSOR OF AEROSPACE ENGINEERING,
> UNIVERSITY OF MARYLAND

In 1955, Cyril Northcote Parkinson wrote a humorous essay in the *Economist* based on his experience in the British civil service. In that essay, Parkinson proposed what became his eponymous law: "Work expands so as to fill the time available for its completion."

If something must be done in a year, it'll be done in a year. If something must be done next week, it'll be done next week. If something must be done tomorrow, it'll be done tomorrow. We plan based on how much time we have, and when the deadline approaches, we start to make choices and **Trade-offs** to do what must be done to complete the task by the deadline.

Parkinson's Law should not be considered carte blanche to set unreasonable deadlines. All projects take time; you can't build a skyscraper in a day or a factory in a week. The more complex the project, the more time it takes—up to a point.

Parkinson's Law is best used as a **Thought Experiment** question. What would it look like if you finished the project on a very aggressive time scale? If you had to build a skyscraper in a day, how would you go about doing it? Answer the question the way you would a counterfactual and you'll discover techniques or approaches you can use to get the work done in less time.

Ingvar Kamprad, the founder of IKEA, once said, "If you split your day into ten-minute increments, and you try to waste as few of those ten-minute increments as possible, you'll be amazed at what you can get done." For small tasks, use what I call Ingvar's Rule—assume each task will take no more than ten minutes to complete, then begin. This includes meetings and phone calls: for some reason, the default time period for meetings is an hour, whether you need it or not. Often you can get just as much, if not more, done if you assume that the basic unit of time for a meeting is ten minutes. Ingvar's Rule is a Thought Experiment—what would you do if you only had ten minutes to get something useful done? Figure out what you can accomplish in that period of time, then do it.

REFERENCE LINK: **personalmba.com/parkinsons-law/**

Doomsday Scenario

What looks large from a distance, close up ain't never that big.

—BOB DYLAN, NOBEL PRIZE–WINNING SONGWRITER AND MUSICIAN

If you're in *Threat Lockdown*, it's hard to get anything done—your mind is fixated on the threat, imagining scenes that would fit right into a bad horror movie.

Let's say you're thinking of starting a business, but you lock up with anxiety whenever you think about striking out on your own. You imagine quitting your job, and your mind pictures investing a lot of money building something that doesn't work, going bankrupt, and becoming homeless. You imagine you won't be able to get another job, everyone will hate you, and you'll spend the rest of your days living in a van down by the river.

How do you encourage your brain to stop trying to protect you if it's overreacting?

A *Doomsday Scenario* is a *Thought Experiment* where you assume everything that can go wrong does go wrong. What if you don't complete the project on time? What if your plan doesn't work? What if you lose everything? What if they all laugh at you?

Doomsday Scenarios are pessimistic for a reason—they help you realize that, in most circumstances, you're going to be okay. *Caveman Syndrome* makes our ancient brains overdramatic, so they assume every potential threat is a life-or-death situation. The reason we get so stressed out is that our brains *Interpret* losing resources, diminishing in status, or being rejected as threats to our survival. That may have been true a long time ago, but it's not anymore. Now you can lose money, screw up, or be rejected hundreds of times a day—and live to tell the tale.

When you examine your worst fears, you'll discover that things won't be as bad as you fear. Creating a Doomsday Scenario is the equivalent of giving a small child who is afraid of monsters under their bed a flashlight—by shedding some light on the subject of their fears, they realize there's nothing to be afraid of.

By *Externalizing* and defining your worst fears, you're exposing them as what they are: irrational overreactions. More often than not, you'll discover that you were scared of something that doesn't really matter. Even if something goes wrong, it's not going to be as bad you think. As soon as you realize you're not going to die, you're free to do much more than you once dared to do.

Once you've imagined your Doomsday Scenario, you can start doing things to improve upon the worst case. If you're starting a business, you can begin defining the actual risks and make plans to mitigate them. Instead of being a victim of your fears, you can use them constructively.

Construct your Doomsday Scenario and you can make your overdramatic brain work *with* you instead of against you.

REFERENCE LINK: **personalmba.com/doomsday-scenario/**

Excessive Self-Regard Tendency

I haven't been wrong since 1961, when I thought I made a mistake.

—BOB HUDSON, POLITICIAN (ATTRIBUTED)

Every few months, television viewers around the world cringe while delusional contestants on *American Idol* show the world how horrible they are at singing.

The most fascinating part of this spectacle isn't the epic display of tone deafness—it's the fact that many of the people auditioning *believe they're talented singers.* The contrast is astounding—how could anyone be so horribly wrong about something so obvious?

Excessive Self-Regard Tendency is the natural tendency to overestimate your own abilities, particularly if you have little experience with the matter at hand. Being optimistic about our capabilities has benefits—it increases the probability we'll try something new. That's how novices sometimes accomplish great things—they do them before realizing how risky or difficult their objective was.

Steve Wozniak, who cofounded Apple Computer with Steve Jobs, built the world's first personal computer. Here's what he had to say about the experience: "I never had done any of this stuff before, I never built a computer, I never built a company, I had no idea what I was doing. But I was going to do it, and so I did it." Woz didn't know what he was doing, but he thought he could, so he did.

Our natural confidence also comes with a cost—the potential for harmful self-delusion.

The Excessive Self-Regard Tendency is even more pronounced if you don't know much about the subject at hand. The more incompetent a person is, the *less they realize they're incompetent.* The more a person knows, the better their ability to self-assess their capabilities, and the more likely they are to doubt their capabilities until they have enough experience to know they've mastered the subject.

According to David Dunning and Justin Kruger of Cornell University, Charles Darwin's famous quip "Ignorance more frequently begets confidence than does knowledge" is literally true. They explain the "Dunning-Kruger effect" as follows:

1. Incompetent individuals tend to overestimate their own level of skill.

2. Incompetent individuals fail to recognize genuine skill in others.

3. Incompetent individuals fail to recognize the extremity of their inadequacy.

4. If they can be trained to improve their own skill level, these individuals can recognize and acknowledge their own previous lack of skill.

People who are "unconsciously incompetent" don't know they're incompetent—they know so little about the subject that they can't fully appreciate how little they know. That's why every barber and taxi driver you meet is an expert on the economy and international politics.

Once you learn a bit more about a new subject, you become "consciously incompetent"—you *know you don't know* what you're doing. As a result, most individuals become less confident in their abilities after learning more about a topic—more knowledge makes it easier to fully appreciate the limits of their knowledge and capabilities.

Developing "conscious competence"—the state of knowing what you're doing—takes experience, knowledge, and practice. When you're consciously competent, you regain your confidence: you know the limits of your knowledge and can assess your abilities in an unbiased way.

A certain amount of humility is a valuable self-correcting quality. Overconfidence sometimes produces greatness, but it's a high-risk bet—without guidance, you're far more likely to find yourself in a bad situation. Cultivating a healthy amount of humility can keep you from assuming you know everything there is to know about everything, then painfully discovering otherwise.

The Excessive Self-Regard Tendency is universal (be very wary if your first impulse is to think *you're* immune to it), so it's important to have trusted advisers who aren't afraid to tell you if you're making a mistake. One of the easiest ways to get yourself in trouble via the Excessive Self-Regard Tendency is estimating deadlines—overconfidence is a major cause of the **Planning Fallacy**. When I agreed to write this book, I thought it would take about six months—but I'd never written a book before, so I had no idea. Several of my more experienced friends and advisers counseled that it would probably take a year, and I'm very glad I listened—they were right.

All of us are prone to overestimating our abilities. Padding your team with yes-men is deadly because people who always agree with you can't help you correct for this tendency—people who always support your decisions won't prevent you from making huge mistakes.

Cultivate relationships with people who aren't afraid to tell you when you're making questionable assumptions or going down the wrong path—they're valuable friends indeed.

REFERENCE LINK: personalmba.com/excessive-self-regard-tendency/

Confirmation Bias

> It ain't what you don't know that gets you into trouble. It's what you know for sure that just ain't so.
>
> —MARK TWAIN, GREAT AMERICAN NOVELIST

One of the best ways to figure out whether or not you're right is to look for information that *proves you're wrong.*

Confirmation Bias is the general tendency for people to pay **Attention** to information that supports their conclusions and ignore information that doesn't. No one likes to learn they've made a bad decision, so we tend to filter the information we pay Attention to.

The more strongly held the opinion or belief, the more we ignore sources of information that challenge that position. That's why you won't find many political conservatives reading liberal sources of news, and vice versa—they already know they don't agree, so why bother? This makes both positions more and more extreme, since neither side seeks information that may challenge their convictions.

Paying Attention to disconfirming evidence is difficult—it means looking for reasons you might be wrong, and we usually hate to be wrong. Seeking disconfirming evidence will either show you the error of your ways or provide additional evidence for why your position is correct—as long as you suspend judgment long enough to learn from the experience.

"Flat Earthers" are a dramatic example of this risk: there is a significant community of people who, for various reasons, believe the Earth is flat, not a spherical body. In the 2018 documentary *Behind the Curve*, filmmakers record two true believers as they conduct an experiment intended to prove the Earth is flat. In an unsurprising turn of events, the results indicate that the Earth is indeed round. Their response?

> Wow, that's kind of a problem . . . We obviously were not willing to accept [the results], and so we started looking for ways to disprove it . . .[10]

Looking for disconfirming evidence is uncomfortable, but it's essential if you want to improve your understanding of how the world works. Paying

Attention to information that conflicts with your current assumptions or beliefs can pay dividends and prevent major errors. If there's no amount of evidence capable of changing your mind, there's nothing tethering your beliefs to reality.

REFERENCE LINK: personalmba.com/confirmation-bias/

Hindsight Bias

Finish each day and be done with it. You have done what you could. Some blunders and absurdities no doubt crept in; forget them as soon as you can. Tomorrow is a new day; begin it well and serenely and with too high a spirit to be encumbered with your old nonsense.

—RALPH WALDO EMERSON, NINETEENTH-CENTURY ESSAYIST AND POET

How do you feel when you realize that you've made a mistake?

Hindsight Bias is the natural tendency to blame yourself for things you "should have known." If you lose your job, you "should have known it was coming." If the price of a particular stock you own drops 80 percent overnight, you "should have sold it." If you launch a **Product** and no one buys it, you "should have known it wouldn't work."

Baloney. If you knew then what you know now, you wouldn't have done what you did.

Every decision you ever make will be based on incomplete information—we have to use **Interpretation** to fill in the blanks. Since you're not omniscient, you'll always have more information when you evaluate the results of your actions than you had when you made the decision.

As a result, it's very easy to feel stupid if things don't turn out the way you expected. It's important to realize that these feelings are irrational—your decisions were based on the best information you had at the time, and there's nothing you can do now to change them.

Don't feel bad about things that you "should have seen" or "should have done." Changing the past is outside of your **Locus of Control**, so there's no sense in wasting energy on self-doubt, wondering what might have been. Hindsight Bias becomes destructive if you judge yourself or others for not knowing the unknowable.

As the saying goes, "Hindsight is 20/20." *Reinterpret* your past mistakes in a constructive light and focus your energy on what you can do right now to move in a positive direction.

REFERENCE LINK: **personalmba.com/hindsight-bias/**

Performance Load

If not controlled, work will flow to the competent man until he sub-merges.

—CHARLES BOYLE, FORMER US CONGRESSIONAL LIAISON FOR THE
NATIONAL AERONAUTICS AND SPACE ADMINISTRATION (NASA)

Being busy is better than being bored, but it's possible to be too busy for your own good.

Performance Load is a concept that explains what happens when you have too many things to do. Above a certain point, the more tasks a person has to do, the more their performance on all of those tasks decreases.

Imagine juggling bowling pins. If you're skilled, you may be able to juggle three or four without making a mistake. The more pins that must be juggled at once, the more likely you are to make a mistake and drop them all.

If you want to be productive, *you must set limits*. Juggling hundreds of active tasks across scores of projects is not sustainable: you're risking failure, subpar work, and burnout. Remember *Parkinson's Law*: if you don't set a limit on your available time, your work will expand to fill it all. If you don't draw the line somewhere, work will consume all of your energy, and you'll burn out.

Limits always have consequences—if you're not prepared to handle the consequences, it's not a limit. If you're working for a manager who expects you to work twenty hours a day, seven days a week, telling them no by setting limits on your working hours may cost you your job. Working that pace is unrealistic, but if you're not willing to accept the possibility of losing the job, you haven't set the limit.

In order to handle the unexpected, you must have unscheduled time to respond to new inputs. The default mind-set of many modern businesses is that "downtime" is inefficient and wasteful—workers should be busy all the time. This philosophy ignores the necessity of handling unexpected events, which always occur. Everyone only has so many hours in a day, and if your agenda is booked solid, it'll always be difficult to keep up with new and unexpected demands on your time and energy.

You can't perform at 110 percent of your capacity at all times—use the *Four Methods of Completion* to eliminate, defer, or delegate marginally valuable work that contributes to Performance Load. By keeping some capacity in reserve, you'll be ready to handle the *Most Important Tasks* immediately.

REFERENCE LINK: **personalmba.com/performance-load/**

Energy Cycles

> We all have times when we think more effectively, and times when we should not be thinking at all.
>
> —DANIEL COHEN, CHILDREN'S AUTHOR

Here's the problem with "time management": time is not what needs to be managed. No matter what you choose to do, time will pass.

The implicit assumption of time-management systems is that every hour is fungible—equivalent to any other. Nothing could be further from the truth: all people are created equal, but all hours are most definitely not.

Throughout the day, your energy level cycles up and down. Your body has natural rhythms during the day, which I call *Energy Cycles*. Most people are familiar with the twenty-four-hour circadian rhythm, which wakes you up in the morning and makes you feel tired at night. Lesser known is the ninety-minute ultradian rhythm, which is described in *The Power of Full Engagement* by Jim Loehr and Tony Schwartz.

The ultradian rhythm influences the flow of hormones throughout your body. When your energy is on an upswing, you're capable of focusing deeply and getting a lot accomplished. When it's on a downswing, all your mind and body want to do is rest and recover. There's nothing abnormal about these changes in energy during the day, but we often act as though being on a downswing is somehow a problem that needs to be fixed.

Nowadays, it's popular to try to "hack" this cycle to get more done by resting less. Attempting to work eight to twelve hours without a break is not uncommon in competitive workplaces. Most of us try to overclock our brains with large doses of sugar and caffeine. Some people even resort to abusing prescription or illegal drugs to work a little bit longer or faster.

Like all biological organisms, humans need to rest and recover for peak performance. Taking a break isn't a sign of laziness or weakness—it's a recognition of a fundamental human need. Paying attention to your natural Energy Cycle will help you perform at your best over long periods of time.

Here are four simple ways to work with your body instead of against it:

1. *Learn your patterns.* Use a notebook or calendar to track how much energy you have during different parts of the day, as well as what you're eating and drinking. If you do this for a few days, you'll notice patterns in how your energy waxes and wanes, allowing you to plan your future work.[11]

2. *Maximize your peak cycles.* When you're in an up cycle, you're capable of getting a lot accomplished, so plan your day to take advantage of that energy. If you're doing creative work, carve out a three- to four-hour block of time during an up cycle to get it done. If your work consists of attending a lot of meetings, plan the most important meetings during the up cycle.

3. *Take a break.* When you're in a down cycle, it's better to rest than attempt to power through it. Rest and recovery are not optional—if you don't rest now, your body will force you to rest later, either by cycling down longer than usual or by getting sick. During a down cycle, go for a walk, meditate, or take a twenty-minute nap. Relaxing on the down cycle can restore your energy, allowing you to take full advantage of the next up cycle.

4. *Get enough sleep.* Sleep deprivation results in a prolonged down cycle, which gets in the way of getting things done. To ensure you get enough sleep each evening, set a timer to go off an hour before you'd ideally be in bed sleeping. When the timer goes off, turn off the computer and/or TV, go through your evening routine, make a

cup of noncaffeinated tea, and spend some time with a book you enjoy. When your reading comprehension starts to go down, you'll know it's time for bed.

Paying attention to your Energy Cycles during the day will help you get the most out of the time you have available. Take maximum advantage of your up cycles and rest on your down cycles, and you'll be amazed at what you can accomplish in a day.

REFERENCE LINK: **personalmba.com/energy-cycles/**

Stress and Recovery

Only those who will risk going too far can possibly find out how far one can go.

—T. S. ELIOT, POET AND PLAYWRIGHT

During my last semester of college—around the time I created the Personal MBA—I pushed myself to the breaking point.

I was taking twenty-two credit hours of classes across three subjects: business information systems, real estate, and philosophy. Every class I took had some kind of capstone project on top of the final exam. Two of the courses I was taking were at the graduate level, and each required a twenty-plus-page paper on a complex topic to pass. I had far too much work to do in the time available.

By the last two weeks of the quarter, I was an absolute wreck: sleep deprived, exhausted, and burned out. Everything got done on time, but the workload took its toll, and it took me a few weeks of doing nothing after graduation to fully recover.

Even though it wasn't pleasant, I'm glad I found my breaking point. Here's why: now I know how much I'm capable of doing and how much is too much. I know more about how my mind and body react to stress, and I'm better able to identify the warning signs of taking on too much before things get out of hand.

As a result, I've learned to keep myself running at about 90 percent capacity, which is enough to get a lot done without burning out. At any given time, I'm writing, consulting, and working on a few interesting side projects. Paying attention to **Stress and Recovery** ensures that I don't take on too much to handle. Learning my breaking point has made it much easier to know when to push and when to slow down.

It's impossible to know how much you're capable of until you decide to push your limits. As long as you stay safe by limiting your experimentation to things that won't kill you or do permanent damage, you can learn a lot about how you work by stretching yourself to the limit. The knowledge you gain will help you make better choices in the future about which projects to take on and how much is too much.

That said, our bodies are not machines that are designed to operate at maximum capacity at all times. It's easy to fall into the trap of comparing your output to an idealized version of yourself who can build Rome in a day, then build the Great Wall of China as a fun side project. If that's your vision of personal effectiveness, you'll always come up short.

You are not a machine—the ideal of human productivity is not acting like a robot. Humans need rest, relaxation, sleep, and play in order to function in an efficient and effective way. Too little of any of these things can seriously diminish your capacity to do good work and impact how much you enjoy your life.

So how do you rest and recover? It's simple: spend time doing something different from your normal activities and responsibilities. The less overlap between your hobby and your work, the better.

During World War II, Winston Churchill was under as much stress as a person can withstand. As prime minister of the United Kingdom, he was responsible for leading the defense of Great Britain from 1940 until the end of the war in 1945. The fate of a country and the freedom of its people depended upon his fortitude and persistence for five long years.

How did Churchill keep from collapsing under such a heavy burden? In *Painting as a Pastime*, Churchill explains how spending time painting helped him recover from the demands of war and politics:

> Many remedies are suggested for the avoidance of worry and mental overstrain by persons who, over prolonged periods, have to bear exceptional responsibilities and discharge duties upon a very large scale. Some advise travel, and others, retreat. Some praise solitude,

and others, gaiety. No doubt all these may play their part according to the individual temperament. But the element which is constant and common in all of them is Change.

Change is the master key. A man can wear out a particular part of his mind by continually using it and tiring it, just in the same way as he can wear out the elbows of his coat. There is, however, this difference between the living cells of the brain and inanimate articles: one cannot mend the frayed elbows of a coat by rubbing the sleeves or shoulders; but the tired parts of the mind can be rested and strengthened, not merely by rest, but by using other parts. It is not enough to merely switch off the lights which play upon the main and ordinary field of interest; a new field of interest must be illuminated.

It is no use saying to the tired mental muscles—if one may coin such an expression—"I will give you a good rest," "I will go for a long walk," or "I will lie down and think of nothing." The mind keeps busy just the same. If it has been weighing and measuring, it goes on weighing and measuring. If it has been worrying, it goes on worrying. It is only when new cells are called into activity, when new stars become the lords of the ascendant, that relief, repose, refreshment are afforded.

If Churchill could find time to paint in the middle of a world war, you can find time in your busy schedule to rest and recover doing something you enjoy. Dedicating guilt-free time to rest and recovery will make your life more enjoyable and more productive.

REFERENCE LINK: **personalmba.com/stress-recovery/**

Testing

Discoveries are often made by not following instructions, by going off the main road, by trying the untried.

—FRANK TYGER, POLITICAL CARTOONIST AND COLUMNIST

I work best after at least eight hours of sleep. After waking up and helping my family get ready for the day, I have breakfast, take a few supplements my body needs to function well, enjoy a cup of peppermint or cinnamon tea, and exercise by going for a morning walk or swinging kettlebells for twenty minutes. Once I'm alert and ready to begin, I turn on my computer, turn off my internet connection, and start working on my **Most Important Task**. Once I get started, I can concentrate for up to six hours without stopping if I'm not interrupted: any longer, and the quality of my work decreases.

I've **Tested** *many* different approaches and variables. This routine is what works best for me, so I've made it a **Habit**. Will this be my method forever? I doubt it—my morning routine has changed many times over the years, and I'm certain I'll find other methods that work even better in the future. My experimentation never stops.

Testing is the act of trying something new—a way of applying the scientific method and the **Iteration Cycle** to your own life. The most happy and productive people I know all have something in common: they're always trying new things to see what works. You can't make positive discoveries that make your life better if you never try anything new.

Testing doesn't have to be complicated. All that's required is choosing some part of your life to focus on, then trying new ways to get what you want. You can Test random approaches, or read about what works for others and then test the approach yourself, **Externalizing** your results in a notebook can help you keep track of what you've tried, what works, and what doesn't.

Here's a simple structure that will help you plan and track your experiments:

▶ *Observations*—what are you observing in your life or business that you want to improve?

▶ *Knowns*—what have you learned from past experiments that might be related to your observations?

▶ *Hypotheses*—based on what you've observed, what situations or factors might cause or contribute to your observations?

▶ *Tests*—what will you try or change to improve your situation? Which hypotheses will this experiment Test?

▶ *Results*—what happened after each Test? Does it support or disconfirm your hypothesis?

Here are a few questions to help you discover things worth Testing:

▶ How much sleep do you need to feel rested and alert?

▶ Which foods make you feel energetic after eating? Which foods make you feel ill or lethargic?

▶ When do you do your most productive work? Are there any patterns in your productivity?

▶ When do you get your best ideas? What are you doing when they occur to you?

▶ What is your biggest source of stress or concern? When do you start worrying, and why?

Once you've found a pattern in one of these areas, it's time to start experimenting. Change your approach to one of these areas of your life and Externalize your results. If you find a change useful, keep doing it—if not, stop doing it and try something else.

Testing is the best way to ensure that your life gets better over time. By trying new things, you're learning what works for you and what doesn't. Over time, you'll discover patterns—things that make your life better and things that make your life worse. The results of your experiments *Accumulate*, until they produce the results you want.

You never know until you try.

REFERENCE LINK: personalmba.com/testing/

Mystique

What grief we'd avoid if we knew how to transfer emotional experience across generations, as we do money or scientific knowledge.

—ALAIN DE BOTTON, PHILOSOPHER AND ESSAYIST

There's a big difference between liking the idea of being/doing something and *liking the actual being/doing*.

It's easy to like the idea of being the CEO of a *Fortune* 500 company. It's harder to like the hours, the responsibility, and the pressure that comes with the top job.

It's easy to like the idea of being a manager. It's harder to like the demands from C-level execs, surprises from your direct reports, and the necessity of defending your turf in a political environment.

It's easy to like the idea of having an Ivy League MBA or law degree. It's harder to like the six-figure debt and the corresponding necessity of getting a stressful sixty-plus-hour-a-week job to make the investment "worth it."

It's easy to like the idea of being self-employed. It's harder to like the fact that 100 percent of your income comes from your own effort and that if you screw up, you're the one who will face the consequences.

It's easy to like the idea of raising millions of dollars of venture capital. It's harder to like the fact that you've given up control over the project you're investing your life in.

It's easy to like the idea of being an author. It's harder to like the solitude, self-doubt, and long hours of "butt in chair, hands on keyboard" that consistent writing requires.

It's easy to like the idea of being a celebrity. It's harder to like the constant scrutiny, loss of privacy, and fear that people will direct their attention away from you in favor of the "next big thing."

Mystique is a powerful force—a little mystery makes most things appear to be a lot more attractive than they really are. Fortunately, there's an easy way to counteract the rose-colored glasses of Mystique: have a real, human conversation with someone who's done what you're interested in doing.

Here's what to ask: "I respect what you're doing, but I imagine it has high points and low points. Could you share them with me? Knowing what you know now, is it worth the effort?"

This conversation will only take a few minutes, but you'll be amazed by what you learn, on both the positive and the negative side.

No job, project, or position is flawless—every course of action has **Trade-offs**. Learning what they are in advance gives you a major advantage: you can examine an option without idealizing it, then choose if it's what you want to do *before you start*. That kind of knowledge is priceless.

REFERENCE LINK: **personalmba.com/mystique/**

Hedonic Treadmill

If thou wilt make a man happy, add not unto his riches but take away from his desires.

—EPICURUS, FOURTH-CENTURY-BCE GREEK PHILOSOPHER

Let's assume that you believe buying a fancy new car will make you happy. In the short term, it might: for the first week or so, you'll probably experience great pleasure when you drive. Over time, however, your joy will fade, a phenomenon psychologists call "hedonic adaptation." Before long, your new car will blend into your surroundings and your mind will fixate on something else to pursue in the quest for happiness.

This cycle is called the **Hedonic Treadmill**: we pursue pleasurable things because we think they'll make us happy. When we finally achieve or acquire what we're seeking, we adapt to our success in a very short period of time, and our success no longer gives us pleasure. As a result, we begin seeking something new, and the cycle repeats.

The Hedonic Treadmill explains why people who achieve wealth, status, and fame continue to seek more. Since we're not satisfied with what we have for very long, it's only a matter of time before we fixate on something else to achieve or possess.

The Hedonic Treadmill is a major problem if you'd like to experience a feeling of success or achievement for an extended period of time. It's possible to work hard, invest, sacrifice, and push your way to the top of your field, only to find yourself restless and despondent. You'd be surprised at how many "successful" people aren't happy with their lives, even after they've achieved everything they set out to do.

Short-circuiting the Hedonic Treadmill is tricky: it's a side effect of **Caveman Syndrome**. There are, however, a few things we can focus on that tend to lead to sustained levels of life satisfaction. Based on the available research, here are five priorities that will contribute to your long-term happiness in a way that minimizes hedonic adaptation:

1. *Work to make "enough" money.* Money contributes to happiness, but only to a certain point. According to a 2010 study by Daniel Kahneman and Angus Deaton, money has a positive correlation with

reported levels of happiness up to an annual household income of approximately $75,000 per year, which represents an income in the top third of US households in 2008–09, the years of the study. Reaching this level of income requires effort, but it's very achievable: median US household income during the years of the study was $71,500.

Once you have enough money to cover the necessities and a few luxuries, you reach a point of **Diminishing Returns**: every additional dollar you earn doesn't provide the same amount of utility. Beyond the point of Diminishing Returns, having more money doesn't increase happiness—in fact, it may decrease it by becoming an additional source of stress and worry.[12]

Knowing your monetary point of Diminishing Returns is useful: by limiting your consumption beyond a certain point and establishing long-term savings, you can reap the benefits of financial security and **Resilience** without spending every waking moment working to pay for pleasures you'll adapt to in less than a month.

As a general rule, experiences contribute more to happiness than material goods. Beyond the point where your needs are met, you'll get a higher emotional return for your dollar by traveling with people you like than by purchasing an expensive luxury item.

2. *Focus on improving your health and energy.* Health is a major contributing factor to happiness: when you feel great, you're more likely to feel happy. The converse is also true: when you feel ill, you tend to experience less pleasure, enjoyment, and life satisfaction.

Experimenting with ways to improve your typical level of health and energy can result in huge improvements in your quality of life. Remember, the human body has **Performance Requirements**: food, exercise, and rest are not optional. If you make it a priority to give your body what it needs to thrive, you'll reap the rewards over the years to come.

3. *Spend time with people you enjoy.* One of the single biggest predictors of happiness is the amount of time you spend with people you enjoy: family, friends, and like-minded acquaintances. The context and environment are less important than the people you spend time with.

Different people need different levels of social contact to feel happy. Extroverted people feel energized by social contact and need to be around others on a regular basis. Introverted people (like me) can go days or weeks with little social contact and get their energy from spending time alone. Still, introverted people benefit from spending time with people they like: regular social time with friends is highly correlated with major, sustained increases in life satisfaction. Long meals and trips with friends are a great use of time.

According to George Vaillant, the project's director, the results of the Harvard Study of Adult Development (the longest-running longitudinal study of mental health) boil down to this: "The only thing that really matters in life are your relationships with other people."[13]

4. *Remove chronic annoyances.* There are many things in life that can wear on your nerves. Examining ways to reduce or eliminate chronic stresses or annoyances can generate significant improvements in life satisfaction.

If you find driving in rush-hour traffic stressful, moving closer to work is a good solution. If you don't like your current job, start looking for another. If you find working with a particular client annoying, fire them. If you always forget to pack your laptop's power cable when you travel, buy a second cable that stays in your travel bag. By finding simple ways to remove unnecessary stress and frustration, you'll spend less time and energy feeling bad and more time feeling good.

5. *Pursue a new challenge.* Most people assume retirees feel overjoyed, but that's often not the case. It's common for people to derive a sense of purpose and enjoyment from their work, and retirees can feel empty and lost when their former career is no longer a priority. Left unresolved, this sense of loss can spiral into depression.

The solution is to take on an exciting new challenge. This challenge can be anything: mastering a new skill, completing a big project, or pursuing a major accomplishment. Whether it's learning a new language, playing an instrument, building something from scratch, or completing a marathon, striving for new achievement is the best way to experience happiness and growth over long periods of time.

Focusing on experiences over material goods goes a long way if you want to step off the Hedonic Treadmill. In the immortal words of Charles Kingsley, a nineteenth-century historian and clergyman: "We act as though comfort and luxury were the chief requirements of life, when all we need to make us happy is something to be enthusiastic about."

REFERENCE LINK: **personalmba.com/hedonic-treadmill/**

Comparison Fallacy

Never compare your inside with someone else's outside.

—HUGH MACLEOD, CARTOONIST AND AUTHOR OF *IGNORE EVERYBODY*

In business and in life, it's easy to compare our situation to others'. Status seeking ensures that we spend energy tracking our relative status to our peers, and most of the time our conclusions aren't favorable.

We tend to fixate on what other people are accomplishing instead of what we need to do next to achieve our *Goals*. When other people we know accomplish big things, it's easy to feel sad for ourselves instead of happy for their achievements, as if their success diminishes us in some way. It doesn't.

The *Comparison Fallacy* is a simple idea: other people are not you, and you are not other people. You have unique skills, goals, and priorities. In the end, comparing yourself to other people is silly, and there's little to be gained by it.

Here's an example: one of my friends is very successful in business and makes about ten times what I make each year. He has received a lot of public recognition for his work. His products sell well, and he enjoys his success. There's a lot to envy.

Here's the other side of the coin: my friend works twelve hours a day, sometimes more. He doesn't have a family. He has a large staff that requires constant attention, and his business's *Overhead* is more than ten times mine. He's overwhelmed with email, phone calls, and meetings. He's under tremendous stress almost all the time.

It's easy to see the benefits of my friend's life, and just as easy to overlook the *Trade-offs*. That's the trick: he is successful in certain areas because he works very hard, and he's willing to pay the price of his success.

If I could swap lives with my friend, I wouldn't: I'd be miserable. His life doesn't mesh with my priorities or how I prefer to live and work. The benefits he enjoys appeal to me, but I'm not willing to pay the price he's paid for obtaining them. Remembering the Comparison Fallacy allows me to wish him well and stay focused on achieving the Goals that are most important to me. I can be genuinely happy for his success and not waste my energy on pointless envy.

The same trick works in any situation that has the potential of generating feelings of envy or inferiority. Whenever you're tempted to compare yourself to an acquaintance, colleague, classmate, or celebrity, it always helps to keep in mind that your goals, preferences, and priorities are not the same. You've lived different lives, and you've each paid a different price for what you've accomplished. Any comparison you try to make renders itself invalid, so you can relax.

The only metric of success that matters is this: are you spending your time doing things you like, with people you enjoy, in a way that keeps you financially sufficient? If so, don't worry about what other people are doing. If not, focus on making changes that are within your *Locus of Control*, so you can start moving in the direction you desire. Remember the Comparison Fallacy and keep moving closer to what you want.

REFERENCE LINK: **personalmba.com/comparison-fallacy/**

Locus of Control

Grant me the serenity to accept the things I cannot change, the courage to change the things I can, and the wisdom to know the difference.

—THE SERENITY PRAYER

No matter how much you want a particular job, after the interview is over, you can't control whether or not you get the job—you've done what you could.

No matter how intently you watch the stock market, you can't will the stock price of a particular company to go up.

No matter how much you'd like to retain a key employee or make a personal relationship work, you can't prevent them from leaving if they want to.

Understanding your **Locus of Control** is being able to separate what you can control (or strongly influence) from what you can't. Trying to control things that aren't under your control is a recipe for eternal frustration.

As much as we'd like to, we can't control everything that happens to us. Natural disasters are a perfect example: if a tornado or earthquake destroys your home, there's nothing you can do about it. As uncomfortable as it is to imagine, the **Environment** contains many things we can't control. It's a fundamental aspect of life that we can't change, no matter how much we might want to.

Focusing on your efforts helps you stay sane; turning results you don't control into **Goals** is a recipe for frustration. One of the reasons that diets drive people crazy is that they involve trying to control a result—weight—that is not under their direct control. If you focus on efforts—eating healthy food, exercising, and doing what you can to manage related medical conditions—your weight will handle itself.

Worrying about things you can't influence or control is a waste of time and energy. One of the best things I've ever done was choose to stop paying **Attention** to the news—99.9 percent of the information you'll find in a newspaper or television newscast is outside of your Locus of Control. Instead of fruitlessly worrying about "what the world is coming to," ignoring the news helps me spend more of my time doing what I can to make things better.

The better you're able to separate what you can control from what you can't, the happier and more productive you'll be. Focus most of your energy on things that you can influence and let everything else go. Keep your Attention on what you're doing to build the life you want to live, and it's only a matter of time before you get there.

REFERENCE LINK: **personalmba.com/locus-of-control/**

Attachment

No trumpets sound when the important decisions of our life are
made. Destiny is made known silently.

—AGNES DE MILLE, DANCER AND CHOREOGRAPHER

Imagine you're on your way up Mount Everest, on the way to achieving
your *Goal*. The night before you plan to summit, a massive storm appears
without warning. Visibility is zero, the temperature is dropping, and conditions are so bad you risk falling or freezing to death if you continue
climbing.

Have you failed?

When something outside of our *Locus of Control* affects our plans or
Goals, it's easy to take it personally. If you have your heart set on summit-
ing Mount Everest *today*, you'll likely meet your doom. Far better to
change your plans and live to climb the mountain another day.

The more *Attachment* you feel to a particular idea or plan, the more you
limit your flexibility and reduce your chances of finding a better solution.
It's good to be dedicated to the pursuit of your goals, but only to a point.
If you become too Attached to the visions you have in your head, you'll
have a hard time adjusting to the inevitable twists and turns of life.

Acceptance requires applying the concept of *Sunk Cost* to yourself.
Imagine losing millions of dollars in the stock market—a horrible situation. No matter how much you rail against greedy bankers, corrupt politi-
cians, or the unfairness of life, it's not going to bring that money back.
Spending time feeling down for not "knowing better" or being omniscient
won't improve your situation.

The solution to Attachment is accepting that your idea or plan is no
longer feasible or useful. The less Attached you are to your plans, Goals,
status, and position, the easier it will be to respond appropriately to inevitable change or unforeseen circumstances.

If you suddenly lose your job, remaining Attached to your previous
position is a hindrance, not a help. It's better to spend your energy doing
what needs to be done to bring in more income.

The more you focus and accept the things that have happened and choose to work on things that you can do to make things better, the happier you'll be.

REFERENCE LINK: **personalmba.com/attachment/**

Personal Research and Development

If a man empties his purse into his head, no one can take it from him.
An investment in knowledge always pays the highest return.

—BENJAMIN FRANKLIN, EIGHTEENTH-CENTURY AMERICAN
POLITICAL LEADER, SCIENTIST, AND POLYMATH

Every successful business dedicates a certain amount of resources to trying new things. Research and development (R&D) is what business leaders around the world count on to determine what the company should work on next. Large companies spend millions (sometimes billions) of dollars in speculative research every year, experimenting with new techniques and processes in order to enhance their capabilities.

R&D exists because it works—companies that make research and development a priority often discover new products to offer their customers or process improvements that meaningfully contribute to the bottom line. If it works for them, it can work for you.

What would it look like if you set aside a few hundred dollars a month as a *Personal Research and Development* budget? Using the techniques discussed in *I Will Teach You to Be Rich*, by Ramit Sethi, it's easy to divert a certain amount of your monthly income into an account earmarked for Personal R&D. That money can then be used—guilt free—for purchasing books, taking courses, acquiring equipment, or attending conferences: anything that will improve your skills and capabilities.

Personal-finance pundits might disagree with me here, but I think having a robust Personal R&D budget is more important than maximizing your savings. I'm all for having a well-funded emergency account and saving enough for future needs, but savings can only get you so far.

Investments in improving your personal skills and capabilities can enrich your life and open doors to additional income sources. New skills create new opportunities, and new opportunities often translate into more income. Your ability to save is limited; your ability to earn is not.

Here's a simple *Thought Experiment* that will help you establish your own Personal R&D budget: What would have to change to be able to dedicate at least 5 percent of your monthly income to personal development and experimentation, assuming your current income stays the same?

Any money-saving tip you find in good personal-finance books or blogs can be used to fund your Personal R&D account. All it takes is a little creativity and budgeting, and you'll be well on your way to funding your own self-directed Personal R&D laboratory.

REFERENCE LINK: **personalmba.com/personal-research-and-development/**

Limiting Belief

Intelligent discontent is the mainspring of civilization.

—EUGENE V. DEBS, LABOR UNION ACTIVIST

In general, there are two primary ways of looking at the world—two mind-sets that influence your response to new experiences.

The first basic mind-set is that your skills and abilities are fixed. If you try something and it doesn't work, it's because you're "not good at that," and you never will be. You were born with innate skills and abilities that will never change.

Using this mind-set, if you experience a challenge or difficulty, you're likely to stop—you're obviously not good at it, so why bother?

The second basic mind-set is that your skills and abilities are malleable. If you try something and it doesn't work, it's because you haven't worked on it very much, but if you keep trying, you'll get better. Your skills and abilities are like muscles—they strengthen with use. If you experience a challenge or difficulty, you're likely to keep going—you might not be good at it yet, but you're always getting better.

These two mind-sets color how you experience everything in the world. In *Mindset: The New Psychology of Success*, Dr. Carol S. Dweck calls these mind-sets the "fixed" and "growth" theories of intelligence. If you have a "fixed" mind-set, challenges are a commentary on your worth as a person—you've been tried and found wanting, which makes trying new things feel threatening. If you have a "growth" mind-set, challenges are an obstacle to be overcome by working harder. The fixed mind-set is an example of a **Limiting Belief**: something you believe is true about the world that holds you back from achieving a **Goal** you value. The fixed mind-set isn't true, but it's capable of holding you back if you choose to believe it.

Some Limiting Beliefs are the result of errors in **Pattern Matching**. Here's a common example: if you believe that wealthy people are superficial, unethical, or corrupt, you'll find it difficult to make money. If you make more money than you make now, you'll become one of "those people," and the thought will make you uncomfortable anytime money is an issue.

If you don't identify the **Conflict** and resolve it, money matters will always make you uncomfortable. Your mind is not malfunctioning: part of your brain is anticipating the future and trying to protect you from something you don't want, but it's going about the task in a counterproductive way. To make progress, you have to identify and eliminate the beliefs that are holding you back.

Everyone has Limiting Beliefs in certain areas. Anytime you use the words "I can't," "I have to," or "I'm not good at," you've discovered a potential Limiting Belief. Most of the time, taking a moment to question the belief is all you need to do to break it. "Is that really true?" and "How do I know that's true?" are very powerful and versatile **Self-Elicitation** questions.

Limiting Beliefs may also appear when you consider doing things that make you uncomfortable, like applying for a new job or selling an offer to a new prospect. Images of rejection and disapproval start flashing through your mind, and your first impulse is to conclude "this won't work" before conducting a single test or gathering real feedback.

Here's a useful rule of thumb for these types of situations: make the other party tell you no. This is a **Habit** worth installing: you may believe you're going to be turned down when you make a request or propose an idea, but make the other party say it instead of assuming it's a given. You'll be surprised at how often you get what you want, even when you believe the odds are slim.

The way you choose to respond to challenges determines how successful you will become. It's important to realize that you have no "fundamental defects"—there's nothing that you're incapable of learning or doing. It may take time and effort, but you'll improve if you make the effort.

Viewing your mind as a muscle is the best way to help it grow.

REFERENCE LINK: **personalmba.com/limiting-belief/**

Malinvestment

Our errors are surely not such awfully solemn things. In a world where we are so certain to incur them in spite of all our caution, a certain lightness of heart seems healthier than this excessive nervousness on their behalf.

—WILLIAM JAMES, NINETEENTH-CENTURY DOCTOR AND
PIONEERING PSYCHOLOGIST

Often, we make decisions that don't turn out the way we expect: unnecessary purchases, bad hires, poor investments, and wasted energy.

This type of error is called **Malinvestment**: a "bad" or "poor" investment. The meaning of bad or poor is variable, but it's almost always tied up with a feeling of "That was dumb . . . what a waste!"

Malinvestment is very common. You can't see the future, and that **Uncertainty** introduces a significant risk of error whenever you make a purchase or investment of time and energy.

It's easy to feel bad about Malinvestment: making mistakes is never fun. Feeling too bad, however, is a form of **Hindsight Bias**: if you knew then what you know now, you wouldn't have done what you did.

Sometimes, Malinvestment looks like a straightforward mistake—an error. You thought the investment was promising, wise, or prudent, and it turns out it wasn't. This usually takes the form of:

▶ Buying items you don't use.

▶ Purchasing a product that doesn't work or malfunctions.

▶ A change in your preferences, needs, or priorities that makes past investments obsolete.

These errors often come from not having enough information before making a purchase decision. You can often prevent these types of errors by:

▶ Collecting more information before you invest.

▶ Being more diligent about evaluating needs and priorities before investing.

▶ Investing only to solve a clear, present, recurring, immediate, or important need or problem.

Other forms of Malinvestment look like inefficiency: an unnecessary waste of resources. This usually takes the form of:

▶ Paying **Insurance** premiums without incident.

▶ Building and maintaining backup systems and **Fail-safes** you never need to use.

It's important to realize that this type of Malinvestment is very common when dealing with **Uncertainty** and risk. Paying Insurance premiums is usually a wise thing to do if you're not able or willing to mitigate certain common or large risks on your own.

If you don't end up collecting a claim on the Insurance, your premiums weren't really "wasted," in the sense that you were paying to mitigate a very real risk. You would've saved money if you could see the future, but you can't. Paying to mitigate major risks is a good decision as long as you don't overpay for the Insurance.

When you're trying to do something new or different, you're bound to make a few mistakes. Investing time, energy, or effort in something that doesn't work out the way you hoped is almost a certainty:

▶ Starting to do something in a certain way, only to find out it won't work.

▶ Doing something one way, then discovering a better way when you're almost done.

▶ Breaking something important, then having to fix it.

In these cases, Malinvestment is a form of tuition: it's the price you're paying to learn more about the topic or area of interest. As long as the tuition costs aren't too steep, a certain amount of error can teach you a lot about what's important, what works, and what not to do in the future.

Often, it's wise to seek out a certain level of Malinvestment as a form of *Exploration*. You'll never have perfect information, and you'll never find the "optimal" or "perfect" strategy before you begin. If you wait until you're 100 percent certain you've found the best possible approach before you begin, you'll never get started.

Here's a useful question that's helpful in overcoming this tendency: "How quickly can I start making mistakes?" The faster you jump in and start trying to do what you want to be able to do, the faster you'll learn— errors and all.

When in doubt, err on the side of imperfect experimentation.

REFERENCE LINK: personalmba.com/malinvestment/

The Necessity of Choice

O! that a man might know / The end of this day's business, ere it come; / But it sufficeth that the day will end / And then the end is known.

—WILLIAM SHAKESPEARE, *JULIUS CAESAR*

We live in a world of *Trade-offs*: you will always have competing demands for your time, attention, and energy. You can learn to use your limited resources in smarter ways, but in the end, you are responsible for deciding what to do and what to drop.

There is no magic formula or perfect system that will allow you to accomplish everything you've ever wanted to accomplish without effort, without stress, without hardship, and without cost.

Once you fully accept the reality that your time, energy, attention, and financial resources are limited, that you are neither omniscient nor omnipotent, and that you always retain the responsibility to think and act for yourself, you're in a good position to make consistent progress toward *Goals* that are important and meaningful to you.

Most time-management and productivity questions boil down to "How can I complete too much work in not enough time, with limited energy?"

The **Necessity of Choice** is a useful way of thinking about this fundamental challenge: it's best to make personal Trade-offs in a conscious and deliberate manner.

You will *always* have too much to do. There will *always* be tasks left undone. If success means "getting everything done," you're in for a lifetime of stress and unsatisfying work. Worse: if getting everything done is a prerequisite for rest and recovery, you're building a prison of your own making.

You always have to choose what to do and what to leave undone: it's a fundamental feature of reality, not something that you can hack in any meaningful way. Reality will force choices upon you by virtue of living in a finite universe. If you don't make informed and clear **Decisions** about what to do and what to avoid, important parts of your life will be determined by chance and circumstance.

The best strategy is to *choose*: to make conscious Trade-offs between things you want in a deliberate, informed way. Choose what you want most and let go of everything that doesn't make the grade.

REFERENCE LINK: **personalmba.com/necessity-of-choice/**

The Arrival Fallacy

Everyone wants to live on top of the mountain, but all the happiness and growth occurs while you're climbing it.

—ANDY ROONEY, JOURNALIST

In talking with business owners, executives, and entrepreneurs, I've noticed a common pattern: no one feels successful or satisfied with their business or career. There's always another milestone to reach for, a new (and larger) sales goal to achieve, or a larger business valuation that represents "true success."

I know many professionals who have set their sights on substantial **Goals**—and have achieved them. Instead of feeling a lasting sense of accomplishment, they find their dissatisfaction persists, and the goalposts shift to a new, even more difficult objective. "When I achieve *that*," they tell themselves, "I'll finally feel successful and happy."

The *Arrival Fallacy* is a way to recognize this pattern and short-circuit the dissatisfaction associated with pursuing Goals. If you recognize that your business, career, and life will never be in a permanent ideal state and there will be no end to your search for meaning and improvement, it becomes much easier to appreciate what you've achieved to date and celebrate the accomplishment of Goals and milestones as they occur.

Think of your current objectives as waypoints, not final destinations: they're useful ways to orient and direct your attention, energy, and effort. When you accomplish your objective, there will always be something else to work on or improve—and that's a good thing. No matter what you choose to do, you will never lack for interesting, productive, or valuable ways to invest your days.

This line of thought also makes it easier to rest, recover, and enjoy your life as you work toward what you want. You won't reach nirvana by working yourself to exhaustion or making severe *Trade-offs* concerning your health, interests, or personal relationships. Ambition and drive can produce wonderful benefits, but they can also lead to self-destructive behaviors if you're not mindful of how you apply them.

"Success" is not a permanent *State of Being*, so it makes no sense to give up everything in a futile attempt to pursue it. Instead, define what you want, and keep moving towards it. When you get there, celebrate your victory, chart a new course, and keep going.

REFERENCE LINK: **personalmba.com/arrival-fallacy/**

8

WORKING WITH OTHERS

Take away my people but leave my factories, and soon grass will grow on factory floors. Take away my factories but leave my people, and soon we will have a new and better factory.

—ANDREW CARNEGIE, NINETEENTH-CENTURY INDUSTRIALIST

Working with other people is an ever-present part of business and life: you can't escape it, even if you want to. Customers, employees, contractors, and partners are all individuals with their own unique motivations and desires. If you want to do well in this world, it pays to understand how to get things done with and through other people.

In this chapter, we'll discuss how to work well with others. You'll learn how to communicate in an efficient and effective way, earn the respect and trust of others, recognize the limitations and pitfalls of group interactions, and lead or manage a team of people to accomplish meaningful objectives.

REFERENCE LINK: **personalmba.com/working-with-others/**

Power

Force is all-conquering, but its victories are short-lived ... Nearly all men can stand adversity, but if you want to test a man's character, give him power.

—ABRAHAM LINCOLN, SIXTEENTH PRESIDENT OF THE UNITED STATES

All human relationships are based on **Power**—the ability to influence the actions of other people. We can never control people in the sense that we discussed in the section on **Perceptual Control**—we don't have direct access to the inner processes that make people do the things they do. All we can do is act in ways that encourage people to do what we suggest.

The use of Power takes one of two fundamental forms: influence or compulsion. Influence is the ability to encourage someone else to want what you suggest. Compulsion is the ability to force someone else to do what you command.

Encouraging an employee to "go the extra mile" out of a sense of loyalty or craftsmanship is influence. Forcing the employee to work over the weekend by threatening to fire them if they refuse is compulsion. The actions that employee takes may be the same, but how they *feel* about taking those actions will be quite different.

On the whole, influence is much more effective than compulsion. The vast majority of people resist being forced to do something against their will or better judgment, so relying on compulsion to get things done is a poor strategy. Bossing people around only serves to make them dislike you, and they'll find ways to retaliate or quit working with you at the earliest available opportunity. Influence, on the other hand, is sustainable— encouraging people to want what you want gets you the results you're looking for without provoking unnecessary ill will.

Like it or not, everyone relies on Power to get things done. Power is a neutral tool—one that can be used for good or ill. Power represents your ability to get things done through other people—the more Power you have, the more things you can do. There's nothing wrong with seeking to increase your Power, provided you respect the rights of other people. The more Power you have, the more you can accomplish, but with great Power comes great responsibility.

The reason that interactions among large groups of people become political is the ever-present nature of Power. If you don't have a plan, your actions will be determined by someone else. By refusing to make the effort to move in the direction you think is best, you're ceding Power to those who *do* have plans. Refuse to understand that Power is important and you're likely to find that any influence you have rapidly disappears. The only way to win is to decide to play.

The best way to increase your Power is to do things that increase your influence and **Reputation**. The more people know your capabilities and respect the Reputation you've built, the more Power you will have.

REFERENCE LINK: personalmba.com/power/

Comparative Advantage

> Be a first-rate version of yourself, not a second-rate version of someone else.
>
> —JUDY GARLAND, ACTRESS AND SINGER

Essential to the idea of working with other people is the question, Why work with other people in the first place? If you can't control them and get them to do what you want them to do all the time, why bother?

The answer is *Comparative Advantage*, a concept that originated in the "dismal science" of economics. Attributed to David Ricardo's 1817 text *On the Principles of Political Economy and Taxation*, "Ricardo's Law of Comparative Advantage" provided an answer to a question of international politics: is it better for the economies of countries to be self-sufficient and produce everything themselves, or specialize in producing certain goods, then trade with one another?

Using Portugal and England as examples, Ricardo calculated that even if both countries were capable of producing cloth and wine, England could produce cloth with much less effort, and Portugal was much better at producing wine. As a result, instead of wasting time and money struggling to do something they weren't good at, Portugal and England would both be better off if they specialized, then traded with each other.

Comparative Advantage means it's better to capitalize on your strengths than to shore up your weaknesses. In *First, Break All The Rules*, by Marcus

Buckingham and Curt Coffman, and *StrengthsFinder 2.0*, by Tom Rath, the authors share the results of Gallup's comprehensive research on human productivity. As it turns out, Comparative Advantage applies as much to individuals as it does to countries: businesses work better if the individuals who operate them focus on what they're best at, working with other specialists to accomplish everything else they need. "Strengths-based management" is just another term for Comparative Advantage.

Comparative Advantage explains why it often makes sense to work with contractors or employees rather than try to do everything yourself. If you want to build a house, it's probably more efficient to hire a general contractor and specialists who do the kind of work the project requires every day. You could try to do it yourself, but unless you know what you're doing, it'll probably take longer, and the results won't be as good.

Comparative Advantage also explains why diverse teams outperform homogenous teams. Having a wide variety of team members with different skills and backgrounds is a major asset: it increases the probability that one of your teammates will know what to do in any given circumstance. If every team member has the same skills and the same background, it's far more likely the team will get stuck or make a preventable error.

Self-reliance improves your flexibility and knowledge over time, but too much self-reliance is a mistake. I'm a huge advocate of self-education and learning how to do things yourself, but taking the DIY ethic to an extreme can do more harm than good. Working with others can help you get more done, faster, and improve the quality of the end result. Even Thoreau left Walden Pond every once in a while to buy things in town.

The major benefit of self-education when working with others is knowing what skill looks like. You may be able to hire a programmer halfway around the world online, but if you've never done any programming yourself, you're going to have a difficult time figuring out whether or not their work is good. Learn a little programming, however, and your ability to identify good programmers will increase, making you more likely to identify skilled colleagues and partners.

In the immortal words of John Donne: "No man is an island." Focus on what you can do well and work with others to accomplish the rest.

REFERENCE LINK: **personalmba.com/comparative-advantage/**

Communication Overhead

> If you had to identify, in one word, the reason why the human race has not achieved, and never will achieve, its full potential, that word would be: "meetings."
>
> —DAVE BARRY, COMEDIAN AND NEWSPAPER COLUMNIST

There's a reason high-performing surgical teams, military units, and sports teams tend to be small and focused: too much time spent in communication and coordination can kill a team's effectiveness.

Communication Overhead is the proportion of time you spend communicating with members of your team instead of getting productive work done. In order to keep everyone on the same page, communication is necessary. The more team members you have to work with, the more you have to communicate with them to coordinate action.

As the number of people you work with increases, Communication Overhead increases geometrically until the total percentage of time each individual must devote to group communication approaches 100 percent. After a certain threshold, each additional team member diminishes the capacity of the group to do anything other than communicate.

Large companies are slow because they suffer from Communication Overhead. If you're responsible for working with a group of more than five to eight people, at least 80 percent of your job will be communicating with the people you work with. Objectives, plans, and ideas are worthless unless everyone involved understands them well enough to take action.

I experienced this phenomenon daily while working at P&G—one of my primary projects involved creating a company-wide strategy on how to measure certain marketing tactics. Because it was a global project, my recommendation required input and/or approval from dozens of individuals across the company before anything could be implemented.

Everyone involved had different ideas, argued endlessly over various approaches, and wanted a share of the credit without having to commit to too much work or expense. I spent three months of full-time effort putting together a workable proposal. In the meantime, *no actual work was being accomplished*—99 percent of my time was spent doing little more than communicating with other members of the group. That's Communication Overhead.

In the book *Beyond Bureaucracy*,[1] Derek Sheane proposed "8 Symptoms of Bureaucratic Breakdown" that appear in teams suffering from Communication Overhead:

1. *The Invisible Decision.* No one knows how or where decisions are made, and there is no transparency in the decision-making process.

2. *Unfinished business.* Too many tasks are started but very few are carried through to the end.

3. *Coordination paralysis.* Nothing can be done without checking with a host of interconnected units.

4. *Nothing new.* There are no radical ideas, inventions, or lateral thinking—a general lack of initiative.

5. *Pseudo-problems.* Minor issues become magnified out of all proportion.

6. *Embattled center.* The center battles for consistency and control against local/regional units.

7. *Negative deadlines.* The deadlines for work become more important than the quality of the work being done.

8. *Input domination.* Individuals react to inputs—i.e., whatever gets put in their in-tray—as opposed to using their own initiative.

If any of these qualities describe your daily work experience, your team is probably suffering from a case of Communication Overhead.

The solution to Communication Overhead is simple but not easy: make your team as small as possible. You'll be leaving people out, but that's the point—including them is causing more work than it's creating in benefits. Removing unnecessary people from the team will save everyone's time and produce better results.

Studies of effective teamwork usually recommend working in groups of three to eight people. In *Peopleware*, project managers Tom DeMarco and Timothy Lister recommend keeping teams "elite and surgical." Small groups tend to be more effective than large groups because Communication Overhead is reduced—each team member adds more networking capacity to the team than they require in communication to be effective. Once group size expands above eight, each additional team member requires more investment in communication than they add in productive capacity.

If you want your team to perform at its best, make your teams as small and autonomous as possible.

REFERENCE LINK: **personalmba.com/communication-overhead/**

Importance

The deepest principle in human nature is the craving to be appreciated.

—WILLIAM JAMES, NINETEENTH-CENTURY DOCTOR AND
PIONEERING PSYCHOLOGIST

Everyone has a fundamental need to feel Important. It doesn't matter if you're dealing with a customer, an employee, an acquaintance, or a friend. The more you emphasize their *Importance*, the more they'll value their relationship with you.

Make someone feel small or unimportant and you'll earn their enmity in record time. How do you feel when you're talking with someone who's checking their phone, or interrupts your conversation to take a phone call?

The more interest you take in other people, the more Important they will feel. The reason you don't feel valued when a sleazy car salesman asks how you're doing is that you know the question doesn't indicate genuine interest—it's a means to close the deal. People want to feel Important even if they don't buy from you, which is where canned sales scripts fail.

Fortunately, making others feel Important is not particularly difficult if you make an effort to be present and curious. It has to do with undivided focus: paying attention, listening intently, expressing interest, and asking questions. Being the complete focus of someone's attention is so rare in today's world that it makes a memorable impact almost immediately.

Cultivating a genuine interest in other people goes a very long way. The more Important you make people feel when they're around you, the more they'll like you and want to be around you.

REFERENCE LINK: **personalmba.com/importance/**

Safety

Consider the people who routinely disagree with you. See how confident they look while being dead wrong? That's exactly how you look to them.

—SCOTT ADAMS, CARTOONIST AND CREATOR OF *DILBERT*

"That's the stupidest thing I've ever heard! Seriously—did you even think that through before you opened your mouth?"

Ever heard a comment like that in a meeting? I have.

This type of interaction happens all the time. In *What Got You Here Won't Get You There*, veteran executive coach Marshall Goldsmith explains that high-level executives often undermine or put down their peers and subordinates to make themselves feel smarter or more **Important**, shutting down effective communication.

Effective communication can only occur when both parties feel safe. As soon as people start to feel unimportant or threatened in a conversation, they start "stonewalling," shutting down communication. The threatened party may continue to interact, but mentally and emotionally, they've withdrawn from the conversation.

The only way to prevent stonewalling is to make the person you're communicating with feel safe being open and honest with you. Just as people have a fundamental need to feel Important, people also have a need to feel safe when expressing what's on their minds and talking about things that are Important to them. The moment they begin to sense they're being judged, evaluated, or looked down upon because of an idea they have or a position they hold, they'll shut down.

In *Crucial Conversations*, a book about maintaining a sense of **Safety** while discussing important issues with colleagues and loved ones, authors Kerry Patterson, Joseph Grenny, Ron McMillan, and Al Switzler recommend using the STATE model to communicate without provoking anger or defensiveness:

1. *Share your facts.* Facts are less controversial, more persuasive, and less insulting than conclusions, so lead with them first.

2. *Tell your story.* Explain the situation from your point of view, taking care to avoid insulting or judging, which makes the other person feel less safe.

3. *Ask for others' paths.* Ask to hear the other person's side of the situation, what they intended, and what they want.

4. *Talk tentatively.* Avoid conclusions, judgments, and ultimatums.

5. *Encourage testing.* Make suggestions, ask for input, and discuss until you reach a productive and mutually satisfactory course of action.

Some people are more sensitive than others. Becoming more aware of your words and actions and how they might be interpreted by people with different attitudes is half the battle. If you want to communicate with someone in such a way that you both benefit from the conversation and get something done, both parties need to feel safe. The best way to make that happen is to avoid passing judgment and focus on making the other party feel Important. Books like *Crucial Conversations*, Dale Carnegie's *How to Win Friends and Influence People*, and Daniel Goleman's *Emotional Intelligence* can help you learn how.

REFERENCE LINK: **personalmba.com/safety/**

The Golden Trifecta

Any fool can criticize, condemn, and complain—and most fools do.
—DALE CARNEGIE, AUTHOR OF *HOW TO WIN FRIENDS AND INFLUENCE PEOPLE*

If people have a fundamental need to feel *Important* and *Safe,* how do you go about making that happen?

The **Golden Trifecta** is my personal three-word summary of *How to Win Friends and Influence People.* If you want to make others feel Important and Safe around you, always remember to treat people with appreciation, courtesy, and respect.

Appreciation means expressing your gratitude for what others are doing for you, even if it's not quite perfect. Imagine that you're designing a product, and your lead designer shows you some mockups that you believe won't work. Bluntly responding, "This is totally wrong—do it again," is a good way to make your colleague feel unimportant and insecure. Instead, express appreciation: "Thanks—it's clear you worked hard on this and I appreciate that. I'm not sure we're there yet, so here are a few ideas that may help . . ." It's the same content, but delivered in a very different tone.

Courtesy is politeness, pure and simple. I once heard courtesy defined as "accepting small inconveniences on behalf of another person," and I think that's a very useful definition. Opening the door for another person is a small inconvenience, but it can have a major impact on how they perceive you. There's no need to make every petty issue a big deal.

Respect is a matter of honoring the other person's status. No matter how you relate to the person you're communicating with, respecting them as an individual is critical if you want to make them feel Important or Safe, no matter how high or low their social status.

It's important to apply the Golden Trifecta to all of your interactions with other people, not just the people you're interested in. If you've ever had lunch or dinner with someone who was nice to you but rude to the waitstaff, you know what I mean. Treating other people poorly sends a clear signal to everyone that you can't be trusted.

If you make it a policy to treat people with appreciation, courtesy, and respect in all circumstances, other people will feel Important and Safe in your presence.

REFERENCE LINK: **personalmba.com/golden-trifecta/**

Reason Why

Civilization advances by extending the number of operations we can perform without thinking.

—ALFRED NORTH WHITEHEAD, MATHEMATICIAN AND PHILOSOPHER

Here's a fascinating quirk about asking people to do something: they'll be far more likely to comply with your request if you give them a reason to do what you ask. In *Influence: The Psychology of Persuasion*, Dr. Robert Cialdini describes an experiment that demonstrates this principle in action.

In the 1970s, Ellen Langer, a psychologist at Harvard University, conducted a set of famous experiments on the subject of compliance—what makes people agree to a request. The experiments centered around a busy copy machine on the Harvard campus.

Langer's students asked people waiting in line to use the copy machine if they could move to the front of the line, using various approaches. A straightforward request was honored 60 percent of the time, but Langer found that adding a *reason* for the request increased the compliance rate to *95 percent*. The technique worked even if the reason was vacuous—"because I have to make copies" worked just as well as "because I'm late for class" or "because I'm in a rush." All the reason had to do was supply a "because," and it was enough to make people agree to the request.

Humans are predisposed to look for behavioral causes. People will be more receptive to any request if you give them a **Reason Why**. Any reason will do.

REFERENCE LINK: **personalmba.com/reason-why/**

Commander's Intent

Never tell people how to do things. Tell them what to do, and they will surprise you with their ingenuity.

—GENERAL GEORGE S. PATTON, COMMANDER OF
THE US THIRD ARMY IN WORLD WAR II

As a rule, people hate to be told what to do. "Micromanagement" is the bane of any worker's existence—if you're a competent professional, nothing is more demeaning than someone else defining and scrutinizing your work to the last detail.

Micromanagement isn't just annoying—it's inefficient. Not only does spelling out every single detail make people feel less **Important**, it impairs their effectiveness. No set of instructions, no matter how detailed, is capable of covering every contingency. When something changes, micromanagement fails.

Think of how overwhelmed a CEO who insists on micromanagement will become—remember, human beings don't **Scale**. The more people who work for the company, the more directions the CEO must give to keep everything moving. If you have ten employees, micromanagement is a hassle. If you have hundreds or thousands, it's a nightmare.

Commander's Intent is a much better method of delegating tasks: whenever you assign a task to someone, tell them *why* it must be done. The more your agent understands the purpose behind your actions, the better they'll be able to respond appropriately when the situation changes.

Commander's Intent originated on the battlefield. If a general tells a field commander in detail how to capture a specific hill and the situation changes, the field commander is forced to return to the general for new orders, which is slow and inefficient. If the general explains the strategy to the field commander and explains *why* that particular hill is important and how it will support the overall strategy, the field commander is free to use their knowledge of the **Goal** and fresh intelligence to act in a new way that supports the original intent.

Commander's Intent alleviates **Communication Overhead**. By communicating the intent behind a certain plan, a leader can make constant communication less critical for the success of the entire team. If everyone understands the purpose of the plan, everyone can act in ways that support the intent without requiring constant attention.

When you communicate the intent behind your plans, you allow the people you work with to respond to changes as they happen.

REFERENCE LINK: **personalmba.com/commanders-intent/**

Earned Regard

You can't build a reputation on what you are going to do.

—HENRY FORD, FOUNDER OF THE FORD MOTOR COMPANY
AND ASSEMBLY-LINE PIONEER

Building **Trust** between individuals takes time and effort. In most situations, other people won't give you substantial **Power**, responsibility, or control until you demonstrate trustworthiness and an ability to deliver.

Earned Regard is a subjective estimate of how much Trust you have built with an individual over time. When you demonstrate competence, reliability, good judgment, skill, or the capacity to deliver positive results, your Earned Regard tends to increase. When you demonstrate the opposite, your Earned Regard with that individual decreases.

In an interview with Shane Parrish, Tobi Lütke, cofounder and CEO of Shopify, explains this idea by way of a metaphor: the "trust battery," which is charged or depleted based on the quality and quantity of interactions over time.[2] This metaphor makes it easier to discuss Earned Regard in a more direct, less emotional way:

> So much about working in teams is the way you communicate working together, and the way you give each other feedback. It's so much easier to say, "Hey, I love working with you and the kind of work you do, but you don't show up to the team meetings, and I just want you to know those two things offset each other. This is why your trust battery with the rest of the team is just not going up, even though you're doing great work." That's a much better conversation than saying, "Hey, do you not care about us?" [. . .]
>
> I want Shopify to be a company [where] people have an enormous amount of personal autonomy. But it's not possible to just bestow that on everyone, because trust needs to be earned. And so, when you have a concept like this where you can say, "Hey, get to 80-90 percent of the trust battery with the majority of the people around you, and then we give you an area to own, and we trust that you own it." That's what people do already. So all we are doing is putting a metaphor into play that people can refer to and give people a goal of saying, "Hey, here's what I get if I build trust with the rest of the team."

It's possible to build Earned Regard in a systematic way. In *The Snowball System*, Mo Bunnell, a veteran sales professional, recommends creating a list of your most important professional contacts, along with a list of people with whom you'd like to establish a new or stronger relationship. This list of VIPs is useful in two ways: it's a practical **Checklist** you can use to ensure you keep in contact and a **Priming** tool that makes it easier to recognize when you come across anything one of your contacts might find useful or interesting. As a result, you'll identify more opportunities to have a positive interaction, interact more often, and strengthen the relationship faster than you would've by leaving future interactions to chance.

The more Earned Regard you accumulate with the people in your life, the stronger your relationships will become, and the more opportunities you'll have as a result.

REFERENCE LINK: **personalmba.com/earned-regard/**

Bystander Apathy

Accountability is about one person taking responsibility. If two people are accountable for the same decision, no one is really accountable.

—GLYN HOLTON, INVESTMENT RISK MANAGEMENT CONSULTANT

Growing up, I was very active in the Boy Scouts. The standard Scout program covers first aid, CPR, and emergency management—basic training that prepares you to handle the most common emergencies you're likely to face.

Outside of specific techniques, I remember two useful principles from this training: (1) step up and take responsibility, unless relieved by a more experienced professional, and (2) always direct commands or requests to *one specific individual at a time.*

If someone appears to be experiencing a heart attack in a crowded store and you yell, "Someone call 911," it's likely that no one will call—the more people around, the more likely everyone will assume that someone else is taking action. It's far more effective to single someone out, make eye contact, point, and say, "YOU—CALL 911." They will.

Bystander Apathy is an inverse relationship between the number of people who *could* take action and the number of people who *choose to act.* The more people available, the less responsibility each member of the crowd feels to do anything about the situation.

The 1964 murder of Kitty Genovese and the 2009 shooting of Petru Barladeanu are dramatic, well-known examples of Bystander Apathy. In both cases, the victims were attacked in the presence of many bystanders, all of whom were hesitant to offer assistance. There's some controversy over how many people witnessed the Genovese murder, but there's no doubt about the Barladeanu case—it was captured on video. As Barladeanu bled to death from a gunshot wound on the floor of a metro station, scores of people who could see what was going on walked past the scene and did nothing to help.

Bystander Apathy explains why anything assigned to a committee never gets done. If you've ever worked with a group of people who have no **Power** over one another, you know what I'm talking about. Unless someone steps up and takes individual responsibility for making things happen and holding individuals accountable for progress, a committee can deliberate for years without getting anything done. Each member of the committee assumes someone else is working on it.

The best way to eliminate Bystander Apathy in project management is to ensure that all tasks have single, clear owners and deadlines. Unless every individual on your team knows what they're responsible for and when it must be done, it's very unlikely that they'll do it.

When delegating responsibilities, *always assign tasks to a single owner with a clear deadline.* Only then will people feel responsible for getting things done.

REFERENCE LINK: **personalmba.com/bystander-apathy/**

Planning Fallacy

Hofstadter's Law: it always takes longer than you expect, even when you take into account Hofstadter's Law.

—DOUGLAS HOFSTADTER, COGNITIVE SCIENTIST
AND PULITZER PRIZE–WINNING AUTHOR

As a rule, people are horrendous at planning. As uncomfortable as this sounds, any plan created by even the most intelligent and skilled CEO or project manager will be inaccurate—even if they've done similar work before.

As Jason Fried and David Heinemeier Hansson quip in their book *Rework*, "Planning is guessing." The reason we're so bad at planning is because we're not omniscient—unforeseen events or circumstances can impact even the most detailed plans. When we create plans, we're guessing and using **Interpretation** to fill in the blanks, no matter how much we cloak that uncomfortable reality in official-sounding language and fancy-looking charts.

The **Planning Fallacy** means that people have a persistent tendency to underestimate completion times. The more complex the project, the more **Interdependencies** the project contains. The more Interdependencies there are, the more likely it is that something at some time will not go according to plan.

When planning, we tend to imagine a scenario in which everything goes well. As a result, we tend to underestimate the likelihood of things that could impact the plan, as well as how much those contingencies will affect the project. Rare is the project plan that contains a line item that says, "Project manager contracts mononucleosis: out for a month."

Most plans drastically underestimate the amount of **Slack** necessary to make the plan accurate. If you're responsible for completing a complex project, including a few months of Slack time is appropriate—unexpected delays, vacations, sicknesses, and other unforeseen events are likely to make things take longer than expected.

The challenge is that including significant Slack time is almost never seen as acceptable or appropriate. If you go to a CEO, customer, or partner with a plan that involves three months of Slack time, the most common response is, "That's not acceptable—get it done faster." The Slack is eliminated, and as a result, almost every project plan is very likely to be wrong.

The inaccuracy of plans doesn't make planning worthless. Plans aren't useful because they help you predict with better accuracy—they're useful because the act of creating the plan helps you understand requirements, dependencies, and risks more thoroughly than when you started. In the immortal words of Dwight D. Eisenhower: "No battle was ever won according to plan, but no battle was ever won without one . . . Plans are useless, but planning is indispensable." The value of planning is in **Mental Simulation**: the thought process required to create the plan itself.

Use plans, but don't depend on them—as long as you keep working with speed and diligence, the project will be done as soon as it's feasible.

REFERENCE LINK: **personalmba.com/planning-fallacy/**

Forcing Function

The schedule you develop will seem like a complete work of fiction
up until the time your customer fires you for not meeting it.

—DAVID AKIN, PROFESSOR OF AEROSPACE ENGINEERING,
UNIVERSITY OF MARYLAND

As a rule, people hate making *Trade-offs* unless the situation requires it. *Options* are valuable, and it makes sense to preserve flexibility and control unless there's a good reason.

A *Forcing Function* is a process or *Constraint* that requires an action, *Decision* or Trade-off within a certain timeframe. Deadlines, project milestones, trial periods, and quarterly or annual reports are common examples of Forcing Functions: the purpose is to encourage or mandate progress that would otherwise not happen in the absence of an external limitation.

Forcing Functions create urgency, but they have limits: you can't speed up creation, discovery, or production processes that take a certain amount of time by setting an artificial end date, even if you devote more resources to the project. Frederick P. Brooks Jr., author of *The Mythical Man-Month*, used a memorable metaphor to explain this inherent limitation: "One woman can make a baby in nine months . . . but nine women can't make a baby in one month." Increasing urgency in situations like this doesn't produce better results and only serves to increase unnecessary stress.

Forcing Functions are best used to place time limits on research and to make Decisions under conditions of *Uncertainty*. If you're not quite sure how to proceed, it's all too easy to put off difficult choices in the name of collecting additional information. By adding an artificial limit to the information-collection phase of the project, it's much easier to move forward and deliver results, particularly if you need to deliver on a deadline.

REFERENCE LINK: **personalmba.com/forcing-function/**

Referrals

The way to get on in the world is to make people believe it's to their advantage to help you.

—JEAN DE LA BRUYÈRE, SEVENTEENTH-CENTURY
PHILOSOPHER AND SATIRIST

When your car breaks down, whom would you rather take it to—a mechanic who's a friend of a friend, or a random operation you found in the phone directory?

Given the choice, people always prefer to interact with people they know and like. **Referrals** make it far easier for people to **Decide** to work with someone they don't know.

Referrals are effective because they transfer the qualities of being known and liked. The reason you're more likely to go to a mechanic your friend recommends is that you know and like your friend, and your friend knows and likes that mechanic. Even if the competing mechanic in the phone book is highly qualified, that doesn't matter as much as being known and liked. The Referral transfers the knowing/liking effect to the recipient—instead of being a risky, unknown quantity, they're a safe, reasonable choice.

Cold calling doesn't work very well because the caller is unknown. Remember, our minds tend to treat unknown people and situations as potential threats, which activates our natural defenses. If someone doesn't already know or like you, you're going to have a tough time convincing them to do what you want.

Even the most obscure commonalities can significantly warm up a cold connection. If someone mentions they're from the same area as you, or that they went to the same college, or know the same person, you'll start to like them more—even though the connection may be very tenuous.

The last year Kelsey sold wedding gowns in Manhattan, over 70 percent of her sales came from Referrals. When you're considering spending $10,000 or more on a designer dress, you want to work with someone you know and like—and Kelsey's previous customers *really* liked working with her. Before they entered the salon, most of Kelsey's prospective customers already knew and liked her—and she closed many more sales as a result.

The more people who know, like, and trust you, the better off you are. Referrals are the best way to expand your network of personal connections.

REFERENCE LINK: **personalmba.com/referrals/**

Clanning

It is a more inspiring battle cry to scream, "Die, vicious scum!" instead of "Die, people who could have been just like me but grew up in a different environment!"

—ELIEZER YUDKOWSKY, ARTIFICIAL-INTELLIGENCE RESEARCHER

In 1954, twenty-two twelve-year-old boys were selected to attend a special summer camp in Robbers Cave State Park in Oklahoma. Here's what made the summer camp special: the camp was a psychology experiment, operated under the direction of Drs. Muzafer and Carolyn Wood Sherif.

Each of the boys was selected to be as similar to the rest of the group as possible—the psychologists ensured that all of the boys had similar IQs, families, and childhood experiences. Before the experiment started, the group of twenty-two was split into two groups and placed on opposite sides of the park. By design, neither group knew the other existed.

The original plan was to let each group coalesce for a while, then make them aware that the other group existed, to see what would happen. The camp counselors were psychologists and graduate students, who would be watching the events unfold up close and personal.

Here's what happened: the groups accidentally discovered each other earlier than planned, and hostilities started immediately. As soon as the boys discovered there was another group in "their camp," they rallied together in preparation and defense.

Humans tend to form distinct groups, a process called **Clanning**. One group of boys began calling themselves "the Eagles," while the other group self-identified as "the Rattlers." Distinct group identities formed to help members identify "insiders" and "outsiders." The Eagles created an image of themselves as the heroic good guys, while the Rattlers took on the persona of misfits and rebels.

With surprising speed, minor provocations like put-downs and stealing the other group's flag turned into chaos: campsite raids and dining-hall fist fights. Competitive activities like sports were a disaster. For the safety of the campers, the researchers tried to find a way to resolve the conflict.

The psychologists introduced challenges and goals that required both groups to work together: solving a water shortage, deciding on a movie to watch, and pushing a broken-down truck back to camp. When the campers started feeling like part of a larger group, the conflicts subsided.

Clanning is a natural human tendency—we are always influenced by the people around us. Identifying ourselves as part of a group and distinguishing ourselves from other groups is an instinct that explains many of the ongoing wars and conflicts featured in the news every day.

Think of sports fans. The players, coaches, and even stadiums and uniforms change so often, it's difficult to understand what the fans are cheering for—the life of a die-hard New York Yankees fan will go on unchanged regardless of whether their team wins or loses. While that may be true, it doesn't feel that way to the fan—when the Yanks win, the fans feel like winners too.

Sports rivalries happen for the same reason. I grew up in northern Ohio, where the Ohio State–University of Michigan rivalry is alive and well. Where I come from, during certain parts of the year, Michigan is *evil* in the eyes of Ohio State fans. If you look at the situation from a distance, it's silly—college kids scrambling for a little, oblong, brown ball while hundreds of thousands of people scream themselves hoarse. In the moment, however, for those two groups the enmity is everything.

Groups form around important issues, positions, or events. Understand the group dynamic or you're likely to be caught up in it.

REFERENCE LINK: **personalmba.com/clanning/**

Convergence and Divergence

The individual has always had to struggle to keep from being over-whelmed by the tribe. If you try it, you will be lonely often, and some-times frightened. But no price is too high to pay for the privilege of owning yourself.

—FRIEDRICH NIETZSCHE, PHILOSOPHER AND AUTHOR OF *THE WILL TO POWER*
AND *THUS SPOKE ZARATHUSTRA*

Over time, you become more and more like those whom you spend time with and less like people in other groups.

Convergence is the tendency of group members to become more alike over time. In business, this is sometimes called a company "culture," in the sense that people who work there tend to have similar characteristics, behaviors, and philosophies.

Convergence also means that groups have a tendency to police them-selves. The **Norms** of the group work like gravity—if they are violated, oth-ers will exert an influence on the rebel to bring them back in line. As the proverb goes, "The tallest blade of grass is the first to be cut."

If you've ever worked for a company with a workaholic culture, you know how powerful Convergence can be. If it's normal for workers to come in at 6:00 in the morning and stay until 10:30 at night, it can be difficult to keep shorter working hours, since violating the Norms is a social signal that you don't belong in the group. One of my clients, who works for a major medical research institution, often has conflicts with coworkers who believe he's not "pulling his weight" because he leaves work at 5:00 p.m. instead of 7:30 p.m., even though he does great work and gets everything done. Instead of being viewed as "working smart," going home at a reasonable hour is seen as a form of treason—sad, but common.

Divergence is the tendency for groups to become less like other groups over time. Since group behavior often evolves to distinguish members of one group from another, the Norms of most groups change to resist being confused with another group or imitator.

Divergence explains why fashions among the socialite class in New York City change so often. In certain social circles, dress is a way to signal your wealth or status. When the latest fashions start appearing in Target so people can imitate the look, fashions change to compensate. This constant Divergence keeps the group affiliation signal valid.

According to the late Jim Rohn, author of *The Art of Exceptional Living*, "You are the average of the five people you spend the most time with." The values and behaviors of the people you interact with on a daily basis exert constant pressures on you to adopt the same values and behaviors.

Convergence can be useful if you choose to spend time with people you'd like to become more like over time. If you'd like to become less shy and more outgoing, spending time with social people in social situations can't help but influence your behavior. You won't become a social butterfly overnight, but you will start to adopt the behaviors and Norms of the people you're spending time with.

Breaking away from groups that aren't serving you is painful but necessary to grow. People who want to quit smoking or drinking often find it difficult to quit because a large portion of their social network engages in those behaviors. Taking a smoke break at 3:00 p.m. or attending a 6:00 p.m. happy hour is a very significant social event—if your friends are expecting you, the temptation is even harder to resist. To make significant changes, it's often necessary to leave one group and find another that's more supportive of where you want to go, which is why joining support groups like Alcoholics Anonymous is a very effective way to change specific behaviors.

Once you realize how powerful Convergence and Divergence are, you can use them to your advantage. If your social circle isn't supporting your goals, change your social circle.

REFERENCE LINK: **personalmba.com/convergence-divergence/**

Social Proof

> If fifty million people say a foolish thing, it is still a foolish thing.
> —ANATOLE FRANCE, NOBEL PRIZE–WINNING NOVELIST AND POET

Have you ever stood waiting for a stoplight to change before crossing the street when the person standing next to you suddenly started walking? Chances are, you started moving too, unless you used willpower to *Inhibit* the response.

In most situations, the actions of other individuals in our situation are a very strong indication that it's okay to behave in a certain way. When a situation is ambiguous, we learn by watching the behavior of others. If you don't know how to act in Rome, doing what the Romans do is a pretty safe bet.

Social Proof can take on a life of its own. Fads often form when one person takes an action and others perceive it as a social signal, then act the same way, creating a social **Feedback Loop**. New fashions, viral videos, and stock market bubbles all gain power via Social Proof—if so many other people like or do something, it's easy to come to the conclusion that you should probably follow suit.

Testimonials are an effective form of Social Proof often used in business to close more sales. There's a reason why Amazon.com and other online retailers feature user reviews: stories about people who have been pleased with a purchase send a clear signal that an item is safe to buy, so more people purchase.

The best testimonials don't necessarily contain superlatives: "amazing," "best," "life-changing," and "revolutionary" have been so overused that people expect them and discount their expectations. The most effective testimonials tend to follow this format: "I was interested in this offer, but skeptical. I decided to purchase anyway and I'm very pleased with the result."

The reason this format is more effective than a litany of people gushing about your offer is that it more closely matches how your prospects are feeling: interested but uncertain. By signaling that the decision was a good one, testimonials tell your prospects that it's safe to buy.

Add a bit of Social Proof to your offers, and your sales will soar.

REFERENCE LINK: **personalmba.com/social-proof/**

Authority

Show respect to all men, but grovel to none.

—TECUMSEH, EIGHTEENTH-CENTURY LEADER OF THE SHAWNEE TRIBE

In the 1970s, Sanka—a popular mass-market coffee brand—hired Robert Young, an actor, to promote the health benefits of decaffeinated coffee.

Young was better known to the public as Dr. Marcus Welby, the lead character of the popular television show *Marcus Welby, M.D.*

Even though Young wasn't an expert on the medical effects of caffeine, people still perceived him as an authority—and purchased Sanka. The approach worked so well that Sanka used "Dr. Welby" to promote their product for decades.

People have an inherent tendency to comply with **Authority** figures. This tendency begins in childhood—we wouldn't survive very long if we didn't obey our parents most of the time. As we grow up, we're socialized to respect and obey other Authority figures: teachers, police officers, government officials, and clergy. As a result, when an Authority figure asks us to do something, we're very likely to comply—even if the request isn't appropriate or doesn't make sense.

People tend to comply with Authority figures even if they'd refuse to take the same action under normal circumstances. In a famously disturbing social psychology experiment, Stanley Milgram proved that most individuals will comply with Authority figures to a surprising degree—even if the request appears to be morally wrong.

In a series of experiments that began in 1961, Milgram placed test subjects in a room with a "scientist" in a white lab coat and another individual, both of whom were actors. The subject was told the study was about the effect of punishment on learning, and one of the participants was "randomly" selected to be the "learner"—the actor. The "learner" was taken to an adjacent room, strapped into a chair, and attached to electrodes.

The test subject's job as the "teacher" was to read the learner questions, then "shock" the learner if they responded incorrectly. The shocks weren't real, but the actor would scream, cry, and beg to be released from the study. Every few minutes, the "scientist" would instruct the teacher to raise the voltage of the shocks. The intent of the study was to see how long the test subject would obey the scientist before refusing to continue.

The results were disturbing: 80 percent of participants continued past the point where the learner begged to stop, and 65 percent continued all the way to the maximum level of 450 volts, which was marked as deadly. Throughout the study, the subjects expressed discomfort with what they were being asked to do. When subjects were *ordered* to continue, they resisted—an example of **Persuasion Resistance**—but when the Authority figure told them continuing the study was important for the "greater good"—the advancement of scientific knowledge—they complied.[3]

In the presence of an Authority figure, people will do things they'd otherwise view as reprehensible, or wouldn't consider in the first place—the source of many a scandal involving famous and powerful people.

If you're in a position of Authority, your Authority will change the way others interact with you. When you express an opinion, your subordinates will be far more likely to *Interpret* your position as a truth or as a command. As a result, people will begin to filter the information they give you based on what they think you want to hear—which may not be what you *need* to hear. This filtering behavior is how Authority figures often end up "living in a bubble"—the combination of Authority and *Confirmation Bias* shelters them from information that contradicts their opinions. As a result, it's difficult for Authority figures to compensate for the *Excessive Self-Regard Tendency*.

Developing a strong *Reputation* in a certain area confers the benefits of Authority. Not all parts of Authority are insidious—if people respect your knowledge and experience, they're more likely to do what you suggest. As a result, developing clear expertise and a strong Reputation can be beneficial—it increases your own influence. Work to establish yourself as an Authority on what you're offering, and people will be more likely to accept your offer.

REFERENCE LINK: **personalmba.com/authority/**

Commitment and Consistency

A foolish consistency is the hobgoblin of little minds.

—RALPH WALDO EMERSON, NINETEENTH-CENTURY ESSAYIST AND POET

A few months ago, Kelsey received a phone call from our alma mater, asking for a donation. Here's the twist: they didn't ask for the donation outright. Instead, they asked if she'd be "willing to donate money to the university in the future." Thinking nothing of it, she agreed—and promptly forgot about the call.

Just before we moved from New York to Colorado, an official-looking "invoice" for $150 from the university appeared in the mail. It said, "Here is your $150 commitment—you can send your check via the enclosed envelope."

Money was tight, since we were paying for movers, buying cars, and purchasing furniture—but Kelsey sent the check anyway. After all, she had promised, right?

No one wants to be considered an "oath breaker." **Commitments** have been used throughout history as a way of binding groups together. Breaking a promise or Commitment can often have a negative impact on **Social Status** and **Reputation**, so most people will do whatever they can to act in ways that demonstrate **Consistency** with previous positions and promises.

Even small Commitments make it more likely that individuals will take actions Consistent with those Commitments in the future. One of my favorite stories about Commitment comes from Michael Masterson, the author of *Ready, Fire, Aim*.[4] On a trip to India, Masterson visited a rug merchant. He entered the shop with a healthy level of skepticism and no intention of buying anything—he was just interested in the experience.

The rug merchant was an excellent salesman and relied on two primary strategies. To break down Masterson's skepticism, he used stories (**Narratives**) of past sales to encourage Masterson to like and **Trust** him before the selling began. Then he used Commitment: Whenever Masterson so much as looked at a rug, the proprietor would have his staff take it down off the racks to examine it closely. The rugs were heavy, and it was clear that the sales staff was working hard on his behalf. By making a small Commitment—expressing interest in a particular rug—Masterson provoked a flurry of action.

As the minutes passed, it became difficult for Masterson to imagine leaving without purchasing a rug—it would be inconsistent with the interest he'd expressed and the work the proprietor's staff were doing for him. The least he could do was engage in **Reciprocation**—how could he tell them no?

In the end, he purchased a rug for $8,200 and walked away a happy customer.

Obtaining small Commitments makes it more likely people will choose to act in a Consistent way later. Salespeople are often taught to do what they can to encourage their customers to start saying yes as soon as possible. By getting a "foot in the door," they increase the probability that their prospect will take further action.

That's why so many activists use opening questions like "Do you care about child safety?" or "Do you care about the environment?" when telemarketing or collecting signatures on a petition. Most people *do* care about these things, so the reply is automatic and swift. Once you've said you care about something, however, it would be rude of you to refuse their request—it's inconsistent with your previous statement.

Obtain a small Commitment and you'll make it far more likely that others will comply with your request.

REFERENCE LINK: **personalmba.com/commitment-consistency/**

Incentive-Caused Bias

Admire Oracles.

—123RD MAXIM OF THE ORACLE OF DELPHI, FOURTH CENTURY BCE

If you're working with a real estate agent or mortgage broker, they're primarily interested in convincing you to buy a house. Most agents won't tell you it's in your best interest to rent,[5] even if it's true.

Incentive-Caused Bias explains why people with a vested interest in something will tend to guide you in the direction of their interest. We touched on the idea of Incentive-Caused Bias when talking about *Buffers*. If you're working with an agent who's paid on commission, it's not necessarily in their best interest to tell you that purchasing something is not a good idea. As the saying goes, "Don't ask the barber if you need a haircut."

Incentives influence the way people act based on how they're rewarded. As a result, the structure of the incentives people are exposed to has a significant impact on behavior. Assuming that the things people are controlling for stay the same, changing the incentives is also likely to change behavior.

In *The Knack*, Norm Brodsky and Bo Burlingham describe how they compensate their salespeople. Most companies compensate salespeople on a commission basis: closing more sales nets the salesperson more money. Under this incentive structure, their salespeople are hyperfocused on closing sales—even if those sales aren't profitable or in the long-term interest of the company. By compensating their salespeople on a salary basis and giving generous bonuses based on long-term performance, Brodsky and Burlingham encouraged salespeople to focus on making *profitable* sales versus sales at any cost.

Sometimes incentives create unintended *Second-Order Effects*. Stock options were created under the theory that executives who had an interest in the company's stock price would act in ways to make the stock go up in value over time, which was in the best interest of the shareholders. That's true, but only to a point: the actual interest of those executives is in making the stock price go up *right before they intend to sell*. Once the options are sold, they no longer care so much, leading to policies that sacrifice long-term stability for short-term gains.

Incentives are tricky because they interact with our **Perceptual Control** systems. For example, giving an employee a bonus or raise for doing something good can create a curious result—they stop doing what got them the reward.

That makes no sense until you realize there was always a reward—they did what they did because they *wanted* to, so the reward was internal. Paying them makes the action part of their job, which reduces their inner drive to complete it for its own sake. In the case of **Conflict**, Perceptual Controls win over incentives every time.

Incentives can be useful if used appropriately, but be careful. If the incentives of the people you work with aren't aligned with your interests, you're bound to have problems.

REFERENCE LINK: **personalmba.com/incentive-caused-bias/**

Modal Bias

> We find comfort among those who agree with us, and growth among those who don't.
>
> —FRANK A. CLARK, MINISTER AND NEWSPAPER COLUMNIST

A few years ago, I was traveling on business with a colleague who was amazed that I was carrying a shoulder bag instead of a rolling suitcase. It was an overnight trip, so I didn't need much—a change of clothes, my computer, and a book. I had everything I needed, and the bag wasn't heavy, so my solution worked just fine.

My colleague thought my solution was absurd and spent the next ten minutes telling me so: "It's much better to carry a rolling suitcase! It would be more comfortable, and there'd be less weight. You should *always* carry a rolling suitcase . . ."

Modal Bias is the automatic assumption that *our* idea or approach is best.

Most of us like to assume we have everything together—that we know what we're talking about, we know what we're doing, and our way of doing things is optimal. Very often, we are mistaken. There is always more than one way to get something done, and good ideas can come from anywhere.

In the absence of evidence to the contrary, decisions are made according to the "Highest Paid Person's Opinion." "HiPPO" is a term coined by Avinash Kaushik in *Web Analytics: An Hour a Day* to explain why it's important to support business proposals and decisions with data. In the absence of data, you'll be forced to do things the boss's way: Modal Bias ensures that the boss always thinks that their way is best, unless you can prove otherwise. In a battle of opinions, the HiPPO always wins.

The best way to avoid Modal Bias in your own decision making is to use **Inhibition** to temporarily suspend judgment. Part of the value of understanding cognitive biases is the knowledge that you're not immune to them, and knowing they exist doesn't make them any less influential. Modal Bias is automatic—we have to use willpower to inhibit it.

If you're a leader or manager, it pays to suspend your judgment long enough to consider the perspectives and suggestions of the people you work with. Otherwise, you're likely to miss important information. Remind yourself to keep an open mind and you'll enhance your ability to make wise **Decisions**.

REFERENCE LINK: personalmba.com/modal-bias/

Attribution Error

> Rare is the person who can weigh the faults of others without putting his thumb on the scales.
>
> —BYRON J. LANGENFELD, WORLD WAR I AVIATOR

Let's assume you hire a contractor to build a house and give him a clear deadline for completion. The deadline comes and goes, and the project isn't done. Three more months go by before the house is complete.

Unless you're feeling charitable, you're likely to think the contractor is unprofessional, lazy, or inexperienced. You tell all of your friends who are interested in building a house not to hire that contractor—he overpromises and underdelivers.

Now imagine the situation from the contractor's point of view. The original plan was to buy lumber from a particular supplier that is trustworthy, but one of their trucks broke down, delaying the shipment. The situation required finding another supplier on short notice, which was difficult, since supplies of the materials were scarce. The contractor moved heaven and earth to get the job done—without the contractor's intervention, the project would have been delayed six months instead of three.

Attribution Error means that when others screw up, we blame their character; when *we* screw up, we attribute the situation to circumstances. By assuming the contractor's actions were due to a character flaw, you made an error in judgment—the contractor went above and beyond the call of duty, given the circumstances. Because you weren't aware of the circumstances, however, you blamed his character.

Avoiding Attribution Error makes it easier to stay on good terms with the people you work with. If you're working with someone who fails to perform to expectations or deliver what they're supposed to on multiple occasions, then you have a legitimate issue that needs to be resolved. Otherwise, it's beneficial to give people the benefit of the doubt unless a particular behavior becomes a pattern. When you understand the reason behind a person's actions, it usually makes you see their behavior in a different light.

When something isn't going as expected, try to find out as much as you can about the circumstances surrounding the behavior you're noticing. More often than not, you'll find that it's a matter of circumstance, not a fundamental character flaw.

REFERENCE LINK: **personalmba.com/attribution-error/**

The Mind-Reading Fallacy

> The single biggest problem with communication is the illusion that it has taken place.
>
> —GEORGE BERNARD SHAW, PLAYWRIGHT AND POLITICAL ACTIVIST

Many people assume that effective employees, contractors, and business partners should be able to anticipate their thoughts, desires, and preferences.

That misconception is responsible for an enormous amount of unnecessary misunderstanding, confusion, frustration, and strife.

The **Mind-Reading Fallacy** is a corollary of **Locus of Control** and **Commander's Intent**: people don't have direct access to your mind, so you must communicate your objectives, priorities, and preferences.

The more responsibility you have and the more people you work with, the more important it is to express your thoughts and desires in a clear and consistent way. Positions of leadership require an enormous amount of communication, particularly as circumstances change over time. If it's important to make sure everyone on your team or in your company knows your current strategy and priorities, constant communication is an absolute necessity.

This principle is also a good rule of thumb for daily life: it can improve the quality of your relationships with loved ones, friends, and acquaintances. By taking full responsibility for expressing your thoughts and feelings and not expecting others to have a perfect understanding of what you need and want, you make it easier for others to interact with you in a productive and beneficial way.

REFERENCE LINK: **personalmba.com/mindreading-fallacy/**

Boundary Setting

> Sometimes it feels like the hardest part of self-employment isn't having the discipline to work, it's having the discipline to *not* work.
>
> —GARRETT DIMON, FOUNDER OF SIFTER.COM AND ADAPTABLE.ORG

Boundary Setting is the practice of defining and informing others of what is and is not acceptable behavior in a given context, then taking action when other parties overstep in those areas.

In order for a boundary to exist, you have to be able to define it and you have to be willing to enforce it. Expected working hours are a common point of tension: companies often require their employees to be at work at a certain time and stay at work until a certain time. If an employee shows up late or leaves early, that's a problem.

Boundary Setting goes both ways: many employers expect a minimum number of work hours but encourage their employees to work additional hours unpaid. If you're willing to work from 9:00 a.m. to 5:00 p.m. on weekdays, but your place of employment expects you to work from 7:00 a.m. to 10:00 p.m. six or seven days a week, there's a fundamental **Conflict**. It's up to you to enforce the boundary, or it doesn't exist.

If you work for yourself, it's important to set artificial boundaries on your work time, or you'll find yourself on the wrong side of **Parkinson's Law**, making severe **Trade-offs** in your personal life for the sake of improving the business. Likewise, if you send an immediate reply to the email your boss sends you at 2:00 a.m., you're sending a clear signal that you haven't set boundaries with respect to your time and attention outside of the office, and that you're available to work at all hours.

Ethics standards, codes of conduct, and other formal behavior policies are examples of Boundary Setting at the organizational or cultural level. If you predefine what is and is not acceptable behavior or activity, it's much easier to enforce boundaries when necessary. This makes it easier to handle difficult situations, whether you're dealing with sensitive interpersonal topics like harassment or shutting down a hacker who's accessing your website a thousand times a second.

Boundary Setting is also useful in defining acceptable behavior that doesn't require oversight. One of the best policies I remember from my corporate days was called the "adult business deal." In essence, you never had to ask for permission or time off to take care of mundane life concerns—going to doctor or dentist appointments, voting, picking up a sick child from school, et cetera. The company assumed by default that you were a responsible adult: you wouldn't have been hired otherwise. As long as you completed your work and didn't abuse the policy, there was no need for strict oversight in these areas. There was no need to guess if something was "okay" or not: the policy was a formal, tangible indicator of **Trust** and had the pleasant side effect of eliminating a huge amount of unnecessary managerial work.

Boundary Setting is important. If you don't define what you're willing to accept and what you're not, you're setting yourself up for unnecessary Conflict and a messy resolution. Be clear about what you expect, and when unacceptable situations occur, be ready to stand up for your values and priorities.

REFERENCE LINK: **personalmba.com/boundary-setting/**

The Principle of Charity

The reason listening is hard is that not-listening doesn't feel like not-listening: it just feels like the other person is wrong.

—ANDREW BADR, PROGRAMMER

Whenever you work with other people, you will often find yourself in disagreement. That's not a huge problem, provided you learn to disagree in a way that's productive for everyone involved.

The **Principle of Charity** is a way to overcome the tendency to disagree in a disagreeable way: instead of picking a fight, it's useful to assume people have reasons for what they say and do. As a result, it's a good idea to understand their position in more detail before assuming bad faith, ignorance, incompetence, or other unsatisfactory qualities.

That's not to say that you have to agree with the other person's point of view: you can take the time to understand their position, *then* come to conclusion that it's ill-informed, inaccurate, or that their proposed solution doesn't work for you. If that's the case, understanding and being able to express the other person's position makes it much easier to learn from the interaction and communicate in a way that preserves their sense of **Safety** and doesn't produce **Threat Lockdown**.

Daniel C. Dennett, the renowned philosopher and cognitive scientist, published an eloquent interpretation of this idea in his book, *Intuition Pumps and Other Tools for Thinking*, which is based on the work of Anatol Rapoport, a mathematical psychologist and systems theorist. Before you criticize someone's work:

(1) You should attempt to re-express your target's position so clearly, vividly, and fairly that your target says, 'Thanks, I wish I'd thought of putting it that way.'

(2) You should list any points of agreement, especially if they are not matters of general or widespread agreement.

(3) You should mention anything you have learned from your target.

(4) Only then are you permitted to say so much as a word of rebuttal or criticism.

This level of understanding takes time and energy, both of which are limited resources. In an ideal world, we'd be able to dig into the details and motivations behind everything others say, but that isn't practical in most cases. Even if you don't have the capacity for extended conversation or deep research, the Principle of Charity is a useful rule of thumb that makes it easier to have productive conversations.

REFERENCE LINK: **personalmba.com/principle-of-charity/**

Option Orientation

The important work of moving the world forward does not wait to be done by perfect men.

—GEORGE ELIOT, NINETEENTH-CENTURY NOVELIST

When something goes wrong, *how* you handle the crisis matters. Mistakes and issues happen all the time, so planning your response in advance goes a long way toward minimizing the impact of the unexpected.

Fixating on the issue is the least productive thing you can do when something goes wrong. By the time you're aware of an issue, preventing it is beyond your *Locus of Control*. The issue has already occurred—the only question is how you plan to respond to it.

Imagine that you report to the CEO of a company that makes microwaves, and you've just received a report that a few of your microwaves have exploded, burning several homes to the ground. That's a major issue. How do you think the CEO will respond if your approach is, "Boss, we have an issue. What do we do? Tell us what to do!"

Unless your CEO is a very patient soul, the response will probably be, "I know we have a $&#@&% issue—help me figure out our options!" Fixate on the hand-wringing and you'll soon be out of a job.

Instead of dwelling on the problem, cultivate an *Option Orientation*. Ruminating on the issue doesn't solve anything; what are you going to *do* about it? By focusing your energy on evaluating potential responses, you're far more likely to find a way to make things better.

Here's an alternate approach your hypothetical CEO is probably going to find more useful:

We've received several reports of fires caused by our microwaves. Here are our options—we can have our engineers run a full diagnostic before we issue a statement and risk further issues, or we can issue an immediate recall. Based on the information we have available right now, it appears our microwaves are at fault and present a major risk to the safety of our customers. Based on our options, I recommend an immediate recall, which we estimate will cost $4 million.

Focusing on the potential options is far more constructive—you're presenting several courses of action and the costs and benefits associated with each, then recommending a solution based on the available information. The CEO (or client) can then review your recommendation and the options you present, ask follow-up questions, then make the best **Decision** possible. Do this often and well, and you'll develop a **Reputation** for clearheadedness in the midst of crisis.

Focus on options, not issues, and you'll be able to handle any situation life throws at you.

REFERENCE LINK: personalmba.com/option-orientation/

Management

Management is doing things right; leadership is doing the right things.

—PETER DRUCKER, FATHER OF MODERN MANAGEMENT THEORY

Much has been made in business schools of "scientific management" and the need for educated, trained managers. In reality, you can't learn to be a competent manager in a classroom—beyond a few simple principles, it's a skill best learned through experience.

Management is simple, but not simplistic. In essence, Management is the act of coordinating a group of people to achieve a specific **Goal** while accounting for ever-present **Change** and **Uncertainty**. It's like taking the helm of a ship during a storm: all you can do is move the wheel back and forth, which is simple, but it takes experience and skill to do it well.

Based on what we've learned thus far, here are six simple principles of effective real-world Management:

1. Recruit the smallest group of people who can accomplish what must be done fast and with high quality. **Comparative Advantage** means that some people will be better than others at accomplishing certain tasks, so it pays to invest time and resources in recruiting the best team for the job. Don't make that team too large, however—**Communication Overhead** makes each additional team member beyond a core of three to eight people a drag on performance. Small, elite teams are best.

2. Communicate the desired **End Result**, who is responsible for what, and the current status. Everyone on the team must know the **Commander's Intent** of the project, the **Reason Why** it's important, and the specific parts of the project they're responsible for completing—otherwise, you're risking **Bystander Apathy**.

3. Treat people with respect. Applying the **Golden Trifecta**—appreciation, courtesy, and respect—is the best way to make the individuals on your team feel **Important** and is also the best way to ensure that they respect you as a leader and manager. The more your team works together under supportive conditions, the more **Clanning** will occur and the more cohesive the team will become.

4. Create an **Environment** where everyone can be as productive as possible, then let people do their work. The best working Environment takes full advantage of **Guiding Structure**—provide the best equipment and tools possible and ensure that the Environment reinforces the work the team is doing. To avoid having energy sapped by the **Cognitive Switching Penalty**, shield your team from as many distractions as possible, which includes nonessential bureaucracy and meetings.

5. Refrain from having unrealistic expectations regarding certainty and prediction. Create an aggressive plan to complete the project, but be aware in advance that Uncertainty and the **Planning Fallacy** mean your initial plan will be incomplete or inaccurate in a few important respects. Update your plan as you go along, using what you learn along the way, and continually reapply **Parkinson's Law** to

find the shortest feasible path to completion that works, given the necessary **Trade-offs** required by the work.

6. **Measure** to see if what you're doing is working—if not, try another approach. One of the primary fallacies of effective Management is that it makes learning unnecessary. This mind-set assumes your initial plan should be 100 percent perfect and followed to the letter. The exact opposite is true: effective Management means *planning* for learning, which requires constant adjustments along the way. Measure your performance across a small set of **Key Performance Indicators**— if what you're doing doesn't appear to be working, experiment with another approach.

Follow these principles well, and your team will be productive. Follow them poorly and you'll be fortunate to get anything useful done at all.

This style of management practice is *not* the command-and-control style of Management most people think of when they hear the term. On TV and in most management literature, managers are high-status executives who spend most of their time telling other people what to do and making important decisions. In practice, those behaviors are telltale signs of poor Management.

The best managers don't act like big-shot executives: they're more like very skilled assistants, whose primary purpose is to keep the people with **Economically Valuable Skills** focused on improving the **Five Parts of Every Business**: that is, doing things that contribute to the company's results. Important decisions are made by the individuals who have the most direct knowledge and experience of the area in question.

In a 2012 essay, software entrepreneur Joel Spolsky explains why managers should stop calling the shots and start letting people do their jobs:

> The "management team" isn't the "decision making" team. It's a support function . . . You don't build a [business] with one big gigantic brain on the top, and a bunch of lesser brains obeying orders down below. You try to get everyone to have a gigantic brain in their area, and you provide a minimum amount of administrative support to keep them humming along.[6]

Management is a unique skill that requires discipline, patience, clear communication, and a commitment to keeping everyone working together without unnecessary distractions. By recruiting a good team and eliminating as much *Friction* as possible, you'll achieve the results you're seeking.

REFERENCE LINK: **personalmba.com/management/**

Performance-Based Hiring

When all is said and done, a lot more is said than done.

—LOU HOLTZ, PROFESSIONAL AMERICAN FOOTBALL
COACH AND SPORTSCASTER

What if you need to build a team? What if you're responsible for recruiting new employees as your company grows? How do you attract and retain the best employees you can find?

Hiring is a tricky business, and there's no foolproof method to find, attract, and retain star employees and contractors. Mistakes in hiring are almost always expensive, and a bad hire can cost you precious time and money and your team's limited energy and patience.

Good employees and contractors are not necessarily the people who have the fanciest résumé or perform the best in a phone screen or interview: the best hires are people who get things done and work well with other members of your team. Ideally, you're looking for an individual who will contribute valuable work, who's excited about the opportunity, and who you'll enjoy working with every day.

Here's the golden rule of hiring: *the best predictor of future behavior is past performance.* If you want to hire people who will perform well for you in the months and years to come, you need to look for people who have performed well in the past. That means digging deep into what the applicant has accomplished, as well as giving each serious candidate a short-term opportunity to work with you before committing to a longer-term engagement.

The first step in *Performance-Based Hiring* is to publicize that you're looking for help. For most companies, announcing the job involves writing a job description, which is either published in a public format or used by a recruiter to search private networks. Either way, don't write the job description like an advertisement: you want to describe what the applicant will do on a day-to-day basis if they work for you, with as much unembellished detail as you can share. You're looking for people who are attracted to the work, and it's difficult for applicants to determine whether or not they'll be a good fit unless you describe what the job involves.

Next, identify a basic "acid test" to screen applicants. In weak employment markets, new job postings tend to be overwhelmed with applicants, many of whom are poor candidates. You'll need a way to identify the most promising candidates without taking too much time per candidate. Screening by degree or GPA is common but ineffective, since these don't tell you anything about the candidate's current level of skill. In the application, ask a few basic questions that require a certain amount of specialized knowledge in the field to answer. The most promising candidates will be easy to identify.

Once you've identified a few promising candidates, ask each one to show you examples of two or three of their best projects to date. These projects don't have to be related to the job in question, but they should be work that the applicant is proud of and that they believe highlights their skills. The idea is to see examples of what the candidate has accomplished to date, which makes it easier to gauge their relative level of experience and work ethic. If a candidate claims that they have "five years of experience" in product development but can't show you something they've created, that's a red flag.

Checking references at this point is a good use of time. Along with the project examples, request the names and contact information of people they worked with in the process. When you contact a candidate's references, your questions should be simple: e.g., Would they work with the candidate again? If they hesitate or talk around the question, it's a no. If you can't reach a reference when you call, leave a message and ask them to contact you if the candidate is extraordinary. If they are, you'll receive a return call. If they aren't, you won't.

Finally, give promising candidates a short-turnaround project or scenario to see how they think, work, and communicate firsthand. Small projects tend to work best for skilled technical employees, while scenarios work best for candidates who will be responsible for product creation, marketing, sales, business development, finance, and management roles. The outcome of the assignment should be a deliverable of some kind: a report, a pitch, an asset, or a process.

Don't put the candidate in an artificial environment: they should be free to use whatever tools or resources they're comfortable using. They should be free to contact you if they have questions. On completion of the project, bring the candidate in to meet you and present their results. This presentation replaces the interview.

The purpose of the project or scenario is to evaluate the candidate's actual work in a realistic environment. What does the candidate focus on first? What do they notice and what do they miss? How do they explain their choices and recommendations? How do they respond when you ask questions or disagree with a conclusion?

Assignments like these should be short, requiring no more than a few hours of work. Respect your applicants: your hiring process should not be a cover to obtain free consulting. If you'd prefer to use longer projects to evaluate a candidate, you can always hire them as a part-time consultant, then bring them on full-time if you're pleased with their work.

This general hiring process is a straightforward, effective way to discover and evaluate promising employees and contractors. It's important to note that this process doesn't rely on résumés or traditional interviews, which only test for how well the candidate writes a résumé and performs in an interview. If you look for past performance and evaluate a candidate's work firsthand, you'll make much better hires.

REFERENCE LINK: personalmba.com/performance-based-hiring/

9

UNDERSTANDING SYSTEMS

You do ill if you praise, but worse if you censure, what you do not understand.

—LEONARDO DA VINCI, INVENTOR, ARTIST, AND POLYMATH

Businesses are complex systems that exist within even more complex systems—markets, industries, and societies. A complex system is a self-perpetuating arrangement of interconnected parts that form a unified whole.

In this chapter, you'll learn common elements of all systems, how *Environmental* factors influence the function of systems, and the ever-present nature of *Uncertainty* and *Change*.

REFERENCE LINK: **personalmba.com/understanding-systems/**

Gall's Law

A complex system that works is invariably found to have evolved from a simple system that worked. The inverse proposition also appears to be true: a complex system designed from scratch never works and cannot be made to work. You have to start over, beginning with a simple system.

—JOHN GALL, SYSTEMS THEORIST

Here's a weekend project for you: build a car from scratch. No premanufactured parts or plans allowed. Just a block of metal, a few simple tools, your knowledge, and your imagination. How do you think your project will turn out?

Even if the project takes a year, chances are it will be a complete disaster—if your car works at all (which is very, very unlikely), it'll be far less efficient and reliable than even the worst car from a commercial manufacturer.

Now imagine building a modern computer, creating a cure for cancer, or cloning a human being from scratch without relying on anything someone else has already discovered. You'll suffer through a series of expensive and demoralizing failures. If you succeed, it'll take decades.

Why is it so hard to build working complex systems from scratch? John Gall, one of the first major complex-systems theorists, provided the answer.

Here's **Gall's Law**: all complex systems that work evolved from simpler systems that worked. Complex systems are full of variables and **Interdependencies** that must be arranged just right in order to function. Complex systems designed from scratch will never work in the real world, since they haven't been subject to environmental selection forces while being designed.

Uncertainty ensures that you will never be able to anticipate all of these Interdependencies and variables in advance, so a complex system built from scratch will continually fail in all sorts of unexpected ways.

Gall's Law is where environmental **Selection Tests** meet systems design. If you want to build a system that works, the best approach is to build a simple system that meets the **Environment's** current Selection Tests first, then improve it over time. Over time, you'll build a complex system that works.

Gall's Law is why **Prototyping** and **Iteration** work so well as a **Value Creation** methodology. Instead of building a complex system from scratch, building a Prototype is much easier—it's the simplest possible creation that will help you verify that your system meets critical Selection Tests.

Expanding that Prototype into a **Minimum Viable Offer** allows you to validate your **Critical Assumptions**, resulting in the simplest possible system that can succeed with actual purchasers. The Iteration Cycle and **Incremental Augmentation**, over time, will produce complex systems that work, even as the Environment changes.

If you want to build a system that works from scratch, violate Gall's Law at your peril.

REFERENCE LINK: **personalmba.com/galls-law/**

Flow

A process cannot be understood by stopping it. Understanding must move with the flow of the process, must join it and flow with it.

—FRANK HERBERT, SCIENCE-FICTION NOVELIST

No matter what a system does, it will have **Flows**—movements of resources into and out of the system. Imagine an automotive assembly line—raw materials like steel, plastic, silicon, rubber, and glass flow in, and a finished car flows out.

Inflows are resources moving into a system: water into a sink, money into a bank account, raw materials into an assembly line, new hires into a company.

Outflows are resources flowing out of a system: water draining from a sink, money flowing out of a bank account, finished goods exiting an assembly line, employees leaving the company due to retirement, termination, or changing jobs.

Follow the Flows and you're on your way to understanding how the system works.

REFERENCE LINK: personalmba.com/flow/

Stock

Goods in any storehouse are useless until somebody takes them out and puts them to the use they were meant for. That applies to what man stores away in his brain, too.

—THOMAS J. WATSON, FORMER PRESIDENT OF IBM

Follow a system's **Flows** and you'll find places where resources tend to pool together.

In this case, a **Stock** isn't a certificate of business ownership—it's a pool or holding tank of resources. A bank account is a good example of a Stock: it's a pool of money waiting to be used. Inventories, queues of customers, and waiting lists are also examples of Stocks.

To increase a Stock, increase inflows and/or decrease outflows. If you want to increase the size of your bank account, put more money in and take less money out. If you're building cars and you start running out of engines, either slow down the line or add more engines to your inventory.

To decrease a Stock, decrease inflows and/or increase outflows. If you have too much inventory, stop producing units or increase sales. If waiting lists are too long, increase **Throughput** or reduce the number of people entering the line.

Find the system's Stocks and you'll discover pools of resources waiting to be used.

REFERENCE LINK: **personalmba.com/stock/**

Slack

A man with a surplus can control circumstances, but a man without a surplus is controlled by them, and often has no opportunity to exercise judgment.

—HARVEY S. FIRESTONE, FOUNDER OF THE FIRESTONE
TIRE AND RUBBER COMPANY

Since **Stocks** are pools of resources, it pays to understand *how many* resources you have to work with. **Slack** is the amount of resources present in a Stock. The more resources you have in a Stock, the more Slack you have.

For a system to operate in an efficient way, Stocks should be just the right size—not too big and not too small. Think of our hypothetical automotive manufacturing system: it's a combination of many smaller systems, each of which is designed to create a Stock of parts.

If there's no Stock of engines waiting to be installed when a car reaches that part of the assembly line, that's an issue—the car will have to wait until an engine is ready, which holds up everything in line behind it. To avoid this issue, it's best to ensure that the Stock is big enough to handle the level of outflows required to keep the system running. Inflows replenish the Stock as it's depleted.

Large Stocks have the most Slack, but that flexibility comes at a cost. If you have five hundred engines waiting around to be installed, you'll have a lot of funds tied up in inventory, which reduces your cash flow. You'll also have to pay for space to store the engines so they aren't lost or damaged, which increases your costs and decreases your **Profit Margin.**

Small Stocks are more efficient but have less Slack. If you only have a Stock of two or three engines, you won't have a huge amount of resources tied up in inventory, but the probability of running out of engines is much higher if the assembly line speeds up or there's a problem with the engine-manufacturing system.

Slack is tricky to manage: too much, and you're wasting time and money. Too little, and your system faces the risk of running out of the resources necessary to continue operating.

REFERENCE LINK: **personalmba.com/slack/**

Constraint

Once you eliminate your number one problem, number two gets a promotion.

—GERALD WEINBERG, COMPUTER SCIENTIST AND SYSTEMS THEORIST

The performance of a system is always limited by the availability of a critical input. Alleviate the **Constraint**, and the system's performance will improve.

In *The Goal: A Process of Ongoing Improvement*, Eliyahu Goldratt explains what he calls the "Theory of Constraints": any manageable system is always limited in achieving more of its **Goal** by at least one Constraint. If you can identify and alleviate the Constraint, you'll increase the **Throughput** of the system.

Creating or increasing the size of a **Stock** in front of a Constraint can help alleviate the issue. If you're running out of engines, increasing the **Slack** in your engine Stock is the best way to alleviate the Constraint. By ensuring that the Constraint isn't "starved," you can increase the performance of the entire system.

In order to find and eliminate a Constraint, Goldratt proposes the

"Five Focusing Steps," a method you can use to improve the Throughput of any system:

1. *Identification*—examining the system to find the limiting factor. If your automotive assembly line is waiting on engines in order to proceed, engines are your Constraint.

2. *Exploitation*—ensuring that the resources related to the Constraint aren't wasted. If the employees responsible for making engines are also building windshields, or stop building engines during lunchtime, exploiting the Constraint would look like having the engine employees spend 100 percent of their available time and energy producing engines, and having them work in shifts so breaks can be taken without slowing down production.

3. *Subordination*—redesigning the entire system to support the Constraint. Let's assume you've done everything you can to get the most out of the engine-production system, but you're still behind. Subordination would be rearranging the factory so everything needed to build the engine is close at hand, instead of requiring certain materials to come from the other end of the factory. Other subsystems may have to move or lose resources, but that's not a huge deal, since they're not the Constraint.

4. *Elevation*—permanently increasing the capacity of the Constraint. In the case of the factory, elevation would be buying another engine-making machine and hiring more workers to operate it. Elevation is very effective, but it's expensive—you don't want to spend millions on more equipment if you don't have to. That's why exploitation and subordination come first: you can often alleviate a Constraint quickly, without resorting to spending more money.

5. *Reevaluation*—after making a change, reevaluating the system to see where the Constraint is located. Inertia is your enemy. Don't assume engines will always be the Constraint: once you make a few **Changes**, the limiting factor might become windshields. In that case, it doesn't make sense to continue focusing on increasing engine production—the system won't improve until windshields become the focus of improvement.

The "Five Focusing Steps" are very similar to **Iteration Velocity**—the faster you move through this process and the more cycles you complete, the more your system's Throughput will improve.

REFERENCE LINK: **personalmba.com/constraint/**

Feedback Loop

> Systems of information-feedback control are fundamental to all life and human endeavor . . . Everything we do as individuals, as an industry, or as a society is done in the context of an information-feedback system.
>
> —JAY W. FORRESTER, SYSTEMS THEORIST AND PROFESSOR AT MIT

Cause and effect are easy enough to consider, but what happens when the effects become causes themselves?

Feedback Loops exist whenever the output of a system becomes one of the inputs in the next cycle. Feedback is how systems learn—if the system is capable of perceiving its **Environment,** that feedback helps the system understand whether it's under control and satisfying the required **Selection Tests.**

Balancing loops dampen each system cycle's output, leading to system equilibrium and resistance to change. Think of dropping a tennis ball from shoulder height: it'll bounce up and down, each bounce smaller than the last. **Friction** and air resistance dampen each cycle until the energy in the system reaches equilibrium and the ball sits at rest upon the ground.

Balancing loops stabilize the system, dampening oscillations and keeping the system in a certain state. **Perceptual Control** systems are usually made up of balancing loops. Going back to the thermostat example: If the temperature of a room is higher than the **Reference Level,** the cooling system will kick in to move the temperature lower. If the temperature is lower than the Reference Level, the heater will turn on to bring the temperature up. As a result, the system tends to maintain a stable temperature, which is its purpose.

Reinforcing loops amplify the system's output with each system cycle. Reinforcing loops tend to lead to runaway growth or decay over time. Think of a price war between two companies, each of which is competing to have the lowest price. Company A lowers its price, then Company B retaliates by moving its price even lower. As long as each company's Reference Level remains "our price must be lower than our competitor's," prices will continue to drop until both companies eliminate their **Profit Margins** on that offering.

Compounding is an example of a positive reinforcing loop. Each cycle of interest payments makes the principal of the next cycle bigger, resulting in even more interest, continuing the cycle. Over time, accumulated interest can build to enormous sums, which is the purpose of the system.

More often than not, the size of every **Stock** is influenced by several loops, all pulling it in different directions. Consider your bank account balance: there are Feedback Loops controlling your income, rent/mortgage, food expenditures, and other expenses. You're evaluating whether each cycle is too much or not enough, which represents a balancing Feedback Loop. Too much or not enough inflow or outflow causes you to jump into action, which affects the next cycle.

Look around you—there are Feedback Loops *everywhere*. Once you start noticing them, you'll fully appreciate the ever-changing complexity of the systems we live in.

REFERENCE LINK: **personalmba.com/feedback-loops/**

Autocatalysis

> The system that will evolve most rapidly must fall between, and more precisely on, the edge of chaos—possessing order, but with the parts connected loosely enough to be easily altered.
>
> —E. O. WILSON, BIOLOGIST AND NATURALIST

Autocatalysis is a concept that comes from chemistry: it's a reaction whose output produces the raw materials necessary for an identical reaction.

An Autocatalyzing system produces the inputs necessary for the next cycle as a by-product of the previous cycle, **Amplifying** the cycle. Autocatalysis is a **Compounding**, positive, self-reinforcing **Feedback Loop**—the system will continue to grow until the system changes in a way that produces less output.

Television advertising from the 1950s to the 1990s is an excellent example of Autocatalysis. Companies could spend $1 in advertising and, via increased demand and distribution, get $2 or more in return. That $2, reinvested in advertising, became $4, which became $8, which became $16, etc. Mass-market consumer goods companies like Procter & Gamble, General Electric, Kraft, and Nestlé used this cycle to become the behemoths they are today.

Now, $1 invested in television advertising is lucky to return $1.20—there are more channels, advertising is more expensive, and people have the technology to filter out unwanted distractions. The loop still works in some circumstances, but it doesn't work as well as it used to.

Autocatalysis doesn't always have to involve money: "network effects" and "viral loops" are also examples of Autocatalysis. Every time someone signs up for a social-media network, they'll invite even more users to the network. Every time someone sees a funny video on the internet, they'll pass it along to several friends. That's Autocatalysis.

If your business includes some Autocatalyzing element, it'll grow faster than you expect.

REFERENCE LINK: **personalmba.com/autocatalysis/**

Environment

> Reality is that which, when you stop believing in it, doesn't go away.
> —PHILIP K. DICK, SCIENCE-FICTION NOVELIST

No system stands alone: every system is affected by all of the other systems around it.

An **Environment** is the structure in which a system operates. The Environment primarily influences or impacts the system's **Flows** or processes, changing the output of the system.

Think of how your body responds when it's either too hot or too cold. Too much or too little heat can kill you: your body must respond to the change in its Environment to keep operating, either by sweating to shed excess heat or by sheltering to preserve it.

When the Environment changes, the system must change with it to continue operating. According to most leading theories, the dinosaurs became extinct because of changes in the Environment, due to either an ice age or a meteorite impact that kicked up enough dust to blot out the sun. Colder temperatures and less sunlight resulted in major food shortages, resulting in mass extinction.

The conditions present in the Environment affect the operation of the system in that Environment. In 2005, oil prices skyrocketed, and many businesses that relied on oil to manufacture plastics or transport goods ran into trouble. The increase in variable costs made many businesses less profitable than they were before, and many businesses that couldn't absorb the increase in costs closed.

If you don't want to go the way of the dinosaur, you must always consider how conditions in the Environment affect your system.

REFERENCE LINK: **personalmba.com/environment/**

Selection Test

> Any one response to the universe, however powerful, becomes inappropriate with time and change. Those who become utterly dependent on one means of mastery will find themselves unable to cope with the future.
>
> —FRANK HERBERT, SCIENCE-FICTION NOVELIST

Self-perpetuating systems (like businesses or organisms) can only self-perpetuate as long as they meet the *Environmental* conditions necessary to exist.

A *Selection Test* is an Environmental *Constraint* that determines which systems continue to self-perpetuate and which ones "die." Mammals like humans have several Selection Tests: breathing enough air, eating enough food, drinking enough water, and retaining enough heat. Businesses also have Selection Tests: enough value provided to customers, enough revenue to cover expenses, enough *Profit* to stay financially *Sufficient*.

Many people think of Selection Tests as "survival of the fittest," but "death of the unfit" is a more accurate description. If a self-perpetuating system fails to satisfy a Selection Test, it will cease to exist. If you can't get enough air, you'll die. If your business can't bring in enough revenue to maintain Sufficiency, it'll die.

As the Environment changes, the Selection Tests change as well. Selection Tests are particularly interesting to watch in the technology market, where the Environment of "what's possible" changes. Businesses that fail to take advantage of major changes in technology find that they're unable to keep up with the new demands customers make for their products.

Changing Environments and Selection Tests are an entrepreneur's best friend—they're what allow small companies to outperform large, entrenched competitors. If you can identify what the Selection Tests in a market are, you'll be able to compete in that market with more success.

Selection Tests are ruthless: satisfy them and you'll thrive. Fail to adapt to changing conditions and you'll die.

REFERENCE LINK: **personalmba.com/selection-test/**

Entropy

> Those who will not face improvements because they are changes will face changes that are not improvements.
>
> —CHARLIE MUNGER, BILLIONAIRE BUSINESS PARTNER OF WARREN BUFFETT, FORMER CEO OF WESCO FINANCIAL, AND VICE-CHAIRMAN OF BERKSHIRE HATHAWAY

Left to their own devices, complex systems fall into disorder.

Entropy is the natural tendency for complex systems to degrade over time. Systems that remain operating over long periods of time require active maintenance and improvement.

This phenomenon has a simple explanation: the **Environment** the system operates within changes over time. Those changes affect both the operation of system itself and the **Selection Tests** the system must pass in order to continue functioning. If the system doesn't change in a way that enables it to continue operating, it will degrade and will eventually stop functioning or cease to exist.

Entropy is everywhere. Without adequate nutrition, movement, and oxygen, your health will suffer. Roads need to be resurfaced every few years or they'll develop cracks, bumps, and potholes. Software needs to be updated and patched, or it will stop functioning as computers are updated and connected systems change. Houses need to be repainted, refinished, and refurbished to keep them in good condition.

Entropy makes maintenance a necessary and valuable activity. In most organizations, creating something new is a high **Social Status** activity, while maintaining existing systems is considered a lower-status activity. That's a huge mistake: the organization is only as strong as its existing systems, which sustain its ability to function. Devoting attention and resources to maintaining and improving those systems is not only important, it's critical for long-term operation and preserving value over time.

REFERENCE LINK: **personalmba.com/entropy/**

Uncertainty

He who lives by the crystal ball soon learns to eat ground glass.

—EDGAR R. FIEDLER, ECONOMIST

What will interest rates look like ten years from now? Where do you think the price of oil will be next year? How about that company stock—is it cheap or overpriced? Is it better to stockpile raw materials now or wait a few months? Businesspeople deal with questions like these daily.

Here's the answer to all of these questions: *nobody knows*. This world of ours is an uncertain place, which is both a blessing and a curse. Anything can happen, for good or ill—we can't know what's around the bend.

There's an enormous difference between risk and **Uncertainty**. In the immortal words of former US secretary of defense Donald Rumsfeld:

> There are known knowns. These are things we know that we know. There are known unknowns. That is to say, there are things that we know we don't know. But there are also unknown unknowns. These are things we don't know we don't know.

Risks are known unknowns. If you're planning to pick up a friend from the airport, the probability that their flight will arrive several hours late is a risk—you know in advance that the arrival time can change, so you can plan for contingencies.

Uncertainties are unknown unknowns. You may be late picking up your friend from the airport because a meteorite demolishes your car an hour before you planned to leave for the airport. Who could predict that?

You can't predict the future based on past events in the face of Uncertainty. Unexpected or random events can occur suddenly, which can have major impacts on your goals and plans.

In *The Black Swan*, Nassim Nicholas Taleb, a former hedge fund manager, describes the perils of Uncertainty. No matter how stable or predictable things seem, unpredictable "black swan events" can change everything in an instant.

The term "black swan" was a common expression in sixteenth-century London for something that was impossible or didn't exist—everyone knew that all swans were white. The problem with the term is what eighteenth-century philosopher David Hume called the "problem of induction": until you see every swan that exists, you can never assume the statement "all swans are white" is true. All it takes is *one* black swan to invalidate the hypothesis, which happened when black swans were documented in Australia in 1697 by Dutch sea captain Willem de Vlamingh.

The moment before they happen, the probability of "black swan" events occurring is close to zero. In the wake of a black swan event, the probability of its occurring is a moot point: the event changes the **Environment** in which the system operates, sometimes drastically changing **Selection Tests** without warning. You can't know in advance if (or which) black swan events will occur: all you can do is be flexible, prepared, and **Resilient** enough to react appropriately if and when they do.

Even the most detailed analysis with reams of historical data can't save you from Uncertainty. The primary drawback of the financial models taught in most MBA programs is Uncertainty: your pro forma, net present value (NPV) or capital asset pricing model (CAPM) calculation is only as good as the quality of your predictions. Many a business has been ruined by financial predictions that turned out to be wrong. How likely is it that your ten-year financial projection predicts everything that will happen with 100 percent accuracy? Who says tomorrow is going to be anything like today?

Many people make a business of selling certainty, which *doesn't exist*. Prediction, forecasting, and other forms of business soothsaying are popular because they provide the illusion that the future is knowable and controllable. Exercises in prediction aren't worth the cost—if there were a foolproof way to predict gas prices, interest rates, or stock prices, the people with that magic knowledge would be multibillionaires and would have no need to sell anything to you.

Absorbing the ever-present nature of Uncertainty is an exercise in seeing the world as it is, not as we want it to be. We all *want* to feel like we know what will happen in the future, particularly given how prone we are to **Loss Aversion** and **Threat Lockdown**. Contemplating Uncertainty feels bad, because not knowing what's going to happen feels like a threat. Instead of fixating on predicting invisible and unknowable threats, it's better to channel your energy into enhancing your ability to handle the unexpected.

Don't rely on making accurate predictions—things can change at any time. Planning for flexibility in response to Uncertainty via **Scenario Planning** is far more useful than pretending to be a seer.

REFERENCE LINK: **personalmba.com/uncertainty/**

Change

> It is not the strongest of the species that survives, nor the most intelligent, but the one most responsive to change.
>
> —CHARLES DARWIN, NATURALIST AND PIONEER OF EVOLUTIONARY THEORY

All systems undergo **Change**—there is no such thing as a system in stasis.

Complex systems are in a constant state of flux. There is a great deal of **Uncertainty** in *how* a system will Change over time, but it is certain that the system *will* Change. Plans that do not take Change into account are of limited value.

Change is a fact of life. Psychologically, it's very difficult to internalize that some things are random: there's no rhyme or reason to many of the things that happen in the world. Because of our natural **Pattern Matching** abilities, we tend to see patterns where none exist and tend to attribute random Changes to skill if the Changes are good or to misfortune if they're bad. As a result, we're *Fooled by Randomness*—the title of Nassim Nicholas Taleb's first book.

You will never develop your business to the point that everything is perfect and unchanging. Many business owners and managers share an unexamined belief that by moving a business "from good to great," it'll be "built to last," continuing to outperform competitors for decades to come. It's a pleasant dream, but measuring yourself against that yardstick is unrealistic—it requires an unchanging world.

The only thing you can do about Change is increase your flexibility to handle a wide variety of different circumstances. The more flexible you are, the more **Resilient** you'll be when things Change.

REFERENCE LINK: **personalmba.com/change/**

Interdependence

> When we try to pick out anything by itself, we find it hitched to ev-
> erything else in the universe.
>
> —JOHN MUIR, NATURALIST

Nothing in the world exists in isolation.

Complex systems almost always rely on other systems in order to operate. Your refrigerator requires electricity to operate. When your local power plant fails, your refrigerator fails as well. That's **Interdependence**.

Highly Interdependent systems are sometimes referred to as "tightly coupled" systems. The more tightly coupled the processes in a system are, the more likely failures or delays will affect other parts of the system.

Tightly coupled systems are often time dependent and rigidly ordered, and have very little **Slack**. There's often only one path to a successful outcome, and a failure in any part of the system can "cascade" to the rest of the system.

If you've ever seen a Rube Goldberg machine or played the children's board game Mousetrap, you've seen a tightly coupled system. In a cascade of dominoes, when one domino fails to knock over the next, the entire system grinds to a halt.

If you've ever heard the project management term "critical path," you know the importance of Interdependencies. The critical path contains only the tasks that must be completed *in order* for the project to be finished on schedule. If something on the critical path changes, that change cascades to everything else on the path. Any delay in a task on the critical path will delay the entire project.

"Loosely coupled" systems have low degrees of Interdependence. Loosely coupled systems are more relaxed: they're not time dependent. You may be able to use "parallel processing," completing multiple steps at a time. There's plenty of Slack, and you may be able to accomplish your goal using many different strategies.

Think of an orchestra, which consists of a conductor and many instrumentalists. If the first violin hits the wrong note, the quality of the performance will be affected, but the mistake won't necessarily cascade to the rest of the orchestra.

You can make a system less Interdependent by removing dependencies. A "dependency" is an input that's required before the next stage of a process can take place. The more dependencies there are in a system, the higher the likelihood of delay or system failure.

Eliminating dependencies makes a system less tightly coupled. Think back to the automotive assembly line example: if you must put in the engine before the windshield is installed, an engine problem will delay the entire system. If it doesn't matter in which order the parts are installed, it's possible to assemble a finished vehicle in more than one way.

Eliminate unnecessary dependencies and you'll reduce the risk of a cascading failure.

REFERENCE LINK: **personalmba.com/interdependence/**

Counterparty Risk

> The man who makes everything that leads to happiness depend upon himself, and not upon other men, has adopted the very best plan for living happily.
>
> —PLATO, FOURTH-CENTURY-BCE GREEK PHILOSOPHER

If your system relies on other people in order to function, that poses a major risk to the operation of your system.

Counterparty Risk is the possibility that other people won't deliver what they have promised. If your house burns down, you can only make a claim on your homeowner's insurance if the company you purchased the insurance policy from is still in business. If it's not, you're in trouble.

If your manufacturing system relies on a third-party vendor to supply certain parts and they're not able to honor their commitments, your manufacturing line stops.

If you outsource work to a contractor and that contractor doesn't perform as promised, your project will be delayed.

Too much Counterparty Risk increases the risk of catastrophic system failure. In the 2008 Wall Street crash, the world's largest investment banks stood on the brink of insolvency because they all relied on one another in the event something went wrong.

Investment banks and financial firms like Goldman Sachs, JPMorgan Chase, and Lehman Brothers made a practice of buying "credit default swaps," a form of financial *Insurance*, from other large firms. If a highly *Leveraged* deal went south, these investment banks thought the Insurance they had purchased would protect them from multimillion-dollar losses, so they took on more and more Leverage, increasing their risk exposure.

When the housing market collapsed and the banks started losing money on the mortgage securities they held, they tried calling in their credit default swaps. Lo and behold, the other banks they had purchased the swaps from had also lost a huge amount of money on mortgage-backed securities and couldn't honor the obligations. Every large investment bank was a counterparty to the risk of the other banks in the system. Because they all relied on one another, when one bank fell, they all fell.

Counterparty Risk is *Amplified* by the *Planning Fallacy*. Your partners can't predict the future any more than you can, and everyone has a tendency to be optimistic regarding plans and deadlines. Make plans and commitments, but always have a plan for when the project doesn't go as expected.

When your system relies on the performance of someone outside of your control, do all that you can to prepare for the possibility that they won't perform as expected.

REFERENCE LINK: personalmba.com/counterparty-risk/

Second-Order Effects

While we are free to choose our actions, we are not free to choose the consequences of our actions.

—STEPHEN COVEY, AUTHOR OF *THE 7 HABITS OF HIGHLY EFFECTIVE PEOPLE*

A few years ago, Kelsey and I had the opportunity to visit the kingdom of Bahrain, a small island country a few miles off the east coast of Saudi Arabia. Now known for its international banking prowess, pearl diving, and international Formula One racing track, it wasn't too long ago that Bahrain was known for its unique ecosystem.

A few decades ago, the interior of Bahrain was lush with natural greenery—an island oasis said to be the original site of the Garden of Eden. Now the interior of the island is a stark desert, and local plant life is maintained via irrigation. What changed?

Bahrain is surrounded by a network of underground freshwater springs, which were responsible both for the island's plant life and for spurring the local oysters to cultivate pearls of remarkable quality. As the country's single large city, Manama, developed, land in the city center became scarce, so developers adopted a process called "land reclamation," which involved excavating dirt from the interior of the island and depositing it on the coast, "reclaiming" land from the sea.

This approach was successful in creating new land, but at a much steeper cost than anticipated—the island's network of springs dried up, turning the country into a desert.

Every action has a consequence, and those consequences have consequences, which are called *Second-Order Effects*. Think of a line of dominoes—a single push causes a chain of events to occur. Once the chain starts, it's difficult (if not impossible) to stop or reverse the cascade of cause and effect.

Rent control in New York City after World War II is another sobering example of unintended consequences. Originally intended to provide returning veterans with affordable housing, the policy capped rent prices (and the ability of landlords to raise them) in certain areas of the city. Affordable housing for veterans is a noble idea, right?

Here's what the city planners didn't expect: every year, the cost to maintain properties in New York City continued to rise, but landlords couldn't raise rent prices to compensate for their increased costs. By law, rent control couldn't be removed unless the original leaseholder moved or the building was condemned, so landlords refused to maintain their property—it was a waste of money. Financially, it was better to let the building deteriorate around the remaining tenants.

The effect of this policy over time was a steep decline in the quality of property, and eventually supply, as buildings were condemned, making housing even more expensive. A policy intended to make housing more affordable destroyed housing supply and made it *more* expensive—the opposite of the original intent.

Changing some aspect of a complex system *always* introduces Second-Order Effects, some of which may be antithetical to the original intent of the change. Elements in a complex system can be interrelated or dependent upon one another in millions of different ways, and **Uncertainty** guarantees that you probably don't know how. Every action has a consequence, and those consequences *always* have consequences—even if you don't know what they are or don't want them to happen.

Approach making changes to a complex system with extreme caution: what you get may be the opposite of what you expect.

REFERENCE LINK: **personalmba.com/second-order-effects/**

Externality

> Our planet is a lonely speck in the great enveloping cosmic dark. In our obscurity, in all this vastness, there is no hint that help will come from elsewhere to save us from ourselves . . . To me, it underscores our responsibility to deal more kindly with one another, and to preserve and cherish the pale blue dot, the only home we've ever known.
>
> —CARL SAGAN, PHYSICIST AND AUTHOR OF *PALE BLUE DOT: A VISION OF THE HUMAN FUTURE IN SPACE*

Between 1868 and 1969, the Cuyahoga River—a large tributary of Lake Erie that runs through the city of Cleveland, Ohio, in the United States— caught fire on at least thirteen separate occasions. The largest of the fires, which occurred in 1952, caused over $1 million of property damage— more than $10 million in today's dollars.

The root cause wasn't a mystery: pollution from petrochemicals, sewage, and manufacturing by-products was so severe that a forty-mile stretch of the river—from Cleveland to Akron—was unable to support fish or other aquatic life. The river was an inexpensive and convenient place to dump garbage, so many factories took the path of least resistance, building pipelines that carried industrial waste into the river in an effort to save money. The river died (and caught on fire) as a result.

The technical term for these events is *Externality*: a side effect of a primary process that affects parties beyond the primary beneficiaries or decision makers. Manufacturing in and around Cleveland was the primary process, and factory owners and employees were the primary beneficiaries: the pollution of the Cuyahoga and the effects of that pollution on other people and creatures were Externalities. The companies responsible for the pollution shifted the cost of waste disposal from their businesses to society at large.

Today, the Cuyahoga River is in much better shape. Improving the situation required significant intervention: laws, policies, and regulations that prevented and punished dumping, lawsuits and fines targeted at violators, and funds for cleaning and restoration efforts. Once the Externality was identified and understood, it was possible to coordinate societal efforts to fix the issue and prevent it from happening again.

Pollution isn't the only type of negative Externality. Here's a common example: many businesses collect Personally Identifiable Information (often abbreviated "PII") as part of their marketing, sales, and customer-support efforts. This data is useful for *Qualification*, *Segmentation*, and outreach, so firms go to great lengths to collect as much information as possible. There is, however, an important Externality to consider: if unauthorized users (like hackers) gain access to this personal information, it can be used for all sorts of nefarious purposes, many of which can create financial and legal issues for the businesses' prospects and customers.

Securing this data is important, but it doesn't contribute to the businesses' bottom line, so there's little direct incentive to worry about it. In the event of a data breach, the businesses' prospects and customers pay the price. That makes PII both an asset and a liability: companies that collect this sort of data have a responsibility to keep it secure and ensure their systems are protected from unauthorized access.

Many negative Externalities can be avoided or mitigated by anticipating potential *Second-Order Effects* and working to prevent unintended consequences. As a general rule: if you anticipate or identify negative side effects that occur (or may occur) as a result of your actions, it's your responsibility to prevent or mitigate those effects as much as possible.

Some Externalities are positive. Consider communications technology like the internet or telephone network: each additional user of the system makes the network as a whole more valuable, creating a "network effect" that benefits every user of the system. Societal policies like widespread literacy and public-health practices (like handwashing and vaccination) have similar benefits: everyone benefits when there are lower barriers to communication and reduced exposure to infectious disease.

Externalities are sometimes difficult to predict in advance, but that doesn't mean you shouldn't try. The benefits and detriments of your actions are real, and it's in everyone's best interest to take full advantage of unexpected opportunities and prevent unnecessary issues.

REFERENCE LINK: personalmba.com/externality/

Normal Accidents

> The problem is not that there are problems. The problem is expecting otherwise and thinking that having problems is a problem.
>
> —THEODORE RUBIN, PSYCHIATRIST AND COLUMNIST

The space shuttle—a vehicle capable of exiting the bounds of Earth's gravity with human travelers aboard—is the epitome of a complex system.

A highly engineered airplane strapped to three rockets holding millions of cubic feet of explosive hydrogen gas is also the epitome of a highly *Interdependent* system. *Any* error has the chance of cascading through the rest of the system, and every time the shuttle is launched, millions of things could go wrong.

In 1986, the space shuttle *Challenger* suffered a catastrophe—a seal in one of the rockets froze, becoming brittle. When the seal was superheated during takeoff, it failed. *Challenger* exploded seventy-three seconds after lift-off, killing everyone aboard.

It's tempting to believe that it's possible to create a system in which nothing ever goes wrong. Real-life systems always prove otherwise—count on it.

The theory of **Normal Accidents** is a more formal way of expressing a universal proverb: shit happens. In a tightly coupled system, small risks accumulate to the point where errors and accidents are inevitable. The larger and more complex the system, the higher the likelihood that *something* will eventually go very, very wrong.

Overreacting to Normal Accidents is counterproductive. When something goes wrong, our instinctive response is to become hypersensitive, locking things down and adding more controls to prevent the unfortunate event from happening again. This response makes things worse: locking things down and adding more systems only makes the system *more tightly coupled*, increasing the risk of future accidents.

NASA's response to the *Challenger* tragedy is instructive: instead of shutting down or adding more systems that could compound the issue, NASA engineers recognized the inherent risk and focused on finding other solutions to the problem that would minimize the risk of the issue reoccurring, without adding more systems that could potentially fail.

The best way to avoid Normal Accidents is to analyze breakdowns or "close calls" when they happen. Instead of going into the systems equivalent of **Threat Lockdown**, which can create even bigger issues in the long term, looking at near misses can provide crucial insight into hidden Interdependencies. By analyzing the issue, it's possible to construct contingency plans in the event a similar situation happens in the future.

In 2003, the space shuttle *Columbia* suffered a catastrophe of a different sort: the carbon-fiber heat shields designed to protect the shuttle as it re-entered Earth's atmosphere failed, and the shuttle disintegrated. Again, NASA focused on how to prevent the issue in the future without making the system even more tightly coupled. When the space shuttle *Discovery* suffered damage to its heat shields on takeoff a few years later, NASA engineers were prepared, and the crew landed safely.

Normal Accidents are a compelling reason to keep the systems you rely on as loosely coupled as you can. There are many positive things to be said for systems, but expecting zero failures is unrealistic in the extreme.

Loosely coupled systems may not be as efficient, but they last longer and fail less catastrophically.

The more complex a system is and the longer it operates, the more likely it is to suffer a major failure. It's not a matter of *if*—it's a matter of *when*. Be watchful for system failure and be prepared to respond to it quickly.

REFERENCE LINK: **personalmba.com/normal-accidents/**

10

ANALYZING SYSTEMS

If you can't understand it, you can't change it.

—ERIC EVANS, TECHNOLOGIST

Before you can improve a system, you must understand how well it's currently operating. That's tricky—it's not possible to stop the world for however long you want while you take careful measurements.

Systems must be analyzed as they're working. Analyzing a system in operation is difficult, but definitely possible—if you know what to look for.

In this chapter, you'll learn how to *Deconstruct* systems into smaller parts you can understand, measure what's important, and discover how parts of the system interact with and depend on one another to function.

REFERENCE LINK: **personalmba.com/analyzing-systems/**

Deconstruction

Out of perfection nothing can be made. Every process involves breaking something up.

—JOSEPH CAMPBELL, MYTHOLOGIST AND AUTHOR OF
THE HERO WITH A THOUSAND FACES

Complex systems, as we've already discussed, are made up of many interdependent *Flows*, *Stocks*, processes, and parts. As a whole, the system may be too complex to take in all at once—if there are more than seven or eight variables or dependencies, **Cognitive Scope Limitation** kicks in and confusion takes over.

If that's true, how can anyone analyze complex systems?

Deconstruction is the process of separating complex systems into the smallest possible subsystems in order to understand how things work. Instead of trying to understand the system all at once, you break up the system into parts, then work on understanding the subsystems and how they interact with one another.

Deconstruction is the reverse-engineering aspect of **Gall's Law**. Remember: complex systems that work evolved from simpler systems that also worked. If you can identify simpler subsystems and focus on understanding how they work and how they fit together, you can eventually understand how the entire system works.

If you know nothing about how cars work, popping the hood of your vehicle and examining the contents is an exercise in confusion—there are so many parts that it's hard to know where to begin. Understanding the system is not impossible, however: identifying important subsystems like the engine, transmission, and radiator can give you valuable insight into how the entire system functions.

Once you've identified important subsystems, isolating them in your mind can help you understand how they work. Instead of focusing on how the entire car works, you narrow your focus to the engine for a while. Where does the subsystem begin? What Flows are involved? What processes take place inside the system? Are there **Feedback Loops** involved? What happens if inflows *don't* come in? Where does the system end? What are the outflows?

It's important not to lose sight of **Interdependence** when using isolation to Deconstruct a system, since each subsystem is part of a larger system. Identifying triggers and endpoints—the parts of the system that interact with other subsystems—is just as important. Triggers teach you what makes a subsystem start operating, and endpoints show you what makes the system stop.

In addition, it's important to understand the conditionals present in a system—if-then or when-then relationships that influence the operation of the system. For example, an engine requires an inflow of gasoline vapor to operate. If that inflow is present, a spark from the spark plug ignites it, providing energy that pushes a piston that powers the rest of the system. If that inflow is absent or a spark doesn't come from the spark plug, the energy is absent and the system stops, making both the inflow of gasoline vapor and the spark from the spark plug conditions of the system's operation.

Creating diagrams and flowcharts can help you understand how each inflow, process, trigger, conditional, endpoint, and outflow comes together. Explaining complex systems in words alone can be limiting—for best results, draw diagrams of the Flows, Stocks, conditionals, and processes involved. Well-constructed flowcharts can help you understand the Flows of a system as it operates, which can go a long way toward helping you fix the system when things break down.[1]

To analyze a system, Deconstruct complex systems into subsystems that are easier to understand, then build your understanding of the system from the ground up.

REFERENCE LINK: **personalmba.com/deconstruction/**

Measurement

In God we trust . . . all others bring data.

—W. EDWARDS DEMING, PRODUCTION MANAGEMENT EXPERT AND
PIONEER OF STATISTICAL PROCESS CONTROL

Once you've understood the parts of the system and how they interact with one another, it pays to ask another question: *How well* is the system operating? To do that, we rely on measuring the system as it's operating.

Measurement is the process of collecting data as the system is operating. By collecting information related to the core functions of the system, it's much easier to understand how well the system itself is performing.

Measurement also allows systems to be compared with one another. For example, it's possible to use several different types of microprocessors to build a computer—which one should you use? By measuring various characteristics of each processor—cycle time, power consumption, heat generation, etc.—it's possible to choose the best processor for your computer, resulting in better performance.

Measurement helps us avoid *Absence Blindness* when analyzing a system. Remember: we have a hard time seeing things that aren't present. Measuring different parts of a system in operation helps to identify potential issues before they arise.

For example, diabetes is a condition that represents a fault in the *Feedback Loop* that controls the body's blood glucose levels. Too much or too little blood glucose is life threatening, so if the body produces too much or too little insulin to keep blood glucose levels stable, that's a major issue.

Even though insulin levels are critical to a person with diabetes, you can't figure out a person's insulin or blood glucose level just by looking at them. Without measurement, Absence Blindness is the rule until the condition becomes bad enough to become visible, which takes the form of the person passing out or going into shock.

To avoid this situation, people with diabetes make a habit of measuring their blood glucose and insulin levels throughout the day.

Measuring something is the first step to improving it. In the immortal words of Peter Drucker, "What gets measured gets managed." It's true. If you don't know how much money your business is collecting or spending, it's difficult to know whether or not any change you make to your business system is an improvement.

Without data, you're blind. If you want to improve anything, you must measure it first.

REFERENCE LINK: **personalmba.com/measurement/**

Key Performance Indicators

It is better to have an approximate answer to the right question than an exact answer to the wrong question.

—JOHN TUKEY, STATISTICIAN

Here's the primary problem with *Measurement*: you can measure a million different things. Measure too much and you'll suffer from *Cognitive Scope Limitation*, drowning in a sea of meaningless data.

Some Measurements are more important than others: *Key Performance Indicators* (KPIs) are Measurements of the critical parts of a system. Measurements that don't help you make improvements to your system are worse than worthless: they're a waste of your limited **Attention** and energy. If your intent is to improve the system you're examining, you don't have to pay Attention to everything—just a few key Measurements that matter.

It's easy to fixate on things that are easy to measure instead of things that are important. Take, for example, a business's revenue—seems pretty important, right? It is, but only to a point: revenue is important only because it's a key component of profit. It doesn't matter if you collected $1,000,000 in revenue if you spent $2,000,000 to collect it. As Theo Paphitis, a serial entrepreneur and host of the hit BBC series *Dragons' Den*, put it: "Profit is sanity. Turnover is vanity." Alone, revenue is not a KPI.

The same thing goes for other in-process Measurements. For example, if you're managing a team of programmers, it's tempting to measure their output in "lines of code"—a visible, easy-to-collect measure. Here's the problem: more code is not necessarily better. A talented programmer can make a program better by rewriting it using *fewer* lines of code. If you fixate on quantity, removing ten thousand lines looks like a setback, even if it's a huge improvement.

The situation gets even worse if you *reward* programmers based on lines of code: **Incentive-Caused Bias** will ensure that your code looks like the programming equivalent of *War and Peace*.

Business-related KPIs are often related to either the **Five Parts of Every Business** or **Throughput**. Here are a few questions I use to identify a business's KPIs:

▸ *Value Creation:* How fast is the system creating value? What is the current level of inflows?

▸ *Marketing:* How many people are paying Attention to your offer? How many prospects are giving you **Permission** to provide more information?

▸ *Sales:* How many prospects are becoming paying customers? What is the average customer's **Lifetime Value**?

▸ *Value Delivery:* How fast can you serve each customer? What is your current rate of returns or complaints?

▸ *Finance:* What is your **Profit Margin**? How much **Purchasing Power** do you have? Are you financially **Sufficient**?

Any Measurements related to these questions are probably KPIs. Anything that's not related to a core business process or a system's Throughput is probably not.

Try to limit yourself to only three to five KPIs per system. When collecting Measurements, it's tempting to build yourself a "dashboard" that contains every piece of information you'd ever want to see. Resist the temptation: if you overload yourself with too much data, you'll be far less likely to see *Changes* that are meaningful and important. You can always dig deeper into the data at your disposal if necessary.

Find your system's KPIs and you'll be able to manage your system without drowning in data.

REFERENCE LINK: personalmba.com/key-performance-indicator/

Garbage In, Garbage Out

> Let us watch well our beginnings, and results will manage themselves.
>
> —ALEXANDER CLARK, NINETEENTH-CENTURY US AMBASSADOR
> AND CIVIL RIGHTS ACTIVIST

If you analyze poor-quality data, the resulting analysis will be worthless at best, and misleading or damaging at worst.

The quality of the input you use always has an impact on the quality of the output. If you build an object from poor-quality materials, that object will be unattractive and unreliable. If you eat a lot of junk food, don't move around much, and pay attention to too much news and reality TV, you'll feel lethargic instead of energetic. If the people working on a project aren't skilled or excited, the end result will suffer.

Garbage In, Garbage Out is a straightforward principle: put useless input into a system, and you'll get useless output. Your ability to understand a system relies on your ability to observe what's going on in that system. The quality and quantity of the data you collect about the system represents an upper limit to how well you'll be able to understand what's happening in the system as it's operating.

If you don't want garbage when you're done, don't use garbage when you begin. Being mindful of what you're starting with can help you ensure that the end result of the process meets your expectations.

To improve your results, improve the quality of what you start with.

REFERENCE LINK: **personalmba.com/garbage-in-garbage-out/**

Tolerance

> The road to wisdom? Well, it's plain / And simple to express: / Err / and err / and err again, / but less / and less / and less.
>
> —PIET HEIN, MATHEMATICIAN AND POET

Many inexperienced businesspeople expect perfection: any sort of mistake or variance, however small, is a cause for concern.

Take, for example, a business's website. Most businesspeople are aghast when their website goes down, an event that prompts concerned calls to the system administrator or responsible party. Often the words "Make sure our website never goes down" are spoken.

That's not realistic: 100 percent reliability is impossible. **Normal Accidents** are a fact of life, so it pays to account for them in planning. The more reliability you need, the more your system is going to cost.

A **Tolerance** is an acceptable level of "normal" error in a system. Within a given range of measurements, the system is performing as intended. As long as the errors don't exceed a certain threshold, urgent intervention is not required.

Tolerances are often referred to as being "tight" or "loose." A tight Tolerance is one in which there's little room for error or variability, which is common if the component or subsystem is critical to the performance of the system. A loose Tolerance allows significant room for error or variability and is common when small mistakes produce no major repercussions.

The reliability of a system is often measured in terms of a percentage. When a system is 95 percent reliable in a given area, it will produce a result within the intended Tolerances nineteen out of twenty times. The higher the reliability, the higher the percentage.

When you hear someone talk about "five nines" reliability, that means the system produces the intended result 99.999 percent of the time. This level of reliability is impressive, and often expensive to achieve. Companies use this reliability measurement as a Tolerance, and they write a contract called a "Service Level Agreement" (SLA) that promises to compensate customers if errors exceed a certain threshold.

Tight Tolerances are very useful and a positive indicator of quality: after all, you don't want mistakes or variations. Work to achieve tighter Tolerances for the critical parts of your system over time.

REFERENCE LINK: **personalmba.com/tolerance/**

Variance

> Keep in mind how fast things pass by and are gone—those that are now and those to come. Existence flows past us like a river: the "what" is in constant flux, the "why" has a thousand variations. Nothing is stable, not even what's right here.
>
> —MARCUS AURELIUS, SECOND CENTURY BCE
> PHILOSOPHER AND EMPEROR OF ROME

Measures that fluctuate at random are often difficult to analyze. Unit sales figures are a good example: If you sell 3,017 units on Monday, 2,967 on Tuesday, and 3,142 units on Wednesday, how do you estimate your "normal" daily sales? Even more challenging: if your sales increase or decrease at random each day, how can you tell if a new marketing or sales strategy is working?

Variance is the degree of fluctuation in a measure or set of data. Measures of **Typicality**, like means or medians, are a natural place to start, but they don't capture the range of fluctuations you're likely to experience. Without establishing the degree of normal fluctuation, you're not equipped to make good decisions.

In *Understanding Variation: The Key to Managing Chaos*, Dr. Donald J. Wheeler describes an approach called "statistical process control" that makes analysis of Variance possible. Starting with a mean or median, it's possible to quantify the size of the fluctuations present in the data set. This gives you a typical value, an upper normal boundary, and a lower normal boundary: a range of expected normal values.

Once you've established an upper and lower bound, you're in a much better position to make decisions. Data points that break the upper bound or lower bound are statistically significant, as are a series of consecutive data points that are close to the boundary. Returning to the daily sales figure example: if your normal upper bound is 3,500 units per day, it's worth looking into a 4,000-unit sales day to see what led to that result. Likewise, if you have five consecutive days that exceed 3,500 units, that indicates you should keep investing in your new marketing plan: it's working.

Measures of Variance are helpful in identifying opportunities or problems when you don't have direct access to or visibility of all of the inputs and outputs. Defect rates are a good example: if you sell a **Product**, you won't be able to test every unit, and **Sampling** may not catch problems that occur in use. If you track the Variance of your customer-support requests, return requests, and warranty requests, you can take immediate action if you see an increase that exceeds normal variation.

REFERENCE LINK: **personalmba.com/variance/**

Analytical Honesty

That which can be destroyed by the truth should be.
—P. C. HODGELL, PROFESSOR AND NOVELIST

My last position at Procter & Gamble involved creating an online marketing **Measurement** strategy: figuring out a way to measure the effectiveness of P&G's advertising on the web. P&G spent millions of dollars every year on banner ads, search-engine advertising, and online video placements. My job was to figure out if the investment was worth it.

One of the things my team discovered while putting together our recommendations was disturbing: the system we were using on most of our websites to measure unique visitors was wrong. Instead of counting human visitors, the system was treating visits from automated search-engine software bots as "visitors" as well, even though they weren't people. Computer programs don't care about (and will never purchase) laundry detergent and shampoo, but the system was counting them as potential customers.

It's not uncommon for search-engine spider programs to visit a website many times a day looking for new information, so the system was overstating how many people were visiting each website by a significant margin.

It was a *Garbage In, Garbage Out* situation, and it made our measurements much less useful.

My team recommended upgrading the tracking system to collect accurate visitor data. Without exception, the business units declined. They knew they were getting crappy data, but they didn't seem to care. Weird, right?

Here's why: installing the new tracking system would make each website's unique-visitors measurement—considered a *Key Performance Indicator* by most teams—decrease by an order of magnitude. Even though the new system was more accurate, installing it would make the team look bad. Instead of correcting the issue, they chose to continue living a lie. As a result, they seriously compromised their ability to improve their website's actual performance.

Analytical Honesty means measuring and analyzing the data you have without emotion or bias. Since humans are social creatures, we tend to care deeply about how others perceive us, which gives us a natural incentive to make things look better than they are. If your purpose is to make things better, this tendency can get in the way of collecting accurate data and conducting useful analysis.

The best way to maintain Analytical Honesty is to have your measurements evaluated by someone who isn't invested in your system. *Incentive-Caused Bias* and *Confirmation Bias* are easy to succumb to if your *Social Status* is on the line. Having an experienced but dispassionate third party audit your measurement and analysis practices is a neat workaround for these tendencies: you might not like what you hear, but at least you'll be fully aware of potential issues.

Don't look at your data through rose-colored glasses: always strive to be honest with yourself about what the data indicates you can improve.

REFERENCE LINK: **personalmba.com/analytical-honesty/**

Context

> If you don't understand something, it's because you aren't aware of its context.
>
> —RICHARD RABKIN, PSYCHIATRIST

You brought in $200,000 of revenue this month. Is that good or bad?

It depends. If you brought in $100,000 last month, it's good. If your expenses are $400,000 this month, it's bad.

Context is the use of related **Measurements** to provide additional information about the data you're examining. In the example above, knowing your monthly revenue isn't very useful without additional information. Knowing last month's revenue and this month's expenses provides necessary Context, giving you a clearer picture of the situation.

Aggregate Measurements almost never tell you anything useful. Aggregate measures are worthless when it comes to making tangible improvements because they lack Context. Knowing two million people visited your website this month tells you nothing useful. Without Context, you can't determine **Change** or effectiveness, which limits your ability to improve the system.

Try to avoid the temptation to focus on a single "magic number" when tracking your results. Relying on a single number sounds like a useful simplification, but it's not—removing Context blinds you to important Changes in the data. Knowing your "total quality score" or that revenue went up or down a few points won't tell you why it happened, whether or not it's important, or if it's due to random fluctuations or a significant Change in the system or its **Environment**.

As a general rule, examine no measure in isolation—always look at them in the Context of other Measurements.

REFERENCE LINK: **personalmba.com/context/**

Sampling

> If you don't believe in sampling theory, next time you go to the doctor and he wants to take a little blood, tell him to take it all.
>
> —GIAN FULGONI, COFOUNDER AND CHAIRMAN OF COMSCORE, INC.

What do you do if your system is too large or complex to collect data on every process?

Sometimes it's not practical to measure the **Flows** of an entire system. If you're managing a scalable system, it's often not possible to test every unit or find every error. How can you identify potential problems when your system is cranking out millions of units or completing millions of transactions?

Sampling is the process of taking at random a small percentage of the total output, then using it as a proxy for the entire system. If you've ever had your blood taken at the doctor's office, you'll have a good idea of what Sampling entails. The doctor or nurse draws a small amount of blood, which is then sent to a laboratory for analysis. If testing reveals anomalies in the sample, it's likely that the same issue is present in the bloodstream in general.

Sampling can help you identify systemic errors without testing all of the output of the system, which can be time-consuming and expensive. If you're manufacturing mobile phones, you don't have to test every single phone that comes off the line. If you test one in twenty phones, you can still identify errors fast enough to fix the system if something goes wrong. Depending on your acceptable error rate, you can increase or decrease the Sampling rate.

Random "spot checks" are also a form of Sampling. Many retail stores employ "secret shoppers" to test customer service or the skills of their sales staff. These shoppers are hired to express interest in specific items, ask certain questions, make a return, or act in annoying ways. Since the staff doesn't know which customers are real and which ones are not, it's an effective way for the management of a store to test their staff without scrutinizing them every second of every day.

Sampling is prone to bias if the sample is not random or uniform. For example, measuring the average household income in the United States by surveying property owners in Manhattan will skew the data considerably higher than if you survey property owners in West Virginia. For best results, use the largest random sample you can.

If you need to test for quality, Sampling can help you collect good data without incurring enormous costs, provided you stay on the lookout for potential bias that can skew the data.

REFERENCE LINK: **personalmba.com/sampling/**

Margin of Error

Everyone generalizes from one example. At least, I do.

—STEVEN BRUST, SCIENCE-FICTION AUTHOR

Suppose you purchase a trick coin from a magician's shop, and you want to be sure the coin is biased to land on heads most of the time.

How can you be sure you didn't buy a dud? You start flipping the coin, of course.

Let's assume that in the first five flips, you get two heads and three tails. Should you ask for a refund?

It's probably worthwhile to make sure your results are accurate before jeopardizing the magician's good name. **Margin of Error** is an estimate of how much you can trust your conclusions from a given set of observed **Samples**.

Since you only flipped the coin five times, you can't be sure it's a dud: your sample size is very small. Each coin flip makes your sample size larger.

If you go on to flip the coin a thousand times, and it comes up tails two thirds of the time, you can be sure that the coin is biased, but not in the way you expected. Since a nonloaded coin should come up heads half the time, your large sample size makes it likely the magician gave you a tails-loaded coin by mistake.

Each additional Sample you make increases your available data and helps ensure your set of observed Samples is representative of the general population you're studying. The more Samples you take, the lower your Margin of Error becomes and the more faith you can have in the conclusions you make from examining the Samples as a whole. Unavoidable biases in Sampling can be accounted for by increasing your Margin of Error.

The math behind how to estimate Margin of Error is beyond the scope of this book. It's easy once you get the hang of it, particularly if you use a spreadsheet or database for your analysis. If you need to calculate Margin of Error or other, related estimates, like "confidence intervals" or "credibility intervals," I recommend picking up *Principles of Statistics* by M. G. Bulmer for an in-depth primer.

In general, beware of misleading conclusions based on small and/or nonrepresentative sample sizes. Whenever you're presented with an average or a probability based on data you're not familiar with, it always pays to investigate the size of the Sample and how it was collected. Sample sets that are too small or biased can significantly influence the final analysis.

When it comes to analytical confidence, more data is always better—collect the largest set of Samples you can.

REFERENCE LINK: **personalmba.com/margin-of-error/**

Ratio

He who refuses to do arithmetic is doomed to talk nonsense.
—JOHN MCCARTHY, COMPUTER AND COGNITIVE SCIENTIST

A **Ratio** is a method of comparing two **Measurements** against each other. By dividing your results by your input, you can measure all sorts of useful relationships between different parts of your system.

For example, assume that for every 30 customers who enter your store, 10 of them make a purchase. Your "closing Ratio" would be 10 divided by 30: 1/3.

Let's say you train your sales staff in techniques that result in 15 paying customers out of 30 who enter the store. Your new closing Ratio is 15 divided by 30: 1/2.

Percentages are Ratios with a base of 100. Your first closing Ratio, converted into a percentage, is 33 percent. Your second would be 50 percent.

HERE ARE SOME USEFUL RATIOS TO TRACK:

—*Return on Promotion*: For every $1 you spend in advertising, how much revenue do you collect?

—*Profit per Employee*: For every person you employ, how much profit does your business generate?

—*Closing Ratio*: For every prospect you serve, how many purchase?

—*Returns/Complaints Ratio*: For every sale you make, how many choose to return or complain?

Financial Ratios are very helpful when examining financial statements. Ratios like **Return on Investment**, return on assets, return on capital, inventory turns, and day sales outstanding are very useful in determining the health of a business. For a full introduction to common Financial Ratios, I recommend *Financial Intelligence for Entrepreneurs* by Karen Berman and Joe Knight with John Case.

Tracking Ratios over time can provide a directional indication of how a system is changing. If your closing Ratio or Return on Investment keeps going up, that's a very good thing. If it's going down over time, it would pay to investigate to find out why.

Be creative: study your business, then construct Ratios that highlight the most important parts of your system.

REFERENCE LINK: personalmba.com/ratio/

Typicality

It ain't what you don't know that hurts you. It's what you know that ain't so.

—WILL ROGERS, AMERICAN COWBOY AND COMEDIAN

The average household net worth of a person who reads the *Wall Street Journal* is approximately $1.5 million.[2] Seems that *Wall Street Journal* readers are well off, right?

Yes, but less than you might think. Bill Gates and Warren Buffett read the *Wall Street Journal*, and their wealth is measured in the billions—significantly more than even the top .01 percent of business professionals. Ultra-high-net-worth executives like Gates and Buffett skew the average much higher than it would be otherwise. If you're relying on the average to tell you how much the typical *Wall Street Journal* reader is worth, you're making a mistake.

Many forms of analysis rely on defining *Typicality*: identifying a normal or typical value for some important measurement. There are four common methods of calculating a typical value: mean, median, mode, and midrange.

A *mean* (or average) is calculated by adding the quantities of all data points, then dividing by the total number of data points available. Averages are simple to calculate but are prone to Gates and Buffett syndrome: the presence of outliers that skew the average too high or low to be representative. (Exclude the outliers, however, and the average becomes more accurate.)

A *median* is calculated by sorting the values in order of high to low, then finding the quantity of the data point in the middle of the range. Medians are a specific form of analysis called a percentile: the median is the value that expresses the fiftieth percentile. By definition, 50 percent of the values in the set will be below the median. Calculating the median and comparing it to the mean can tell you if the average is being influenced by a few heavy hitters.

A *mode* is the value that occurs most frequently in a set of data. Modes are useful for finding clusters of data—a set can have multiple modes, which can alert you to potentially interesting **Interdependencies** in the system that produced that data.

A *midrange* is the value halfway between the highest and lowest data points in a set of values. To calculate the midrange, add the highest and lowest values, then divide by two. Midranges are best used for quick estimates—they're fast, and you only need to know two data points, but they can be skewed by outliers that are abnormally high or low, like Bill Gates's bank balance.

Means, medians, modes, and midranges are useful analytical tools that can indicate typical results—provided you're careful enough to use the right tool for the job.

REFERENCE LINK: **personalmba.com/typicality/**

Correlation and Causation

Correlation isn't causation, but it sure is a hint.

—EDWARD TUFTE, STATISTICIAN AND INFORMATION DESIGN EXPERT

Imagine a billiards table: if you know the exact position of every ball on the table and the details of the forces applied to the cue ball (impact vector, impact force, location of impact, table friction, and air resistance), you can calculate how the cue ball will travel and how it will affect other balls it hits along the way. Professional billiards players are skilled at creating a **Mental Simulation** of these relationships so well that they can clear entire tables with little effort.

That's **Causation**: a complete chain of cause and effect. Since it's possible to calculate a complete chain of causality, you can say that striking the cue ball *caused* a ball to fall into the corner pocket. If you hit the cue again in the same way in the same situation, you'll get the same result every single time.

Here's another **Thought Experiment**, using hypothetical data: people who suffer heart attacks eat, on average, 57 bacon double cheeseburgers every year. Does eating bacon double cheeseburgers cause heart attacks? Not necessarily. If people who suffer heart attacks take 365 showers a year and blink their eyes 5.6 million times a year, does taking showers and blinking your eyes cause heart attacks?

Correlation is not Causation. Even if you notice that one measurement is associated with another, that does not prove that one thing *caused* the other.

Imagine you own a pizza parlor and you create a thirty-second advertisement to air on local television. Just after the commercial goes live, you notice a 30 percent increase in sales. Did the advertisement cause the increase?

Not necessarily—the increase could be due to any number of factors. Maybe a convention was held in town that day, so there were more visitors in town than usual and they needed a quick place to eat. Maybe school let out and families went out to eat to celebrate. Maybe you offered a special two-pizzas-for-the-price-of-one promotion at the same time, and that's what brought more people in the door. So many things happened at the same time, it's hard to be certain.

In fact, the commercial may have caused a *decline* in sales—maybe people found it unappealing or offensive, but another factor caused such a huge increase in sales that it overshadowed the decline.

Causation is always more difficult to prove than Correlation. When analyzing complex systems with many variables and *Interdependencies*, it's often difficult to find true causality. The more changes that happen in a system over a period of time, the higher the likelihood that more than one change had an impact on the result you're trying to analyze.

Adjusting for known variables can help you isolate the potential causes of a change in your system. For example, if you know that families go out to celebrate the end of school or that an annual convention is coming up, you can adjust for that seasonality by using historical data.

The more you can isolate the change you made in the system from other factors, the more confidence you can have that the change you made caused the results you see.

REFERENCE LINK: **personalmba.com/correlation-causation/**

Norms

Those who cannot remember the past are condemned to repeat it.

—GEORGE SANTAYANA, PHILOSOPHER AND APHORIST

If you want to study the effectiveness of something in the present, it's often useful to learn from the past.

Norms are measures that use historical data as a tool to provide **Context** for current **Measurements**. For example, by looking at past data you may discover trends in your sales data related to the date the sale was made, which is called *seasonality*. Seasonality is a good example of why Norms are often useful. If you're in the business of selling Christmas ornaments, comparing sales during Q4 (the last quarter of the year—October through December) to Q3 sales (August through September) isn't useful—no one purchases Christmas ornaments in August. Far better to compare this year's Q4 sales with last year's Q4 sales to see if you performed better than last year's comparable period.

When Measurement practices **Change,** Norms based on the previous Measurements are no longer valid. At P&G, we had a method of evaluating the effectiveness of certain types of advertising. Drawing on several years' worth of data, it was possible to compare new advertisements with old advertisements that had been successful. If the new advertising didn't beat the Norm in testing, it wasn't used.

If the company suddenly decided to use a different testing methodology, the Norms would no longer be valid—it would be comparing apples and oranges. Change the Measurement methods and you invalidate any Norms based on them. If you still want to use Norms, you must build your database of historical information once again.

Past performance is no guarantee of future performance. Remember, we're dealing with complex systems—things always Change over time. Just because something was useful in the past does not mean it will continue to perform as well in perpetuity. For best results, reexamine your Norms at regular intervals to make sure they're valid.

REFERENCE LINK: **personalmba.com/norms/**

Proxy

How many legs does a dog have if you call the tail a leg? Four. Calling
a tail a leg doesn't make it a leg.

—ABRAHAM LINCOLN, SIXTEENTH PRESIDENT OF THE UNITED STATES

What do you do if it's not possible to measure something in a direct way?

A **Proxy** measures one quantity by measuring something else. For example, in democratic political systems, votes are used as a Proxy to measure the "will of the people." It's not possible to subject every citizen in the country to a brain scan that reveals their preferences in detail, so votes are used as the **Next Best Alternative**.

Proxies are used all the time in scientific measurement. Ever wonder how scientists know how hot the sun is, or how old certain rocks are? They measure Proxies like the wavelength of electromagnetic rays or the decay of known radioactive isotopes, then apply proven relationships and formulas to determine the answer.

Useful Proxies are closely related to the primary subject—the closer, the better. Take website analytics—you may want to know how long people pay **Attention** to different parts of the webpage, but again, you can't scan the brain of each visitor to your website. Tracking the position of the mouse cursor, however, can be a useful Proxy for Attention. According to a study done by researchers at Carnegie Mellon University:

> 84% of the times that a region was visited by a mouse cursor, it was
> also visited by (users') eye gaze. In addition, 88% of regions that
> were not gazed by the eye were also not visited by a mouse cursor.[3]

Because mouse movements and eye fixation (i.e., Attention) are highly **Correlated**, mouse movements are a good Proxy for visitor Attention. The better the Correlation, the better the Proxy.

For best results, ensure that the Proxy is related to the intended subject. Proxies can be tricky or misleading if they seem to measure one thing but actually measure another. Think back to the example of trying to measure programmer productivity by counting lines of code as a **Key Performance Indicator**. As we discussed earlier, "lines of code" is a Proxy for programming effectiveness, but more code is sometimes an *inverse* signal of productivity, making it a useless **Measurement** for the stated objective.

Used with care, Proxies can help you measure the immeasurable—just be sure your Proxy is Correlated with the subject of interest.

REFERENCE LINK: **personalmba.com/proxy/**

Segmentation

Analytics nirvana rule: never report a metric (even God's favorite KPI) without segmenting it . . . There is no KPI so insightful all by itself, even in a trend or against a forecast, that can't be made more impactful by applying segmentation.

—AVINASH KAUSHIK, DATA-ANALYTICS EXPERT AND ENTREPRENEUR

Very often, aggregate data sets contain hidden nuggets of gold—if you can find them. **Segmentation** is a technique that involves splitting a data set into well-defined subgroups to add additional **Context**. Splitting the data into predefined groups can uncover previously unknown relationships. For example, knowing that orders increased by 87 percent this month is good, but knowing that 90 percent of those new orders came from women in Seattle is even better. Find out what made those women order and you'll be able to use that information to further capitalize on your success.

There are three common ways to Segment customer data: past performance, demographics, and psychographics.

Past performance Segments customers by past known actions. For example, you can Segment customer sales data using previous sales data, comparing sales to new customers with sales to customers who have already purchased from you. **Lifetime Value** calculations are a form of Segmentation by past performance.

Demographics Segment customers by external personal characteristics. Personal information like age, gender, income, nationality, and location can help you determine which customers are your **Probable Purchasers**. Knowing that your best customers are males between the ages of twenty-three and thirty-two who live in major metropolitan areas and have more than $2,000 per month in disposable income can be quite useful—you can focus your marketing efforts on reaching more prospects who have those characteristics.

Psychographics Segment customers by internal psychological characteristics. Typically discovered via surveys, assessments, or focus groups, psychographics are attitudes or world views that influence how people see themselves and the world at large.

Psychographics can be very useful in creating or adjusting your value creation, marketing, and sales strategies. For example, if you're selling home security systems, it's likely that your Probable Purchasers will believe statements like "the world is a dangerous place" and feel somewhat in danger even when in their homes. Experimenting with promoting your product in survivalist and self-defense magazines and websites—markets whose customers might have similar beliefs—might not be a bad idea.

Segment your data and you'll find many useful hidden connections worth investigating.

REFERENCE LINK: **personalmba.com/segmentation/**

Humanization

People are the center of the universe. Not stuff.

—STOWE BOYD, SOCIAL TECHNOLOGIST

Analyzing data is comforting to the quantitative-minded, but to use data properly, you must go beyond juggling numbers to understand what they're telling you.

When analyzing data from a system, it's easy to forget that it often pertains to the actions of real human beings. For example, imagine a customer service department that answers customer complaints by telephone. Reducing hold times from ten minutes to eight minutes sounds great—that's a 20 percent improvement!

Put the champagne away: what the data-centric viewpoint misses is the fact that you still have a dissatisfied customer waiting on the phone for eight minutes, which still *feels* like an eternity. Every minute on hold makes that customer angrier, which affects their perception of the company. That 20 percent improvement pales in comparison to the **Reputation** hit your business takes every time that customer tells their friends and associates how horrible your company is to deal with.

Humanization is the process of using data to tell a story (**Narrative**) about a real person's experience or behavior. Quantifiable measures are helpful in the aggregate, but it's often necessary to reframe the measure into actual behavior to understand what's happening.

Many businesses Humanize by developing a series of personas: fictional profiles of people developed from data. When I developed home cleaning products for P&G, market research data told us that two broad **Segments** existed: people who valued regular deep cleaning ("Unless I'm on my hands and knees cleaning with bleach and elbow grease, I'm not satisfied") and people who wanted cleaning to be quick and convenient ("I'm too busy to clean—as long as it looks good enough, I'm happy").

Using this information, we combined these characteristics with other data like household income, family statistics, and hobbies to create a profile of a fictional person. Once the profile was developed, it became easier to use the data we had to make decisions—instead of relying on statistics to evaluate an idea, we could rely on our intuition by asking ourselves if "Wendy" would like it.

Don't just present data—tell a story that helps people understand what's happening and you'll find your analysis efforts more useful.

REFERENCE LINK: **personalmba.com/humanization/**

11

IMPROVING SYSTEMS

In theory there's no difference between theory and practice.
But, in practice, there is.

—BENJAMIN BREWSTER, EPISCOPAL BISHOP

Creating and improving systems is the heart of successful business practice. The purpose of understanding and analyzing systems is to improve them, which is often tricky—changing systems can often create unintended consequences.

In this chapter, you'll learn the secrets of *Optimization*, how to remove unnecessary *Friction* from critical processes, and how to build systems that can handle *Uncertainty* and *Change.*

REFERENCE LINK: **personalmba.com/improving-systems/**

Intervention Bias

For every complex problem there is an answer that is clear, simple, and wrong.

—H. L. MENCKEN, ESSAYIST

Before making a change to a system, it's important to understand that human beings are predisposed to do something rather than nothing. As we discussed, **Absence Blindness** leads us to value things we can see over things we can't. This predisposition affects how we work on systems: **Intervention Bias** makes us likely to introduce changes that aren't necessary in order to feel in control of a situation.

Many corporate policies have their roots in Intervention Bias. When something bad happens, it's tempting to "fix" the situation by installing additional layers of limitations, reporting, and auditing. The result isn't an improvement in **Throughput** or efficiency: it's an increase in **Communication Overhead**, waste, and unproductive bureaucracy.

The best way to correct for Intervention Bias is to examine what scientists call a "null hypothesis": examining what would happen if you did nothing or assumed the situation was an accident or error.

Imagine a company that allows its employees to purchase any book they want or need, no questions asked. Books are inexpensive sources of high-quality information, so making it easy for employees to obtain them makes sense.

All is well until one employee abuses the privilege and orders hundreds of novels for personal enjoyment. What should be done?

Many companies would respond by eliminating the policy and requiring a manager's approval for all book purchases. But this change wouldn't fix the situation, because it isn't a widespread issue. Instead, it would annoy or anger employees who use the benefit responsibly, waste time for everyone by increasing paperwork and bureaucracy, and reduce employee productivity by increasing the amount of time it takes to find information they can use to improve the business.

The correct response in this case is to do *nothing*. One employee made an irresponsible decision, so the situation can be handled with a single discussion, without a major change in policy. The damage is limited, and there's no sense in penalizing everyone for a single person's poor judgment. It is a **Normal Accident**, so overreaction is counterproductive.

Examining the null hypothesis before intervening will help you avoid Intervention Bias and ensure you make the best possible decisions.

REFERENCE LINK: **personalmba.com/intervention-bias/**

Optimization

Premature optimization is the root of all evil.

—DONALD KNUTH, RENOWNED COMPUTER SCIENTIST

Optimization is the process of maximizing the output of a system or minimizing a specific input the system requires to operate. Optimization revolves around the systems and processes behind your **Key Performance Indicators**, which measure the critical elements of the system as a whole. Improve your KPIs and your system will perform better.

Maximization focuses on the system's **Throughput**. If you want to earn more money, create more units to sell, or serve more customers, you're Optimizing for Throughput. Making **Changes** to the system that increase Throughput means your system is performing better in a specific, measurable way.

Minimization focuses on in-process inputs required for the system to operate. If you're trying to increase your **Profit Margin**, costs are one of the key inputs. Minimize your costs and your margins will increase.

By definition, if you're trying to maximize or minimize more than one thing, you're not Optimizing—you're making **Trade-offs**. Many people use the term Optimization to mean "making everything better," but that definition doesn't help you *do* anything.

In practical terms, trying to Optimize for many variables at once doesn't work—you need to be able to concentrate on a single variable for a while, so you can understand how the Changes you make affect the system as a whole. You're trying to find **Causation** (not **Correlation**) in your Changes, and hidden **Interdependencies** can make it difficult to understand which Changes produced which results.

Remember: you can't Optimize a system's performance across multiple variables at once. Pick the most important one and focus your efforts.

REFERENCE LINK: **personalmba.com/optimization/**

Refactoring

Elegance is necessarily unnatural, only achievable at great expense.
If you just do something, it won't be elegant, but if you do it and then
see what might be more elegant, and do it again, you might, after an
unknown number of iterations, get something that is very elegant.

—ERIK NAGGUM, COMPUTER PROGRAMMER

Not all changes to a system are designed to affect the system's output. Sometimes it's more effective to reengineer a process without changing the *End Result* at all.

Refactoring is the process of changing a system to improve efficiency without changing the output of the system. The term comes from computer programming—programmers will spend hours rewriting a program that, if all goes well, does *the same thing* when they're finished. What's the point?

The primary benefit of Refactoring isn't improving the output—it's making the system itself faster or more efficient. By rearranging the processes the system uses to produce the result, it's possible to make the program run faster or require fewer resources while operating.

Refactoring starts by *Deconstructing* a process or system, followed by a search for patterns. What are the critical processes that must be done right in order to achieve the desired objective? Do those processes have to be completed in a certain order? What are the current *Constraints*? What appears to be particularly important? Collect as much information about how the system works as you can, then sit with it for a while.

More often than not, you'll start to notice things about the system that don't make sense—things that you've done a certain way because it seemed like a good idea at the time but that aren't the best way to approach the task now.

Once patterns begin to emerge, you can rearrange the system to group similar processes or inputs together. Think of rearranging an assembly line: if you have to stop what you're doing and travel all the way across the factory to obtain a necessary component, rearranging things so the component is always close at hand is probably a good idea. The system will still produce the same thing when you're done, but you'll have removed a little inefficiency from the system that adds up to significant losses in productivity.

If your *Goal* is to make the system faster or more efficient, Refactoring is one of your best tools.

REFERENCE LINK: **personalmba.com/refactoring/**

The Critical Few

Typically, causes, inputs, or effort divide into two categories: (1) the majority, that have little impact, and (2) a small minority, that have a major, dominant impact.

—RICHARD KOCH, BUSINESS CONSULTANT AND
AUTHOR OF *THE 80/20 PRINCIPLE*

Vilfredo Pareto was a nineteenth-century economist and sociologist who was very interested in the topic of land ownership and the social distribution of wealth. After collecting and analyzing a great deal of data, Pareto found a curious pattern: over 80 percent of the land in Italy was owned by less than 20 percent of the population. The Italian economy wasn't distributed evenly, or in the bell curve–shaped distribution many people assumed: wealth was highly concentrated among a relatively small group of individuals.

As Pareto studied other areas of life, he found the same pattern: in Pareto's garden, for example, 20 percent of the pea pods produced 80 percent of the peas. What was going on?

In any complex system, a minority of the inputs produce the majority of the output. This pattern of persistent nonlinearity is now called the Pareto principle, or the 80-20 rule. I prefer to call it the *Critical Few*.

Once you understand this common pattern, you'll find it in many areas of life:

▶ In many businesses, less than 20 percent of the customers account for more than 80 percent of annual revenue.

▶ Less than 20 percent of a business's employees do 80 percent or more of the most valuable work.

▶ You wear less than 20 percent of the clothing in your closet over 80 percent of the time.

▶ You spend over 80 percent of your time communicating with less than 20 percent of your personal contacts.

The nonlinearity of the Critical Few can often be extreme. For example, less than 3 percent of the world's population is in possession of over 97 percent of the world's total wealth. Over time, political power (in both countries and companies) also tends to concentrate in the hands of a few people, which results in a very small group of individuals making decisions that affect the lives of hundreds of millions of people. Far less than 1 percent of movies ever produced become blockbusters, and less than 0.1 percent of books ever written become bestsellers.

For best results, focus on the critical inputs that produce most of the results you want. In *The 4-Hour Workweek*, Timothy Ferriss explains how he used the Critical Few to identify his best customers. Out of the 120 customers Ferriss was serving, 5 accounted for 95 percent of the business's revenue. By focusing on those top-performing wholesalers and putting the rest of his customers on "autopilot," Ferriss doubled his monthly revenue and cut his work time from eighty hours to fifteen hours a week.

The same approach is often useful to weed out results you *don't* want. While conducting his business analysis, Ferriss realized that two particular customers accounted for most of his frustration and stress. "Firing" these energy-sucking customers, even though they represented significant sources of volume, liberated his time and energy. As a result, he was able to secure distribution with three additional high-volume customers that boosted the bottom line without the constant headaches.

Noncritical inputs are significant **Opportunity Costs**. If you're spending most of your time in unproductive meetings, for example, you're wasting time that could be used to get important things done. The same goes for noncritical expenses: they represent money that you could be using to far greater effect.

Find the inputs that produce the outputs you want, then make them the focus of most of your time and energy. Eliminate the rest.

REFERENCE LINK: **personalmba.com/critical-few/**

Diminishing Returns

The last 10 percent of performance generates one-third of the cost
and two-thirds of the problems.

—NORMAN R. AUGUSTINE, AEROSPACE EXECUTIVE AND FORMER
UNDERSECRETARY OF THE U.S. ARMY

If you have $10 in your bank account, finding $5 in the pocket of your
freshly laundered pants is a cause for celebration. If you have $10 million
in your bank account, the same situation is a non-event.

In a similar vein, eating one cookie is great. Eating two cookies is even
better. Eating a hundred is worse. More is not always better. (The same
relationship applies to drinking beer and taking vitamins.)

All good things are subject to *Diminishing Returns*—after a certain point,
having more of something can be detrimental. When I was in marketing at
P&G, we spent a lot of time and effort analyzing the results of our advertising. In the first few weeks of running a television commercial, it was easy to
see if it was performing as expected. If the commercial was performing well,
we'd allocate more money to it, but that would only work for so long.

No matter how much people liked the commercial, at a certain point it
would "wear out," and the company would no longer produce $1 of revenue
for every dollar the company spent showing that ad. That was the "point
of diminishing returns"—if we spent more dollars showing the same commercial, the company would start losing money. Far better to spend those
funds promoting the product in a different way.

It's always better to spend a little time and energy to get the big wins
than to do nothing. In *I Will Teach You to Be Rich*, Ramit Sethi recommends applying what he calls the "85% Solution." So many people get
wrapped up in making the perfect decision that they wind up overwhelming themselves and doing nothing. Focus on doing a few simple things that
will produce most of the results you're looking for, then call it a day.

Don't feel like you have to *Optimize* everything to perfection. Optimization and *Refactoring* are affected by the *Critical Few* as well—a few small
changes can produce enormous results. After you've picked the "low-hanging
fruit," further Optimization can cost more in effort than you'll reap in returns. That's a good point to stop. Perfectionism is a trap for the unwary.

Optimize and Refactor up to the point you start experiencing Diminishing Returns, then focus on doing something else.

REFERENCE LINK: **personalmba.com/diminishing-returns/**

Progressive Load

Little by little, one travels far.

—SPANISH PROVERB

It's not a good idea to run a marathon the first time you lace up your running shoes, or attempt to lift four hundred pounds the first time you go to the gym. The most effective (and lowest-risk) strategy is to start with a small but manageable challenge, work at that level until it becomes easy, and increase the level of challenge over time as your body adapts.

The term for this strategy is *Progressive Load*: increasing the amount of total capacity in a system by gradually increasing demand on the system, prompting the system to *Change* to adapt to the new demands over time.

Progressive Load is a universal approach that works in areas well beyond fitness. Businesses are often tempted to solve problems by hiring additional employees, particularly in areas like sales and customer support, but it takes time and training for new employees to reach their maximum effectiveness. Instead of increasing capacity, hiring too fast can cause new problems instead of solving them.

Untrained salespeople have a higher risk of making promises the business can't deliver on, and untrained customer-support staff aren't well equipped to handle frustrated customers, communicate company policies, and make exceptions to those policies when the situation warrants it. Effective training requires instruction, communication, and oversight from managers or experienced staff, increasing demands on current staff. That investment often pays off in the medium- to long term, but at the cost of stress in the short term. Adding too much stress can lead current employees to look for other options, and the loss of key employees can result in the loss of important experience and capacity.

The most effective way to add capacity is to add small amounts in a consistent way over time, which increases capacity without adding demands that are beyond the system's current ability to handle. Instead of hiring several new employees to a team at once, adding an additional employee a few times per year is often a better approach.

Consistent improvements **Accumulate** into large improvements. When in doubt, start small and build over time.

REFERENCE LINK: **personalmba.com/progressive-load/**

Friction

The world is wide, and I will not waste my life in friction when it could be turned into momentum.

—FRANCES E. WILLARD, EDUCATOR AND SUFFRAGIST WHO SPEARHEADED
THE CAMPAIGN TO ADOPT THE EIGHTEENTH AND NINETEENTH
AMENDMENTS TO THE US CONSTITUTION

Imagine a hockey puck on the ground in front of you. You're armed with a hockey stick, and the objective is to move the puck from its present location to the goal, which is located one mile away.

First, assume the puck is sitting in a field of tall grass, which is waving in the wind. Each whack of the hockey stick will move the puck only a few feet, since the tall grass robs the puck of energy. At this rate, you'll have to hit the puck thousands of times before you get to the goal, and you'll exhaust your energy quickly. It'll take you many frustrating hours to reach the goal.

Now let's assume you mow the field until the grass in front of you is very short. Each time you hit the puck, it goes twenty feet or more—a huge improvement. The puck comes in contact with less grass, which means that it travels a longer distance with every strike. You'll still have to work to get the puck to the goal, but you'll achieve your objective faster and with less effort.

Finally, let's assume you flood the field with water and freeze it, until the landscape is a smooth plane of ice. Now the puck will travel hundreds of feet every time you hit it, because the ice doesn't rob the puck of energy—the puck glides along the surface. At this rate, you'll only need to hit the puck a few times before you've achieved the objective, and you won't be tired when you're done.

Friction is any force or process that removes energy from a system over time. In the presence of Friction, it's necessary to continue to add energy to a system to keep it moving at the same rate over time. Unless additional energy is added, Friction will slow the system down until it comes to a stop. Remove the Friction and you'll increase the system's efficiency.

Every business process has some amount of Friction. The key is to identify areas where Friction currently exists, then experiment with small improvements that will reduce the amount of Friction in the system. Removing small amounts of Friction over time *Accumulates* into large improvements in both quality and efficiency.

Removing even small amounts of Friction from your marketing, sales, and value-delivery processes can generate major improvements in *Profit*. For example, retailers like Amazon go to enormous lengths to minimize the amount of effort it takes for a customer to place an order. From allowing customers to purchase items with a single click (which charges and ships the order to the customer's default credit card and address on file) to recommending related items for purchase, Amazon aims to make it as easy as possible for its customers to buy online.

Amazon Prime, a service that upgrades every order a customer places to two-day shipping, is a textbook example of the benefits of reducing Friction. In exchange for a small annual fee, Prime customers receive their purchases by mail in two days or less, without spending time in a retail store.

When a customer signs up for Amazon Prime, that customer's annual order volume doubles. 46 percent of Prime members purchase items from Amazon at least once per week, and 31 percent of Prime subscribers browse the retailer's website on a daily basis . . . all thanks to reducing Friction in the buying process.[1]

Introducing *intentional* Friction can sometimes encourage people to behave in a certain way or make a particular decision. For example, adding a small amount of Friction to your returns process, like requiring the customer to provide a receipt or explain the reason for the return, can decrease the number of people who return your product. You don't want to add too much, since that can negatively impact your *Reputation*—customers get angry if you make them work too hard for a refund—but a little Friction in the right place can help prevent frivolous returns.

Work on removing Friction from your business system where appropriate and you'll generate better results for less effort.

REFERENCE LINK: **personalmba.com/friction/**

Automation

The first rule of any technology used in a business is that automation applied to an efficient operation will magnify the efficiency. The second is that automation applied to an inefficient operation will magnify the inefficiency.

—BILL GATES, COFOUNDER AND CHAIRMAN OF MICROSOFT

Remove enough **Friction**, and people may not have to be involved in a process at all.

Automation refers to a system or process that can operate without human intervention. Factory production lines, utility networks, and computer programs use Automation to minimize the amount of human involvement necessary to complete a task. The less human effort required to operate the system, the more efficient the Automation.

Automation is best for well-defined, repetitive tasks. For example, if I had to reply to a letter or email every time someone wanted to read my list of recommended business books, I'd go insane. Fortunately, I can just put the list up on my website—every time someone requests the list, it's delivered to them without any effort on my part. My reading list has been viewed by hundreds of thousands of readers from around the world, and Automation is what makes it possible.

Find a way to Automate your system and you open the doors to **Scale** via **Duplication** and **Multiplication**, improving your ability to create and deliver value to more paying customers.

REFERENCE LINK: **personalmba.com/automation/**

The Paradox of Automation

One machine can do the work of fifty ordinary men. No machine can
do the work of one extraordinary man.

—ELBERT HUBBARD, AUTHOR OF *A MESSAGE TO GARCIA*

Automation can be great, but it has very important drawbacks worth understanding.

Imagine a fully Automated production line that makes computer processors that sell for $200 per unit. All the human operators have to do is push a button, and the production system starts cranking out 2,400 finished products per minute. Life is good, right?

Yes, with a *very* important caveat. Imagine that a drill used to bore holes in the silicon wafer becomes misaligned and starts drilling microscopic holes through the middle of the processor core. Every second the system keeps working, forty chips are ruined.

Assume each processor costs $20 in raw materials—that means the factory starts losing $800 every second the error isn't found. Every minute the system keeps running, the company loses $48,000. And that's just the direct cost. If you take into account that each processor would sell for $200, the company is losing $528,000 a minute: $48,000 in direct costs and $480,000 in **Opportunity Costs**.

Sound farfetched? Consider this: In late 2009, Toyota identified a major issue with the accelerator pedal in several popular vehicle models, which were top sellers for many years. The error was **Multiplied** across every vehicle Toyota made, and the recall cost *more than $5 billion*.

Before the recall, Toyota was considered the best automotive manufacturer in the world. They still are in many respects, but their **Reputation** and financial situation suffered a major blow. Even the best can fall if costly mistakes are allowed to Multiply.

Here's the **Paradox of Automation**: the more efficient the Automated system, the more crucial the contribution of the human operators of that system. When an error happens, operators need to identify and fix the situation or shut the system down—otherwise, the Automated system will continue to Multiply the error.

Dr. Lisanne Bainbridge, a psychologist at University College London, was one of the first to rigorously study the ramifications of efficient and reliable systems.[2] She was the first to identify and express the "paradox" of Automated systems: efficient Automated systems reduce the need for human effort but make human involvement even more critical.

Efficient Automation makes humans *more* important, not less.

REFERENCE LINK: **personalmba.com/paradox-of-automation/**

The Irony of Automation

There will always be a set of circumstances that was not expected, that the automation either was not designed to handle or other things that just cannot be predicted. As system reliability increases, the more difficult it is to detect the error and recover from it.

—DR. RAJA PARASURAMAN, PROFESSOR OF PSYCHOLOGY
AT GEORGE MASON UNIVERSITY

Efficient **Automated Systems** make skilled human intervention essential to prevent the **Amplification** of errors, so it's best to keep skilled operators on hand at all times, right?

That's easier said than done: businesses don't pay highly skilled employees to sit around in a room all day doing nothing, which is what they'll be doing as long as the system appears to be reliable. Even if they do, the operators will spend most of their time being bored out of their skulls.

Here's the **Irony of Automation**: the more reliable the system, the less human operators have to do, so the less they pay **Attention** to the system while it's in operation. Remember the Mackworth Clock and the vigilance studies conducted on British radar operators in World War II from our discussion of **Novelty**? Humans get bored if things stay the same, and the more reliable the system, the *more things stay the same*.

Reliable systems tend to dull the operator's senses, making it very difficult for them to notice when things go wrong—the moment when their Attention is required. As a result, the more reliable the system, the lower the likelihood that human operators will notice when something goes wrong—particularly if the error is small.

Left long enough, small errors can become the "new normal," which is how a company like Toyota ends up with a $5 billion recall. (By the way, don't fall prey to **Attribution Error** and think that Toyota's engineers were stupid or careless—if you rely on Automated systems, it could happen to you.)

The best approach to avoid major Automation errors is rigorous, ongoing **Sampling** and **Testing**. Remember, **Normal Accidents** can and will occur. If you assume that errors will be made and plan a battery of tests to find the most critical errors, you can keep your system operators engaged and increase the probability of finding important errors quickly.

Keep your Automated system's operators mentally engaged, and they'll be far more likely to notice when errors occur.

REFERENCE LINK: **personalmba.com/irony-of-automation/**

Standard Operating Procedure

The measure of success is not whether you have a tough problem to
deal with, but whether it's the same problem you had last year.

—JOHN FOSTER DULLES, FORMER US SECRETARY OF STATE

What do you do when a customer has a complaint or asks for a refund? What happens when you run out of toner for the laser printer? Who takes the helm if the manager is out of town and there's an emergency?

A **Standard Operating Procedure (SOP)** is a predefined process used to complete a task or resolve a common issue. Business systems often include repetitive tasks, and having a standard process in place can help you spend less time reinventing the wheel and more time doing productive work.

Well-defined Standard Operating Procedures are useful because they reduce **Friction**. Instead of wasting valuable time and energy solving a problem that has already been solved many times before, a predefined SOP ensures that you spend less time thrashing and more time adding value.

Standard Operating Procedures are also effective ways to bring new employees or partners up to speed quickly. Having a central source of SOPs can help new employees or partners learn how you work with less formal training. Storing your SOPs in some sort of central electronic database is best—it ensures that everyone can reference the most up-to-date procedures available.

Don't let your Standard Operating Procedures lapse into bureaucracy.

Remember, the purpose of an SOP is to minimize the amount of time and effort it takes to complete a task or solve a problem. If the SOP requires effort without providing value, it's Friction.

For best results, review your SOPs on a periodic basis—once every two to three months is ideal. If you find outdated, wasteful, or unnecessary work in your SOPs, change them. Neither you nor your customers are served by unnecessary red tape.

Create Standard Operating Procedures for important recurring tasks, and you'll see your productivity skyrocket.

REFERENCE LINK: personalmba.com/standard-operating-procedures/

Checklist

> No matter how expert you may be, well-designed checklists can improve outcomes.
>
> —STEVEN LEVITT, COAUTHOR OF *FREAKONOMICS*

Want to make sure an important task is done correctly every single time? Create a checklist.

A **Checklist** is an **Externalized**, predefined **Standard Operating Procedure** for completing a specific task. Creating a Checklist is enormously valuable for two reasons. First, Checklisting will help you define a system for a process that hasn't yet been formalized—once the Checklist has been created, it's easier to see how to improve or **Automate** the system. Second, using Checklists as a normal part of working can help ensure that you don't forget to handle important steps that may be overlooked when things get busy.

Pilots have detailed Checklists for takeoff and landing for a reason: skipping a step is easy but can have major consequences for everyone on board. Even pilots with decades of flying experience always use Checklists to make sure everything is done right and in the proper sequence. As a result, plane crashes are rare—it's safer to travel via a commercial airline than it is to drive.

Even simple processes can benefit from **Systemization** and the use of Checklists. In 2001, Dr. Peter Pronovost conducted a study on the effects of Checklisting, which was described in detail in Dr. Atul Gawande's *The*

Checklist Manifesto and in an article Gawande published in the *New Yorker*.[3] The study was conducted in a hospital in Detroit that had the highest rate of ten-day IV line infections (a costly and life-threatening condition) in the country. Pronovost's objective was to determine whether or not using Checklists would reduce the rate of infections.

Here's the entirety of the intervention: whenever a doctor inserted an IV line, they were instructed to use the following Checklist.

Step 1: Wash hands with soap.

Step 2: Clean the patient's skin with chlorhexidine antiseptic.

Step 3: Put sterile drapes over the entire patient.

Step 4: Wear a sterile hat, mask, gloves, and gown.

Step 5: Put a sterile dressing over the catheter site once the IV line is in.

These steps aren't complicated. In fact, many doctors resisted the study, since they felt that being forced to use a Checklist for such a simple procedure was insulting, given their status as highly trained specialists. Even more insulting, the head nurse was empowered to stop the doctor if they weren't using the Checklist—an unusual role reversal that had many doctors fuming.

Nevertheless, the results of this study over two years were astounding: the ten-day IV line infection rate dropped from 11 percent to 0 percent and saved the hospital more than $2 million in related costs. As it turns out, forgetting even basic, commonsense procedures is easy in a busy, stressful **Environment**.

Checklisting can produce major improvements in your ability to do quality work, as well as your ability to delegate work. By taking the time to describe and track your progress, you reduce the likelihood of major errors and oversights and prevent **Friction** associated with figuring out how to complete the same task over and over again. In addition, once your Checklist is complete you can use it as the basis for full or partial Automation of the system, which will allow you to spend time doing more important things.

For best results, create explicit Checklists for the **Five Parts of Every Business**, then make sure they're followed every single time.

REFERENCE LINK: **personalmba.com/checklisting/**

Process Overhead

Do not believe that it is very much of an advance to do the unnecessary three times as fast.

—PETER DRUCKER, FATHER OF MODERN MANAGEMENT THEORY

It's possible to have too much of a good thing.

Processes aren't free: every procedure or *Checklist* in a system has a cost that is paid in time, energy, and *Attention*. *Process Overhead* is the amount of system capacity spent on internal processes instead of other value-creating activities.

Business systems often have significant amounts of Process Overhead: mandatory status meetings, reports, rules, and paperwork. These practices are adopted for valid reasons: communicating information is important and valuable, as is tracking progress toward shared *Goals* and eliminating preventable errors by following *Standard Operating Procedures*. The problem appears when all of those separate practices *Accumulate* to the point where they represent the bulk of the organization's capacity and effort.

Processes have a point of *Diminishing Returns*, so it's useful to identify and eliminate processes that are no longer necessary. Processes should not be defined via top-down mandate or maintained just because they exist. It's best to keep your processes flexible and expect that they'll change or become unnecessary over time. Once a process outlives its usefulness, *Cessation* is valuable and warranted.

The people who are most qualified to create and maintain processes are the people closest to the work: give them the flexibility and control necessary to update or remove processes that no longer serve the intended purpose.

REFERENCE LINK: **personalmba.com/process-overhead/**

Cessation

There is nothing so useless as doing efficiently that which should not be done at all.

—PETER DRUCKER, FATHER OF MODERN MANAGEMENT THEORY

Sometimes the best way to improve a system is to stop doing so much.

Cessation is the choice to stop doing something that's counterproductive. Due to **Absence Blindness**, we're predisposed to attempt to improve a system by doing something—it "feels wrong" to do nothing. That doesn't mean that doing nothing is a bad strategy: it's often more effective.

In *The One-Straw Revolution*, Masanobu Fukuoka wrote about his experiments with natural farming, which involved letting nature take its course and intervening as little as possible. While most farms were introducing chemicals and machinery into agriculture, Fukuoka was doing *nothing*—and reaping the rewards of high yields and increased soil richness. Here's what he had to say about the virtues of Cessation:

> Human beings with their tampering do something wrong, leave the damage unrepaired, and when the adverse results accumulate, work with all their might to correct them. When the corrective actions appear to be successful, they come to view these measures as splendid accomplishments. People do this over and over again. It is as if a fool were to stomp on and break the tiles of his roof. Then when it starts to rain and the ceiling begins to rot away, he hastily climbs up to mend the damage, rejoicing in the end that he has accomplished a miraculous solution.

Instead of trying to do too much, Fukuoka only did what was necessary. As a result, his fields were among the most productive in the area.

Cessation takes guts. It's often unpopular or unpalatable to do nothing, even if doing nothing is the right solution. As an example, "pricing bubbles" are often caused by government intervention in certain markets, which has the **Second-Order Effect** of artificially decreasing the costs of certain actions, leading to rampant speculation. When reality sets in and the bubble "pops," as it did with dot-com companies in 2000 and the housing market in 2008, it's politically unpopular for the government to do nothing, even though *doing something is what caused the situation in the first place*. More often than not, the government acts, which causes another, bigger bubble a few years later.

Firing customers, quitting your job, discontinuing a product, or pulling out of a market you can't succeed in are all tough decisions, but these decisions may put you in a better position in the long run.

Doing something is not always the best course of action. Consider doing nothing instead.

REFERENCE LINK: **personalmba.com/cessation/**

Resilience

Placing a system in a straightjacket of constancy can cause fragility to evolve.

—C. S. HOLLING, ECOLOGIST

Turtles aren't the sexiest creatures in the animal kingdom. They can't run fast. They can't fly. They don't have big, sharp teeth or claws. They can't puff themselves up to look menacing or poison their enemies with deadly venom. Compared to the raw power of a tiger or a falcon, turtles are rather lame.

What turtles *do* have is a variety of protective strategies—they can swim, use camouflage, snap with their jaws, and, if all else fails, retract into their shell and wait for the threat to pass.

Creatures elsewhere in the animal kingdom are in big trouble if they're cornered by a predator. Turtles have a fighting chance—they win because they're the armored tanks of nature. They can also eat many different things and go into hibernation when times get tough. That's why they live so long.

Tigers, on the other hand, rely on their strength, power, and speed to chase down their prey. When times are good, tigers are the kings of the jungle. If prey becomes scarce or they lose their hunting prowess due to age or injury, death takes them without mercy—no second chances.

What the business world needs is more turtles and fewer tigers.

The world is a fundamentally **Uncertain** place. Unexpected things happen—some good, some bad. You never know when Mother Nature, Lady Luck, or a hungry predator will decide that today is not your day.

Resilience is an underrated quality in business. Having the toughness and flexibility to handle anything life throws at you is a major asset that can save your skin—literally and metaphorically. Your ability to adjust your strategy and tactics as conditions **Change** can be the difference between survival and disaster.

Resilience is never "optimal" if you evaluate a system solely on **Throughput**. Flexibility always comes at a price. A turtle's shell is heavy—it could move faster without it. Giving it up, however, would leave the turtle vulnerable in the moments when moving a little faster just isn't fast enough. In an effort to chase a few more dollars, many businesses trade Resilience for short-term results—and pay a hefty price.

The big investment banks are a classic example. Keeping cash reserves on hand to handle the unexpected has become "ultraconservative" and "inefficient"—it's become a "best practice" to **Leverage** the entire company many times over times to squeeze out a few more cents in earnings per share each quarter, leaving the business vulnerable to a very small decline in revenues.

Operating a business with no cash reserves, no insurance, and high levels of debt may improve your returns for a few months or quarters, but the moment your revenues decline even by a little or someone decides to sue the business, you're sunk.

Leverage works just like rocket fuel—depending on how it's used, it can propel your business to dizzying heights or make the entire operation explode. Many of the advanced financial manipulation tactics taught in business schools implicitly trade Resilience for on-paper returns—and once-successful businesses pay the price by going out of business when times get tough.

Preparing for the unexpected makes you more Resilient. On a personal level, investing in a home emergency/first aid kit, car kit, and extra resources like food and water isn't paranoid—supplies like these are cheap insurance for the intelligent. The same goes for purchasing **Insurance** and building up cash reserves for unexpected events. You may never need them, but you'll be glad they're there if you do.

HERE'S WHAT MAKES A BUSINESS RESILIENT:

—*Low (preferably zero) outstanding debt*

—*Low overhead, fixed costs, and operating expenses*

—*Substantial cash reserves for unexpected contingencies*

—*Multiple independent products/industries/lines of business*

—*Flexible workers/employees who can handle many responsibilities well*

—*No single points of failure*

—*Fail-safes/backup systems for all core processes*

Planning for Resilience as well as performance is the hallmark of good management. Resilience is not sexy, because the benefits suffer from **Absence Blindness**. It can, however, save your hide when times get tough.

Think less like a tiger and more like a turtle and your business will be able to withstand pretty much anything.

REFERENCE LINK: **personalmba.com/resilience/**

Fail-safes

> "Always" and "never" are two words that you should always remember never to use.
>
> —WENDELL JOHNSON, PSYCHOLOGIST AND PIONEER OF SPEECH PATHOLOGY

Every Wednesday at noon, a generator kicks on outside of the house I grew up in. If all goes well, it'll run for ten minutes, then turn off until the next testing cycle, ready to spring into action if the power goes out.

My father once worked as a firefighter and emergency medical technician, and has refined "being prepared" into a high art. The generator is designed to turn on the moment the primary electricity to the house fails, taking over the house's electrical demands in seconds if an outage occurs. The generator is fed via a propane tank behind the garage, which has enough fuel to keep the generator running for a week. If a storm knocks out power to the area, Dad is prepared to handle it.

Dad's preparedness rubbed off on me. Now that we live in the mountains of Colorado, we have to be prepared for the possibility of our car breaking down somewhere remote or cold and we can't rely on AAA (or cell phone coverage) to save us.

Kelsey often makes fun of me for stocking our vehicles with extra clothing, sleeping bags, snowshoes, and satellite-driven personal locator beacons, but I don't mind. If something happens, we'll be glad we were prepared—I consider the investment in equipment a cheap, durable *Insurance* policy.

A *Fail-safe* is a backup system designed to prevent or allow recovery from a primary system failure. If the primary system fails in some way, well-designed Fail-safes can keep the system from collapsing unexpectedly. You can find backup systems anywhere consistent performance is critical.

Actors in high-profile Broadway shows have understudies. If "the show must go on," it pays to know you'll always have a replacement for any actor who can't perform. Most shows even have a few "swing" actors—performers who are ready to play *any* role at a moment's notice.

External hard drives back up critical computer data. If the hard drive in your computer crashes, you can still access the data via the backup drive, so you won't lose everything. Some businesses even take the precaution of storing backup drives off-site in case of fire or natural disaster.

Airplanes have a system that senses a failure in cabin pressure, which deploys face masks attached to an oxygen tank. If the airplane's pressurized cabin fails for some reason, the passengers won't lose consciousness—a very good thing indeed.

Fail-safes are not efficient, in the sense that you're investing time and resources in a system you hope you'll never use. Backup systems and Insurance, from one perspective, can be seen as a waste of money—why spend valuable resources on something you hope you'll never need?

Here's why: by the time you need a Fail-safe, it's too late to develop one. In order to be effective, Fail-safes must be developed *before* you need them. If you wait to develop backup systems until you need them, it's too late to make a difference. Paying for homeowners' insurance can feel like a waste of money until your house burns down. If you wait to buy Insurance until something bad happens, it's already too late.

Try to separate your Fail-safe and primary system as much as possible. One of the reasons people rent safe deposit boxes in banks is to protect certain items from loss in the event of fire or theft—if something happens to the house, the items in the safe deposit box will still be okay. The practice of backing up data to an off-site data center serves the same purpose: if something happens to the business's primary computers, the data is still safe in another location.

Fail-safes that are highly **Interdependent** with the primary system can introduce additional risks. One of the worst things you can do is make your backup system a part of the system you're trying to protect. For example, it wouldn't do my father much good if a failure in the generator cascaded to the house's primary electrical system and knocked out the power. An **Automated** computer backup system doesn't do you any good if installing it risks deleting all of your original files.

As much as possible, *never have a single critical point of failure.* If your system relies on critical inputs or processes in order to function, it's a good idea to plan for situations where those inputs aren't available or those processes are disrupted. What would you do if the primary system failed?

Plan in advance to develop Fail-safes for all critical systems, and you'll make your system as **Resilient** as you can.

REFERENCE LINK: **personalmba.com/fail-safe/**

Stress Testing

> To make no mistakes is not in the power of man; but from their errors
> and mistakes the wise and good learn wisdom for the future.
>
> —PLUTARCH, FIRST-CENTURY GREEK HISTORIAN AND ESSAYIST

Let's say you've developed what you believe is a robust, **Resilient** system, but you want to ensure that your preparations work. How would you go about **Testing** it?

Stress Testing is the process of identifying the boundaries of a system by simulating specific **Environmental** conditions. Instead of staying in systems-engineer mode, Stress Testing inverts your mind-set to "demon mode." What would it take to break what you've built?

In the early days of the Personal MBA, every time I launched a new version of my recommended reading list,[4] my web server would go down in a blaze of glory—the system couldn't keep up with all of the people trying to visit the website. I upgraded to several different systems, but each time, it wasn't enough.

I continued having server issues until I got serious about Stress Testing. Instead of waiting for an influx of traffic that would cause my site to go down, I started "breaking" my website on purpose, then trying different approaches to make the system more Resilient under stress.

Using an **Automated** tool,[5] I simulated a huge number of visitors hitting my website at the same time. The tool increased the number of virtual visitors requesting my website every second, then tracked how long my website took to respond to each request. As the volume of requests increased, my site's performance decreased until the server failed.

Using the data I collected from Stress Testing, I made several major improvements to my website's infrastructure and systems. Now, thousands of people can visit my site at once without affecting performance—a huge improvement.

Stress Testing can help you learn more about how your system works. If you're in the manufacturing business, you could simulate an unexpected order of ten thousand units—could you fulfill it? If you're doing customer support, you could simulate a massive influx of questions or complaints— how would you handle it? Your ability to test is only limited by your available time and imagination—let your inner demon run wild, then fix any major problems you find before they affect real customers.

REFERENCE LINK: **personalmba.com/stress-testing/**

Scenario Planning

A danger foreseen is half avoided.

—ENGLISH PROVERB

As we've discussed many times in this book, no one can predict what will happen tomorrow, let alone ten years from now. That's a problem when your plans and **Goals** depend on things outside of your **Locus of Control.** What can you do to prepare for an **Uncertain** future?

Scenario Planning is the process of systematically constructing a series of hypothetical situations, then creating a **Mental Simulation** of what you would do if they occurred. You may not be a seer, but **Thought Experiments** give you a powerful capability: imagining things that *might* occur, then figuring out what you'd do if they did. Scenario Planning is detailed, thorough, and systematic Thought Experiments applied to major decisions.

Scenario Planning always starts with a simple question: "What would I do if . . . ?" The "what if" part is called a "counterfactual," and it's what kicks your planning brain into gear, helping you imagine possible responses. By writing down all of your potential courses of action in that circumstance, it's possible to develop several responses to any situation you can imagine.

Scenario Planning is the essence of effective strategy. Trying to base your actions on predictions of interest rates, oil prices, or stock values is a fool's game. Instead of trying to predict the future with 100 percent accuracy, Scenario Planning can help you prepare for many different possible futures. Instead of rigidly focusing on only one option, your business will become more flexible and **Resilient**, improving your ability to **Change** and adapt to a changing world.

Most large businesses use Scenario Planning as the basis of a practice called "hedging": purchasing various forms of **Insurance** to reduce the risk of unfavorable future events. For example, manufacturers care about oil prices because they increase the cost of importing raw materials and shipping finished products to their customers, both of which decrease their **Profit Margins**. By purchasing financial instruments called "futures," the businesses can make money if the price of oil goes up, which helps to offset the losses they would incur in their primary line of business if oil prices increase.

Scenario Planning is easy to skip, particularly if you already have a lot of work to do. The time you spend in Scenario Planning can be some of the most valuable time you spend building your business, but it's easy to overlook if you're struggling to keep your head above water. Regular, non-negotiable time to step back and plan for the future is always time well spent—don't skip it.

Don't waste time trying to predict an unknowable future—construct the most likely scenarios and plan what you'll do if they occur and you'll likely be prepared for whatever happens.

REFERENCE LINK: **personalmba.com/scenario-planning/**

Exploration / Exploitation

We must conquer the truth by guessing, or not at all.

—C. S. PEIRCE, NINETEENTH-CENTURY PHILOSOPHER AND MATHEMATICIAN

Figuring out which changes or investments will give you the best outcomes is a major area of study in probability theory, which is best illustrated through the "multi-armed bandit" problem.

Imagine walking into a casino to play the slot machines—"one-armed bandits." There's a row of machines, each of which has a different probability of paying a reward when you pull the lever. Some machines pay more—some *much* more—than the others, but you're not sure which machine has the highest return.[6]

If you knew the best machine in advance, you'd just pull that lever all the time, but you don't know which lever is best, and no one is going to tell you. The only way to discover the best lever is to start pulling levers at random, keep track of what works and what doesn't, and analyze the results.

There's an important **Trade-off** inherent in this approach: when you choose to pull a lever you haven't pulled before, you get new information about that particular option, and that information is valuable in finding the best overall machine. Pulling the less tested lever, however, has an **Opportunity Cost**: you're *not* pulling the lever you currently think will give you the best return. There's a risk that the lever you pull will return less than what you would've brought in pulling the current optimal lever, and that's a very real cost.

Information is valuable, but it comes at a price: experimentation is sometimes a form of **Malinvestment**. That insight is the key to solving the bandit problem.

Without going into the math, the solution to the bandit problem is easy to understand: the optimal strategy is to start with a period of **Exploration**, where you pull levers at random and gather information. Once you have more information about what works and what doesn't, you shift to spending the majority of your time pulling the best lever you've discovered so far (*Exploitation*), but you keep exploring the other options in case your current best option isn't the very best that exists.

It's important to emphasize the last part of the optimal strategy: *the Exploration phase never stops*. Even if you're certain you've found the best possible option, you never stop experimenting because the information you gather by experimenting is always valuable. The only way to beat the bandit is to keep trying new things.

In real-world circumstances, you have a major advantage over the situation in this *Thought Experiment*: other people are playing the same game, and you can watch what they do to gather information about what works and what doesn't without having to try same approach. Learning from the actions of others—and observing their results—is an efficient way to gather useful information.

Extending this approach to day-to-day decisions is straightforward: experiment as much as possible, with as much variation as you can, and pay close attention to the experiments other people are doing. As you find things that appear to produce the outcomes you want, spend more time and energy doing them. As your efforts produce results and your certainty in a given option increases, increase your investment in that option. The more you experiment, the more you learn, the more information and options you'll have at your disposal, and the better chance you'll discover the things that will produce the outcomes you desire.

You can't make positive discoveries that make things better if you never try anything new. Start experimenting and never stop.

REFERENCE LINK: **personalmba.com/explore-exploit/**

Sustainable Growth Cycle

After victory, tighten the straps on your helmet.

—TOKUGAWA IEYASU, FOUNDER OF THE TOKUGAWA SHOGUNATE
OF EARLY SEVENTEENTH-CENTURY JAPAN

It's a mistake to assume any system can grow without limit. Systems tend to have a natural size, and exceeding this size can cause many problems. Elements of a system that are out of control need to be eliminated.

Take cell growth, for example. The cells in your body tend to grow to a certain size and to multiply at a rate that ensures new cells replace cells that die. When these proportions are in balance, your body works quite well. When cells grow or multiply out of control, the situation can threaten the existence of the entire system. Cancerous cells need to be removed to ensure the health of the body.

Businesses and biological organisms have many things in common: they're made up of many interrelated parts and systems that change and grow over time. If the **Five Parts of Every Business** grow out of control or out of proportion to one another, the situation can threaten the health of the organization.

The **Sustainable Growth Cycle** is a pattern I've noticed in businesses that are able to grow year after year without major difficulties. This cycle has three distinct phases: expansion, maintenance, and consolidation.

In an *expansion* phase, the company is focused on growing. New offers are created and tested. New markets are explored. New business units are built and staffed, and future plans are created. Early data about what works is collected for later use.

In a *maintenance* phase, the company is focused on executing the current plan. The marketing, sales, and value-delivery parts of the business are in full swing, and emphasis is placed on fully exploring the potential of the current business structure. Systems are put in place to ensure proper execution.

In a *consolidation* phase, the company is focused on analysis. Information about the performance of the business is examined in detail in an attempt to figure out what's working and what's not. Things that aren't working are cut back or eliminated, and things that are working are given more resources.

Think of plant cultivation: the best gardeners allow plants to grow, ensure they have enough resources to thrive, then cut back the plants that don't. This cycle repeats, season after season. Every cycle is essential.

Many entrepreneurs become frustrated when their business seems to hit a "plateau" and growth appears to stop. Spending time on maintenance or consolidation seems like a waste, or a flaw in the business idea. That's not the case at all: these phases are necessary to ensure the business succeeds, and they should be respected.

A business that fixates on expansion but shortchanges maintenance and consolidation will experience the commercial equivalent of cancerous growth. Parts of the business will grow out of control, consuming too much time, energy, and resources compared to what they contribute to the health of the business. New opportunities will be explored while proven opportunities are ignored or forgotten.

Maintenance and consolidation are necessary to bring the system into balance. Once the system is humming along, the growth cycle tends to kick in, and the process repeats.

A healthy business cycles among expansion, maintenance, and consolidation often. No matter which part of the cycle you're in, it's important to recognize that it's necessary and essential to the health of the business. By giving each cycle the appropriate time and attention, you'll ensure the long-term success of the business.

REFERENCE LINK: personalmba.com/sustainable-growth-cycle/

The Middle Path

> A master in any art avoids what is too much and what is too little; they search for the mean and choose it.
>
> —ARISTOTLE, FOURTH-CENTURY-BCE GREEK PHILOSOPHER

Business is never easy—it's an art as much as a science.

The **Middle Path** is the ever-changing balance point between too little and too much—just enough. No one can tell you what the Middle Path is—you have to be walking the path to know, and it changes all the time. Getting the balance right in the midst of **Uncertainty** is the difference between a competent business professional and a great one.

The best approach to anything almost always lies somewhere between "too little" and "too much." Just as in cooking, "business recipes" can only teach you so much. You may know the ingredients, the techniques, and the tools, but cooking a dish still requires attention, effort, and taste.

No one has it "all figured out." No one is certain that something will work or has a complete lack of fear that things won't work out as planned.

The people who experience the most success in this world are the people who accept the Uncertainty and fear as best they can, learn from their experiences, and keep trying new things.

Try to find the Middle Path, then stay on it as best you can. Find the right balance, and you can accomplish anything.

REFERENCE LINK: **personalmba.com/middle-path/**

The Experimental Mind-set

The only way you learn to flip things is just to flip them!

—JULIA CHILD, WORLD-RENOWNED CHEF, AFTER FLOPPING A POTATO
PANCAKE ONTO THE FLOOR DURING HER TV SHOW

When improving yourself or your business, it's often not clear what approach will create the intended result. That's where the *Experimental Mind-set* comes in handy.

Constant experimentation is the only way you can identify what will produce the result you desire. Often, the best (or only) way to learn things is to jump in and try. At the beginning, you may be in over your head, but there's no faster way to learn what works. Once you're committed to exploring something, you'll learn faster than if you'd cowered on the sidelines.

You learn the most from what doesn't go well. As long as your mistakes don't kill you, paying **Attention** to what doesn't work can give you useful information you can use to discover what does. All failures are temporary—what you learn in the process always helps you move forward.

Experimentation is learning through play. There's no need to build yourself up as a "serious businessperson" who cringes at the thought of the slightest mistake. You'll make thousands of mistakes over the course of your career, and that's okay. Every experiment teaches you something new, and every new lesson you learn increases your capability to accomplish great things.

Experimentation is the essence of living a satisfying, productive, fulfilling life. The more you cultivate an Experimental Mind-set, the more you learn and the more you'll achieve.

REFERENCE LINK: **personalmba.com/experimental-mindset/**

NOT "THE END"

A truly good book teaches me better than to read it. I must
soon lay it down, and commence living on its hint. What I
began by reading, I must finish by acting.
—HENRY DAVID THOREAU

Many of my readers and clients ask me:

"This business education stuff is great, but when will I be done?"

Wrong question, Grasshopper. Self-education, whether it's about business or anything else, is a never-ending process. There's never a point where you'll say, "Okay, I'm done—no more learning for me." Every new concept you come across is a gateway to thousands of other opportunities for exploration.

That's what makes self-education so fun and rewarding: there's always something new to learn.

In Eastern philosophy, *Tao* means "way" or "path"—a journey you're in the process of undertaking. Tao has no beginning and no end—it just is. Educating yourself about anything is a Tao—there's no end to the process. The journey itself is the reward.

Even masters of the art of moneymaking like Warren Buffett are always looking for new things to learn. When asked in an interview with students from the University of Nebraska–Lincoln about what superpowers he'd like to have, Buffett answered: "I'd like to be able to read faster." Most of what Buffett does on a daily basis is read financial reports and learn new concepts, looking for new ways to increase the value of his company.

Even the wealthiest people on earth have things to improve and more to explore. That ongoing curiosity is what made them successful in the first place.

There will be milestones along your path: completing a book, acquiring a new skill, launching a business, closing a sale. Eventually, however, you'll find that there's a new path for you to take, and the journey will continue.

There's never a limit to how much you can grow.

Now that you've read this book, I recommend visiting personalmba .com and subscribing to the Personal MBA email list. I revise my recommended reading list and publish new research on a regular basis. There's no cost to subscribe, and I'd be happy to keep you up to date with the most useful business information I discover.

I'd like to leave you with a few words of wisdom from B. C. Forbes, the founder of *Forbes* magazine, who wrote an essay in 1917 called "Keys to Success." I refer to it often and find that it's a great reminder of what business and life are all about:

> Your success depends on you.
> Your happiness depends on you.
> You have to steer your own course.
> You have to shape your own fortune.
> You have to educate yourself.
> You have to do your own thinking.
> You have to live with your own conscience.
> Your mind is yours and can be used only by you.
> You come into this world alone.
> You go to the grave alone.
> You are alone with your inner thoughts during the journey between.
> You make your own decisions.
> You must abide by the consequences of your acts . . .
> You alone can regulate your habits and make or unmake your health.
> You alone can assimilate things mental and things material . . .
> You have to do your own assimilation all through life.
> You can be taught by a teacher, but you have to imbibe the knowledge. He cannot transfuse it into your brain.
> You alone can control your mind cells and your brain cells.

You may have spread before you the wisdom of the ages, but unless you assimilate it you derive no benefit from it; no one can force it into your cranium.

You alone can move your own legs.

You alone can move your own arms.

You alone can utilize your own hands.

You alone can control your own muscles.

You must stand on your feet, physically and metaphorically.

You must take your own steps.

Your parents cannot enter into your skin, take control of your mental and physical machinery, and make something of you.

You cannot fight your son's battles; that he must do for himself.

You have to be captain of your own destiny.

You have to see through your own eyes.

You have to use your own ears.

You have to master your own faculties.

You have to solve your own problems.

You have to form your own ideals.

You have to create your own ideas.

You must choose your own speech.

You must govern your own tongue.

Your real life is your thoughts.

Your thoughts are your own making.

Your character is your own handiwork.

You alone can select the materials that go into it.

You alone can reject what is not fit to go into it.

You are the creator of your own personality.

You can be disgraced by no man's hand but your own.

You can be elevated and sustained by no man but yourself.

You have to write your own record.

You have to build your own monument—or dig your own pit.

Which are you doing?

I hope you've enjoyed this book and found it useful—if you have, please pass it along to friends and colleagues who might benefit from learning more about business. If you have questions or comments, don't hesitate to reach out—you can contact me at josh@personalmba.com.

Thanks for reading, and best wishes on your journey through the fascinating and ever-changing world of business.

Have fun!

ACKNOWLEDGMENTS

To Kelsey: we did it. Thank you for your unwavering love, confidence, and support.

To Mom and Dad: thanks for teaching me to read at such an early age. I owe my curiosity about the world and open heart to your example.

To Seth Godin: thanks for the inspiration, and for changing my life in all sorts of remarkable ways.

To Charlie Munger: thanks for sharing what you know with the world; I'm a better person because of it.

To Todd Sattersten and Jack Covert: thanks for introducing me to the team at Portfolio—without your generosity, this book wouldn't exist.

To Ben Casnocha and Ramit Sethi: thanks for encouraging me to take on this project, reviewing rough drafts, introducing me to Lisa, and inspiring me with your example.

To Carlos Miceli, who assisted in creating the website that accompanies this book.

To Lisa DiMona: your reputation preceded you, and it's not difficult to see why. Your enthusiasm, dedication, and patience are world-class. Thanks for everything you do.

To Adrian Zackheim: thanks for taking a chance on a young man with a crazy idea, and for publishing great work. The books you've published have improved my life, and I'm happy to be able to contribute to the cause. I hope it sells a million.

To David Moldawer: I expected an intelligent, experienced, and tough editor. You're all that and more: a trusted friend. Thanks for your keen eye and sharp wit: you left this book much better than you found it.

To Will Weisser, Maureen Cole, Richard Lennon, Joseph Perez, Oliver Munday, Jaime Putorti, Noirin Lucas, Michael Burke, and everyone behind the scenes at Portfolio: many years ago, I promised myself that if I ever decided to write a book, I'd only work with a publisher if I could work with the best. Your experience and professionalism in taking this book to market is astounding—I couldn't ask for a better team.

To Eric Gonzalez, Enoch Ko, Steven McGuinnity, Peter Millonig, Denver Rix, Marina Murray, Joseph Magliocco, Tim Shadel, Joel Masters, Sweeney Amenya, Tony Guntrip, Amy Hay, Eric Rogstad, and Tudor F. Dumitrescu: thanks for your help in identifying and correcting errors in previous editions. I appreciate your sharp eyes, attention to detail, and suggestions for improvement.

Special thanks to Chase Karpus, Niki Papadopoulos, David Moldawer, Molly Lindley Pisani, Lisa DiMona, and Kelsey Kaufman for their editorial help and assistance in preparing the 2020 edition for publication, and to Pete Garceau for the updated cover design.

To my clients and readers: without you, this book wouldn't exist. Thanks for your support, feedback, and encouragement—I hope you find this resource useful and that you accomplish everything you set out to achieve.

HOW TO CONTINUE YOUR BUSINESS STUDIES

We write by the light of every book we ever read.

—RICHARD PECK, AUTHOR

The next best thing to knowing something is knowing where to find it.

—SAMUEL JOHNSON, ESSAYIST

This book is a high-level overview of a large body of business literature: it's the beginning of your business studies, not the end. If you found this book useful, I recommend reading additional books in the areas you found most interesting and helpful.

The best place to start is the Personal MBA recommended reading list, which I publish online at **personalmba.com/best-business-books/**

If you'd like to be notified when I update the reading list, sign up for email updates on that page or at: **joshkaufman.net/newsletter**.

Happy reading!

FORTY-NINE QUESTIONS TO IMPROVE YOUR RESULTS

Good questions help your brain look at the world in a different way. By holding a question in your mind and pondering potential answers, you can find unexpected paths to get from where you are now to where you want to be.

Below is a list of questions I created for myself a few years ago. The intent of the list was to help me figure out what I wanted to improve about my life, both as a person and as a professional. These questions helped me figure out who I was and what I wanted during a particularly difficult time in my career, and I hope they help you as much as they've helped me.

DO I USE MY BODY WELL?

- ▶ What is the quality of my current diet?
- ▶ Do I get enough sleep?
- ▶ Am I managing my energy well each day?
- ▶ How well am I managing daily stress?
- ▶ Do I have good posture and poise?
- ▶ what can I do to improve my ability to observe the world around me?

DO I KNOW WHAT I WANT?

- ▶ What achievements would make me excited?
- ▶ What states of being do I want to experience each day?

- ▶ Are my priorities and values well-defined?
- ▶ Am I capable of making decisions fast, and with confidence?
- ▶ Do I focus my attention on what I want versus what I don't want?

WHAT AM I AFRAID OF?

- ▶ Have I created an honest and complete list of the fears I'm holding on to?
- ▶ Have I confronted each fear to imagine how I would handle it if it came to pass?
- ▶ Am I capable of recognizing and correcting self-limitation?
- ▶ Am I appropriately pushing my own limits?

IS MY MIND CLEAR AND FOCUSED?

- ▶ Do I externalize (write or record) what I'm thinking about?
- ▶ Am I making it easy to capture my thoughts as I have them?
- ▶ What has my attention right now?
- ▶ Am I regularly asking myself appropriate guiding questions?
- ▶ Do I spend most of my time focusing on a single task, or am I toggling among multiple tasks?
- ▶ Do I spend enough time reflecting on my goals, projects, and progress?

AM I CONFIDENT, RELAXED, AND PRODUCTIVE?

- ▶ Have I found a planning method that works for me?
- ▶ Am I "just organized enough"?
- ▶ Do I have an up-to-date list of my projects and active tasks?
- ▶ Do I review all of my commitments on a regular basis?
- ▶ Do I take regular, genuine breaks from my work?
- ▶ Am I creating positive habits?
- ▶ Am I working to shed nonproductive habits?
- ▶ Am I comfortable with telling other people "no"?

HOW DO I PERFORM BEST?

- ▶ What do I particularly enjoy?
- ▶ What am I particularly good at doing?
- ▶ What environment(s) do I find most conducive to doing good work?
- ▶ How do I tend to learn best?
- ▶ How do I prefer to work with and communicate with others?
- ▶ What is currently holding me back?

WHAT DO I NEED TO BE HAPPY AND FULFILLED?

- ▶ How am I currently defining "success"?
- ▶ Is there another way of defining "success" that I may find more fulfilling?
- ▶ How often do I compare myself with my perceptions of other people?
- ▶ Am I living within my means?
- ▶ If I could only own one hundred things, what would they be?
- ▶ Am I capable of separating necessity and luxury?
- ▶ What do I feel grateful for in my life and work?

Pick up a notebook, set aside an hour, and spend time with yourself answering these questions. Make it fun: treat yourself to a nice lunch or dinner at a restaurant you like and write as you eat. By the time the check arrives, you'll have more than a few new ideas about how to change your life or business for the better.

NOTES

INTRODUCTION: WHY READ THIS BOOK?

1. This epigraph was misattributed to Ralph Waldo Emerson in the first and second editions. Special thanks to Garson O'Toole of the blog Quote Investigator for tracing the original source ("The Man Who Tries Methods, Ignoring Principles, Is Sure to Have Trouble," July 17, 2015, https://quoteinvestigator.com/2015/07/17/methods/).

2. Seth Godin, "Good News and Bad News," *Seth's Blog* (blog), March 14, 2005, https://seths.blog/2005/03/good_news_and_b/.

3. Josh Kaufman, "The Personal MBA Recommended Reading List: The 99 Best Business Books," *The Personal MBA*, https://personalmba.com/best-business-books/.

4. Warren Buffett, "The Superinvestors of Graham-and-Doddsville," *Hermes*, May 17, 1984, https://www8.gsb.columbia.edu/articles/columbia-business/superinvestors.

5. Janet Lowe, *Damn Right: Behind the Scenes with Berkshire Hathaway Billionaire Charlie Munger* (Hoboken, NJ: John Wiley & Sons, Inc., 2003), 75.

6. *Outstanding Investor Digest (New York, NY: Outstanding Investor Digest, Inc.)*, December 29, 1997.

7. Peter D. Kaufman, ed., *Poor Charlie's Almanack: The Wit and Wisdom of Charles T. Munger*, 3rd ed. (Virginia Beach, VA: The Donning Company Publishers, 2005), 64.

8. See "College: Big Investment, Paltry Return" by Francesca Di Meglio, *Bloomberg Businessweek*, June 28, 2010, https://www.bloomberg.com/news/articles/2010-06-28/college-big-investment-paltry-returnbusinessweek-business-news-stock-market-and-financial-advice. This is not just a problem with business schools: it's a problem with college in general. College tuition has increased 7 to 14 percent annually since the 1980s, while salaries have stagnated, so the return on investment of college education has decreased.

9. Bill Gates didn't graduate from college and doesn't have an MBA. Most successful and wealthy individuals didn't go to business school—they started as entrepreneurs and taught themselves.

10. The Institute for College Access & Success, "Student Debt and the Class of 2017: 13th Annual Report," September 2018, https://ticas.org/files/pub_files/classof2017.pdf.

11. National Center for Education Statistics, "Trends in Graduate Student Loan Debt," *NCES Blog*, August 2, 2018, https://nces.ed.gov/blogs/nces/post/trends-in -graduate-student-loan-debt.

12. "Find the Best Business School," U.S. New, accessed January 29, 2020, https://www .usnews.com/best-graduate-schools/top-business-schools.

13. Marc Ethier, "How Much Does a Top MBA Now Cost? Nine Schools Are in the $200K Club," *Poets&Quants*, December 24, 2018, https://poetsandquants.com/2018 /12/24/cost-of-an-mba-program/.

14. For more on how top universities bias the admissions process in favor of wealthy and well-connected applicants, I suggest reading *The Price of Admission* by Daniel Golden (New York: Crown, 2006), who was awarded a Pulitzer Prize in 2004 for his reporting on the issue.

15. Shahien Nasiripour, "Top U.S. B-School Students Pile on Debt to Earn MBAs," *Bloomberg Businessweek*, June 17, 2019, https://www.bloomberg.com/news/articles /2019-06-17/top-u-s-b-school-students-pile-on-debt-to-earn-mbas.

16. Christian Schraga, "A Wharton grad's caveat emptor for prospective MBAs," *MBA—Think Carefully Before Taking the Plunge* (blog), June 2, 2005, https://web .archive.org/web/20181220151724/http://mbacaveatemptor.blogspot.com/2005/06 /wharton-grads-caveat-emptor-for.html.

17. Jeffrey Pfeffer and Christina T. Fong, "The End of Business Schools? Less Success Than Meets the Eye," Academy of Management Learning & Education 1, no. 1 (September 2002), http://www.aomonline.org/Publications/Articles/BSchools.asp.

18. Dan Rasmussen and Haonan Li, "The MBA Myth and the Cult of the CEO," *Institutional Investor*, February 27, 2019, https://www.institutionalinvestor.com/article /b1db3jy3201d38/The-MBA-Myth-and-the-Cult-of-the-CEO.

19. See Daniel Pink's book *Drive: The Surprising Truth About What Motivates Us* (New York: Riverhead, 2009).

20. Including perceptual control theory, which we'll discuss in chapter 6.

21. Noam Scheiber, "Upper Mismanagement," *New Republic*, December 18, 2009, http://www.tnr.com/article/economy/wagoner-henderson.

22. Leverage is the use of debt to amplify financial return on investment (ROI), which has a side effect of amplifying downside risk if the business doesn't succeed. We'll discuss leverage and ROI in detail in chapter 5.

23. For an example of how this works, read Julie Creswell, "At Simmons, Bought, Drained and Sold, Then Sent to Bankruptcy," *New York Times*, October 4, 2009, http:// www.nytimes.com/2009/10/05/business/economy/05simmons.html.

24. "Frequently Asked Questions," US Small Business Administration Office of Advocacy, September, 2019, https://cdn.advocacy.sba.gov/wp-content/uploads/2019/09/24153946/Frequently-Asked-Questions-Small-Business-2019-1.pdf.

25. "Small Businesses Drive Job Growth In United States; They Account For 1.8 Million Net New Jobs, Latest Data Show", US Small Business Administration Office of Advocacy, April 24, 2019, https://advocacy.sba.gov/2019/04/24/small-businesses-drive-job-growth-in-united-states-they-account-for-1-8-million-net-new-jobs-latest-data-show/.

26. "Frequently Asked Questions," US Small Business Administration Office of Advocacy, September, 2019, https://cdn.advocacy.sba.gov/wp-content/uploads/2019/09/24153946/Frequently-Asked-Questions-Small-Business-2019-1.pdf.

27. "Small Businesses Generate 44 Percent Of U.S. Economic Activity," US Small Business Administration Office of Advocacy, January 30, 2019, https://advocacy.sba.gov/2019/01/30/small-businesses-generate-44-percent-of-u-s-economic-activity/.

28. Lavelle, Louis. "Is The MBA Overrated?" *Bloomberg Businessweek*, March 20, 2006. https://www.bloomberg.com/news/articles/2006-03-19/is-the-mba-overrated.

29. For detailed tips on how to take good notes while you read, see "3 Simple Techniques to Optimize Your Reading Comprehension and Retention" at https://personalmba.coma.com/resources/.

CHAPTER 1: VALUE CREATION

1. For an example of how I do this, see "How to Create a Basic Business Plan" at https://personalmba.com/resources/.

2. A legally binding contract or promise not to share information about a business or business idea with others.

3. Louviere called the approach "MaxDiff" testing. You can find an explanation of how it works here: Sarah Littler, "Maximum Difference Scaling (MaxDiff)", Select Statistical Services, accessed December 3, 2019, https://select-statistics.co.uk/blog/maximum-difference-scaling-maxdiff/.

4. For an example of how to conduct Relative Importance Testing for your business idea, see "How to Conduct Relative Importance Testing" at https://personalmba.com/resources/.

5. "Arizona Outdoors Interview: Brief Biography of Patrick Smith," Kifaru International, September 2001, http://www.kifaru.net/radio.htm.

6. Miguel Caballerousa, YouTube channel, http://www.youtube.com/user/miguelcaballerousa.

CHAPTER 2: MARKETING

1. Amy Cortese, "Wiggling Their Toes at the Shoe Giants," *New York Times*, August 30, 2009, https://www.nytimes.com2009/08/30/business/30shoe.html.

2. Jaya Saxena, "130 Years Ago, Elephants Solved Panic on the Brooklyn Bridge," *Behind the Scenes* (blog), New-York Historical Society Museum and Library, May 29, 2014, http://behindthescenes.nyhistory.org/elephants-panic-brooklyn-bridge-1883/.

3. "The Elephants Cross the Bridge," *New York Times*, May 18, 1884, https://www.nytimes.com/1884/05/18/archives/the-elephants-cross-the-bridge.html.

4. You can see examples of Billy's commercials at https://www.youtube.com/watch?v=91K8MvN01b4.

5. See https://www.progressive.com.

6. Kevin Kelly, "Amish Hackers," *The Technium* (blog), February 10, 2009, https://kk.org/thetechnium/amish-hackers-a/.

CHAPTER 3: SALES

1. Edon Ophir, "507-Carat Cullinan Heritage Diamond Sells for $35.3 Million," IDEX Online, March 1, 2010, http://www.idexonline.com/FullArticle?id=33728.

2. You can find the formula here: "Discounted Cash Flow (DCF)," Investopedia, June 19, 2019, https://www.investopedia.com/terms/d/dcf.asp.

CHAPTER 4: VALUE DELIVERY

1. For an example of how I do this, see "Diagramming a Value Stream/Flowcharting a System" at https://personalmba.com/resources/.

2. David A. Garvin, "Competing on the Eight Dimensions of Quality," *Harvard Business Review*, November 1987, https://hbr.org/1987/11/competing-on-the-eight-dimensions-of-quality.

3. Drew Harwell, "America's Best-Selling Cars and Trucks Are Built on Lies: The Rise of Fake Engine Noise," *Washington Post*, January 21, 2015, https://www.washingtonpost.com/business/economy/americas-best-selling-cars-and-trucks-are-built-on-lies-the-rise-of-fake-engine-noise/2015/01/21/6db09a10-a0ba-11e4-b146-577832eafcb4_story.html.

4. It's important to note that not all businesses use satisfaction throughput in the same way. Luxury experiences, like fine dining, often involve much longer periods of time (and cost much more) than a quick meal at a casual restaurant. The lavish amount of time and attention spent on customers in these instances is a Quality Signal designed to increase the customer's satisfaction and tend to promote feelings of importance and Social Status.

5. Before the advent of the printing press, Bibles were copied and illuminated (decorated and illustrated) by cloistered monks, who spent years working on a single copy.

6. Kevin Kelly, "Better Than Free," *The Technium* (blog), January 31, 2008, https://kk.org/thetechnium/better-than-fre/.

7. We'll discuss Toyota's recall woes later, in The Paradox of Automation.

8. "2018–2019 CMI Annual Report," Can Manufacturers Institute, accessed January 27, 2020, http://www.cancentral.com/sites/cancentral.com/files/public-documents/2018CMIAnnualReport.pdf.

9. Felix Richter, "The Terminal Decline of BlackBerry," Statista, June 26, 2017, https://www.statista.com/chart/8180/blackberrys-smartphone-market-share.

10. Dr. Peter J. Meyers, "How Often Does Google Update Its Algorithm?," *Moz* (blog), May 14, 2019, https://moz.com/blog/how-often-does-google-update-its-algorithm.

CHAPTER 5: FINANCE

1. If you're interested in how this works, I recommend *Venture Deals* by Brad Feld and Jason Mendelson (Hoboken, NJ: John Wiley & Sons, Inc., 2013).

2. James Carland et al, "Fraud: A Concomitant Cause of Small Business Failure," *Entrepreneurial Executive* 6, 2001, http://citeseerx.ist.psu.edu/viewdoc/download?doi=10.1.1.201.3276&rep=rep1&type=pdf#page=79.

CHAPTER 6: THE HUMAN MIND

1. For details on my approach to strength training, see https://joshkaufman.net/strength-training-for-non-athletes/.

2. I use the Philips GoLITE BLU light-therapy device and highly recommend it. It's small, bright, and easy to travel with, and it works wonders.

3. For more on the neurophysiology of the brain, check out *Kluge: The Haphazard Construction of the Human Mind* by Gary F. Marcus (New York, NY: Houghton Mifflin Harcourt), 2008.

4. Suzanne McGee, "Go for Gold, Wind Up Broke: Why Olympic Athletes Worry About Money," *Guardian*, August 7, 2016, https://www.theguardian.com/sport/2016/aug/07/olympic-games-rio-athletes-personal-finance-struggle; Charles Riley, "Olympians Face Financial Hardship," *CNN Money*, July 10, 2012, https://money.cnn.com/2012/07/10/news/economy/olympic-athletes-financial/index.htm.

5. "Pedestrian Counts," Times Square: The Official Website, accessed October 24, 2019, https://www.timessquarenyc.org/do-business/market-research-data/pedestrian-counts.

6.   Adam Hayes, "Dutch Tulip Bulb Market Bubble", Investopedia, June 25, 2019, https://www.investopedia.com/terms/d/dutch_tulip_bulb_market_bubble.asp.

7.   Adam Hayes, "Dotcom Bubble," Investopedia, June 25, 2019, https://www.investopedia.com/terms/d/dotcom-bubble.asp

8.   Jim Chappelow, "The Great Recession," Investopedia, July 25, 2019, https://www.investopedia.com/terms/g/great-recession.asp.

CHAPTER 7: WORKING WITH YOURSELF

1.   I've used several different internet blocking software applications over the years: some of them block the entire internet, and others can be configured to block specific websites on a predetermined schedule. I'm using Cold Turkey Blocker (https://getcoldturkey.com) as I write this.

2.   "The Pomodoro Technique," Francesco Cirillo, accessed October 24, 2019, http://www.pomodorotechnique.com/.

3.   Karin Foerde, et. al., "Modulation of Competing Memory Systems by Distraction," *Proceedings of the National Academy of Sciences of the United States of America* 103, no. 31 (August 1, 2006), http://www.pnas.org/content/103/31/11778.abstract.

4.   "Drivers on Cell Phones Are as Bad as Drunks," University of Utah, June 29, 2006, https://archive.unews.utah.edu/news_releases/drivers-on-cell-phones-are-as-bad-as-drunks/.

5.   "Maker's Schedule, Manager's Schedule," Paul Graham, July 2009, http://www.paulgraham.com/makersschedule.html.

6.   "The Emergent Task Planner," David Seah, July 20, 2015, http://davidseah.com/pceo/etp.

7.   Oren Harari, "Quotations from Chairman Powell: A Leadership Primer," Gov Leaders.org, accessed December 1, 2019, http://govleaders.org/powell.htm.

8.   For a complete look at my personal productivity system, see "Josh Kaufman's Personal Productivity System," https://personalmba.com/resources/.

9.   "The Autofocus Time Management System," *Get Everything Done* (blog), http://www.markforster.net/autofocus-system/.

10.   Andrew Whalen, "'Behind the Curve' Ending: Flat Earthers Disprove Themselves with Own Experiments in Netflix Documentary," *Newsweek*, February 25, 2019, https://www.newsweek.com/behind-curve-netflix-ending-light-experiment-mark-sargent-documentary-movie-1343362.

11.   For an example of how I do this, see "How to Track Your Time and Energy Cycles" at https://personalmba.com/resources/.

12.   For examples of how money can decrease happiness, read *Fables of Fortune: What Rich People Have That You Don't Want* by Richard Watts (Austin, TX: Emerald Book Company, 2012).

13.   Joshua Wolf Shenk, "What Makes Us Happy?," *Atlantic*, June 2009, http://www.theatlantic.com/magazine/archive/2009/06/what-makes-us-happy/7439/3/.

CHAPTER 8: WORKING WITH OTHERS

1.   Derek Sheane, *Beyond Bureaucracy*, Organization Research, 1976. The first edition of this book attributed the source of this list to Dr. Michael Sutcliffe of the University of Cambridge. Many thanks to Marina Murray for the correction.

2.   Shane Parrish, "The Trust Battery: My Interview with Shopify Founder Tobi Lütke," in *The Knowledge Project*, episode 41, podcast, MP3 audio, 1:45:56, http://fs.blog/tobi-lutke/.

3.   For a detailed examination of the context of the Milgram experiment, including audio from the experiments themselves, listen to Jad Abumrad and Robert Krulwich, "The Bad Show," January 9, 2012, in *Radiolab*, podcast, MP3 audio, 1:07:28, https://www.wnycstudios.org/story/180092-the-bad-show.

4.   Mark Morgan Ford, "Lessons From a Persian Rug Merchant in Jaipur," *Early to Rise* (blog), November 30, 2007, http://www.earlytorise.com/2007/11/30/lessons-from-a-persian-rug-merchant-in-jaipur/.

5.   Mike Bostock, Shan Carter, and Archie Ise, "Is It Better to Rent or Buy?," *New York Times*, http://www.nytimes.com/interactive/business/buy-rent-calculator.html.

6.   Joel Spolsky, "The Management Team—Guest Post from Joel Spolsky," *AVC* (blog), February 13, 2012, http://www.avc.com/a_vc/2012/02/the-management-team-guest-post-from-joel-spolsky.html.

CHAPTER 10: ANALYZING SYSTEMS

1.   For an example of how I do this, see "Diagramming a Value Stream/ Flowcharting a System" at https://personalmba.com/resources/.

2.   "WSJ.com Audience Profile," Dow Jones & CO, Inc., accessed December 4, 2019, https://images.dowjones.com/wp-content/uploads/sites/183/2018/05/09164150/WSJ.com-Audience-Profile.pdf.

3.   Mon Chu Chen, John R. Anderson, and Myeong Ho Sohn, "What Can a Mouse Cursor Tell Us More?: Correlation of Eye/Mouse Movements on Web Browsing," *CHI EA '01: CHI '01 Extended Abstracts on Human Factors in Computing Systems*, March 2001, 281–82, http://portal.acm.org/citation.cfm?id=634067.634234.

CHAPTER 11: IMPROVING SYSTEMS

1.   Rahul Chadha, "Nearly Half of US Households Are Now Amazon Prime Subscribers," eMarketer, June 26, 2018, https://www.emarketer.com/content/nearly-half-of-us-households-are-now-amazon-prime-subscribers.

2.   Lisanne Bainbridge, "Ironies of Automation," Department of Psychology, University College London, 1983, http://www.bainbrdg.demon.co.uk/Papers/Ironies.html.

3.   Atul Gawande, "The Checklist," *New Yorker*, December 2, 2007, http://www.newyorker.com/reporting/2007/12/10/071210fa_fact_gawande.

4.   You can see the current version of my recommended reading list at https://personalmba.com/best-business-books/.

5.   LoadImpact.com is a load and performance testing service for websites, web or mobile apps, or application programming interfaces. Tools like this make it easy to simulate hundreds (or thousands) of simultaneous users, allowing you to identify bugs and performance issues the system will experience under heavy load.

6.   Slot machines are sometimes referred to as "one-armed bandits," which is how the "bandit" problem got its name. I don't recommend playing slot machines, by the way—there's a reason casinos are profitable. Under standard odds and given a long enough period of time, the house always wins, so the only way to win is to refuse to play. Let's assume, for the sake of this Thought Experiment, you're not paying to play—each game only costs you the time it takes to pull the lever and see the result.

INDEX

ABOUT THE AUTHOR

Josh Kaufman is the bestselling author of books on business, entrepreneurship, skill acquisition, productivity, creativity, applied psychology, and practical wisdom. His work focuses on helping people make more money, get more done, and have more fun in life and work.

Before creating PersonalMBA.com, Josh worked in brand management, product development, and marketing measurement for Procter & Gamble, where he launched major new products and developed P&G's global online-marketing measurement strategy. He lives in Fort Collins, Colorado.

You can find more of Josh's research and writing at joshkaufman.net.